ISLAM IN THE CONTEMPORARY WORLD

ISLAM
in the Contemporary World

Edited by
Cyriac K. Pullapilly
Saint Mary's College, Notre Dame

CROSS ROADS BOOKS

Published by Cross Roads Books
P.O. Box 506
Notre Dame, Indiana 46556

© Copyright 1980, by Cross Roads Books.

All rights reserved. This book, or parts thereof,
must not be reproduced in any form without permission.

Printed in the United States of America
by Rink Riverside Printing, Inc., South Bend, Indiana.

Typography by Vicki Cooper
Cover Design by Stephen A. Walker
Map illustrations by Sandy Knoll

First Printing, 1980
Second Printing, 1980

Preface

This volume is not meant to be a systematic study of the history or theology/philosophy of Islam. What it is, is a collection of answers to common sense questions which laymen today ask about the Islamic world. Although those who address these questions are highly respected specialists in their fields, the questions themselves are posed from the perspective of non-specialists, and the answers are couched, as far as possible, in non-technical language. Thus, it is hoped, that a combination of scholarly depth and readability is achieved.

The idea of the book came from a conference on contemporary Islam that was hosted by Saint Mary's College, Notre Dame, in the Spring of 1980. Subsequently, a conference on Islamic revival that was held under the auspices of the Center for Middle Eastern Studies at the University of Chicago in early summer 1980 served as an added stimulus. The majority of the articles in this book originated in one form or another at these two conferences. Other articles were subsequently commissioned for this volume. None was previously published.

From the beginning, focus was set on an overall theme for the book which is expressed in a two-pronged question: What is and what is happening in the Islamic world today, and what is and what should be the West's relationship with this world. All articles are written or rewritten to address these questions.

From the beginning, too, a determination was made that all questions in this book would be asked and answered with due respect to a great world religion whose contributions to the progress and preservation of civilization is to be properly recognized, not ignored, in the course of disputes about specific issues. It is hoped that we succeeded in this.

Another important consideration was to find the most qualified scholar to address each significant question that is raised in the book, and, if there are two opposing sides to an important issue, find two equally eminent experts to argue the case. No effort or expense was spared in this regard, thanks to an understanding publisher. As a result we are able to present two sides of most controversial questions, but in some instances we are not as time limitations prevented several scholars of note from contributing to this collection.

Nevertheless, I must assume, as editor, responsibility for all failures and omissions in this book. There were extenuating circumstances. Pressure to get the book out fast came, not from the authors, but from many other persons in this country and Europe. Enquiries came from the White House and from many private citizens. An impatient patron even reproduced five thousand copies of one article (authorized?) for private circulation. The temptation to yield to partisan journalistic interest had to be countered by principles of responsible scholarship.

The pressures only confirmed our conviction that the questions raised in the book touched the nerves of history. It would be presumptuous to say that anyone would learn anything from this book that cannot be learned elsewhere, but we can say confidently that the issues between the Islamic world and the West that are systematically treated in this volume — issues which men and women, both in the East and the West, are seeking to understand — are given ample clarification herein, thanks to the expertise of the contributors.

Finally, I must admit that this has been a labor of love for me. Bringing East and West together, as I have attempted to do in other historical works, has, in this, come to be a living experience — for which I am gratified.

Saint Mary's College
Notre Dame, Indiana
November 30, 1980

Acknowledgements

The twenty-five contributors to this volume deserve a note of thanks before anyone else. Many of them presented their papers at the Saint Mary's College or the University of Chicago meetings, but were requested to rewrite them for publication on short notice. Others were requested to start entirely new projects just for this volume, on even shorter notice. Some authors had as little as one week to finish their articles. None took more than a day to read the proof of his/her essay. Besides the constraints of time, some authors were called on to tolerate substantial revisions of their essays to suit the thematic and structural design of this book. All during the process of editing and printing the book I have received full and cordial cooperation from the contributors. I am deeply grateful to them.

As indicated elsewhere the majority of articles in this volume came from the two conferences. The Saint Mary's College conference was organized with the support of various colleagues on campus. Chief among them is Vice President William A. Hickey. Others include my colleagues in the Department of History, Professor Anthony Black, Brother Bernard Donahoe, C.S.C., Professor Jack Detzler, Professor Charles Poinsatte and Reverend James Zatko; Professors Craig Hartzer and Louis Tondreau from the Government Department; Professor Frank Yeandel from the Business-Economics Department; Professor Harold Weiss from the Religious Studies Department; and Professors Michael McKee and John Thorp from the Sociology-Anthropology Department. My gratitude to all of them.

The Saint Mary's College conference was funded through grants from the Indiana Committee for the Humanities, the Indiana Consortium for International Programs, Saint Mary's College History Department and the Office of the Vice President for Academic Affairs, Saint Mary's College. Support from these organizations came through the cooperation and help of their officers — Ms. Donna Bucove, Associate Director of ICH; Dr. Allen Maxwell, Executive Director of ICIP; Brother Bernard Donahoe, Chairman, Department of History; and Dr. William A. Hickey, Vice President for Academic Affairs, Saint Mary's College. To all of them my deep appreciation.

As organizer of the University of Chicago conference, Dr. Richard Chambers, Director, Center for Middle Eastern Studies, not only did extend his hospitality to me but also assisted in many ways to obtain for this volume the papers presented there. In addition, he has been helpful with his counsel throughout the two conferences and during the preparation of this book. I am much indebted to him.

The person on whom I depended at every stage of the production of this book — revision, design and proofreading — was Professor Jack Detzler of the Saint Mary's College History Department. Without his generous help the publication of the volume would have been much delayed. My deepest thanks to him.

Dr. David Waas who recently returned to his old position as Executive Director of the ICIP and Bonnie Tinsley, the new Director of Public Information of ICH, helped publicize the book through announcements in their respective news bulletins. For this I am grateful to them.

Dr. Dilaver Berberi of the Modern Languages Department of Saint Mary's College and Mr. Samir Sayegh, a Ph.D. candidate in the Physics Department at the University of Notre Dame, were kind enough to spend much time clarifying some Arabic terminology for me. To them I am grateful.

Mr. Wilbur Warne West of South Bend was kind enough to permit us to use the valuable Mughal painting from his private collection on the cover of this book. I am grateful to him for his generosity.

Throughout the production of the book, Donald Rink of Cross Roads Books and his staff, Charles Lightner, Stephen A. Walker, Vicki Cooper, Tom Woltman, Tom Pettit, Sandy Knoll, and Maryann Kiska extended to me exceptional cooperation, help and courtesy. We share in the pride of bringing out this book in such a short time, something which other publishers thought impossible.

Finally, I must thank my family, my wife Elizabeth and the children Kavita, Anand and Gita, and Mrs. Gladys Klatt whom the children consider and call their "aunt" for tolerating my many interruptions of family routine and for keeping me healthy and sane during the several difficult months that it took me to get this book in shape.   — *CKP*

A Special Note to the Reader from the Editor

Consistency in style and structure has been a chief concern of the editor all during the preparation of this book. Yet some inconsistencies, especially in orthography, had to be allowed. They reflect either the preferences of the authors or the usages common in the regions with which the articles deal. Inconsistencies in the inclusion of footnotes also reflect the preferences of authors. It was difficult to resolve some of these problems through correspondence with authors as many of them were in such distant places as Cairo, Karachi, Paris, Istanbul and Jakarta. Apart from these, I must assume responsibility for all errors.

—*CKP*

Contents

Preface v
Acknowledgements vii
Note From the Editor ix
Contents x
Introduction xiii
    Islam and Islamic Civilization, An Historial Sketch
                Cyriac K. Pullapilly

I.	Islam in the Islamic World, An Overview	1
	Seyyed Hossein Nasr	
II.	Religious Revivalism in Islam: Past and Present	21
	Victor Danner	
III.	Islam and Other Religions	44
	Richard L. Chambers	
IV.	Martyrdom in Arabic Literature	54
	Salih J. Altoma	
V.	Theocracy in Islam	70
	Bert De Vries	
VI.	The Islamic World and the West Today	86
	C. Ernest Dawn	
VII.	The Political Economy of Middle Eastern Oil and the Islamic Revival	105
	Karim Pakravan	
VIII.	The Islamic World, Israel, and the United States	126
	Frank Tachau	
IX.	The Arabian Peninsula and the Islamic "Revival"	143
	Manfred W. Wenner	
X.	Islamic Revival in Egypt and Greater Syria	158
	Ibrahim Ibrahim	
XI.	Shi'i Social Thought and Praxis in Recent Iranian History	171
	Shahrough Akhavi	
XII.	The Scourging of the Shah	199
	Russ Braley	

XIII.	Religion and Atheism Among Soviet Muslims *Alexandre Benningsen*	222
XIV.	Religion and Ethnic Consciousness Among Turks in the Soviet Union *Ilhan Başgöz*	238
XV.	Islam and the Struggle for Afghan National Liberation *Richard S. Newell*	251
XVI.	Islamic Revival in Pakistan *Mumtaz Ahmad*	261
XVII.	Islam in African History *Ralph A. Austen*	274
XVIII.	African-American Muslims and the Islamic Revival *Umar A. Hassan*	284
XIX.	Islamic Law and Islamic Revival in Libya *Ann Elizabeth Mayer*	296
XX.	Islam in Iraq's Public Life *Daniel Pipes*	306
XXI.	Atatürk's Secularizing Legacy and the Continuing Vitality of Islam in Republican Turkey *Howard A. Reed*	316
XXII.	Islam in Indonesia: Challenges and Opportunities *Nurcholish Madjid*	340
XXIII.	Islam in the Philippines *William L. Yam, S.J.*	358
XXIV.	Women in Islam: Yesterday and Today *Darlene May*	370
XXV.	*Concluding Statement* Islam: Legacy and Contemporary Challenge *Fazlur Rahman*	402
Index		416

INTRODUCTION
ISLAM AND ISLAMIC CIVILIZATION: AN HISTORICAL SKETCH

Cyriac K. Pullapilly

Islam was born in the semi-desert trading post of Mecca in western Arabia among the prosperous caravan merchants as the ultimate revelation of God to mankind. Muhammad, God's final messenger to humanity, brought this revelation. Thus, from its origins Islam carried the indelible imprints of the character of Arabia and the personality of the Prophet.

Caravan trade between the spice-rich southern Arabia and the vast Mediterranean markets had been going on for many centuries before Christ. Many towns on the western, Red Sea coast of the peninsula that sprung up along this caravan route — such as Ta'if, Mecca, Yathrib (Medina) and Petra — were direct beneficiaries of this trade. Mecca also benefited from another source, the Kaaba, the chief focus of religious veneration and pilgrimage in Arabia for quite some time before the Christian era. The black stone embedded on a corner of the cube-like structure had been, according to Arabian folklore, the object of veneration to all mankind, from Adam on. Legend also had it that Abraham and his illegitimate offspring, Ishmael, were the architects of the Kaaba. Thus it was mythically, and to the believers mystically, placed in the very center of human history. This epicenter of human history, so sacred as it was, had come under the control of the tribe of Kuraish several generations before the time of Muhammad who was born into that tribe, though as a member of a poor clan, sometime around 570 A.D.

Bereft of his father even before his birth and his mother when he was only six, Muhammad grew up as the ward of his grandfather and uncle and entered at an early age in what was perhaps the best career open to young men in Mecca, caravan driving. Accompanying the caravans of a rich widow, Khadijah, he traveled to distant regions, perhaps as far away as Syria and Egypt, absorbing all along the beliefs and values which he found appealing from the communities of Christians and Jews with whom he traded. These outside influences only strengthened his already growing doubts about some of the worse practices of the Arabs, Meccans in particular — infanticide, bloody feuds, greed and idol worship. Soon he began to see himself as the appointed messenger of God to save Arabs, and perhaps humanity itself, from the depths of evil. Marriage to Khadijah offered him the leisure to think, a receptive ear to his views and above all time to listen to the voice of God. This God was Allah, the imageless deity in the Arabian pantheon of gods, whom Muhammad had envisioned as the one resembling closest the Jahve of Jews and Christians and had come to elevate over the years above all other gods of the Arabs as the only true God. This god, on "The Night of Power and Excellence", in the cave at the foot of Mount Hira, commenced to give Muhammad his revelation through his messenger the archangel Gabriel, a revelation which through many such subsequent encounters grew into the Koran, the holy book of the Muslims.

The Koranic revelation is simple: there is no god but one God, Allah, and Muhammad is his Prophet. Its moral themes are: kindness to neighbors, leniency to debtors, honesty and forgiveness. Its injunctions are: against infanticide, eating unclean food (pork), intoxicant beverages and blood feuds. Its enjoiners: almsgiving to the poor, praying five times a day facing Mecca, fasting during the days of the month of Ramadan, and a once in a lifetime pilgrimage to Mecca for those who have the health and the funds for travel. Those who follow the path laid out in the Koran, with purity of heart, belong to the religion of Islam, "submission", and they are called Muslims, "those who submit", to Allah.

Not many were inclined to submit to this revelation when Muhammad first announced it in the Kaaba to the Meccans. Nor did a decade of daily preaching gain him many converts outside of his own household. Instead, the prominent factions of the Kuraish tribe, finding his revelation a threat to the idols of the Kaaba and to the revenues they brought to Mecca, began to take punitive measures against Muhammad. His life, fortunes, and the new revelation in danger, Muhammad looked for a safer haven. After several years of search, finally, at the Ukaz fair, during the season of truce in the year

620 A.D. Muhammad met six men from Yathrib, a city about three hundred miles north of Mecca on the caravan route. They were looking for a leader who could impose discipline on the fighting factions of the city, and Muhammad was looking for an opportunity to exercise leadership. The meeting was auspicious. In two years the people of Yathrib were readied to accept Muhammad. In 622 Muhammad and his family and followers undertook the *Hijra* (migration) to Yathrib, which marked the beginning of the Islamic era. Yathrib would from then on be called Medina (*Medina an nabi*, City of the Prophet). Muhammad was, finally, accepted as Prophet of God by an important Arabian city.

Having established himself the unquestioned ruler of Medina in both religious and temporal matters, Muhammad, in 630, prepared to take Mecca. A surprise attack on a Meccan caravan, a Meccan attempt to siege Medina, and Muhammad's march on Mecca — it was all over. In an instant Muhammad became the most respected tribal leader in all of Arabia. In addition he was also the Prophet of Allah. Tribes from far and wide came to 'submit' voluntarily or were brought to submission. Much of Arabia obeyed Allah and his Prophet by the time Muhammad died suddenly in 632.

By then also the basic patterns of Islamic life had been established. The house of worship, as the one he erected in Medina for daily prayer, the calls to private prayer from the mosque's roof five times a day, five daily prayers facing Mecca and prostrate on earth, Friday gathering of the whole community in the mosque for common prayer, collection of alms for the poor and for the cause of Islam — all these became marks of Muslim communities in every town and village.

In addition, Muhammad's practice of exercising both religious and secular authority himself became a precedent for his successors *(caliphs)*, although they did not have his prophetic mission. So too, his practice of using the sword to bring unbelievers to the submission of Allah.

It was only in the centuries that followed that Muslim teachers pieced together Islam's articles of faith. Their sources for this were the Koran, the examples set by the Prophet, collectively known as the *Sunnah*, and the *Hadiths* or the traditions about the Koranic passages, sayings of the Prophet and events in the first generation of Muslim history. The articles are generally placed under three headings — doctrine *(īmān)*, religious duty *('ibādāt)* and right conduct (ihsan). Very simply described, Islamic doctrine entails the belief in Allah (*La ilāha illa Allāh*, "there is no god but Allah"), his Prophet, Muhammad, and his revelation in the Koran and through the angels; resistance to *Iblis*, the fallen angel, the tempter; and belief in the last judgment. Religious duty is contained in the "Five Pillars" — repetition of the formula ("There is no god but Allah, and Muhammad is the prophet of Allah"), prayer, almsgiving, fast during the sacred month of Ramadan and pilgrimage. Right conduct means that Muslims should follow faithfully Muhammad's comprehensive teachings and examples on all aspects of life.

Muhammad did not envision a priesthood or religious hierarchy for Islam. But the need for religious leadership was obvious. So too was the need for learned minds to interpret Islamic teachings as they applied to the various and complex situations of Muslims' lives. To meet these needs, there arose in early Islamic era the *Ullama*, religious scholars, whose training, functions and position in society are by no means standardized even today from country to country. Nevertheless, they have played important roles throughout Muslim history as sages, teachers, ascetics and even as political forces.

The rise of the *Ullama* coincided with the gradual growth of the Islamic legal system or the *Shari'a*. Solidly based in the Koran, the *Sunnah* and the *Hadiths*, the *Shari'a* governs all aspects of Muslim life and all persons in the Muslim community, although a uniformity in its interpretation or application has never been achieved from age to age and region to region.

The sudden death of Muhammad in 632 could have destroyed the whole movement. He had selected no successor *(caliph)* nor had he established any procedures for it. There arose three factions representing three different criteria for selecting a *caliph*. The first, composed of Muhammad's early companions and emigrants from Mecca, thought the ancient Arabian custom of election should be followed and a successor should be chosen from their ranks. Another group advocated a hereditary principle, that is selection from Muhammad's descendants through Fatima, his daughter (as Muhammad left no male heir) and her husband Ali. A third group would have chosen someone from the Umayyads, leaders of Muhammad's tribe. But the first group being most influential at this point, a successor was elected, Abu Bakr, one of Muhammad's first converts and a faithful supporter from his early days in Mecca.

Abu Bakr's election proved most auspicious for Islam. He brought all of Arabia into submission in a matter of months and sent a huge army into Syria before his death in 634. Umar, the next caliph, also elected, witnessed the brilliant victories of this ill-equipped Islamic army over the forces of the Byzantine Emperor, Heraclius, and the capture of Damascus in 635. Emboldened by the fall of Damascus, the first major city to fall to the Arabs, and encouraged by the Prophet's twin promises to his soldiers — one-fifth of the booty to those who survive and Paradise to those who perish — Muslim armies marched on. Good military leadership was a factor — General Khalid ibn al-Walid, the conqueror of Damascus was an example — but perhaps even more decisive a factor was the religious fervor the like of which has seldom been displayed in warfare. City after city fell before the Bedouin conquerors — Jerusalem in 638, Caesarea in 640, and all the towns and hamlets of Palestine soon thereafter. Muslim armies then turned toward Egypt. In just three years (639-41) they overran the Nile Delta and started a push through North Africa towards the Strait of Gibraltar. In less than a century they would not only cross the Strait into Europe but also occupy much of Spain. In the Near East itself, the Arab armies took Iraq in 637, all of Persia between 640 and 649 and Asia Minor between 640 and 652. In another century Muslim forces would extend their sway all the way across Central Asia into Mongolia in the northeast and the borders of India in the southeast. And in the west, except for Charles Martel's narrow victory over them in the Battle of Tours (732), they would have captured France and moved on to the rest of Europe. Thus, in a hundred years after the death of Muhammad, Islam could lay claim to nearly one third of the civilized world.

Yet, in a sense these great victories of Islamic armies themselves were a cause for the house of Islam to fall asunder. As a result of these victories enormous amounts of wealth began to flow into Medina, into the coffers of the caliphate. Umar, the second caliph, established a system of distributing these riches among all Arabs. But his assassination by a Christian captive in 644 occasioned a political maneuvering by the Umayyads who succeeded in the selection of one of their own, Uthman, to become caliph. Although he had excellent credentials, as a son-in-law and close associate of the Prophet, Uthman yielded to corruption and the angered faithful assassinated him in 656. Next, another son-in-law, Ali, the candidate of the legitimists who advocated a hereditary principle for caliphate (as Ali was the father of two sons, the only male descendants of Muhammad) was selected over many rivals. But one rival, Mu'awiyah, the Umayyad governor of Syria, declared war against him. Ali led a force against Mu'awiyah but offered to negotiate with him, magnanimously, when Mu'awiyah was just about ready to accept defeat. Upon which Ali's angered followers assassinated him. Mu'awiyah immediately claimed the caliphate and moved its seat to Damascus. The Umayyad caliphate which thus ensued came to an end in 750 when the Shiites (followers of Ali and advocates of the hereditary principle) overthrew the dynasty and raised in its place the Abbasids, a family distantly related to the Prophet. The Abbasids moved the caliphate to Baghdad, the oriental city on the Tigris River.

Several generations of feud over the issue of succession had by then driven a wedge between the Sunnites (those who followed the principle of election for succession) and the Shiites. What is more, both groups also had developed new theological positions — for example, the Sunnites considered both the Koran and the *Sunnah* of the Prophet as the basis of religious belief while the Shiites would accept nothing but the Koran. In addition a new mystical trend also developed in Islam militating against the increasing legalism, rationalism and worldliness of the Sunnites and the Shiites, which would subsequently find expression in the Sufi orders.

Such tensions only increased the fissility of the fabric of Islam. Finally, in early tenth century when the Abbasid caliphate was languishing under the weight of its own corruption, the Umayyads whose only possession since 750 remained Spain, declared an independent caliphate in Cordova. This was in 929. Shortly thereafter the descendants of Fatima and Ali established themselves as sovereign rulers of Egypt and Morocco. The Abbasids themselves surrendered their temporal powers in 1057 to the newly rising power in the region, the Seljuk Turks. The Seljuks ruled these vast regions until the middle of the twelfth century when they were replaced by the Ottoman Turks. The Ottoman rule lasted till 1918.

The end of the Abbasid rule marked the end of Arab domination of the Islamic world. The torch of Islam and the sword would now be carried by other tribes. But the Arabs left a lasting legacy for civilization. Having inherited Greek learning in philosophy and sciences from the Syrians and Persians whom they conquered, the Arabs encouraged their intellectually inclined subjects to engage in creative pursuits. In philosophy they produced a synthesis of Aristotelianism and Neo-Platonism to establish such basic principles as the superiority of reason over faith, the eternality of the universe, emanation of the universe from God, the absolute justice and goodness of God, and the mortality of individual souls. In the ninth and tenth centuries the Baghdad caliphate provided patronage for such great names as Al Kindi (d. 870), Al Farabi and Avicenna (b. 980). In the West the

Spanish caliphate patronized Averroës of Cordova (1126-1198) whose influence on the fathers of Scholastic philosophy — Albertus Magnus, St. Thomas Aquinas, Duns Scotus — was profound. The impact of the Arabs on sciences was even more significant. They made unprecedented advances in mathematics, astronomy, physics, chemistry and medicine. They were the ones who popularized the notion of the earth rotating on its axis around the sun; who developed an accurate calendar (Omar Khayyam being chiefly responsible); who made great advances in algebra and trigonometry; who adapted the "Arabic" numerals (although Indian Brahmins were the inventors); who made brilliant discoveries in optics; who developed the science of chemistry and invented the ways to make sulphuric acid, nitric acid, alum, carbonate of soda, mercury, borax and many other useful chemical compounds; and who started to use the chemical processes of filtration, sublimation and distillation. In the field of medicine, two names were supreme in the Middle Ages — Avicenna and Rhazes (850-923). Avicenna's *Canon* was the most sought after medical book in Europe until the late seventeenth century, and his discoveries in the nature of tuberculosis, nervous diseases, pleurisy and the contagious character of many ailments advanced the medical science immeasurably. Rhazes, the most famous practitioner of medicine in the Middle Ages, in East or West, correctly described the nature of smallpox and established precedents for the prevention and treatment of other contagious diseases. It was through the influence of Rahazes and other Arab physicians that well organized hospitals, with wards, dispensaries and libraries — prototypes of modern Western hospitals and just as efficient — were established in practically all major cities of the Arab empire. In these hospitals, licensed physicians and surgeons, the only ones in the world in those days who had the benefit of systematic medical training, diagnosed and treated all ailments from food-poisoning to cancer of the stomach, introduced the use of cauterization and styptic agents and instructed people on the infectious nature and the ways of transmission of the plague.

The literature of the Arabic empire reflects the simplicity of desert life on the one hand, which was by now only a distant and romantic memory, and the lavishness of the oriental courts on the other. Omar Khayyam's (d. ca. 1124) *Rubayat* is the best example of Arabic poetry and the *Book of the 1001 Nights* the best example of their prose. Both have a central place in world literature.

Just as the tales of the *1001 Nights* came from every part of the world, so did inspiration for Arabic art. Since the painting and sculpturing of human figures was discouraged by Islam, only architecture and the minor arts flourished. The bulbous domes, horseshoe arches, twisted columns and minarets that adorned Arabic palaces, mosques, schools, hospitals and private mansions from Spain to Mongolia bespoke the eclectic character of Islamic art. Embellished by the use of sensuous colors, mosaics, interlacing geometric designs, Arabic calligraphy, animal and plant figures, black and white stripes, and stone traceries, Arab edifices stood as examples of rich and exquisite taste. No less tasteful were the brocaded silks and tapestries, enameled glasswares, painted potteries, inlaid metal works and pile carpets Arab craftsmen manufactured and sent all over the civilized world.

The rich everywhere dreamed of silks from Damascus ("damask"), swords from Toledo, leather goods from Morocco, jewelry and glassware from Baghdad and cotton from Mosul. And Arab merchants were eager to sell these and a host of other products — perfumes and drugs, rugs and tapestries, satins and woolens, inlaid metals and cut glasses — that their craftsmen produced. Caravans of camels carried these cargoes across the Central Asian highlands into India and China and, to the south, into sub-Saharan Africa. Also, laden with these wares, Arab ships sailed into the Indian Ocean and the China Sea, not to speak of the Mediterranean and the Caspian Sea, touching a thousand ports. Not until the European age of discoveries in the sixteenth century would the world see again such extensive sea travels.

So extensive a network of trade routes indicated not only the Arabs' knowledge of geography and climatic conditions and the excellence of their navigational skills but also the strength of their industry and economy. In fact they introduced such institutions and practices of modern economy as banks and credits, checks and receipts, joint-stock companies and craft guilds, and accounting and bookkeeping several centuries before the Europeans copied them.

No less were the achievements of the Arabs in agriculture and horticulture. It was not just the Arabian desert and the barren wastelands of the Middle East that they turned into blooming paradises, but also the exhausted ancient lands as Egypt and the rocky mountain slopes of Iberia. Orchards, vegetable gardens, ornamental shrubs and trees and flowering bushes of endless varieties brought from every part of the world ringed the ornate palaces of the sheikhs of Araby, whether they be in the Middle East, Mongolia or Persia. Some of them established vast estates as far away as Ceylon where serfs and slaves helped to grow various crops for export far and wide — coffee, cotton and sugar for example.

Indeed, the inspiration of Islam and the genius of Arabia met and produced a glorious moment in history the brilliance of which has shone all over the world. But no other part of the world, outside of the Islamic world, has benefited as much from the Arab-Muslim civilization as Western Europe. How the Islamic philosophers helped the development of medieval Scholasticism has been noted. Even more influential was Islamic science — mathematics, physics, chemistry, botany, astronomy, navigation and medicine. Furthermore, Islamic writings inspired the courtly lyrics of medieval Europe and some of its most popular prose works as the *Canterbury Tales*. Every Gothic cathedral carried marks of Islamic influence — ribbed vaulting, pointed and cusped arches, arabesques — and every medieval castle was designed at least in part after Muslim mansions. Finally, without the economic stimulus provided by Muslim commerce, industry and agriculture and without the spirit of adventure which the Arabs inspired, Western Europe would not have emerged as quickly as it did from the feudal age into the age of discoveries and into the modern era.

The Islamic world also benefited from interaction with the Christian world. Yet the first meetings of the two were armed confrontations — in the East the battle for Damascus in 635 and in the West the battle of Tours in 732. These confrontations continued through the Crusades and into the fifteenth and sixteenth centuries culminating in such historic turning points as the capture of Constantinople, the capital of the Christian Byzantine Empire by Muslim Turks (1453) and the Battle of Lepanto (1571) in which the European Christian powers defeated Ottoman Turkey. Even as the rapid expansion of the Arabic empire brought vast Christian populations under Muslim control, Islam exhibited remarkable religious tolerance. Muhammad himself, having been the beneficiary of Christian and Jewish ideals and having accepted the Old and New Testaments as divinely inspired books, had felt kinship towards Christians and Jews. Accordingly the "People of the Book" were given a special status, not being forced to convert if they submitted to Muslim rule and paid special taxes. As Muslim victories brought people of other great religions, such as Zoroastrians, Hindus and Buddhists, under Islamic governments, they too, were extended the same kind of toleration. Yet, it must be said that pressure, discriminatory taxation and occasional persecutions resulted in the conversion of virtually the entire populations of many Christian territories — North Africa and the Byzantine territories, for example. The same thing also happened to the Zoroastrians in Persia and the Hindus in many parts of India.

Yet, it must be noted that it was not by sword or pressure alone that Islam spread. Some of the largest Muslim communities in the world accepted Islam willingly, through a process of assimilation that lasted over periods of several centuries. Indonesia is the chief example of this. Other such Muslim communities exist in Malayasia, the Philippines, Ceylon and South India. Arab merchants implanted Islam in these regions, at first in their own commercial settlements. From these settlements Islam spread, through intermarriage between Middle Eastern Muslim settlers and natives, through commercial contacts, and as a result of Islam's superior posture over the animistic religions of the natives, into many islands of Indonesia, the Philippines, and most communities of the Malay Peninsula. To a lesser degree Islam also spread around the coastal cities of Ceylon and South India.

The fall of the Abbasids and the destruction of the extensive Arab Empire did not mean instant decline for Islam. Instead, several great Islamic empires arose from the ashes of the first. Of these the greatest was founded by the Turks. Even though the nomadic Turks had established a khanate spanning much of western and central Asia before the time of Muhammad, it was not until the late century that they became politically and culturally prominent. The conversion of the Seljuks, a clan of Orghuz Turks, in 960, through the efforts of the separatist Samanid dynasty which ruled the eastern provinces of the Abbasid empire in its declining years, was a landmark. So was the Battle of Manzikert in 1071 in which the Seljuks dealt a shattering blow to the Byzantine Empire. Thus arose the second Turkish empire, now Islamic and, since the 1057 Abbasid capitulation, the official rulers of the Islamic heartlands. It was the fortunate rise of the Seljuks that saved the Middle East for Islam from the Christian crusaders (although it must be noted that it was the ill-treatment of Christians by the Seljuks, fervent new converts to Islam, in contrast to the tolerance of their Arab predecessors, that provoked the Crusades). But the Seljuks were not able to defend Islamic lands from another invading army, the Mongols. On New Year's Day, 1256, the Mongol general, Hulagu, marched on to Baghdad, sacked the city and murdered the last Abbasid caliph, who was thrown under the hoofs of horses, all rolled up in a carpet, as the superstitious Mongols were afraid of shedding the blood of a religious figure. It remained to the

Mamelukes, another Turkish clan that rose to prominence after the fall of the Seljuks, to avenge this atrocity and kill Hulagu in a surprise attack on September 3, 1260, thus shattering the myth of Mongol invincibility. It was also the Mamelukes who revived the caliphate in Cairo, the first caliph being selected from the house of Abbasid, thus once again providing a central authority figure for Islam. Yet it was not the Mamelukes, but another Turkish clan, the Ottomans, who inherited the mantle of the fallen Arab Empire and provided another great era in Islamic history.

The founder of the clan, Osman (Othman), was one of those wandering warlords inhabiting the no-man's land between the Seljuk and Byzantine empires. Islamic, but fiercely independent, the followers of Osman did not allow themselves to be ruled by the Seljuks, instead when the Seljuk empire began to crumble they started to prey upon it. By 1326, Osman's son, Orkhan, held enough territories to declare himself a sultan. His power was such that the Byzantine Emperor called on him three times for help and gave him one of his own daughters in marriage. Yet it was one of Orkhan's successors, Muhammad II, the Conqueror, who dealt Byzantium the fatal blow by capturing Constantinople in 1453. From then on the Ottomans ruled, as emperors, from the throne set up symbolically in the Hagia Sophia, the famed cathedral of Emperor Justinian.

The conquest of Constantinople was the culmination, indeed the crowning point, symbolically and really, of a series of victories the Ottomans had won over the previous one hundred and odd years. The new stature they thus achieved assured them of the leadership of the Islamic world. In fact, the Ottoman Sultans had assumed the title of caliph from the time of Murad I (1362-89). Furthermore, they imposed their supremacy over the entire region of the fallen Seljuk empire and conquered Muslim territories that had become independent, since the decline of the Seljuks, such as Egypt. In addition, they confronted and conquered much of Christian Eastern Europe, and at one point, from July 17 to September 12, 1683, even encircled Vienna, the seat of the Holy Roman Emperor. Only the heroic effort by a combination of Western Christian forces, led by King John Sobieski of Poland and supported by the pope and the Germans, succeeded in breaking the siege. In the Mediterranean, the Ottomans built a navy through the help of the corsair pirate Khayr-ad-Din Barbarossa, which forced the Venetians out of their Aegean possessions and persistently threatened the coasts of Europe. Although the European powers were able to deal a decisive defeat to the Sultan's navy in the Battle of Lepanto in 1571, the Ottomans continued to remain a formidable force in the sea into the eighteenth century.

Astounding though the success of the Ottomans in empire building, their cultural legacy was limited to some advancements in the science of geography and to their concept of religious toleration. Although the Turkish literature originated as early as the eleventh century and although even some of the great sultans — Muhammad II, for example — were patrons of poetry and *belles lettres,* no great classic was produced by Turkish writers. Nor was the contribution of the Ottomans significant in the arts or the sciences. Perhaps their greatest achievement was the preservation of Islam in the Islamic heartlands in the aftermath of the collapse of the Seljuk empire.

While the Ottomans created a great empire in the western half of the old Arab empire, in the east another Turkish tribe, the Safawids, named after its fourteenth century conquering chief, established a vast empire centered in Persia. Ismail, its founder, entered Tabriz, after a series of conquests, and declared himself Shah in 1501. The empire reached its zenith during the reign of Abbas the Great who ascended the throne in 1587. The splendid new capital that he built, Isfahan, became a center of culture and luxury, rivaling any in the world. Once again literature and philosophy flourished in Persia. Religiously, the Safawids favored Shiism which, in the time of Abbas' successors, led to serious problems — increase of the power of the Shiite *ullama,* intolerant treatment of the non-Shiite Muslims, secession of the Sunnite Afghanis and the conquest of Persia itself by the Afghan leader Mahmud who declared himself Shah in 1722. Persia would never recover, except for a brief period during the reign of the great Turkish conqueror, Nadir Shah; instead, it would soon fall prey to European intrigues and the greed of Russia and Turkey.

Further east, still another great Muslim empire sprang up in the sixteenth century, the Mughal Empire of India. Its founder, Babur, partly a Turk from the line of Timur on the father's side and partly Mongol from the line of Genghis Khan on the mother's side, started as a princeling in southern Turkestan. Advancing through Afghanistan and through the mountain passes into India in 1525, he conquered most of Northern India by 1530. This was not the first time India saw Muslim conquerors, however. Even as early as the eleventh century, Turkish and Afghan Muslim raiders swooped down to the rich cities of the Indian plains in seasonal frequency. From the thirteenth century on, several Turkish and Afghan dynasties were also established in Northern India, the chief among them being the Sultanate of Delhi. In conquering India Babur put an end to this sultanate, by then severely wounded by the sack of Delhi by Timur (Tamerlane) a century earlier (1398-99) and further afflicted since then by internal problems. Babur died even before he completed his conquest, but in the five years he spent in India he established a strong foundation for the Mughal Empire. This empire reached its apogee by the middle of the sixteenth century, during the reign of Babur's grandson, Akbar (1556-1605). After Akbar the empire slowly declined over a period of two centuries, until the last of the Mughals, only nominally a ruler, was deposed by the British in 1857.

The Mughal period is noted for its extraordinary cultural achievements. Fostering a cosmopolitan atmosphere in their courts, employing in their administration Hindus, the majority population, and tolerating, in most cases, cultural and religious diversity, the Mughals achieved a synthesis of Persian, Arabic, Turkish, Byzantine and Indian cultures the marks of which are still seen in the art and literature of India. Three hundred years of Mughal rule and three hundred years of earlier Muslim rules helped also the spread of Islam, so much so that before its division into Pakistan (and Bangladesh) and India (1947) the subcontinent was home for the largest Muslim population anywhere in the world.

The decline of the Ottoman, Safawid and Mughal empires coincided with — in part it was caused by — the rise of European colonialism. No part of the Islamic world was spared from European penetration. In some areas it was outright occupation — India, Indonesia, Malaya and North Africa, for example; in others strong economic and cultural presence — Egypt, Persia and the Middle East. After the First World War, even some of these latter areas were brought under direct European control or supervision. In all cases Western influence intensified.

One reason for the West's increasing influence in the Islamic world was the appeal of Western science, technology and economic prosperity to the elite classes and the intelligentsia. For this reason large numbers of Western style educational and cultural institutions were introduced in Islamic lands. In some instances these institutions were introduced by the European overlords of these territories — the French in Algeria and the British in India, for example; while in others they were assiduously sought by native Muslim leaders who were eager to raise the level of their peoples to that of Europeans, as in the case of Egypt. In all cases, however, the result was a massive importation of European science, technology, philosophy, art and value system. Only a few pockets of the Islamic world, such as Saudi Arabia, remained relatively unaffected. Western cultural superiority was simply taken for granted.

Yet, one underlying purpose of the importation of Western culture was to gain for Islamic peoples an equal footing with the Westerners so that they may compete with and overcome the West on its own grounds. This introduced a new dimension in the meeting/confrontation of Islam and the West — nationalism. A Western idea, to be sure, but political nationalism began to be adopted by Islamic peoples from the late nineteenth century on as still another way of overcoming the West.

It must be noted, however, that it was not the methods adopted from the West alone that Islamic peoples used in their confrontation with the West. They also drew upon Islam's own resources. Chief among these was the concept of religious revival. Deeply rooted in the Koran and Islamic tradition, this concept was viewed variously — as the reappearance of an Imam as Mahdi or as the revitalization of Islamic faith and practices, for example — by various factions within the world of Islam. In the context of European colonialism, it was the traditionalists and the masses outside the urban centers — who viewed the lowly state of Islamic peoples as the result of corruption within Islam, caused by Western influence — who adopted this concept as the solution for Islam's problems. It was for this reason that the appearance of a Mahdi in Sudan in late nineteenth century was greeted with much enthusiasm by the desert peoples; and the Wahhabi movement of the eighteenth century had such a great impact on Arabia, resulting, in the twentieth century, in the creation of the modern Saudi state.

European withdrawal from all parts of the Islamic world after the Second World War was cheered by all factions of Muslims. But the house of Islam was divided by then on the issue of Islamic identity. The modernist view of an Islam that reconciled with Western values prevailed at first as the modernists, as beneficiaries of Western education and skills and as leaders of nationalist movements, inherited the positions of power vacated by the Europeans. Their success is marked by the Western style constitutions, legal systems and governmental structures that were adopted in many newly independent Islamic countries — Pakistan and Egypt, for example — with some modifications to accomodate Islamic values. But this situation was not going to last very long. The traditionalists rose to question the validity of Western style institutions in Islamic lands and to challenge the modernists' right to leadership. Within the past decade, this traditionalist challenge to modernism has become widespread throughout Islamic countries, assuming the characteristics of a religious revival. It is in the background of this revival that we should study the dramatic events that are taking place in the Islamic world.

I

ISLAM IN THE ISLAMIC WORLD TODAY, AN OVERVIEW

Seyyed Hossein Nasr

> *In the aftermath of the Iranian revolution and the upheavals in Mecca and the Asian and African countries with strong Muslim populations the question has been raised whether what we are witnessing is an Islamic revival of universal proportions. But the forces at work are so diverse and their philosophies and programs so conflicting that it would be difficult to perceive them all as parts of a larger Islamic movement although all of them lay claim to an Islamic heritage. In the face of these conflicting claims it is important to define what the Islamic heritage is and how the various movements in the Islamic world do or do not relate themselves to this heritage. Professor Nasr approaches this question from "the traditional point of view" and provides an overview of Islam in its history and contemporary manifestation.*
>
> *Seyyed Hossein Nasr is qualified to provide such an overview, perhaps more than any other Islamic scholar. Brought up in Teheran, Iran, educated in the United States, at M.I.T. and Harvard, trained in science and philosophy, having held distinguished professorships in Teheran and at the American University in Beirut, and being the author of over twenty books and two hundred articles, Nasr is recognized as one of the foremost authorities on Islam in the world. He delivered the Charles Strong Memorial Lectures in Australia in 1970 and is scheduled to deliver the Gifford Lectures in Edinburgh in 1981. He is currently professor of religion and Islamic studies at Temple University.*

The events of the last few years in various parts of the Islamic world have brought the question of the meaning and pertinence of Islam in the contemporary world to the forefront of international concern. Many people who had never known anything about Islam are now faced with the name, if not always the reality, practically from morning to night. But this very "current" concern which places Islam under the category of "current events" has itself caused a bewildering array of mis-statements and misrepresentations while at the same time providing an unparalleled opportunity to explain the teachings of Islam to a much larger audience than was previously possible. In a situation in which there is both the possibility of greater comprehension resulting from awakened interest and the danger of distortion and even the blemishing of the name of Islam as a result of all that passes under its banner, it is important to turn once again to the Islamic reality itself and to examine that reality in the context of the Islamic world and the external ideas, concepts and forces which have played and continue to play a role in that world and to which that reality has responded and is responding today.

As far as Islam itself is concerned, its meaning is clear from the traditional point of view which is that of this essay. Islam is a divinely revealed religion whose roots are contained in the Holy Quran, and the traditions of the Blessed Prophet — both written and oral — and whose branches embrace fourteen hundred years of a sacred and religious history which in its orthodoxy has embraced both Sunnism and Shi'ism as well as the esoteric dimension of the tradition contained in Sufism and which has produced not only the schools of law *(Sharī'ah)* but also theology, philosophy, a whole array of arts and sciences, a distinct educational system not to speak of political, economic, social and family structures and ethical and moral norms to which those structures are related. The roots of this tree have also produced a sacred and traditional art, both auditory and visual, ranging from the various methods of chanting the Holy Quran to calligraphy and architecture and finally various forms of Islamic literature. While Islam remains a trans-historical reality, it has also had this long historical deployment which has linked and continues to link every generation of Muslims to the Origin through time as the direct access to the spiritual world made possible by the rites and the *barakah* issuing from the Quranic revelation links each Muslim to the Origin through a hierarchic "space" which is present and accessible here and now. Islam is at once that inexhaustible trans-historical reality and the whole of the Islamic tradition as reflected in Islamic history and including not only roots but the trunk, branches and fruits which have issued from the roots.

As for the Islamic world, that term too needs some elucidation. In traditional Islamic terms the world would be divided into *dār al-islām*, the "abode of Islam" or where Islam rules as a majority religion, that is, where the Islamic sacred law or *Sharī'ah* governs human life; *dār al-sulh*, the "abode of peace" where Muslims live as the minority but where they are at peace and can practice their religion freely; and finally *dār al-harb*, the "abode of conflict or war", where Muslims are not only in a minority but where they are in a state of conflict with and struggle against the external social and political environment in order to be able to practice their religion. Had there not been the intrusion of secularism into the Islamic world since the nineteenth century, one could have simply defined the "Islamic world" as *dār al-islām*. But today the situation is made complicated by the fact that in many parts of *dār al-islām* itself non-Islamic forces have gained a footing sometimes under the name of a foreign ideology or a Western form of nationalism and sometimes even under the name of Islam itself which during the last few years has been used more and more in a clever and sometimes insidious fashion to hide the real nature of the forces in question. Moreover, Muslims in both *dār al-sulh* (such as India and parts of Africa) and even *dār al-harb* (such as Muslims in Europe) have come to play an important role in *dār al-islām* and modern means of communication have linked in a new fashion the Muslims in the three "worlds" or abodes defined above. It is therefore not so easy to define exactly what is meant by the Islamic world. For the sake of this discussion, however, let us define it as that part of the world in which there is either an Islamic majority or a substantial Muslim population even if the degree of attachment of the Muslims in all these regions to Islam is not exactly the same.

This question of the kind and degree of attachment of Muslims to Islam is itself a crucial question in the discussion of the role of Islam in the Islamic world today. Before modern times the degree of penetration of Islam within a particular region or ethnic group was mostly a question of the length of the process of Islamization. For example, in parts of Indonesia or Black Africa where Islam had penetrated for only a century, the process of Islamization had not been as complete as where this process that commenced let us say four centuries before. But in parts of the Islamic world in which Islam had had time to sink its roots and establish its institutions, the attachment of Muslims to Islamic practices was of such intensity that one could not easily say whether let us say the Egyptians or Syrians or Persians or Punjabis were more strongly attached to Islam although some communities emphasized more the formal, legal aspects and others inner attachment and faith according to the emphasis of the different schools of law and theology which they followed. Wherever the orthodox schools of Islam, whether Sunni or Shi'ite, were firmly rooted, the complete practice of Islamic precepts and attachment to the teachings of Islam were taken for granted. Differences existed only in such questions as pietistic attitudes, emphasis upon secondary forms of worship such as pilgrimage to local shrines or certain superogatory prayers, theological speculations, expressions of sacred art etc. which often demonstrated as much local variation as differences between various Islamic communities and ethnic groups and which at the same time reflected positive elements of the ethnic genius of the people in question, elements which Islam did not destroy but allowed to flower within the context of the Islamic universe.

In modern times, however, forces such as Western-styled nationalism, tribalism, and linguistic affinities as well as the different manner in which various parts of the Islamic world have experienced the modern world and such forces as colonialism, secular nationalism, racialism and Western lay humanism have caused a significant variation in the manner and degree of attachment of many Muslims to Islam. There are Muslims who never miss their daily prayers and live as much as they can by the Sharī'ah and consider their manner of following Islam as the only manner. But in contrast to days of old, there are also others who do not follow all the injunctions of the Sharī'ah and do not even pray regularly yet consider themselves as being definitely Muslim. And there are even others who do not do anything specifically Islamic except to follow a kind of "humanistic" ethics which is vaguely Islamic and who yet call themselves Muslims and would protest if called anything else. And again there is another group which performs the Islamic rites meticulously and yet breaks many of the moral injunctions of the Sharī'ah including for example, honesty in business while claiming to be ever devout.

From another point of view there are the majority for whom Islam is essentially an all-embracing ethical and social code, a way of life embodied in the Sharī'ah, and for those who wish to follow the spiritual life in the Tarīqah. And there are those for whom it is felt more than anything else as a culture and now, as a result of Western influence and a reaction against it, an ideology and political force with which to combat other ideologies. There are authentic as well as anti-traditional and modernistic interpretations and there are as a result many kinds and degrees of attachment to Islam especially in those parts of the Islamic world which have been long exposed to various types of modernistic influences. Those who speak of a "monolithic" Islam or a uniform wave of "fundamentalism" sweeping over the Islamic world or who try to scare the West by depicting Islam as a violent enemy unified to oppose the rest of the world are all too unaware of the differences and nuances which exist in the perception of

Islam and attachment to it by contemporary Muslims. If Islamic history has taught anything in this domain it is that even in traditional times no part of *dār al-islām* could speak for the whole and that the reaction of the whole of the Islamic world to such major events and forces as the introduction of Graeco-Hellenistic learning into the Islamic world, the Crusades or the Mongol invasion was never uniform. How much more is this true today when the degree of exposure of a college student in any cosmopolitan center of the Middle East to non-Islamic elements is totally different from the exposure of a villager from the same country not to speak of radical differences in the degree and manner of modernization and secularization in let us say the Yemen and Turkey.

Another point of central importance in the study of Islam in the Islamic world today is that because of the all-embracing nature of Islam, despite the recent process of secularization which has influenced the degree and manner of attachment of many Muslims to Islam, especially in the big cities which are centers of decision-making, for most Muslims all of their other relations and concerns are intertwined with their understanding of their religion as a reality inseparable from these other relationships. For example, a traditional Muslim has bonds to his family, city, nation, business, friends, etc. which he does not juxtapose to religion but sees in the context of a totality which for him is in one way or another, Islam. He does not see Islam *only* as an ideal, although it *is* of course an ideal especially as far as the ethical norms exemplified by the Blessed Prophet and the great figures of the religion are concerned. But for the ordinary Muslim it is more than anything else a reality with which he lives day and night. Therefore, in many cases he makes use of religious sentiments to solve family problems or further his economic or social goals or for the exercise of power if he feels that such sentiments will aid in reaching his aims. There are of course many Muslims who practice their religion only for the fear and love of God. But it would be a dangerous idealization of Islamic society and the forgetting of human frailty to think that every person who makes an ostentation of his attachment to Islam has nothing but the satisfaction of God in mind and that he would continue such ostentatious acts were the rest of his life, work, family, etc. disrupted or destroyed. For many people all of these forces, bonds and relationships are intertwined in a manner which can cause unexpected social and political upheavals in the name of religion but at the same time rapid changes of direction and aim without the religious elements appearing to be sacrificed or compromised.

Precisely because Islam is still a powerful force which pervades the lives of its believers, the misuse of it to further various personal and group interests is always a possibility, one which in fact has been and is being made use of not only by some Muslims themselves but also by many forces outside of the Islamic world. Obviously this kind of recourse to religious sentiments and practice is very different from the following of religion only for the sake of God, a difference which can result in devastating effects upon the whole world if there is a manipulation of Islam for non-Islamic ends.

With these general traits of the Islamic world in mind it is now necessary to turn to the more particular types of reactions which have been created within that world as a result of its encounter with the modern West, reactions which must be elucidated and fully understood if we are to grasp the nature of Islam in the Islamic world today. During the first twelve centuries of its historic existence Islam lived with full awareness of the truth and realization of God's promise to Muslims that they would be victorious if they followed His religion. Such verses as "There is no victor but God" *(Lā ghāliba illa'Llāh)* which adorns the walls of the Alhambra also adorned the soul and mind of Muslims. They were victorious in the world, the Crusades and the short conquest of the Islamic world by the Mongols not withstanding since the Crusaders were defeated and the grandson of Hulagu, Uljaytū, became a Muslim and in fact a patron of Islamic learning and the arts. The authenticity of the Quranic message was born out by the experience of history.

Then came the conquest of various parts of the Islamic world by the British, the French, the Dutch and the Russians not to speak of the more peripheral conquests of the Portuguese and the Spanish. Although Muslims were at first somewhat indifferent to the long range significance of these events, the conquest of Egypt by Napoleon caused a shock which made Muslim leaders aware of the dimension and meaning of the Western conquest of Islam. In the early 19th century the Muslim intelligentsia realized that clearly something had gone wrong which as mentioned by W. C. Smith, among other Western scholars of Islam, was on the dimension of a cosmic crisis. How was it that the Islamic world was being defeated by non-Islamic forces everywhere and in such irreversible fashion? Logically one of three attitudes could be taken:

1) Something had gone wrong with the world as God Himself had mentioned in His Book concerning the end of the world and the Blessed Prophet had described in his traditions. In such a case the

eclipse of Islam was itself a proof of the validity of the Islamic message which, however, also foretold of the imminent appearance of the Mahdi and the final eschatological events leading to the end of the world.

2) Muslims had ceased to follow Islam properly and should return to the practice of their religion in its pure form and with full vigor so as to defeat the non-Islamic forces and escape the punishment they were receiving in the hands of God for their negligence of their religion. Such a reaction resulted mostly in the Wahhābī and Neo-Wahhābī movements associated with the Deoband school in India, the followers of Muhammad 'Abduh and the Salafiyyah in Egypt and Syria etc. but was also connected with the much less studied inner revivals within Sufi orders or establishment of new ones such as the Darqāwiyyah and Tījāniyyah in Morocco and West Africa, the Sanūsiyyah in Libya, the Yashrūtiyyah in the Arab Near East, the Ni'matallāhiyyah in Persia, the Chishtiyyah and Qādiriyyah in India and many others.

3) The Islamic message had to be changed, modified, adopted or reformed to suit modern conditions and be able to adapt itself to the modern world so as to overcome Western domination. Out of this attitude grew all of the different types of modernism influenced by the French revolution and the rationalism of such men as Descartes and Voltaire in some quarters, and Locke and Hume and later Spencer and Bergson in others. The so-called Arab liberalism as well as modernistic movements in Turkey, Persia and the Indian subcontinent were also results of this third possible reaction to the subjugation of the Islamic world by the West.

In some cases these elements mixed with each other, Mahdiism, puritanical or "fundamentalist" tendencies and modern reformist elements combining together in the thoughts and teachings of a single figure or school. Sometimes even Sufi figures had a Mahdiist aspect as the study of the life of such figures as 'Abd al-Qādir in Algeria, Usman dan Fadio in Nigeria and al-Hājj 'Umar of Futa Toro in East Africa reveals. In such cases Sufism itself undertook the task of reviving the Islamic community as a whole, a task which has not received nearly as much attention by Western scholarship as the fruit of the efforts of the Neo-Wahhābī and modernistic reformers.

These reactions continued to animate certain segments of Islamic society for the next century until the Second World War although the wave of Mahdiism gradually died down after giving birth to such diverse phenomena as the Ahmadiyyah movement in India and

Pakistan, the Bābī-Bahā'ī movement in Persia and the Mahdiist state in the Sudan.

With the end of the Second World War certain events took place which revived or altered the movements which had grown out of the original reaction of Islam to its domination by the West. First of all nearly the whole of the Islamic world became politically "independent" but as national states along the model of European states. This apparent freedom brought with it the expectation of greater cultural and social independence especially as the less Westernized elements of Islamic society began to gain political and economic power. Secondly, the vast array of wealth pouring into much of the Islamic world brought with it the acceleration of the process of industrialization and modernization and heightened the tensions already present between Islam and the ethos of modern Western civilization, tensions which had not been solved either intellectually or socially and which had been mostly glossed over by the well-known earlier figures usually known as "reformers" as well as by the *'ulamā'* (religious scholars) who had hardly concerned themselves with them.

These events within the Islamic world were complemented by transformations within the Western world itself which were also to have profound consequences for movements within the Islamic world. From the moment the West conquered the Islamic world until the Second World War, the Islamic world saw in the West another model or philosophy for human existence which, while many in that world rejected, the modernists in it accepted wholeheartedly. But few doubted the success of this model at least from the point of view of man's life on earth whatever the consequences might have been for man's immortal soul. Before the Second World War few Muslims were seriously affected by Spengler's *Decline of the West* which in fact had been translated into Arabic and Persian and fewer still had read the gloomy description of Western civilization by such literary figures as T. S. Eliot although this poet has exercised a great influence on certain Arab poets during the past few decades. And practically no one save a small circle in Cairo had read the "prophetic" works of R. Guénon such as *The Crisis of the Modern World* and *The Reign of Quantity and the Signs of the Times* predicting the collapse of the modern world, although Guénon had moved permanently to Cairo in 1931. It was only after the Second World War that the Islamic intelligentsia became aware that within the Western world itself there were profound criticisms of that civilization and that the Western model which so many Muslims had tried to emulate was itself breaking down.

This movement in the West was combined with an attempt on the part of many to seek their roots once again, to rediscover tradition and to regain access to the sacred. So, while much of what remained of the Western tradition was floundering and giving place to despair and nihilism, there was also a reassertion of traditional teachings, a rediscovery of myth and symbols, a positive appreciation of non-Western religions and even a reappraisal of the medieval Western heritage which ceased to appear as dark as its purblind Renaissance and 18th century critics had made it to be. All these developments were bound to and in fact did affect the few but influential intellectual and religious leaders, critics, writers, scholars, and other leaders within the Islamic world.

Finally, a change began to appear in the attitude of non-Islamic powers, both Western and communist, toward the forces within the Islamic world. After the Second World War for some time Islam as a religion was belittled as a possible force to be reckoned with by the outside world but various nationalistic forces, which in most cases were in fact combined with religious sentiments in one way or another, were manipulated in every conceivable way to aid the cause and aims of the powers in question to the extent possible. The history of the various forms of Arab nationalism during the past decades is a good example of the way these forces were at work. Then, as the situation changed, the same policy of manipulation began to be used in the case of religious forces themselves through indirect aid or hindrance of a particular religious school or organization or sudden aggrandisement of a particular force or movement and belittling of others which might not be of immediate political or economic benefit to the interested powers. This external manipulation, although relying on existing movements, tendencies, forces and personalities in the Islamic world has played and continues to play an important role in the manner in which these forces and processes develop and change and the way the personalities in question are able or not able to exercise influence and leadership. This manipulation is not the only factor but certainly an important one to be reckoned with if one wishes to understand the present state of Islam and Islamic forces within the Islamic world.

With the earlier reactions of the Islamic world to the West in mind and with full consideration of the new forces and changes brought upon the scene since the Second World War, it is now possible to describe the present state of forces, movements and tendencies within Islam as they affect and mold the contemporary Islamic world.

There are first of all a number of forces, differing in many basic features among themselves, which are more or less heir to the type of the earlier Wahhābī reaction against the Western world and which are usually termed "fundamentalist" although this term has particular Christian and in fact Protestant connotations which do not apply exactly to the Islamic situation. These forces share in common a disdain for the West, a distrust of foreign elements, a strong activist tendency and usually opposition or indifference to all the inward aspects of Islam and the civilization and culture which it created, aspects such as Sufism, Islamic philosophy, Islamic art, etc. They are all outwardly oriented in the sense that they wish to reconstruct Islamic society through the re-establishment of external legal and social norms of an Islamic nature rather than by means of the revival of Islam through inner purification or by removing the philosophical and intellectual impediments and obstacles which have been an obstacle on the path of many contemporary Muslims. These movements, therefore, have rarely dealt in detail with intellectual challenges posed by Western science and philosophy although this trait is not by any means the same among all of them, some being of a more intellectual nature than others.

Politically also there has not been a uniformity of program among them. Some have sought to revive the caliphate, others have supported other traditional forms of government such as the sultanate or amirate and yet others have opted for a Western type of democracy in an Islamic context while still others have a violent and revolutionary political nature in some of which the most fanatical and volcanic elements of Western nationalism and Marxist revolutionary theories and practices have been set in what the followers of these groups consider as an Islamic setting. There is only one political aim in which these so-called "fundamentalist" forces are united, and that is the unification of the Islamic world or what is called Pan-Islamism. In this sense they are all heirs to the campaign of Jamāl al-Dīn Astarābādī known as al-Afghānī who in the 19th century called for the reunification of the Islamic world. But although pan-Islamism has remained an ideal espoused by nearly all Islamic leaders and intellectual figures during the past century and remains encrusted in the traditional Islamic vision of the perfect state to be established by the Mahdī before the end of time, the manner of its execution as part of a practical political program has hardly been agreed upon by the diverse groups who speak of it. Some preach the re-establishment of a single caliphate or central political authority as during the time of the four "rightly-guided caliphs" *(khulafā' rāshidūn)*. Others speak of a commonwealth of Muslim nations and yet others while using pan-Islamism as a slogan to arouse the religious sentiments of the people, remain deliberately vague as to how it would be carried out in practice. The manipulation of these so-called "fundamentalist" Islamic forces by external powers to achieve ends as diverse as creating a wall of defense against communism and making certain that what is called economic development in current parlance does not move past a certain stage is particularly dangerous because of the ambivalent and vague aspect of the political dimension of these forces. The effect that such manipulations are having and will have upon the Islamic community is bound to be very different from what so-called experts who provide the programs for such manipulation have envisaged.

Of the "fundamentalist" forces the oldest are without doubt those which inherited the earlier Wahhābī movement and have carried that movement to our own day. These forces that are centered mostly in Saudi Arabia which follows officially the Wahhābī interpretation of Islam and which from the beginning were associated with a group of Islamic scholars in the Hejaz and especially Medina, include neo-Wahhābīs in Egypt, Syria, Jordan and other countries of the Arab Near East, many of whom were influenced by the Salafiyyah movement whose base was in Egypt and Syria until the Second World War and which withdrew later into the Hejaz. Its influence is felt directly in many Muslim seats of learning such as al-Azhar, but it is less of a distinct political force of an activist nature than it was in the 19th century.

In the subcontinent of India this type of "fundamentalist" movement has had many expressions of which perhaps the most significant today is the *Jamā'at-i islāmī* (literally "Society of Islam") of Pakistan founded by Maulānā Abu'l-'Alā' Maūdudī. This organization is closely knit and of a semi-secret nature, its purpose being the revival of the Islamic way of life. It has direct political and social goals and is of an activist nature although it is milder than the violent revolutionary movements and is more interested in the consideration of the more intellectual dimensions of the confrontation between Islam and modernism. There are organizations of a similar nature among Muslims of India itself as well as in Indonesia with close links to the Pakistani "society".

An organization of a somewhat longer history but more limited political power at the present moment is the famous Muslim Brotherhood *(al-Ikhwān al-Muslimīn)* founded in Egypt before the Second World War but later extended to other Muslim countries especially the Persian Gulf region where many of its members settled after the execution in Egypt of its leader, Sayyid Qutb during the rule of Jamāl 'Abd al-Nāsir. This organization which has also been involved in political plots of various kinds and even accused of political assassinations, has also produced a religious literature which has had some influence among some of the young in the Arab world and even elsewhere. Adherents to its cause are also found in the Arab countries of North Africa although in much smaller numbers and an organization called the *Fadā'iyān-i islām* (literally "those who sacrifice themselves for Islam") was founded in Iran in the 40's on the model of the *Ikhwān* and following the same programs including the elimination of certain political figures.

In Turkey the appearance of a remarkable politico-religious figure, Sayyid Sa'īd Nūrsī, during the time of Ataturk and the outward secularization of Turkey made possible the founding of a secret organization whose aim was the protection of Islam from secularism. The members of this organization grew rapidly in number and represent today a very significant voice in Turkey. They are usually given much more to Islamic education and the rejuvenation of the Islamic faith based on the Quranic commentary of their founder, than to political activism or direct violence. There are, however, Islamic movements in Turkey which use violence especially when faced with Marxists, and who espouse the cause of the re-establishment of the caliphate abolished by Ataturk.

The nature of this type of "fundamentalism" in Iran is of a more complicated nature since Iran is mostly Shi'ite and traditionally Shi'ism always disdained political power and kept aloof from it. Until just a short time ago the majority of Shi'ite scholars followed the traditional interpretation of Shi'ism, leaving it to the Mahdī to actually take the reign of power in his hands. Moreover, protest over modernism as a threat to Islamic values, the intrusion of the so-called "Islamic Marxism" into the arena of Islamic action, the direct participation of non-Islamic powers, both communist and Western oriented, in the guise of Islam in events which have been carried out in the name of Islam and many other complications have created a remarkably complex mixture in which genuine Islamic sentiments have become combined with all kinds of extraneous forces. Only the passage of time will allow the sifting of these elements and judgment upon the nature of the forces at play.

The type of "fundamentalism" thus far described, can also be found in other Muslim countries not cited here such as in the Sudan and

Nigeria or among the Afghans before and even after the Soviet invasion. The only part of the Islamic world where such forces have made no headway at all, in contrast to the hope and expectations of certain elements in the West which have sought to manipulate these forces, is among the Muslims of the Soviet Union and China. As far as the former is concerned, the cause for the continued presence of Islam and its vitality is in fact to be sought not at all in some kind of externalized, "fundamentalist" revival but in the Sufi orders which have kept the flame of faith burning within the heart of men despite adverse external circumstances.

"Fundamentalist" movements have also been related in many ways to the several international Islamic conferences, leagues and the like which have their centers in such places as Saudi Arabia, Pakistan and even in Europe and whose goal is the unity of the Islamic world. Although the political perspective of these organizations is not the same, they share the goal of achieving some form of unity and bringing the Islamic peoples closer together. They therefore often attract people who are also attracted to one form or another of the neo-Wahhābī, puritanical or "fundamentalist" movements although there is no necessary link between the two and one can in fact remain a completely traditional Muslim and yet strive for the unity of the Islamic peoples as is in fact the case in many instances. But there is also no doubt that many of the leaders and administrators of these international Islamic organizations are also those who are leaders of various kinds of "fundamentalist" movements. This nexus seems in fact to be found most often in the Indo-Pakistani world and Southeast Asia.

The second reaction spoken of earlier in this essay, namely the espousal of one form or another of modernism, has also led to the creation of powerful forces within the Islamic world today, forces whose nature and degree of Islamicity has, however, been open to debate. Since the Second World War the very advent of political independence of many Islamic countries brought to the fore once again the question of the relationship between nationalism and Islam. From this debate have grown several forms of what can be called "Islamic nationalism", that is, a way of thinking which accepts both Islam and a particular nationhood and seeks to weld them together. The experience of Pakistan is the most outstanding example of such a wedding between the idea of a nation or state in the modern sense and Islam. Because Pakistan was created for the sake of Islam, obviously its nationalism could not be anti-Islamic as certain earlier forms of virulent nationalism like that of Turkey. But many Pakistanis give a positive connotation to their wedding of Islam and nationalistic sentiments and consider this type of coupling of sentiments as positive both from an Islamic point of view and the geo-political realities of this century. The same attitude can be found among most Persians, Malays, Senegalese, etc. In fact in many Islamic countries where a sense of nationhood or at least separate existence as an autonomous entity preceded the intrusion of the modern European concept of nationalism, Islamic and national sentiments have developed a *modus vivendi* which has allowed Islam to flourish in its authentic, traditional form within the state without being abused for ends beyond itself.

As for Arab nationalism, since it is already based not on an actual political entity such as Egypt, Syria or Iraq, but upon the unification of present day states into a bigger unit, it is of a unique nature and has created a phenomenon which is different from other types of nationalism within the Islamic world. But what is interesting from the point of view of this essay is that earlier Arab nationalism was essentially a secular movement led often by Christian rather than Muslim Arabs. It has left behind at least one important political expression which is the Ba'th party. Later Arab nationalism, whether in the form of Nasserism or Qadhafi's version or any other brand has become more and more Islamic in nature. For most Arabs today it is impossible to separate their "Arabism" *('urūbah)* from Islam and in fact among the masses when they use *'urūbah* the connotation in their minds is practically completely Islamic. Arab nationalism has in a sense nationalized Islam with all the dangers that such an act implies for the universal teachings of Islam which are opposed to all forms of parochialism especially the fanatical and narrow form of nationalism which grew out of the French Revolution in contrast to the natural love of man for his nation and country to which the Prophet of Islam referred when he said, "The love of one's nation comes from faith (in religion)." Nevertheless this process has caused most Arab nationalistic sentiments and forces to possess also strong Islamic elements although the secular type of Arab nationalism is of course also still very much present especially in the eastern Arab countries.

Another type of movement that has grown from the modernizing quarters within the Islamic world and which has been in vogue among many young Muslims during the past two decades is the so-called "Islamic socialism" and lately "Islamic Marxism". Those who follow these movements have been influenced of course by the Soviet and socialist worlds and their apparent espousal of pro-Arabic and pro-Islamic causes in such matters as the Arab-Israeli question but without regard for the plight of Muslims within the socialist world itself. Many people who accept the slogan of "Islamic socialism" understand by socialism social justice and in their desire to promulgate justice in their own societies adopt an "Islamic socialist" stance. In certain states this ideological position is directly supported by the state and is made use of by existing political forces more or less sympathetic to the Soviet world. Although the theoretical constructs upon which this movement is based have come mostly out of leftist circles in France and, the movement itself is strongest among Islamic countries which were culturally French originally such as Algeria and more recently Iran (as far as a circle educated in France is concerned), it can also be found in the Arab Near East where Islamic socialism has come to replace the Arab socialism of two decades ago (and still surviving in Syria and Iraq). There are also defendants of this amalgamation of Islam and socialism in Pakistan, India and Southeast Asia.

As for Islamic Marxism, this thesis is of a much more recent origin associated with certain extremist groups in the Middle East which consider themselves as Muslims but which use a nearly completely Marxist political ideology and also means of achieving their goals. In fact the so-called "Islamic Marxists" interpret Islam itself as a political revolutionary force in the sense that revolution has been understood in the context of Marxist and post-Marxist schools in European history. This movement has naturally received much attention as well as support from the so-called intellectually Marxist circles in France and other European countries and the figures whose works have been used by the Islamic socialist and Marxist groups have been in close contact with leftist circles in the West. Today, this type of modernism within the Islamic world is an important force to contend with, not because of the number of its adherents or the degree of its popularity among the mass of the people, but because of its being used as a means of allowing totally un-Islamic and in fact anti-Islamic forces to gain access to power within certain of the Islamic countries.

The cataclysmic events of recent years have also brought back to life the movement of Mahdiism which had been dormant for over a century since the wave caused by the first encounter between Islam and the modern world. The fact that much of the Islamic world is under the cultural and economic domination of non-Islamic forces, that the very attempt to free oneself from this domination through industrialization and the like brings with it a greater destruction of Islamic values, that the world as a whole seems to be confronted with so many apparently insoluble problems such as the ecological crisis, and that forces of destruction have become such that all peoples are threatened with extinction at all times have all aided to bring back a sense of the imminent appearance of the Mahdī, the one who will destroy inequity and re-establish the rule of God on earth. The fact that this year is the year 1400 of the Islamic calendar and that the Blessed Prophet had promised that at the beginning of every century, a renewer *(mujaddid)* would come to revive Islam from within has only strengthened this feeling of expectation of the Mahdī. Already in the fall of 1979, the holiest cite in Islam, namely the House of God in Mecca, was captured in the name of the Mahdī although the forces at work were far from being those of simply pious Muslims helping to bring about the parousia. During the Iranian Revolution also many simple people believed that the coming of the Mahdī was imminent. Without doubt, as the forces of destruction in the world increase, as the natural system strains ever more under the burden of a technology which is alien to the natural rhythms of the life of the cosmos and as movements which speak in the name of Islam itself fail to create the ideal Islamic order which they always promise, this sense of expectation of the Mahdī and movements associated with it will increase among traditional and devout Muslims. This force is certainly a reality among present day Muslims and is bound to continue as a powerful force in the future.

Finally, there is a fourth kind of force or presence in contemporary Islam which must be mentioned especially since it has received practically no attention so far. This force is the revival of the Islamic tradition from within by those who have encountered the modern world fully and who with full awareness of the nature of the modern world and all the problems of a philosophical, scientific and social nature which it poses, have returned to the heart of the Islamic tradition to provide answers and to revive the Islamic world as a spiritual reality amidst the chaos and turmoil created throughout the world by what is called modernism. The number of this group has of necessity been small. Their theatre of action has been not mass meetings or political gatherings but the hearts and minds of individuals gathered in small circles. For this group Islam is traditional Islam with its roots sunk in heaven and its branches spread through a vast world stretching in a space from the Atlantic to the Pacific and in a time span covering fourteen centuries. They reject nothing of the Islamic tradition whether it be its art or sciences or philosophy not to speak of Sufism which they consider as the heart of the whole body of Islam whose limbs governed by the *Sharī'ah* are animated by the blood flowing from this heart. To this group it is Islamic metaphysics which provides an answer to problems posed by such modern ideologies and "isms" as rationalism, humanism, materialism, evolutionism, psychologism and the like. For them the revival of the Islamic world must come with the revival of the Muslims themselves. Their idea of reform is not the modern one which always begins with the outward, which wishes always to reform the world but never man himself. They emphasize inner reform of Islamic society as a whole. Their attitude to the world, including the modern world, is not that of passive acceptance. They criticize the modern world in the light of immutable principles and view it as a canvas alluring from afar but shown to be of an illusory nature when its texture is examined from close by. They stand at the center of Islamic orthodoxy and consider all violent movements which incorporate the worst elements of Western civilization to combat that civilization as a disservice to Islam and below the dignity of God's last revelation.

This group believes in inner revival *(tajdīd)* which is a traditional Islamic concept and not external reform *(islāh)* which is a modern idea grafted upon the body of Islam. The model for this group is an al-Ghazzālī, an 'Abd al-Qādir al-Jīlānī or a Shaykh Ahmad Sirhindī and not some 19th century or 20th century leftist revolutionary who would simply be given a Muslim name. This group acts without acting in the sense that its function is more that of knowledge and presence than action, but it is from this group that there has flowed and continues to flow some of the most profound and religiously significant Islamic responses to the modern world. And it is this group that in the long run will leave the deepest effect upon the Islamic community as has been the case in the past.

The four types of groups or movements within the Islamic world today, namely the "fundamentalist", "modernist", "Mahdiist" and "traditional" are not of course always exclusive of each other although certain positions such as the traditionalist excludes others such as the modernist. For example, in the "fundamentalist" camp there are those who are attached to Sufism and close to the traditionalist perspective, others who share certain elements with the modernists and yet others who are strongly attracted by the Mahdiist type of sentiment. If all of these forces have been divided into these four categories, it has been to facilitate discussion and also to point to four fundamental types or attitudes which are discernible in the Islamic world today. Of course it is essential to remember that in many parts of the Islamic world the majority of Muslims continue their lives in the traditional manner and are not involved in any of the theological, religious or political reactions to the modern world already mentioned. The vast number of Muslims whose belonging to the Islamic tradition is still defined in terms of the traditional Islamic categories rather than as reactions to modern ideologies and thought patterns must always be kept in mind.

Islam is still very much alive in the Islamic world today; but also there are so-called "Islamic forces" within the Islamic world which are often manipulated and altered in such a manner that although they remain forces, it is doubtful that they are still Islamic. Not everything that happens to occur in the Islamic world is Islamic nor is every birth in that part of the world an Islamic renaissance. After all, according to authentic Islamic traditions, the anti-Christ is also to be born in the Islamic world. Close attention must be paid to the Islamic character of all that is chosen to be called Islamic in a world in which the use and misuse of practically anything can take place as long as it serves the aims of the powers that be. In any full discussion of Islam today, one must ask in every instance what is meant by "Islamic". Islam is not a vague idea. It is a religion with its Sacred Book, traditions of its Blessed Prophet, sacred law, theology, mystical paths and a specific manner of looking at the world of nature and of creating art. There are certainly such things as Islamic orthodoxy and orthopraxis and therefore their opposites. There are traditional forces and anti-traditional forces and such fundamental differences cannot be glossed over by the simple use of the term "Islamic".

Today we are witness to a vast religious community which is still alive and whose teachings on all levels from the most esoteric to daily laws are kept intact. But we are also witness to the destruction of certain elements of this religious world not only through modernistic forces alien to its genius but also to modernistic forces which in order not to appear as alien put on the guise of Islamicity in order to enter within the citadel of Islam. It will serve neither the interest of the Islamic world, nor of Christianity nor of even the secularized West to remain oblivious to fundamental differences between forces at play and to use mass media dominated by a new version of triumphalism to blind people to the difference between Islamic forces seeking genuine political and social expression and totally anti-Islamic or at best non-Islamic political forces using the guise of Islam to further their own ends. Nor is it wise to neglect the more hidden forms of inner revival and rejuvenation which have always been and will always be at the heart of every authentic religious regeneration.

It is the hope of every Muslim concerned with the future of Islam that the energy and vitality of Islam will react in a constructive manner with other religions faced, like Islam, with the withering effects of modern secularism and not that this vitality be channelled into volcanic eruptions and violent reactions which will in the long run leave both the Islamic world and the world at large impoverished spirtually whatever advantage they might serve in the short run to serve the immediate aims of present-day world powers. Let us hope that Islamic movements and groups will channel and guide their activities in a manner which is worthy before the sight of God and not according to the expediency of the moment and what might appear as politically or economically opportune. Islamic history stands as witness to the fact that only those acts have had and will have an enduring effect upon the heart and soul of Muslims and the Islamic world at large that have been performed in the light of eternity and according to the Will of the One, the surrender to whose Will has given rise to *islām* itself.

Suggestions for Further Reading

Ahmad, A., *Islamic Modernism in India and Pakistan.* London, 1967.

Brohi, A. K., *Islam in the Modern World,* Karachi. 1968.

Cragg, K., *Counsels in Contemporary Islam,* Edinburgh. 1965.

Gibb, H. A. R., *Modern Trends in Islam.* Chicago, 1945.

Jameelah, M., *Islam in Theory and Practice.* Lahore, 1967.

——————————————, *Islam versus the West.* Lahore, 1968.

Lings, M., *A Sufi Saint of the Twentieth Century.* Los Angeles, 1975.

Nadwi, Abdul Hasan Ali, *Saviours of Islamic Spirit.* trans. M. Ahmad, Lucknow, 1971.

al Naquib at-Attas, S. M., *Islam and Secularism.* Kuala Lumpur, 1978.

Nasr, S. H., *Ideals and Realities of Islam.* Boston, 1973.

_____, *Islam and the Plight of Modern Man.* London, 1976.

_____, *Islamic Life and Thought.* London, 1980.

Rahman, Fazlur, *Islam.* London, 1966.

Schuon, F., *Understanding Islam,* trans. D. M. Matheson. Baltimore, 1974.

Smith, W. C., *Modern Islam in India.* Princeton, 1957.

II

RELIGIOUS REVIVALISM IN ISLAM: PAST AND PRESENT

Victor Danner

> *The answer to the question of whether the upheavals in the Islamic world represent an authentic revival or reformation of the religion lies at least in part in a determination of whether the Prophet himself or the Quranic Revelation presupposed such revivals/reformations. Professor Danner affirms such a presupposition and contends that genuine restorations of Islamic religion after periods of decay always did, and perhaps always will, come about through the work of the live Sufi orders who have accomplished a healthy integration of the sacred Law and the sacred Path of Islam. While challenging the authenticity of various forces at work today in the Muslim countries as agents of such a renovation of Islamic religion and culture Danner nevertheless emphasizes the need and even the inevitability of a revival of Islam.*
>
> *Victor Danner is professor in the Department of Near Eastern Languages and Cultures at Indiana University.*

Revivalism implies that old beliefs and ways, which had lain dormant for some time, can be revived through the influence of an individual or a movement. But there are different types of revivals. At times, a revival in one domain spells death in another; at times, a revival has nothing to do with the traditional way of life, and is even counter to it; and finally, at times, a revival is a genuine rebirth of the religion as a whole.

For example, the application of the Islamic law so that it leads to the destruction of the Sufi mystical orders (that constitute the Path of contemplation in Islam) might be considered a revival in the eyes of certain religious authorities, but it is, at the same time, a death of the mystical life in the country where the eradication of Sufism occurred.

Another example: the reinterpretation of the Islamic traditional political theories in such a way as to produce an "Islamic republic" which does away with the long-established monarchical institutions of that religion could hardly be called a revival of Islam. Republican regimes never existed in the traditional Islamic civilization. In abolishing the Persian monarchy, the Shi'ite religious chief, al-Khomeini, has created a political structure that is called an "Islamic republic," with himself as the real chief, but it has nothing to do with the traditional political institutions of Islam nor is it recognizable as a republican regime, in the normal sense of the word.

Normally, a revival within any religion should have spiritual results that are recognizably such by virtue of the criteria laid down in its Scriptures and the traditional doctrines. Within Islam, the great sages and saints are the ones whose writings throughout the course of the centuries have furnished the spiritual interpretations of the Quran. Their exegesis, for the most part, has been mystical in nature, to be sure, but at the same time it has been faithful to the deeper aspects of the Quranic Revelation. There have also been, side by side with the mystical commentaries, the more popular, non-mystical commentaries of the Quran, and they have been responsible for maintaining a traditional outlook easily grasped by the knowledgeable and pious Muslims. In either case, whether we are talking about mystical or non-mystical exegesis of the Quran, we are concerned with the eminent traditional authorities of Islam. They were anxious to transmit, in more developed fashion, the truths imbedded in the original Revelation, which was the Quran, and that transmission is really what is meant by tradition.

But a religion is not simply a doctrine — or an ensemble of revealed truths. It is also a way of life in keeping with those truths. In other words, the original Message of Islam, like that of other religions, is both belief and practice, and these two can be interpreted either mystically or non-mystically, according to perspective. It is in the light of the tradition as a whole — that is, as both a system of beliefs and practices — that one should evaluate revivals or declines. The traditional doctrines of Islam and its way of life are what give us the criteria that permit speaking objectively of any socio-religious phenomenon appearing on the historical scene of the Islamic faith at the present day, or in the past, for that matter. One should recall that the traditional doctrines of Islam cover an immense domain: Islam has its own theological, philosophical, mystical, cosmological, sociological, political, and other teachings, that cover a wide gamut of intellectual and spiritual perspectives which remain mostly unknown by modernist and even conservative Muslims of recent times. The rediscovery of these teachings, by the way, is perhaps the single most important problem facing the intellectual leaders of the Muslim world in these times, whose ideas are generally drawn from the many conflicting ideologies that circulate in the modern Western civilization, and these are hardly compatible with Islamic teachings and ways of life. That being so, and since the phrase "Islamic revival" is often abusively employed even in relation to movements that are antitraditional in nature, we would do well to examine just how Islam itself looks upon the question of revival, which implies also knowing how it looks upon the corollary question, that of decline.

The question of religious revivalism in Islam is intimately bound up with the foundations of the Islamic religion itself, namely, the Quran and the Norm of the Prophet, or the *Sunnah*. The Quranic Revelation is a pure monotheism that states the principle of the Oneness of the Divinity, or *Allah*, with compelling force. The *Sunnah* of the Prophet sets down the way of life that must be followed by the Muslim and the Islamic community in general. The Quran gives us the theory, the *Sunnah* gives us the practice of Islam. The two go together, for the Quran without the *Sunnah* of the Prophet would be ineffective in establishing the rituals and other prescriptions of the faith; and the *Sunnah* without the Sacred Text would be like an ensemble of actions without transcendent principles to back them up.

If all revivalism in Islam is always related somehow to the Quran and the *Sunnah*, this in no way implies that these two foundations of Islam are interpreted by all parties in a uniform fashion. When we consult the history of that faith, we see emerging from the original Revelation two great traditions, the spiritual esoterism or mystical way of life that later on would be called Sufism, and the religious exoterism that would manifest itself in the various schools of jurisprudence, such as Hanbalism, Hanafism, Shafiism, and Malikism. The esoteric aspect of the Islamic Revelation is the spiritual Path *(tariqah)* that preaches union with the Divinity through direct knowledge and love gained in contemplation. The exoteric aspect of the Islamic Revelation is the sacred Law *(shari'ah)* that governs man's actions in view of salvation at the hour of death, which leads to the beatific vision of God in the paradisal states. The spiritual Path deals with both contemplation and action, and therefore presents a total view of the Islamic faith; the sacred Law deals only with action, namely the action prescribed for salvation, but it has nothing to say about the contemplative life, and as a result its view of Revelation is restricted.

Like all other religions, Islam has had its ups and downs, spiritually speaking, for no religion remains eternally fresh, as it was when it first came into this world. The process of worldliness, which flows from forgetfulness, affects Islam as much as it affects other great religious traditions. Revivals of religion are really rebirths in keeping with the spiritual perspectives and traditions of the faith. Decadence is what happens when forgetfulness of those principles comes over a considerable proportion of the population in a given region or even a vast area. In Islam, revivals and declines have come and gone throughout its fourteen centuries of existence: the revivals have always been characterized by their acceptance of the Quran and the *Sunnah* as the final arbiters of all beliefs and conduct, and the declines have always been characterized by their indifference to the Quran and the *Sunnah* in one way or another.

The Prophet said that every generation after his would be worse than the preceding one. He was clearly referring to the fact that the momentum of fallen mankind would begin once again after his time and gradually increase in its intensity as the sequence of generations in every century went by. But he also said that at the beginning of each century God would raise up in his community a sage who would revive its tradition. This seems to be in contradiction with the first remark, but is only so in appearance, for the two tendencies are cyclical movements reflecting the ups and downs of spiritual life in a religious community that cannot but exist in the historical fabric of its earthly existence. Even so, the process of spiritual decline affects greater and greater numbers of the community with the passage of time; the revival at the beginning of each century, or even within the century itself, affects fewer and fewer numbers of the community. If things did not proceed in that fashion, in accordance with the laws of cyclical unfolding, then the Quranic teachings on the Last Judgement — or the Hour, as the sacred Text would say — would make no sense: the Last Judgement falls on a mankind that is spiritually exhausted and beyond spiritual redemption. If we reflect long enough on the Quranic doctrine, the fall of mankind — or the expulsion from the Garden of Eden — set in motion a long series of consequences both for mankind and the cosmos it lives in that would eventually lead to the terminal stopping point called the Day of Judgement. In the meantime, from the Fall to the Day of Judgement, we witness a whole series of Revelations brought by the Messengers and the Prophets, so that we do not see simply a decline of mankind but also a series of rebirths corresponding to the arrival of new religions into this world. Islam sees itself as the very last religion to be revealed to mankind before the coming of the end of the ages; it considers its Prophet as the Seal of the Prophets, the one who brings the entire cycle of Prophecy, beginning with the Prophet Adam, to an end with his own person. The finality of the Islamic Message and its Messenger points to the fact that, had Revelation been allowed to continue, so that new religions affecting vast multitudes would have come into the world, the whole cyclical process of mankind would have gone on indefinitely through the constant alternation between decline and rebirth. What we see, instead, in the Quranic cyclical teachings is that the momentum of forgetfulness, which is what feeds the fallen state of mankind, gradually increases its erosive power and this in turn leads straight to the Day of Judgement. Man eventually is devoured or consumed by the Fall. That being the case, the ups and downs of the Islamic community alluded to previously in the remarks of the Prophet are not of indefinite duration. By cyclical coincidence, the Day of Judgement marking the end of the Islamic community is the same Day that closes the earthly existence of the other religious traditions in the world. We cannot understand the cyclical necessity of the Day of Judgement if we have not grasped the whole doctrine of the Garden of Eden, for the two events constitute the beginning and terminal points of the human cycle, or of the sacred history of mankind. The Fall of mankind from the Garden of Eden is the *terminus a quo* (starting point) of the story of man, and the Day of Judgement is the *terminus ad quem* (ending point) of that Fall. It was such notions as these that were behind the Prophet's statements about the declines and revivals of his community.

If the first decline in the history of Islam came with the disappearance of the Prophet and his great Companions from the scene, which set in motion a whole new set of conditions, the first revival comes around a century or two later. It is at that moment that we see the vast Islamic imperial civilization, with its symbiosis of Arab religion and Persian culture, stretching from Spain in the West to Central Asia and beyond in the East. By then, tens of millions had entered the ranks of Islam. A great need was felt for the codification of everything from Arabic poetry to the *hadiths* of the Prophet. But above all, it is at this moment that we see the separation of the Path (or *tariqah*) and the Law (or *shari'ah*). The Path would call itself Sufism, and would remain in the Islamic community right down to the present day with its own authorities, its own books, its own teachings and practices reposing on the Quran and the *Sunnah*, interpreted spiritually. The Law would split up into a number of schools, or *madhhabs*, called by different names, such as the Malikite *madhhab*, and they would have their own authorities, their own teachings and practices reposing on the Quran and the *Sunnah*, interpreted literally, for the most part, and in any case not mystically.

The separation of the two never meant divorce in the sense that each went its separate way. The great Sufi teachers, in all epochs, have always combined contemplation and action, which is as much as to say that the *tariqah* cannot be pursued in a void, but is in need of the *shari'ah*, or of a certain degree of the *shari'ah*. The religious scholars, on the other hand, whether they be called the *ulamā* or the *muftis* or the *fuqahā*, while they might ignore the whole realm of the inner spiritual life in their interpretations of Islamic teachings and its Law, could not ignore the Quran and the *Sunnah*. There have always been *ulamā* hostile to the Path as represented by Sufism; but at the same time, there have always been *ulamā* who recognized that the *shari'ah* of Islam could not possibly be the whole story of the Islamic Revelation, and that, consequently, Sufism had the answer to the contemplative or spiritual questions provoked by that Revelation itself. In any case, by the third or fourth century of the Hijrah (ninth or tenth century A.D.), the reconciliation between the Path and the Law had already taken place, as in the works, for example, of Abu Talib al-Makki, particularly his *Qut al-Qulub* ("The Nourishment of Hearts"), which speaks of both the Path and the Law. But this reconciliation between the life of contemplation and the life of action did not take place just one time: it had to take place in every century, so to speak. Thus, the *Ihya ulum ad-din* ("The Revival of the Religious Disciplines") of al-Ghazali in the fifth century was yet another attempt to reconcile the Law and the Path, although it was indeed a powerful one. In any case, for al-Ghazali, as for all the other traditional renovators of the Islamic faith, whether before or after him, it is always the Quran and the *Sunnah* that are indispensable to their renovative efforts. Additional principles, such as those of "consensus" *(ijma')*, implying the consensus of opinion on given matters by the notables of early Islam, and "argument by analogy" *(qiyas)*, or arriving at conclusions by the use of precedents analogous to those found in the Quran and the *Sunnah*, and yet other principles, would be added to the Quran and the *Sunnah*, but obviously it was these that formed the foundation stones of the Islamic tradition.

Around the sixth and seventh centuries of the Hijrah (the twelfth and thirteenth centuries A.D.), there arose on the Islamic scene a host of Sufi orders, or *turuq*, such as the Suhrawardiyyah, the Qadiriyyah, the Shadhiliyyah, the Chishtiyyah, and so on, that effected an impressive spiritual renovation of the entire world of Islam, a renovation visible in all domains, including the arts and architecture, to say nothing of literature and intellectuality in general. What makes that epoch so important is that it provided the principles and institutions for spiritual revival to take place within the Islamic community for centuries to come. The principles were embodied in the Sufi Path and its doctrines, which were intellectually gnostic in nature, if we go by their deepest expression, and that therefore declared gnosis to be the most profound fruit of faith. All of the Sufi orders had great masters, or *Shaykhs*, who were authors of important works on Sufi doctrines, and these would circulate throughout the Islamic world or else in particular cultural regions. Ibn al-Arabi, Rumi, Ahmad Sirhindi, and so on, left behind an intellectual and spiritual legacy in their compositions that had enormous influence on the Islamic community, especially Ibn al-Arabi, whose teachings on *Wahdat al-Wujud* ("Oneness of Being") penetrated almost everywhere in the community of Muslims.

Such, then, were the principles provided by that remarkable epoch for the future generations, and even centuries, of the Islamic faith. But it also provided the institutions through which revival could take place, and these were the *khaniqahs* and *zawiyahs* of the different Sufi orders. For centuries later, an endless series of saintly masters are to be found in these institutions teaching their disciples and a vast multitude of non-Sufi audiences the finer points of the Islamic Revelation. It is their radiance that kept Islam alive and even explosively so: the Ottoman Empire, the Mughal Empire of India, the Safavid Empire in Persia, and other contemporaneous dynasties elsewhere in the Muslim world show the direct or indirect influence of Sufism in all walks of life.

To put matters differently, what these Sufi orders were really saying is that all attempts to renovate Islam without them were doomed to failure, for such attempts would leave out the entire spiritual or contemplative nature of the religion. It is that spiritual life of Islam that Sufism represents. Of course, it can be either gnostic or devotional, according to perspective, for Sufism is universal in its coverage of the inner needs of the community. Perhaps the greatest number of Sufi adherents throughout the history of Islam have been more devotional in orientation than gnostic, and this is no doubt what has made them more accessible to the great mass of Muslims. When we realize that some of the Sufi orders of the past and even of the present day have hundreds of thousands of adherents, we are compelled to admit that it is not the mystical philosophy of an Ibn al-Arabi that attracts them to Sufism so much as it is the atmosphere of piety and fervor and devotionalism that draws them to the Path.

The nineteenth century (the 13th century of the Hijrah) saw numerous revivals of the Sufi orders here and there in the world of Islam, as in North Africa, for example, and Central Asia, just to cite a couple of places. But it is doubtful if the spiritual renovation effected by them could have embraced more than particular regions of the Muslim world. By then, a certain interior weakness, the cumulative effect of generations of worldliness, and therefore of decline, had become manifest throughout the Islamic world. What Sufism could do, under such circumstances, was not to revive the entirety of the Community and bring it back to a fresh understanding of the Quran and the *Sunnah* within the framework of the tradition as a whole. No, that seems to have been a task beyond Sufism at that point in the history of Islam. Rather, it appears that Sufism throughout that century and well into the twentieth century (the fourteenth century of the Hijrah) could only effect regional renovations, involving smaller numbers of the faithful.

Moreover, the weakness that was evident throughout the Islamic world was to be found in some of the Sufi orders themselves, the ones that the Sufis call "the sleeping orders" *(turuq na'imah)*, in contrast to the orders that are spiritually "alive" *(turuq salikah)*. The sleeping orders had no real masters presiding over their *zawiyahs*, while the others, the ones that were alive, had competent teachers who could guide their disciples in the spiritual path. Perhaps in the period of Islamic decadence that began a century or so back, the sleeping orders stole a march on the living Sufi orders and began to predominate all over the Islamic world. The Sufi phrase "dead orders" *(turuq mayyitah)* proves that some of the orders reached a point where non-spiritual practices crept into the picture and eventually subverted everything from top to bottom. When Sufism speaks of its role as the renovator of the Islamic faith, it has in view the living Sufi orders, not the other two categories of sleeping and dead orders, though it has to be admitted that the sleeping orders at least play a conservative role in that they preserve, to a certain extent, the traditional structures of the Path and the Law.

However that may be, it was in the same nineteenth century that the arrival of Western imperialistic civilization, with its colonialist aspirations, gradually brought the greater part of Islam under the domination of the Western world. Throughout the Islamic world, Sufism fought the Western colonialist regimes of the Russians, the French, the English, and the other European States that were bent on carving out colonies for themselves at the expense of Muslim lands. The intrusion of modern Western industrial civilization, with its dogmas of progress, republicanism, revolutionism, and materialism, into the very substance of Islam, which still had its own lingering civilization, was to have a traumatic result. For one thing, the Islamic civilization, which had become spiritually weakened from within by a long process of decline antedating the arrival of Western civilization, was given a lethal blow from which it would never recover. With a few exceptions here and there, the lights of that civilization began going out with the coming of the West. What was happening was that the traditional structures of that Islamic culture — its arts and architecture, its garments, its literature of the classical type, its whole style of life and its cosmic perspective — all of this was either wiped out by the coming of modern Western civilization or else eroded to the vanishing point. By the end of the First World War, that civilization, in so far as it had constituted a traditional homogeneous matrix, had been brought to its knees, for the most part, and in many regions of the Islamic world it was to all intents and purposes a dead corpse.

For another thing, while the traditional framework, or civilization, that had supported Islam for over a thousand years in many glorious flowerings of culture, had caved in and disintegrated under the impact of modern Western civilization, the religion — ironically enough — survived the maelstrom, and even began to expand all over the globe. The predictions of Western specialists on Islam that the process of Westernization would lead eventually to the disappearance of the faith has simply not happened at all. On the contrary, Islam is now the fastest-growing religion on the face of the globe. This is still the traditional Islam of some fourteen centuries ago, as regards the external forms dealing with rituals and other observances, or the Five Pillars of religion.

But a religion is an ensemble of beliefs, moral attitudes, and rituals, and not just simply rituals. When one speaks of esoteric or exoteric Islam, that is to say, of the contemplative life or of the active life in that faith, one has in view those three things: a set of teachings, a morality, and rituals of different types. Sufism, in this respect, simply takes these three things and gives to them a spiritual explanation — a depth, if one wills — which does not exist in exoteric Islam, the Islam of the *ulamā*. But throughout the centuries, the *ulamā* always gave to those three elements of faith an interpretation which, while not very profound, nevertheless kept them within the perspective of the Islamic Revelation and its on-going tradition. In other words, the traditional interpretations of Islam were either quite shallow or else strikingly profound, but they were always recognizable as traditional, that is to say, there was always an element of truth that shone through them.

There is a fourth element which relates also to Revelation, and that is art. In Islam, art manifests itself in the mosques and in everything dealing with the liturgical forms. All spiritual art is meant to express symbolically the truths of the religion in a visual or auditive sense; it is also called upon to house the ritual life of the community, as the mosques and the *zawiyahs* and *khaniqahs* do, for they are primarily concerned with the collective aspects of liturgical observance, to which sacred art gives an ambiance of beauty and serenity that detach these ritual aspects from the world of profane man. In any case, while it is possible to extract a theory of sacred art from the Islamic Revelation, it is obvious that it was taken for granted throughout the lifetime of the traditional Islamic civilization, so that no theologian and no Sufi had to draw attention to it in the same fashion as they would allude to the beliefs and the practices of Islam. This was because the spiritual art of Islam supplied static models, for the most part, such as mosques and the like, that were not immediately subject to the ups and downs of the Muslims themselves. In periods of decline, the mosques remained intact; it was the souls of the Muslims that forgot the teachings of Islam, its morality, and its general liturgical nature. When the period of rebirth set in, generally brought on by some Sufi revival, the mosques were still there, as before; but now, the beliefs and morality were once again in line with the Quran and the *Sunnah*.

To understand what is happening in the modern world of Islam, one has to remember that these four elements just mentioned — the beliefs, the moral attitudes, the rituals, and the arts — have a *normative* reality of their own, independently of their expression in this epoch or that, or here and there. The traditional teachings and way of life, throughout the entire history of Islam, are simply external expressions of these spiritual norms themselves. What makes us recognize this or that traditional belief as being normative is simply the fact that it squares with a Quranic scriptural text, on the one hand, or else with the evidence of logic, on the other. A normative Islam, in other words, is on the side of tradition. Mention has already been made, however, that tradition, in the Muslim world, is not one-dimensional, but multi-dimensional. One and the same Quranic text can give rise to a plurality of meanings, which is what we find in the Islamic tradition, and these meanings can range from the literal to the mystical, without this altering in any way the truth manifesting itself in the literalist or mystical interpretations. Needless to add, the four elements of Revelation — for they all stem from the same Revelation — can be seen from either the exoteric or esoteric viewpoint, the latter giving them their deepest interpretation.

So long as contemporary Islam moves within the bounds that tradition has established, it remains within its normative vitality. This is no doubt the case for the overwhelming mass of believers, especially in the out-of-the-way places of the Muslim world. It is certainly not the case for the modernistic Muslim, whose ideological formation is Western, whatever might be his ritual observance. It is here where Muslims separate into traditional and anti-traditional types, with a whole gamut of intermediate types possible also. Frequently it is assumed that the Muslim who observes the ritual prescriptions is also somehow being traditional in a total sense, whereas in reality he is being traditional only in the ritual sense. In the other traditional senses — in attitudes of mind flowing from the Islamic beliefs, in his morality, and the like — he may be perfectly anti-traditional and even flagrantly so. Some of the *mullahs* of Central Asia, in the Soviet Union, for example, are very observant of the ritual prescriptions of Islam; but their Marxist-Leninism, which they got from the Russians, is in brutal contradiction to all the traditional doctrines of Islam, and this means that their attitudes are themselves suspect.

We do not have to go to the Soviet Union to see this principle of inner contradiction at work in the Islamic community. Wahhabism, for example, is often referred to as a fundamentalist, puritanical movement within the Islamic Arab world of Saudi Arabia. It is certainly a conservative version of Islam, if we contrast it with the socialistic ideologies — or the so-called "Islamic socialism" — of other regimes. Wahhabism, however, suffers from an interior fissure in its teachings that could never compensate for its ritualistic and legalistic exactitude. Sufism, for Wahhabism, is the real agent of Islamic degeneration: get rid of it and everything returns to normal. That is precisely what the Wahhabis did, and in the process, they stripped Islam — or their Islam — of all of its spiritual plasticity and beauty. Wahhabism is said to have been a form of Islamic revivalism, beginning in the eighteenth century with its founder Muhammad Abd al-Wahhab, and finally breaking out into the Bedouin world of the

Arabian Peninsula in the twentieth century. But it is not through the destruction of the Sufi institutions and shrines of Arabia that one reawakens the inner spark of the religion. The error of the Wahhabis was not so much that they reduced Islam to the *shari'ah*, but that, in so doing, they reduced the entire structure of beliefs within that faith to the most fundamentalist dogmatism conceivable, surpassing even the Hanbalite dogmatists of the Medieval Age, and then, like all puritans, insisted that this was the *true* Islam. Compared with the communist *mullahs* of Central Asia, or the socialist *ulamā* of other Islamic lands, the religious scholars of Saudi Arabia — or at least those who are pious and sincere — seem conservative enough. But their Islam is not normative Islam either, for it lacks a Sufi heart, which is as much as to say that it lacks the whole spiritual message of the Revelation, and this is quite a lack.

Whatever one might see in Wahhabism that is counter to the spiritual and intellectual doctrines of the Islamic tradition, it is nevertheless something positive when compared with the so-called revival of Islam that has taken place in Persia under al-Khomeini. Here, too, we encounter a characteristic feature of modernistic Islam, namely, the reinterpretation of the religion in keeping with ideologies borrowed from the Western world, in this case the world of socialism and republicanism. For Khomeinism, Islam is a kind of socialistic ideology that also prescribes five daily prayers and other ritual observances. At the sight of everybody praying in the streets of Persia, Westerners immediately concluded that Islam was being revived by the *mullahs* of that land. In reality, it was not the rebirth of Islam but its death that was taking place: the people praying were doing so with the attitudes fostered by Khomeinism, and those attitudes were incompatible with traditional Islam, to say the least. For the Shi'ite world of Persia, over which Khomeinism now reigns temporarily, republicanism was the solution to all the ills of society, and this meant the end of the monarchic form of government. But the traditional form of government in the history of the Islamic religion has always been monarchic, and this, from the very beginning. The Prophet himself was a monarch — a Prophet-King, if you will, but a monarch nevertheless; and his simplicity of life must not delude us in this respect. Likewise, his Companions, such as Abu Bakr, Umar, Uthman, and Ali, were all monarchs: as Caliphs, they reigned and ruled. What makes Khomeinism so sad to witness is its trivialization of the Islamic faith and its reduction of everything simply to socio-political and economic questions. We are far removed here even from Shi'ite theological beliefs, from the normal manner of acting within the Islamic faith, and even from the aesthetic aspects of that religion. That Khomeini's demagogic version of Islam should have been considered as a resurgence of religion is simply another proof that Islam remains largely misunderstood in the Western world.

Previously, mention was made of the disintegration of the Islamic traditional civilization, which had lasted for over a millenium when it finally collapsed by the end of the First World War. While it is true that Islam, as a religion, is now the fastest-growing faith in the world, this should not lead us to believe that, for some magical reason, it is immune to the corrosive influence of the modern world on all religions. Reference has already been made to the introduction of modern Western ideologies of one type or another into the Islamic world, and therefore into the mind of the Muslim, whether he is anti-Western or not. All Muslims who have succumbed consciously or unconsciously to modernist notions that originated in the Western world carry within their minds the seeds of revolt against many of the basic doctrines of the Quran and the *Sunnah*. For example, Islam is not an evolutionistic religion — no religion is, though at the present day many modernists in all religions would like to reinterpret them along evolutionistic modes of thought, of which Darwinism is simply a postulate affecting the biological world. Evolutionism, in its widest sense, is the fundamental ideology of modern Western civilization, and it affects everything, from religion to science to art to morality to philosophy to political systems, and so on. It is a kind of belief that things change, somehow for the better, and that the example of what is better is to be found in the West, especially in its cult of science, technology, republicanism, progress, and all the rest of the numerous ideologies that arise in the West with distressing ease.

Now, the Muslim whose mind harbors such evolutionistic thoughts, even if they be unconscious, cannot but disbelieve in the Quranic doctrine of cyclical decline leading to the Day of Judgement. How could one say to him that the modern world, in all of its entirety, is nothing but the product of men whose fallen nature made this civilization possible? One could not easily do so, and it is for this reason that one must conclude that the religion of Islam, to the extent that it is subverted in its system of beliefs by the modern ideologies of the West, likewise suffers from the malaise that all religions of the world suffer from. The only remedy for this, of course, lies in the exposition of the traditional intellectual, cosmological, spiritual, and even cyclical concepts of Islam, that are often ignored totally by many of the so-called Muslim thinkers. Herein lies one of the pressing problems in the Islamic world of today: it is time now to express, yet once again, the traditional doctrines, of incredible depth and beauty, which have lain hidden for so long. It is only through these teachings that a veritable Islamic world-view can be re-established in the minds of thinking Muslims, a world-view that is compatible with all respects of the Islamic Revelation.

Be that as it may, the fact of the matter is that the Islamic tradition in the twentieth century is to be found only in Sufism, and this for the simple reason that Sufism contains both the Path and the Law. It is generally thought that Sufism is a mystical Way, which of course it is, providing that one quickly adds that there is no way of contemplation without action, for everyone must act, including the most enlightened sage; and if everyone must act, the Sufi masters must deal with the Law, which contains the prescriptions for action within the Islamic faith.

In the past, outside of Sufism, one found a brilliant Islamic civilization with the Law and its authorities. But neither the civilization nor the Law represented the entire Islamic tradition. The civilization did not represent it because the arts and architecture, the philosophy and literature, the music and the other cultural phenomena of the world of Islam were not directly bound up with the task of salvation, which was the whole point of the Islamic Message. And the Law and its authorities did not represent the entire Islamic tradition for the simple reason that the Law has nothing to do with the contemplation of the Divinity, which is what the Path is all about. Nevertheless, the Law was concerned with the question of salvation, and still is; and in this respect, it is infinitely superior to the civilizational framework upholding it and surrounding it during the Middle Ages of Islam. Thus, it has always been Sufism, and Sufism alone, that has contained within itself the integral Islamic tradition. In reality, any Sufi order, considered in the abstract, contains within itself an entire Islamic community, in the sense that the whole Message of the religion is to be found therein, not only as regards the socio-religious Law but also as regards the mystical Way.

In our days, the problem of revivalism is stymied in advance because of the hostility towards Sufism that one can detect here and there in the Islamic world. The hostility is motivated by sometimes different and even contrasting causes. In the case of the Young Turks, or of the movement later on taken over by Ataturk, Sufism was seen as the major obstacle to the secularization of Turkey along Western lines, which meant of course the de-Islamicization of that land. Even pitched battles were fought by Ataturk's armies against the dervishes and their chiefs who opposed his secularist and anti-Islamic measures. Certainly no one regime in the non-communist world could match the Russian communist imperialism against the Muslims of Central Asia: the Russians closed down hundreds of mosques, killed off all dissidents, and imposed heavy restrictions on the practice of Islam. Even so, if a comparison were made between what took place in Turkey under Ataturk and what took place in Central Asia, one has to admit that the Turkish secularist nationalism was not too far behind. In any case, there are regions in Central Asia where practically half the population belongs to one of the Sufi orders. One certainly cannot say this of modern-day Turkey under Ataturk's program.

The example of Turkey is one extreme; the other example, that of the Wahhabis of Saudi Arabia, represents another extreme. For the Wahhabis, it was not a question of re-making Arabia into a secularized version of the West, as the Turkish nationalists wanted to do; rather, it was a question of re-making Islam into a puritanical and fundamentalist faith devoid of any mystical elements, and for this to take place, it was necessary to destroy Sufism. The hostility towards Sufism in Turkey, during the days of Ataturk, came from the fact that it represented the bastion of the entire Islamic faith: attack it and destroy it, and the way is clear for the introduction of Western secularistic values. For the puritanical Wahhabis, on the other hand, the destruction of Sufism in Arabia was considered a pious deed, because in the eyes of the Wahhabis Sufism had nothing to do with Islam but was merely one of the historical accretions that had been superadded to the purity of original Islam. Take Sufism away and that purity, represented by Wahhabism, comes back into its own once again, which is what the Wahhabi regime of Arabia set out to do with dispatch.

Turkey and Saudi Arabia represent the two most contrasting attitudes of hostility towards Sufism. In between come the usual antagonistic thoughts of most modernist movements in the world of Islam. If it be asked: "Why does Sufism draw the ire of most reformers or would-be reformers or even of most educated Muslims of the present day?" The answer is complex. Let us recall what was previously said about the threefold division of the Sufi orders into living, sleeping, and dead orders *(salikah, na'imah,* and *mayyitah).* Islam can do without the dead orders, to be sure, because they contribute nothing to the inner life of the community and of course nothing to their own members. They represent deviations from the normative orders of Sufism. In the Middle Ages of Islam, as in Mughal India, or elsewhere, it was in these dead orders that we find the drug-taking dervishes, to say nothing of other illicit activities. With the passage of time, and the proliferation of dead orders here and there, an image of generalized immorality spreads over the face of Sufism. Those who are hostile to the Sufi orders, and even those who should know better, point the finger at all of Sufism, as if the entire Sufi tradition were to be blamed for the rot to be found in the dead orders.

Then, there are the sleeping orders, who have no competent teachers to guide others, but who preserve some of the forms of Islam. In the past, it was often in these orders that one found a great preoccupation with various kinds of white magic — as distinct from black magic — and allied phenomena. This in turn characterized many of the sleeping orders as exclusively concerned with magical or semi-magical activities. Obviously, a sleeping order could easily glide into a dead order. But, when one considers that the dead orders indulged in illicit and even subversive activities, while the sleeping orders were concerned to a great extent with magical practices of one kind or another, we can understand that a certain incomprehension should arise in the minds of those who could not grasp the role of Sufism in Islam.

What makes things complex is that certain orders, like the Qadiriyyah or the Shadhiliyyah, actually span continents and have hundreds of thousands of adherents and scores of *Shaykhs* or *Pirs* or *Qutbs* as their chiefs. The Qadiri order in the Soviet Union, for example, has numerous chiefs — or masters, if you will — and literally hundreds of thousands of adherents. Perhaps one of those masters might be a real spiritual guide, in which case we would say that his *tariqah* is alive, whereas the same Sufi order in Turkistan or Uzbekistan or in Azerbaijan would not have authentic masters, but only chiefs holding down the fort, so to speak. Outside the Soviet Union, the Qadiris are strong here and there in the Islamic world. We are forced to conclude that this great *tariqah*, because of the immensity of its geographical distribution, can be classified as alive, sleeping, and dead, at one and the same time, depending on region, *zawiyah*, *khaniqah*, or teacher. So long as there is one Qadiri master who is a real spiritual guide, we can hope that the order will not in the long run perish. In any case, it is the presence of a real spiritual guide in an order that determines whether it is alive or not, at least in this or that region.

Strictly speaking, the live Sufi order is the sole representative of

Sufism. If Sufism contains the entire Islamic tradition, it is obviously only the Sufism found in the live Sufi orders that does so: to say that a sleeping order represents the entire Islamic tradition — both Law and Path — would be to utter absurdities. A sleeping order, however, to the extent that it is faithful to the past, has at least the role of preserving the traditional forms, if nothing else. But it is really the live Sufi order that is the pivotal center of Islam, for it contains both the Path and the Law.

The coming of modern Western industrial civilization to the world of Islam poses immense spiritual, religious and social problems for the Muslims. Just as the rise of modern civilization in the sixteenth and seventeenth centuries in Western Europe eventually led to the collapse of the Christian civilization in the eighteenth century through the French Revolution and the Industrial Revolution, so similarly modern Western civilization has demolished the traditional Islamic civilization of the past to the point where only debris and remnants of the old culture are all that can still be seen, apart from the mosques and other architectural monuments of the past that are still standing.

Various attempts have been made to force Islam to conform to modern industrial civilization, the theory being that Islam and technology are perfectly compatible. The modernists of the Christian religion sometimes make the same claim for Christianity. In reality, the Christian modernist is more plausible in claiming that his religion and the modern world are compatible, for Christianity has never had a sacred Law, like Islam, and thus the Christian can more easily take on the coloration of his ambiance. The Muslim is in more difficult straits precisely because his sacred Law (the *shari'ah*) governs the individual and society at one and the same time. The entire history of modernism in the Islamic world has been the history of the erosion of that Law in both society and the individual, an erosion that took place by the importation of Western legal codes and also by the Westernization of Islamic society. Granted that, once the colonialist regimes left the Muslim world, the Muslims attempted to round off the legislative systems left behind by the West so as to bring them more into line with the spirit of Islam. But this, after all, is only a rear-guard battle designed to prevent Islam from disappearing altogether from the societal framework of a given country. In any case, this can hardly be called the "revival" of Islam. What is called the compatibility of Islam and modern industrial civilization is simply the process that results in the residualization of Islam and the triumph of technology everywhere.

But things are not that simple. The modern Western world, when it came to the East, began to create a new kind of personality: this was the Westernized Muslim, who was more at home in modern Western culture than he was in the traditional culture of Islam, which he tended to look at through the prism of Western thinking. At first, he was in a minority in the Muslim world, but with the passage of time and the establishment of Western systems of education, the mentality that he represented became widespread and eventually determined the outlook of the governing minority and even of the cultivated classes. This was so not only as regards the so-called liberal or progressivist class of Muslims but also as regards the conservative leaders. In other words, the psyche that the modern world actually created in the collective mentality of the Muslims is not the traditional mentality, which was the fruit of the old Islamic culture of the past, but rather a special psyche that has reinterpreted Islam within the categories of thought brought to the Muslim world by the West; but the reinterpretation is not Western — nor is it Eastern, for that matter. It is neither fish nor fowl. The previously-mentioned Marxist-Leninist *mullahs* of Central Asia, for example, see the revival of Islam as the end-product of a series of stages through which the community must go, one of those stages being communism. Thus, the communist way of life is provisional and not, as the Western Marxist-Leninists would have it, definitive and conclusive. It is simply a stage on the way to the creation of an Islamic scheme of things. Obviously, the *mullahs* of Central Asia, and the other Muslims there who agree with them, have borrowed a leaf from the communist book on tactics and strategy and simply reversed the procedure: instead of Islam being a provisional halting-place on the way to the perfect communist society, it is communism that is a provisional step before the dawn of a purified Islam on the horizon. For the Western theoreticians of communism — that is to say, the Russians, who, after all, are Western colonialists in Central Asia — the Muslim brand of Marxist-Leninism sounds crazy, for it is neither pure communism, as they have known it, namely, an ideological movement based on atheistic premises and utterly hostile to religion of any kind, nor is it traditional Islam with its own *shari'ah* that is absolutely opposed to a Marxist-Leninist society.

This neither-fish-nor-fowl approach of many contemporary Muslims, whether they be what are called the reactionaries or their opposites the revolutionaries, is the ultimate consequence of the invasion of the mental lands of the Muslims by the modern Western world. We have to remember that imperialism is not simply a territorial expression of

Western civilization; it also involved an aggression against the mental territory of the East, an aggression which succeeded in establishing a Western colonialism in the very minds of the East. The departure of Western colonialism after the Second World War from the Islamic lands took place only after long strife, but it was finally accomplished, except for the Russian colonialist regime in Central Asia. But the physical departure of the West was one thing; the departure of the West from the mental world of Islam is another thing. That departure has been slow in coming: but the fact that many contemporary Muslim thinkers carry a kind of *Dār al-Harb* ("The World of Warfare", or the non-Islamic world) inside their own minds signifies that their versions of Islam are predetermined by modern Western models as seen by Muslims. This explains why Islamic republicanism, socialism, communism, democracy, feminism, evolutionism, and the like, which are all of Western origin, come out in the writings of Muslims as hybrid and impure products of minds that seem to inhabit a no-man's land that is neither Eastern nor Western.

But that is not the whole problem: There is also the very real question that revivalism, for the different schools of thought derived from Western ideologies, springs from mutually destructive points of departure. The Muslim Marxist-Leninist or socialist is not the same as the Muslim capitalist, and therefore their respective versions of the ideal society are in direct opposition. What has happened in the Islamic world of the post-World War epoch has been that the Western ideologies of numerous stripes and brands have all been transferred to the Islamic lands with incredible ease, due to the speed with which modern communications operate. There is no homogeneity of opinion on what constitutes the ideal Islamic world, nor can there be any, given the fact that Western ideologies, while they are all more or less secularist and even downright materialistic, are not in agreement on the ideal state, and indeed, the image of that ideal state changes with the tempo of technological transformations themselves, which are, in the final analysis, the real arbiters of modern man's destiny. That same technological transformation of society has now attacked the substance of Islamic culture in numerous areas of the Muslim world, and the end is not yet, since industrial civilization requires for its continued existence — whether in *Dār al-Islam* ("The World of Islam") or outside of it — a constant transformation, not only of the natural world, but of the social order as well, which means the reduction of Islam to a residual shadow of its former self.

From these reflections, it is clear that Westerners have misunderstood such movements as Khomeinism in Persia, interpreting it as a kind of resurgence of Islam due to a reaction against the process of over-industrialization or over-modernization in Iran. In reality, the Khomeinists are less Islamic, to say the least, than the previous monarchic system that prevailed in Iran: their republicanism, if really understood by a Westerner, would be seen as a frightening demagogic totalitarianism, all the more monstrous in that it is skillfully clothed in the robes and turbans of the Shi'ite *mullahs* of Iran. Far from being opposed to the whole industrial system of modern times and its devastating effects on mankind, Khomeinism is all for it. If the Marxist-Leninist *mullahs* of the Soviet Union sound strange to modern Western ears, the Khomeini version of Islam is yet another example of the process of hybridization that modern civilization produces in all religions when they abandon the traditional intellectual and spiritual principles that had sustained them for centuries, to say nothing of abandoning the traditional political and economic structures that had given them such stability. Instead of readapting such traditional systems so as to make them strong in the face of the devastating imperialism of modern civilization, the world religions have too often discarded them, leaving the religions open to the invasion of modern ideologies and demagogues.

From all of this, it can be seen that the root of all the real problems facing the revivalists of Islam at the present day comes from the West, whether that West be inside their minds or in the world outside their minds. It is the West inside their minds that prevents them from rediscovering the traditional Islamic intellectual and other doctrines and that forces them to view Islam from the point of view of this or that Western ideology. It is the West outside their minds, in the form of modern industrial civilization, that obliterates the landmarks and artistic ambiance of *Dār al-Islam*. The remedy for the West inside the mind lies within the corpus of Islamic doctrines that the Muslim sages spun around the Quranic teachings, and they are diverse, as was said earlier, ranging from the philosophical to the mystical to the cosmological to the psychological to the theological to the sociological, and the like. This is a vast, largely unexplored cultural heritage that needs to be understood and applied with rigor to all problems created by the modern world.

The remedy for the West outside the mind is not as easy as the remedy for the West inside the mind: the individual Muslim is responsible for his own mental territory, and hence, he can control, to a greater or lesser extent, what he imports into it and what he exports;

but he cannot control the demolition of the traditional Islamic culture, for that is beyond his own power to stop. There is only one realm where a kind of control could be practiced, and that is in architecture: clearly, the preservation of a traditional Islamic architectural style, even if it be somewhat simplified, should figure in any attempt to conserve the millennial legacy of Islam. Let us recall that the Islamic religion, like other religions, is also an art and even an aesthetic approach to the world, as witness the great marvels of mosque architecture in Islam, or the miniatures of Persia and Mughal India, or the urban and domestic architecture that can still be found in such cities as Fez and Isfahan — these are all the fruits of the Islamic spirit acting in the forms of this world. They are as definitive and inspirational for the Islamic community as were the theological dogmas and philosophical formulations of the Muslim sages. It is a historical fact that no Revelation we know of is without its artistic manifestations. The sacred art of Islam is certainly necessary to house the liturgical life of the community, but the traditional domestic and urban architecture of the Islamic faith was also a necessity in the preservation of the entire Islamic way of life. While it might not be possible to impose a simplified traditional architecture on an entire land overnight, it is certainly a possibility for the individual Muslim who has grasped the necessity for the artistic forms of Islam in his own ambiance to arrange his own home in such a fashion that it becomes a real bastion of *Dār al-Islam* instead of a direct manifestation of *Dār al-Harb* in his private life. One of the most salient features of the so-called modern reformers of the Islamic faith is their total silence on the importance of Islamic architecture and art for the spiritual vitality of the Muslims, and this, at a time when silence is tantamount to a conspiratorial alliance with the West and its architectural or artistic fashions. However that might be, it is easier for the Muslim to reaffirm his own architectural heritage than it is for the Westerner, for the Muslim is only now seeing that heritage disappear in the world around him, whereas the Westerner saw it disappear long ago.

If all Revelations, like the Islamic one, eventually are reducible to beliefs, morality, rituals, and art, and if these four elements are interpretable either in an esoteric or mystical sense as well as an exoteric or literal sense, then clearly it is to the Islamic tradition that one must go to learn how these elements are to be arranged for the continued vitality of the faith. A revival of Islam that attempts to side-step the traditional solutions and to recreate the religion in the image of this or that modern pattern of thinking is not really a revival of Islam: it is simply another effort to participate in the decadence that overwhelms all religions at different moments in their existence, a decadence that is largely the spiritual forgetfulness of the aforementioned traditional elements. There is no authentic revival of Islam at any period in its history that did not involve the renovation of the traditional framework of the faith. In his work, *Ihya ulum ad-din* (The Revival of the Religious Disciplines), al-Ghazali (11th century A.D.) did not present a novel approach to Islam; quite the contrary, to an age that tended to forget the mystical or spiritual aspects of the Islamic Revelation, he revived the complete Message of Islam, presenting the integral tradition as Path and Law.

Earlier on, it was explained that Islam has a complex cyclical doctrine that connects the Fall of mankind (from the Garden of Eden) with the Day of Judgement through a series of spiritual ups and downs, or revivals and declines, that intervene between the beginning and the end of the sacred history of mankind. Whatever might have been the previous declines of the Islamic world, and the rebirths that followed them, it is historically obvious that they took place within a traditional Islamic civilization that no longer exists anywhere on the face of the globe, except in fragmentary cultural expressions here and there. The disappearance of that civilization coincides with the disappearance of many other traditional cultures the world over. This should be a sign, to paraphrase the Quran, for those who can reflect that, cyclically speaking, we are living in exceptional times, and even in apocalyptic times that have no precedence in the past, for it is the entire globe nowadays, and not just this or that humanity, as was the case in the past, that stands in need of a spiritual renovation. So Islam is not alone in this respect. All of the Islamic traditional doctrines are still intact and serve as landmarks for those who want to know how that renovation can affect their lives here and now. Without those teachings, how could the Muslim distinguish between the true and false faith? The Prophet said that, in the last days, the Anti-Christ would arise preaching a new religion, with Heaven and Hell as posthumous states, except that the Heaven he talks about is really Hell, and his Hell is really Heaven — the classic subversion of all anti-traditional teachings. In that eschatological image, we have an indication that all anti-traditionalism leads straight into the realm of subversion.

The question of revivalism in the Muslim world at the present day is really an individual problem, as far as the tradition is concerned. The individual Muslim alone can understand the traditional doctrines and practices, whereas the society at large obeys the tempo set by the industrial age and follows passively the promptings of its collective nature, a nature which may be good or bad, but which in any case is without any conscious understanding. The revival of Islam is actually the revival of the individual Muslim, for a decadent Islam could never revive anyone. This means that the religion is perfect; it is the individual Muslim who is imperfect, and that of course is the well-known thesis of the Muslim Sufis and the theologians. It is religion, as transmitted by tradition, that provides the teachings and practices necessary to overcome the effects of the Fall, of the decline of man. It is certainly not the decadent Muslim who is going to revive Islam. Thus, there is nothing to revive in the Islamic religion as such: this was always a self-evident truth to the great Muslim sages, whose quest for wisdom began with the realization that they were themselves decadent and imperfect and that it was only in the traditional doctrines and modes of behavior that they could find the ideas and means wherewith to perfect themselves and revive their inner spiritual life.

Bibliography

Burckhardt, Titus, *Introduction to Sufi Doctrine*. Wellingborough, England: Thorsons Publishers Limited, 1976.

_____, *The Art of Islam: Language and Meaning*. World of Islam Festival Publishing Company, 1976.

Lings, Martin, *A Sufi Saint of the Twentieth Century*. London: Allen & Unwin, 1971.

_____, *The Quranic Art of Calligraphy and Illumination*. World of Islam Festival Publishing Company, 1976.

Nasr, Seyyed Hossein, *Ideals and Realities of Islam*. London: Allen & Unwin, 1966.

_____, *Sufi Essays*. London: Allen & Unwin, 1972.

Schimmel, Annemarie, *Mystical Dimensions of Islam*. University of North Carolina Press, Chapel Hill, 1975.

Schuon, Frithjof, *Understanding Islam*. London: Allen & Unwin, 1963.

_____, *Dimensions of Islam*. London: Allen & Unwin, 1970.

_____, *Islam and the Perennial Philosophy*. London: World of Islam Festival Publishing Company, 1976.

III

ISLAM AND OTHER RELIGIONS

Richard L. Chambers

> Since the late nineteenth century the dominance of Western powers over much of the Islamic lands and the growing hold of Western style nationalism and ideas of democracy on Islamic peoples had made the question of how Islam treats people of other religions not too urgent if not irrelevant. But the scene has changed since the Second World War. The rise of new Islamic theocracies and the current sweep of Islamic revivalism in Muslim nations make the question important again. Professor Chambers discusses here the guidelines for treatment of non-Muslims established by Prophet Muhammad himself and his successors, their usage in history and their contemporary relevance.
>
> Richard L. Chambers, who has done extensive work in the history of the Ottoman Empire is currently professor and director of the Center for Middle Eastern Studies in the Department of Near Eastern Languages and Civilizations at the University of Chicago.

Americans have inherited from Europe a distorted and generally negative picture of Islam. Our educational system and the mass media have, on the whole, done more to reinforce than to correct that image. Islam is usually seen as alien, hostile, fanatical, and backward; and only rarely do Americans recognize how closely akin Islam is to Christianity and Judaism.

These three great religions sprang from common roots in the Semitic Middle East. All are monotheistic. All are revealed religions, God's revelations being transmitted to mankind by means of prophets and preserved in holy scriptures. While all share a belief in an afterlife, they are also concerned with ethical and moral behavior in this world and have developed rules or even laws to regulate the lives of their adherents. They have all spread, although under radically different circumstances, far beyond their common birthplace in the Middle

East. Over centuries they have undergone varying degrees of change and development. Sectarian movements, schisms, and heresies, together with geographical diffusion and exposure to other cultural traditions, have compromised the original unitary nature of these faiths without, however, destroying their most fundamental and characteristic principles.

These similarities stand out boldly when Judaism, Christianity, and Islam are juxtaposed to the other great world religions — Hinduism, Buddhism, Confucianism — whose origins lie in the civilizations of East Asia, in India and China. But we should not allow the resemblances to obscure the very real differences which set Judaism, Christianity, and Islam apart. The exclusiveness of Judaism stands in marked contrast to the universality of its two sister faiths. It is true that there is a tendency to equate Islam with the Arabs, and certainly in its early years that identification was valid. The Prophet Muhammad was an Arab; the Koran was written in Arabic; and it was the Arabs who initially embraced Islam, spread it from the Arabian peninsula through Syria, Iraq, and Egypt to North Africa and Spain in the West and to Persia, Central Asia, and India in the East, thereby creating an Arab Islamic empire. But conversion to Islam on a massive scale accompanied or followed political conquest, and Islam has continued until today to spread even further through Muslim missionary activities and commercial contacts. In the process, the Arabs were not only reduced to a numerical minority within the Islamic community but for centuries they were replaced by Muslim Persians, Turks, Mongols, Berbers, and others as the military-political elite in most of the Islamic World. Yet the Arab contributions to Islam were such that the identification has persisted. Christianity, on the other hand, has no comparable identification with one ethnic-linguistic group.

Perhaps partially at least because of its exclusiveness, Judaism has rarely enjoyed the status of dominant religion of a state and never of an expansive world empire. More often it has been the religion of a barely tolerated or persecuted minority. Christianity suffered a similar fate for some three centuries before the conversion of the emperor Constantine and, through him, the Roman Empire. ✳Muhammad, however, was the founder of a religion and of a state; he was both prophet and ruler. Within a few years after his death, the state he had established expanded to become an empire, and Islam grew to be not just the religion of the conquerors but the faith of the majority of the empire's peoples. In Islam, then, faith and state were one from the very beginning. Muhammad was both the religious and political head of the Islamic community; and while his successors, styled Caliphs, were endowed with none of his prophetic qualities, they, too, combined within themselves both spiritual and temporal authority. Thus Jesus' injunction to his followers to "render unto Caesar the things which are Caesar's and unto God the things which are God's" is utterly meaningless in the traditional Islamic context.

Whereas Jesus is regarded by Christians as the Son of God and therefore divine, to Muslims he is but one of a succession of God's prophets or messengers; and the message he brought was superseded by that of the final messenger, the Seal of the Prophets, Muhammad. Because for Muslims the oneness of God is indivisible no aura of divinity is attached to Muhammad. Nor are any miracles associated with him other than the miracle of God's revelation, dictated to Muhammad by the angel Gabriel and embodied in the Koran.

Based upon the Koran and the practice *(Sunna)* of the Prophet — it being assumed that all of Muhammad's actions and statements were also divinely inspired — a comprehensive legal and ethical system was developed. Known as the *Shari'a*, this "Holy Law" reflects once again the inseparable coupling in Islam of the religious and secular spheres. It incorporates the Muslim's religious obligations and his political obligations. It regulates his relations with God, with the Islamic community and state, with his fellow Muslims, and even with non-believers. As the law of God, it became the fundamental law of the Islamic community and its government.

For reasons which should now be obvious, Islam never developed a corporate ecclesiastical structure separate from the state which is comparable to "the Church" in Christendom with its pope or patriarch, councils or synods, bishops or priests. In the absence of a clergy, Islam produced learned men *('ulama)* versed in the religious sciences and particularly in the law. Although they were held in high esteem, served as jurisconsults and as judges in the *Shari'a* courts, staffed Muslim schools, and usually led the prayers and delivered the Friday sermon in the mosques, they were not ordained and were set apart from other Muslims only on account of their learning and, ideally, their piety.

These examples of similarities and differences between Islam, Christianity, and Judaism are by no means exhaustive and could be elaborated upon but must suffice for present purposes. What should be noted, however, is that Muslims, Christians, and Jews would account for them in different ways. Whereas Jews and Christians might attribute the similarities simply to borrowing from their own traditions by the early Muslims and consider the differences as heretical deviations from divine revelation, the Muslims would argue otherwise. They would contend that it was the failure of the Jews and Christians to comprehend completely or to implement fully God's plan for mankind which required a succession of revelations culminating in the Koran. It would follow that the similarities shared by Islam with one or both of its sister religions are not borrowed but represent the portions of the divine plan which, although previously understood, were reiterated in the final revelation, while the differences are attributable to God's acting through Muhammad to correct past errors of comprehension or deliberate distortion of His message. In short, Islam is not a debased or heretical form of Judaism or Christianity but rather the purified and perfected version of God's revealed will.

There is a second and quite different aspect of Islam's relations with other religions which requires attention. What was the basis of the Muslim's attitude towards non-Muslims? During Muhammad's lifetime, precedents were established for dealing with the non-Muslims with whom the infant Islamic community came into contact. Whereas Arab pagans were required either to accept Islam or be killed, a third option was open to Christians and Jews, the so-called People of the Book *(Ahl al-Kitab)*, that is, members of the other revealed religions. In return for submission to Muslim rule and the payment of tribute in the form of a poll-tax *(jizya)* levied on adult males, they were guaranteed protection of their lives, property, and religion. This compact or treaty was called *dhimma* ("obligation" or "responsibility") and the non-Muslims covered by it were known as *dhimmis*.

As Islam spread beyond Arabia, initially at the expense of the Byzantine Empire, this formula of protection in return for submission was extended to the Christian and Jewish inhabitants of the conquered lands. For example, the Caliph 'Umar made a compact with the people of Jerusalem in 636 A.D. in which he accorded them protection "for their persons, their property, their churches, their crosses, their sound and their sick, and the rest of their worship.... No constraint shall be exercised against them in religion nor shall any harm be done to any among them.... The people of Aelia [Jerusalem] must pay the *jizya* in the same way as the people of other cities.... This document is placed under the surety of God and the protection *[dhimma]* of the Prophet, the Caliphs and the believers, on condition that the inhabitants of Aelia pay the *jizya* that is due from them."[1]

A problem was raised by the collapse of Sassanian Persia before the Arab Muslim armies. The Persians were Zoroastrians. Were they to be considered pagans and given the option of conversion or death, or were they to be treated as People of the Book and accorded *dhimmi* status? The Arab historian al-Tabari relates that the commander of the Muslim army sent a letter to the border-chiefs of Persia in which he said, "Become Muslim and be saved. If not, accept protection from us and pay the *jizya*. If not, I shall come against you with men who love death as you love to drink wine."[2] The same author records the compact made by the Muslim commander with the people of Isfahan in 642 A.D. It reads as follows:[3]

> In the name of God, the Merciful and the Compassionate.
> A letter from 'Abdallah to the Fadhusafan and the inhabitants of Isfahan and its surroundings.
> You are safe as long as you discharge your obligations, which are: to pay the *jizya*, which you must pay according to your capacity every year, paying it to whoever is the governor of your country, for every adult male; you must also guide the Muslim [traveler], keep his road in repair, lodge him for a day and a night, and provide the walker with a mount for one stage.
> Do not assert your authority over any Muslim. What you owe to the Muslims is your goodwill and the payment of your dues; you have safe-conduct *(aman)* as long as you comply. But if you change anything, or if anyone among you changes anything and you do not hand him over, then you have no safe-conduct. If anyone insults a Muslim, he will be severely punished for it. If he strikes a Muslim, we shall kill him.
> Written and witnessed by 'Abdallah ibn Qays, 'Abdallah ibn Warqa', and 'Isma ibn 'Abdallah.

For what must have been largely pragmatic reasons, it is clear that Zoroastrians were considered *dhimmis*. This extension of the *dhimmi* concept was repeated time and again when other faiths were encountered in Central and East Asia. The original tripartite division (Muslims, People of the Book, and pagans) of the peoples under Muslim rule was thus reduced to two (Muslims and *dhimmis*), although there continued to be a certain precedence or "pecking order" within the *dhimmi* ranks — People of the Book, followed by Zoroastrians, with pagans at the bottom of the heap.

All lands under Muslim rule were known collectively as the World of Islam *(Dar al-Islam)*, while the areas beyond the borders of the Islamic Empire were called the World of War *(Dar al-Harb)* and the people inhabiting it "infidels" or *harbis*. In theory, an unceasing state of war existed between these two worlds; the ultimate goal of the Muslims' striving (*jihad*, usually translated as "holy war") was the extinction of the World of War by conquest and absorption into the World of Islam. Actual hostilities, however, were frequently interrupted by periods of truce and both *harbi* and Muslim traders carried on a thriving business across frontiers.

Harbis who entered the World of Islam for whatever purpose were protected by a temporary safe-conduct or pledge of security *(aman)* which any adult, sane Muslim, male or female, free or slave, could grant. The holder of an *aman* was called a *musta'min* and enjoyed the same protection as a *dhimmi* but did not have to pay the poll-tax *(jizya)*. Should the *musta'min* remain within the World of Islam more than one year, however, he was considered a *dhimmi* and was obliged to pay the poll-tax. Furthermore, an *aman* might be revoked by the Muslim ruler if he found it to be inconsistent with the interests of Islam.

The specific restrictions and obligations placed upon *dhimmis* in return for protection varied from time to time and place to place, sometimes because the regulations themselves differed or were variously interpreted, but more often because they failed to be implemented fully. The most essential obligation of the *dhimmi* was payment of the poll-tax, but there were other ways in which *dhimmis* were constantly reminded of their inferior status. In theory if not always in practice, they were obliged to wear distinctive clothing and forbidden to carry arms, ride horses, build their houses higher than those of Muslims, build new houses of worship, or behave publicly in such a way as to scandalize Muslims. Marriage between a *dhimmi* man and a Muslim woman was prohibited, but a Muslim man could marry a *dhimmi* woman. They were, on the other hand, exempt from all specifically Muslim obligations including military service. They were free to worship and to follow the rules of their own religious law administered by their own judges, to educate their children as they deemed appropriate, to live where they wished (except that *dhimmis* were removed from the vicinity of the holy cities of Mecca and Medina and not allowed to live there), and to engage in the occupation of their choice.

In brief, *dhimmis* were legally inferior to Muslims and endured humiliation and discrimination at the hands of the dominant Muslims, but they enjoyed an exceptional amount of autonomy and relative security — considerably more than any religious minority in Christian

Europe was accorded. Islamic history is not without occasional periods of intolerance and incidents of violence directed against one or another religious minority, but the very selective nature of these occurrences suggests that they stemmed from something more than just Muslim fanaticism or religious intolerance. The fact that the social and political organization of the World of Islam was communal and based on religious lines has often led outside observers, rarely impartial to begin with, to the conclusion that any hardships suffered by its non-Muslim inhabitants can be attributed solely to Muslim religious intolerance. More careful analysis would argue otherwise. Political disintegration, economic stagnation, and foreign invasion in the medieval period, for example, created chaos in the Islamic World and brought with it insecurity and hardship for all of its inhabitants, Muslim and non-Muslim alike. Social, economic, and political instability, fear, and suspicion undermined the traditional relationships between individuals, communities, and governments and released accumulated antagonisms and grievances. The non-Muslim minorities were not infrequently the targets.

It is one of the ironies of history that the expulsion of the Muslims and Jews from Spain and the religious wars in Europe (15th-17th centuries) coincided with the restoration of order in most of the Islamic Middle East by the Ottoman Turks and the revival in a modified form of the earlier Muslim-*dhimmi* symbiosis. Sephardic Jews in large numbers found refuge in the Ottoman Empire where Jews were recognized as a distinctive religious community *(millet)* under the leadership of a grand rabbi. Eastern Orthodox Christians and Armenian Christians were similarly organized as *millets*, each with a patriarch at the top of an ecclesiastical hierarchy. The *millets* were given almost complete autonomy in managing their intra-communal affairs. They retained their own religious laws and courts, educational institutions, and welfare services, and *millet* officials were even empowered to apportion and collect the taxes imposed on the *millet* by the Ottoman government, one of these being the poll-tax *(jizya)*. Jews, Greeks, and Armenians prospered as merchants and financiers, as ecclesiastical officials with wide-ranging authority over their co-religionists, and as imperial interpreters, envoys, and advisers. Christian youths were recruited by the Ottomans in their Balkan and, to a lesser extent, Anatolian provinces and trained to fill the highest military and administrative posts of the empire, converting to Islam in the process. From the mid-16th century, the Ottoman Empire entered into formal commercial treaties with European states which provided protection and guarantees to merchants and other foreigners temporarily resident in Ottoman lands. These treaties, known as "Capitulations," embodied in a collective sense the traditional concept of the *aman* or safe-conduct for *harbis* in the World of Islam. The Ottomans thus preserved the legal distinctions among Muslims, *dhimmis*, and *harbis* while accentuating the autonomous communal organization of society along religious lines.

Between the late 16th and the early 19th century, the once powerful and efficient Ottoman Empire suffered a series of economic, political, and military reverses which left it weakened and shaken. Under the influence of European ideas and with European support, the Christian minorities of the Ottoman Empire embraced the Western concept of nationalism and sought to establish independent nation-states. The Ottomans attempted to prevent the dismemberment of the empire by the use of military force but also by reforms which had as their *leitmotif* the legal equality of all Ottoman subjects, regardless of their religion. The guarantees of equality were ineffective in curbing the separatist nationalism of the Christian minorities, and they were resented by Muslims who were unwilling to be put on a par with *dhimmis*. Violence, warfare, massacre and counter-massacre between Christians and Muslims was the result. First the Greeks, then the Serbs, Bulgars, Armenians, and others were infected by secular nationalism. As most of these, usually with the aid of one or more of the European Great Powers, achieved their independence, new streams of refugees flooded into what remained of the crumbling Ottoman Empire to escape political or religious oppression, but this time they were Muslims fleeing the Balkans, the Crimea, the Volga region, and the Caucasus.

It is revealing that Ottoman Jews were virtually unaffected by these Christian-Muslim conflicts. In Turkey proper and even in the Arab provinces they proved to be more reluctant than European and American Jews, perhaps because of the relative security and prosperity they enjoyed, to embrace Zionism, Jewish political nationalism which emerged at the end of the 19th century in Europe and culminated in the establishment of the state of Israel after World War II.

The Arabs were also late in opting for nationalism, although they experienced a cultural reawakening in the 19th century in which Christian Arabs played a prominent but sometimes exaggerated role. Only in the aftermath of the 1907-1908 Turkish revolution and the ensuing adoption by the Young Turk government in Istanbul of a policy of Turkish nationalism did the growing self-awareness of the

Arabs begin to take the form of separatist nationalism. The Arab-Israeli conflict was triggered by the head-on clash of Arab nationalism and Jewish nationalism in Palestine. The deterioration of the condition of Jews in the Arab Middle East and their flight *en masse* from Arab countries dates from this confrontation. Once again, the basic issue was political, although it had religious overtones and implications.

Likewise, the protracted conflict in Cyprus is an example of two national communities, Greeks and Turks, inhabiting the same island but differentiated by ethnic origin, language, and culture as well as religion, which seem incapable of resolving their conflict and finding a way to live together in peace and security. To view the Cyprus problem in terms of Muslims pitted against Christians is as misleading as to see the Palestine problem in a religious context of Muslim versus Jew.

The course of history has radically altered the World of Islam. Muslims have witnessed in recent centuries what must have appeared to them as a reversal of the divinely-ordained historical process — the expansion of the World of War at the expense of the World of Islam. Military defeats, foreign domination, and the political, social, economic, and cultural changes of revolutionary proportions which these produced were accompanied by a loss of self-confidence and by challenges to traditional beliefs and practices. The secular nationalism of the West has made inroads in the religiously-based modes of individual and communal identification of the World of Islam and, in so doing, has undermined the traditional relationships between Muslims and non-Muslims. Complex movements variously described as "the resurgence of Islam," "Islamic Fundamentalism," "Islamic Modernism" and "Islamic Revivalism" have emerged and in recent years commanded increasing attention throughout the world. Where these will lead Islam and how Islam's relations with other religions will be affected by them in the final analysis are questions which cannot yet be answered, but one thing is certain: there can be no going back to the medieval world inhabited by Muslims, *dhimmis* and *harbis*.

Footnotes
[1]Bernard Lewis, ed. and trans., *Islam from the Prophet Muhammad*

to the *Capture of Constantinople.* New York: Harper & Row, 1974, vol. I, pp. 235-236.

[2]*Ibid.,* p. 228.

[3]*Ibid.,* p. 238.

Suggested Readings

Grunebaum, Gustave E. von., *Medieval Islam, A Study in Cultural Orientation.* 2nd Revised Edition. Chicago, 1953.

——————, *Modern Islam, The Search for Cultural Identity.* New York, 1964.

Hasluck, F. W., *Christianity and Islam under the Sultans.* 2 vols. Oxford, 1929.

Itzkowitz, Norman, *Ottoman Empire and Islamic Tradition.* Chicago, 1980.

Khadduri, Majid, *War and Peace in the Law of Islam.* Baltimore, 1955.

Levy, Reuben, *The Social Structure of Islam.* Cambridge, England, 1957.

Lewis, Bernard, *The Arabs in History.* New York, 1967.

——————, (ed. and trans.). *Islam from the Prophet Muhammad to the Capture of Constantinople.* 2 vols. New York, 1974.

Schacht, Joseph, *An Introduction to Islamic Law.* Oxford, 1964.

IV

MARTYRDOM IN ARABIC LITERATURE

Salih J. Altoma

> Young Palestinian revolutionaries risking their lives either in hijacking airplanes or attacking Israeli settlements, masses of unarmed marchers challenging government tanks and gunships either in Jordan or Iran, Afghani Muslim fighters holding out against infinitely more powerful Soviet troops, pious Shi'ite masses flagellating themselves, young fanatics sacrificing their lives in the Grand Mosque of Mecca — these have been familiar scenes from the Islamic world in recent years. It is important to understand what moves them to put their lives on the line so easily, whatever may be the causes that they perceive as so noble. This force, as Professor Altoma points out, comes from the promise of martyrdom which is a most cherished attainment for Muslims and as such much romanticized in Islamic religious and secular literature of all times and places. Recently the trend in Arabic literature has been to draw a parallel between much venerated martyrs/saints of Islam and the modern revolutionaries who risk their lives for more secular causes. Thus the desire for martyrdom and secular militancy come together in the current Islamic revival.
>
> Salih J. Altoma who has written extensively on modern Arabic literature is currently professor in the Department of Near Eastern Languages and Literatures at Indiana University.

Martyrdom as a symbol or theme recurs frequently in modern Arabic literature, evoking defiance against oppression, suffering in quest of renewal, or expectation of man's ultimate triumph against evil. Indeed the frequency and the intensity with which this symbol is used border on the obsession leading inevitably to considerable repetition of themes, imageries or motifs. Such a literary phenomenon can be attributed to the active influence of Islam as a religion, as well as to the climate of unresolved tension or crisis which has dominated the Arab/Muslim world throughout its modern history. However, other factors also seem to have contributed to its growth including ancient Near Eastern myths or rituals which relate to death and renewal or resurrection, and Christ's passion and crucifixion.

In this paper, we will attempt to identify, first, the Islamic influence and, second, the use of different types of martyrs — religious, mystic and political — particularly in poetry.

Martyrdom in Islam is defined as the believer's voluntary act of death in the way of God defending his faith. The Quran does not use the world "shahīd" (martyr) but it refers unmistakably to the act of martyrdom and the merits of the martyrs in several instances: "And say not of those who are slain in the way of God: 'They are dead.' Nay, they are living, though ye perceive (it) not." (Sura ii, 154). "And if ye are slain or die in the way of God, forgiveness and mercy from God are far better than all they could amass. And if ye die, or are slain, it is unto God that ye are brought together." (Sura iii, 157-158). "Think not those who are slain in God's way as dead. Nay, they live, finding their sustenance in the Presence of their Lord. They rejoice in the Bounty provided by God: and with regard to those left behind, who have not yet joined them [in their bliss] they [martyrs] glory in the fact that on them is no fear, nor have they [cause to] grieve. They glory in the Grace and the Bounty from God, and in the fact that God suffereth not the reward of the faithful to be lost." (Sura iii, 160/171). "But those who are slain in the way of God He will never let their deeds be lost. Soon will He guide them and improve their condition and lead them into Paradise which He has announced for them." (Sura xlvii, 4-6).

The traditions of the Prophet Muhammad contain numerous references to the martyr, his privileges or merits and the importance of his martyrdom to the community's well being. The martyr is promised a number of prerogatives: forgiveness of his sins, one of the highest ranks in Paradise, freedom from the trial of the grave, the crown of honor, one jewel of which is worth more than the world and all that is therein, and the right of intercession on behalf of his relatives. Other characteristics attributed to the martyr include his painless death, his desire to return to the world to seek martyrdom anew, and the inspiring role of his act as a living reminder: his blood will never dry up and "the light is seen on the martyr's grave" (Wensinck, pp. 146-48; Bjorkman, pp. 259-61; Guillaume, pp. 111-13). Such exaltation of martyrdom expressed in the two primary sources of Islamic teaching defines not only the motivation and the aspirations of the martyr, but also some of the salient symbols or motifs recurrent in Arabic literature: the joyful expectation of death in the way of God, self-defense, or in combating injustice; the bliss the martyr experiences and the rewards he anticipates through his martyrdom; the inspiring role his act, his blood, and his radiant tomb play in the life of his community; and the notion that martyrs never die. Although different types or degrees of martyrdom are identified, it is the fighting martyr who has received the highest honor and to whom countless number of literary works or references have been devoted. Perhaps the most important single event which reinforced martyrdom in Islam and kept it vividly alive in the minds of many Muslims is the tragic death of Husayn, the Prophet's grandson on 10 Muharram A.H. 61/10 October 680 at Karbala, Iraq. Husayn's death encompasses both the religious and political dimensions of martyrdom in that it was the result of his refusal to acknowledge the legitimacy of a ruler (Yazid) widely known for his violations of Islamic teachings, and of his revolt in quest of righteousness and justice. What seems to have turned his martyrdom into a Christ-like passion, a paragon of suffering, is not simply his close relation to the Prophet, his virtues, the justice and nobility of his cause, his betrayal by the same followers who invited him to lead them, but also the barbarity to which he was subjected before and after his death, and the ruthless treatment the women of his camp received as captives. According to most accounts of his martyrdom, Husayn was the last to die on the tenth of Muharram after witnessing painfully the death of all the male members of his camp (72) with one exception, Ali, the only surviving son. Furthermore, it seems that he was killed gradually, his corpse dismembered and trampled under the hoofs of horses, stripped of his clothes and left unburied for three days, and that his severed head, along with the heads of other supporters, was carried in a peculiar procession to Damascus and was subjected to an infamous treatment by Yazid. Such atrocities have been repeatedly dramatized in Islamic literatures as the following lines from a nineteenth century Persian poem illustrate:

> What rains down? Blood! Who? The Eye! How? Day and Night! Why?
> From grief! What grief? The grief of the Monarch of Karbalā!
> What was his name? Husayn! Of whose race? 'Ali's!
> Who was his mother? Fātimā! Who was his grandsire? Mustafā!
> How was it with him? He fell a martyr! Where? In the Plain of Māriya!
> When? On the tenth of Muharram! Secretly? No, in public!
> Was he slain by night? No, by day! At what time? At noontide!
> Was his head severed from the throat? No, from the nape of the neck!
> Was he slain unthirsting? No! Did none give him to drink? They did!

Who? Shimr! From what source? From the source of Death!
Was he an innocent martyr? Yes! Had he committed any fault?
No!
What was his work? Guidance! Who was his friend? God!
Was not the dagger ashamed to cut his throat?
It was! Why then did it do so? Destiny would not excuse it!
Wherefore? In order that he might become an intercessor for mankind!
What is the condition of his intercession? Lamentation and weeping!
Were any of his sons also slain? Yes, two!
Who else? Nine brothers! Who else? Kinsmen!

(Browne, pp. 180-181)

It was, therefore, inevitable that Husayn, of all other Muslim martyrs, should stand out as the martyr par excellence, the father of martyrs, their king or seal, and become the subject of continuously growing literature of martyrologies. The extensive literature devoted to Husayn has, from the start, underlined not only the Islamic (political and religious) significance of his martyrdom, but also its cosmic or universal dimension by means of supernatural, mythical and eschatological interpretations or accounts. To the latter belong, for example, the notion that Husayn's matyrdom was sympathetically anticipated by, or revealed to, Adam, Noah, Abraham, Moses and Jesus among others, and that "all sufferings before are but a prelude to his and sufferings after him are only modes of participation in his martyrdom." (see Ayoub, pp. 27-36). There are also the marvels connected with his death such as the grief which the seven heavens and earths expressed when he fell on the battlefield, or the marvels about his severed head illuminating and speaking in a manner that impressed a Christian monk to embrace Islam, or the misfortunes which afflicted all men who had taken part directly or indirectly in his death. Such elements which are still incorporated in elegies or *Ta'zias* (passion plays) serve basically to renew the faith of his devotees and their loyalty to his cause, to remind them of the divine or universal sympathy or support Husayn enjoys and to assure them of his (as well as their) ultimate triumph against injustice, evil or tyranny. Today, as in the past, Husayn's martyrdom is reenacted or commemorated in a variety of expressive forms, especially among the Shi'ites: elegies, memorial services, pilgrimage rituals (visit to his shrine in Karbala), processions, self-flagellation, passion plays, and other mourning ceremonies, whether during the days directly related to his martyrdom or any time throughout the year.

To illustrate some of the features shared by these forms, we shall briefly describe elegiac poetry and cite a few examples. Elegies, recited mainly on the occasion of Husayn's anniversary, are intended to keep his memory alive and express grief for his suffering. Both remembrance and sorrow are emphasized not only because they lead to salvation but also because they are regarded as an extension of Husayn's struggle, a participation in his suffering. This notion has its roots in the early Shi'ite traditions attributed to the various Imams and has, over the years, been reinforced and amplified by other commentaries and practices. One of the earliest traditions is attributed to Husayn's only surviving son, Ali, the fourth Imam: ". . . any man of faith whose eyes shed tears until they run down copiously on his face for a harm we have suffered at the hands of our enemies, God will ensure for him a place of righteous mansions to dwell therein for countless ages in Paradise. And any man of faith who may suffer harm for our sake and his eyes shed tears for such harm . . . God would surely take away all pain from his face on the Day of Resurrection and would protect him from His wrath and the fire." Similarly, the eighth Imam is quoted to have counseled one of his disciples: "If it would please you to have the reward of those who were martyred with Husayn, say whenever you remember: Oh how I wish I were with them that I may have achieved great victory! . . . If you wish to be with us in our high stations in Paradise, rejoice for our joy and grieve for our sorrow. . . ." (Ayoub, pp. 143, 147). In other words, elegies are expected to narrate Husayn's martyrdom in all of its aspects recalling events, sufferings and virtues of the martyred and other pertinent themes even at the risk of considerable repetition. However, modern poets have tended to relate Husayn's martyrdom to the modern situation and adapt elegy as an instrument of political protest or resistance against internal or external oppression. A recent poem (1972) by Mustafa Jamal ad-Din entitled "Destination of the Martyrs" invokes the act of betrayal Husayn suffered only to suggest that the Palestinians were the victims of a similar act of betrayal when they were suppressed in Jordan in the early 1970's. Another poem by Salih al-Ja'fari, dedicated to Husayn, universalizes his martyrdom as a living spirit active in every struggle for a just cause: "O symbol of boundless sacrifice/ the fluttering banner of every rebel/ the ebullient blood in every revolutionary/ liars are those who said you were defeated/ the world rages with its rebels/ you are in their midst, no longer alone/ if the closest to you betrayed the covenant/ the farthest from you have been more faithful/ here is proud Vietnam pledging/ to stir up the world and here is Guevara/ they see you a towering leader/ they follow your steps as a fearless rebel."

The literary use of Husayn's martyrdom may be direct and didactic as the lines cited above indicate or may assume a more suggestive tone alluding to the city where he was buried, Karbala, or his severed head as a cross-like symbol of suffering, or other landmarks or symbols associated with his tragedy, the river Euphrates and thirst. Perhaps Ahmad Dahbour's poem "Return to Karbala" represents one of the more successful and subtle attempts in which Husayn's ordeal is interwoven into the predicament of the Palestinians without naming either one.

> I am coming — my love has preceded me
> I am coming — my hands reaching ahead of me
> I am coming in spite of my thirst
> In my provision: the fruits of the palm trees
> Let the buried water come to me
> Let it be my guide.
> O Karbala, touch my face with your water
> You will feel the martyr's thirst
> You will see in the wounds of my forehead a trust
> which dictates my steps
> You will see my steps.
> It was said: reaching you is a miracle
> It was said: the earth has been sealed
> It was said . . .
> I said: you are mine
> The world eats of your fruits, but not I.
> I came — my love ahead of me
> Don't ask my new face: How the loved ones are!
> Shepherd's garments, wolf's intention!
> We have pledged to seek death
> to undo the suffering of your death
> in a prolonged captivity
> They divided the fruits of the palm trees
> No one but I alone died
> I witnessed them, I had witnesses: you, water turning blood
> the blood that became water, and the palm trees
> I witnessed them: a merchant, a gambler, a masked face
> All were the gold of the intruder
> I have entered my death alone, turning into
> a homeland, a massacre, an exile.
> I came, Karbala, my hands preceding me
> and within me a restless flame,
> remembering how the faces turned around
> They knew the antagonist . . . they witness him
> sinking in my flesh, drinking of my blood
> they were mad at him during the hours of my death
> but they crowned him when I died
> they exchanged my head

> only to return to me bearing the noble wound
> and I return
> they will never lead in my name
> for my wound is back to deny them, my eyes to renounce their deeds
> O Karbala, city of massacres, joys, camps, love
> all the faces unmasked/ unmasked are the faces
> I saw them all who sold you, who sold us both in an auction
> yet we remained indivisible
> I was the river within you, my banks merged with your grass
> I was murdered in you, I am the martyred river
> Let the buried water come to me
> Let it be my guide.
> You have my memory, unseal it,
> you will seal the time of lamentation
> Reaching you is not a miracle, a step forward
> and the impossible wall crumbled
> here I am, carrying my joy, the gifts, and sorrows
> I am coming — my love has preceded me
> I am coming — my hands reaching ahead of me
> coming in spite of my thirst
> in my provision: the fruits of the palm trees
> let the buried water come to me
> let it be my guide.

As expected, poems totally or mainly devoted to Husayn's martyrdom, innumerable as they are, are not the only forms dealing with the subject, for there are, likewise, innumerable instances in which reference is made to Husayn for one purpose or another as in the following fragments by the Syrian-Lebanese poet Adonis (Ali Ahmad Said):

1. The Head's Mirror (A conversation between a man and his wife held on October 680)

> I returned home / my wife Nuwar opened the door
> — you left me lonesome for too long . . .
> — rejoice! I brought you the world, the treasure of the world
> — from where? how? Where?
> — his head . . .
> — Husayn's? woe to you on the day of resurrection, woe to you /
>   after today, no path, no dream, no bed will ever unite us.

And Nuwar went away.

2. The Witness's Mirror

> When lances pierced Husayn's heart
> and the horses trampled every spot of Husayn's corpse
> and Husayn's garments were pillaged and divided
> I saw every stone bending over Husayn
> I saw every flower sleeping at Husayn's shoulder
> I saw every river walking in Husayn's funeral.

3. A Mirror for Husayn's Mosque

> Don't you see the trees walking
> in ecstasy, in patience
> to witness the prayer?
> Don't you see a sheathless sword
> crying?
> an armless swordsman
> circling around Husayn's mosque?

Husayn's severed head recurs frequently as a symbol of both suffering and redemption in a manner that resembles, to a certain extent, the literary use of the cross and crucifixion. Such use may be reflected in a line or two within a poem or may be pursued in greater detail throughout a poem as in the case of "The Exodus of Husayn's Head from the Cities of Treason" by Qasim Haddad, a leading poet from Bahrain. Published in a collection bearing the same title (Beirut, 1972), the poem draws upon imageries and allusions indicating Husayn's suffering to highlight a world that lacks justice, equality and compassion.

> We move on, we know how to split the earth
> to sow within it new creations
> we are Husayn journeying from Karbala
> we are Husayn's head, torn between Damascus and the gulf
> we carry it, pause at the wall of mummies
> and walk on along with our triumphant banner
> coming out from every hut on this gulf
> entering all the castles
> let the rose of the ashes bloom
> the ashes that conceal fire, youthful lives, the starved.
> beneath it we lived for a thousand years
> turning to a heap of ash
>
> Hunger will receive Husayn's head, the gate of fire opens
> and Husayn's head steps in
> the land becomes a bride having a thousand children
> a thousand lovers
> (Love prevails everywhere but falls victim at the moment
> of confrontation . . .)
>
> We march on, we waited too long, we were killed
> but rose from the grave, we were killed
> again we rose . . . we were never defeated
> we walked with the head to every region unwavering
> carrying Husayn's besieged head in every foreign land
> walking to the cities of fire, burning their walls
> writing on the hands of their children verses of love,
> a journey on the road without wavering . . .

Poetry seems to be best suited for the dramatization of martyrdom as a theme in modern Arabic literature and as such it is more often used than any other genre. There are, however, a few dramatic or fictional works which have dealt with the martyrdom of Husayn or other martyrs such as al-Hallaj, the Muslim mystic who was put to death in Baghdad in the year of 922. Most famous among them are two plays: *God's Revenge* by the Egyptian novelist Abd al-Rahman al-Sharqawi and *The Tragedy of al-Hallaj* by the Egyptian poet Salah Abd al-Sabur. Both plays are in verse.

Sharqawi's play offers a fairly detailed account of Husayn's story in two parts: *Husayn as a Rebel* and *Husayn as a Martyr* (Cairo, 1969). In the first part Husayn finds himself in a quandary now that Yazid has assumed power and seems to have ensured the allegiance of many Muslims through terror or by means of tempting promises. He is invited by Yazid's representative, the governor of Medina, to pay homage for the sake of preserving the peace and unity of the community. He also was extended a promise of generous material rewards in case of compliance and a threat of adverse consequences, his death and the persecution of his family, in case of non-compliance. From the beginning Husayn is drawn as a righteous man deeply troubled by the fate that awaits Islam and the faithfuls under a rule of corruption and oppression and is unwilling to resign himself to a passive role under such conditions. Yet, he appears uncertain as to the course he should follow. He turns to the Prophet while meditating at his grave seeking guidance: "I do not know what I should do . . . help me/ If I pay homage to the impudent/ to save my life, the life of others/ I would commit blasphemy/ I would disobey you in what you have conveyed from God to men/ Should I refuse to pledge allegiance/ I would be killed/ If I stay here to mobilize men against him/ the blood of the innocent would flow around you." Husayn finally resolves the question by his decision to leave his city, to go out in the hope of reaching men who would respond to his call: "Save the world/ this senseless world has strayed/ save it from chaos and the tyranny of fear/ save the community from this hell." With this decision made, Husayn seems to have taken the crucial step toward his martyrdom for he soon reveals that in his dream he saw his grandfather, the Prophet, urging him to act against falsehood and calling him "the Chief of the Martyrs." Having been reassured that he would be acting in God's interest, that with his martyrdom he would be defending God's religion, Husayn from now on insists upon pursuing his cause in a journey that leads him to Karbala where he would meet his martyrdom. Nothing would deter him from his course, be it personal and family sufferings, the human weakness reflected in the betrayal of would-be followers or in the sympathetic, but passive, expression of devotion, or the premonition he hears regarding his fate. The second part of the play deals in detail with the sequence of events which took place in Karbala, after Husayn's arrival and lead to his martyrdom. Aside from idealizing Husayn's cause, the play gives prominence to the widely held belief that Husayn did not die in vain and that his death would be avenged by God as the final scene amply indicates. Here, five years after Husayn's death, Yazid appears haunted by his crime, facing Husayn in a desert as he suffers thirst and dies a helpless king. When all other antagonists responsible for Husayn's death are punished, the scene concludes with Husayn exhorting his devotees to uphold faithfully truth and justice: "Remember me not by bloodshedding / but by rescuing truth from the tyranny of falsehood / by struggling on the path / so that justice may prevail / . . . Remember me when virtues become homeless / and vices alone become the favorite beloved / Remember me when defamation, deceit and falsification become signs of success / and the cowardice of the humiliated mark of wisdom / Remember me when you are invaded in your homeland as you watch / when the usurpers feel secure in your midst while your youth pursue shameless acts / Remember then and rise up in the name of life / to raise the banner of truth and justice / remember my great revenge / seek it from the tyrant / only then life triumphs / If you acquiesce to deception, if man accepts humiliation / I will be massacred anew / I will be killed every day a thousand times / . . . And a new Yazid will continue to rule you / to act as he wishes / and upon you will be cast the damnation of the martyr's wound / for failing to fulfill the martyr's vengeance." Needless to say, these selected lines from Husayn's exhortative farewell serve not only to sum up the human essence of Husayn's movement or to stress the socio-political implication of his martyrdom but also — and perhaps more importantly — to relate it to current conditions in Egypt and the Arab world in general.

Al-Hallāj represents another notable example of historical figures glorified as martyrs in Arabic literature. Accused of heresy and subsequently put to death, in 922 in Baghdad, al-Hallāj has not been elevated by the general public to the rank of martyrs. Judgments or opinions regarding his doctrine or his martyrdom are largely divided into three groups: condemnation, affirmation of his sainthood and suspension of judgment. Nonetheless, he assumes in the modern literary context, more often than not, the role of an inspiring martyr concerned with both spiritual and social issues as illustrated in Sabur's play, *The Tragedy of al-Hallāj*. The play in two acts opens with the shock of al-Hallāj hanging dead from a tree to the bewilderment of casual bypassers. This confusion as to the reason for the "old man's" death leads to the eventual unraveling of events preceding the hanging and a discussion of the purpose or reason behind it. That responsibility for his death is claimed separately by a group of townspeople, a group of his sufist devotees, and his fellow mystic, Shiblī, only adds to the mystery. With succeeding scenes we find al-Hallāj alive and in discussion with Shiblī as to the purpose of his path toward self-realization. While Shiblī insists upon his solitary path of devotion, al-Hallāj senses a responsibility to share and disseminate his enlightened understanding toward a universal social good. He appears incapable of closing his eyes to a world that has been conquered by evil. When later he is warned of the state's suspicion, and the danger to which he exposed himself, he responds: "Is it because I converse with my friends / saying to them: the ruler is the heart of the community? / that the community attains righteousness through his own righteousness? / Telling them: if you rule do not forget / to pour the wine of authority into the cup of justice." Before the first act ends al-Hallāj is arrested and led to jail for heresy while conversing with a group of people about his mystical experience. The second act ensues with al-Hallāj in prison winning over his guard and two other prisoners. This scene serves two main purposes: first, to develop further al-Hallāj's social oriented mysticism and second, to face and resolve the question of how to fulfill his vision. Should he remain content to preach to the people about his vision, or should he go among the populace, taking action, raising his "sword" against the wrongs that surround them? Al-Hallāj rejects the latter course, declaring in his conversation with his fellow prisoners that only by spiritual consciousness can man conquer evil. This becomes clear when he presents his defense in the final scene before the Sultan's tribunal.

> I saw poverty howling in the streets
> destroying the spirit of man.
> I asked myself: What should I do?
> Should I call upon the poor
> to thrust the sword of vengeance
> into the hearts of the unjust?
> But how pitiful it would be
> if we were to meet evil with evil
> to cure a sin with a sin?
> What should I do?
> Should I call upon the unjust
> to rid his people of injustice?

> But can a word open a heart
> sealed with a golden lock?
> What can I do?
> I have nothing but to converse
> Let the wandering winds carry my words
> Let me affirm them upon papers —
> A testimony from a man of vision
> perhaps they inspire the thirsty heart
> of a notable from the community
> so he may spread them
> so he may protect them if he rules,
> reconciling power with vision
> uniting wisdom with action.

The court's proceedings expose the hypocrisy of the system as the judges appear, with the exception of one, intent on condemning al-Hallāj under any pretext. When a message from the Sultan arrives declaring that the state has pardoned al-Hallāj for his acts of sedition, the chief judge decrees, in response to the vizier's request, that he should be tried for heresy. Undeterred by the protestation of a fellow judge who insists that such an act can be vindicated or judged only by God, not man's law, he proceeds to sentence al-Hallāj to death in the name of paid witnesses declaring that the public demanded his death not the state or the state's judges.

As this brief summary indicates, the play imparts to al-Hallāj's martyrdom overtones that have relevance to the modern world. Through them al-Hallāj appears not simply as a hero from the past worthy of exaltation but also as a man of vision who has much to say to his audience. This is achieved by skillfully bringing into focus two central viewpoints: al-Hallāj's insistence on socially activating his mystical ideas for the community's well-being in contrast to both the state's insensitivity toward the suffering of its citizenry and the preoccupation of righteous men with their solitary path of salvation.

Although the theme of martyrdom is basically religious in origin and orientation, it has increasingly tended to stress the secular or political issues. This is reflected in the manner religious martyrs are invoked or reinterpreted as well as in the frequent elevation to martyrdom individuals who meet their death for a political cause. There are "martyrs" of one ideological movement (party) or another seeking to refashion society in its image, or of a broader national struggle against a regime or foreign domination. Such martyrs are often extolled, individually or collectively, in elegies, memorial studies or other literary works, irrespective of their standing in society. The Palestinian poet Ibrāhīm Touqān (1905-1941) devoted, as early as the

1930's, a poem to "The Martyrs" which idealizes fallen patriots in familiar terms. "Perhaps death snatched him / as a hostage in a prison / without farewell of a tear or home / Perhaps he was buried shroudless / you know not where / In valleys or on mountaintops / Ask not where his corpse lies / Eternity echoes his name / He is a star of guidance / glimmering in nights of calamities."

Another poet, Abd al-Rahīm Mahmūd (d. 1948), who met his death in a battle near Jerusalem, has likewise stressed martyrdom as a price for his homeland's survival and renewal in a poem entitled "The Martyr," declaring, "I will carry my soul on my hands / and throw it into the path of death / To attain either life, pleasing my friends / Or death, annoying my enemies." More recently Mahmoud Darwish uses the martyr as a symbol which enshrines the predicament of the Palestinians and their spirit of defiance under Israeli rule, as in his poem "The Song's Martyr."

> I am not the first to wear the crown of thorns,
> to say: cry!
> For my cross may become
> a courser's back
> and the thorns on my forehead,
> adorned with blood and dew
> may turn into a crown of laurel!
> And may I be the last to say:
> "I have longed for death."

Martyrdom embraces also the use of cross, crucifixion, "Fedayyin" (self-sacrificing) and other related symbols which recur in modern Arabic poetry in general. "The singer on the cross of pain / With his wound shining like a star / said to the men around him: / Anything you ask but repentance / Thus I die standing / Like a tree I die standing / Only thus the cross becomes a platform / A melody, and strings." (From Darwish's poem, "The Singer Said").

Darwish's poetry abounds in many allusions to Palestinian martyrs who died or seek their death in the defense of their homeland.

> If I perish on the cross of my worship
> I shall return a saint in a fighter's uniform.
>
> How did the pool of blood
> turn into stars and trees?
> None but the murderer died.
>
> Let me be a martyr
> defending the grass, love,

the dust of the streets, of the trees,
the eyes of women,
the movement of the rocks.

Examples dealing with martyrdom in other contexts such as internal conflicts, revolutions and wars of independence are too numerous to cite here — they tend, however, to evoke the same patriotic tone or use similar symbols or ideas in extolling the virtues of martyrdom as may be seen from the following specimen:

> We were on the road of martyrs
> carrying a coffin on our shoulders,
> It was a wedding,
> It was a throne
> You were the king, we were your subjects
>
> We have resumed our waiting for you
> You are coming back — coming back to your homeland,
> like a star — now turning westward,
> only to rise from the East
> You are a branch
> Withering in a season,
> but shall return in the season
> of your flowering.
>
> Abd al-Mu'ti al-Hijazi (Egypt)
from his poem, "A Martyr Who Did Not Die"

> Who can wash the blood in the streets?
> This eternal blood who can conceal it?
> Who can rob the martyr of his tomb?
>
> This naked blood on the cross flows,
> flows ceaselessly,
> through the winds,
> across the streets,
> the doors
> and will blossom one day,
> Like a wild flower.
>
> Sa'di Yusuf (Iraq)
"Blood in the Street"

> When I saw the night in his blazing eyes,
> And found no palm trees in his face,
> no stars,
> I whirled around his head like a wind,
> and broke like a reed.
>
> Adonis (Syria-Lebanon)
"The Martyr"

O land of emerald and pearls
Remember:
The ruby is your most precious jewel
the season of your birth; your loftiest season,
when thousands of eyes lose, in an instant,
the flash of life.

They were human like others
Human in their faults, resolution, aspirations,
when evil dashed their dreams
And a harsh question challenged them:
"Shall it be truth (justice) and evil's death?
or the death of aspiration?
submission to live? or refusal and defiance?
They gathered their resolve
the barren tombs were filled
with fresh youth, with fragrance,
with verdant hopes . . .
with lives.

Salma al-Khadra' al-Jayyusi (Palestine)
"Elegy to the Martyrs"

Martyrs never die
they are the seed and the rose
in the soil of redemption
the sea, the seashore, the verse
whenever darkness reigns
Baghdad bursts forth, in its night of calamity,
a river of light
whenever blood is shed
gardens blossom, poors rebel

Abd al-Wahhab al-Bayati (Iraq)
"Martyrs Never Die"

In conclusion, martyrdom as a literary theme continues to dominate modern Arabic literature and perpetuate much of the overtones, symbolism and appeal associated with the early Islamic doctrine of martyrdom: self-sacrificial acts against injustice and oppression, faith in the victory of the martyr's cause, the self-fulfilling and inspiring role of martyrdom. In pursuing this theme, modern writers draw heavily on earlier conventions except in their tendency to emphasize the secular or patriotic implications of martyrdom, to adapt ancient Near Eastern myths or Christian symbols, and to become more suggestive in their tone. To them as well as to their audience, martyrdom seems to provide an outlet for their sense of helplessness, failure and frustration, and to act as an effective "myth" which, in time of crisis, sustains their faith and renews their hopes and aspirations.

Selected Bibliography

Abd al-Sabūr,Salāh, *Murder in Baghdad* (Ma'sāt al-Hallāj), Tr.Khalil I.Semaan. Leidin, 1972

Ayoub, Mahmoud, *Redemptive Suffering in Islam: A Study of the Devotional Aspects of 'Ashūra'in Twelver Shi'ism*. The Hague, 1978.

Bjorkman, W., "Shahīd", *Ency. of Islam*. 1st Edition. Vol. IV pp. 259-261

Browne, Edward G., *A Literary History of Persia*. Cambridge, 1930. Vol. IV esp. pp. 172-192

Ende, Werner, "The Flagellations of Muharram and the Shi'ite Ulamā", *Der Islam* 55 (1978) pp. 19-36

Grunebaum, G. E. von., *Muhammadan Festivals*. London, 1951. esp pp. 85-94

Guillaume, Alfred, *The Traditions of Islam: An Introduction to the Study of the Hadith Literature*. Beirut, 1966

The Holy Quran, Tr. Abdullah Yusuf Ali. 2 Vols. Cambridge, Mass., 1946

Jafri, S.H.M., *The Origins and Early Development of Shi'a Islam*. London and New York, 1979. pp. 174-221 on "The Martyrdom of Husayn".

Massignon, L. & L. Gardet, "Al-Hallādj", *Ency. of Islam*, New Edition. Vol. III pp. 99-104

Thaiss, Gustav, "Religious Symbolism and Social Change: The Drama of Husain", *Scholars, Saints and Sufis*. ed. Nikki R. Keddi. Berkeley, 1972. pp. 349-366

Vaglieri, L. Veccia, "Al-Husayn B. 'Alī B. Abī Tālib", *Ency. of Islam*. New Edition. Vol. III pp. 607-615

Wensinck, A. J., *Handbook of Early Muhammadan Tradition*. Leiden 1927.

THEOCRACY IN ISLAM

Bert De Vries

In 1947 when Pakistan was created as a Muslim state the Western world, especially the British who were relinquishing their political control of the subcontinent of India, wondered what shape it was going to take. For that matter even the leaders of the new nation had no clear idea of what it should be or would be. That is the reason it took so long and so many efforts for them to thrash out the various constitutions of Pakistan. As it turned out the makers of these constitutions increasingly fell back on the medieval model of Islamic theocracy.

In contrast, when in 1979 the Islamic republic was declared in Iran the process was simple, quick and direct. In a matter of weeks a theocratic constitution was adopted by overwhelming popular majority. One reason for this was the religious nature of the Iranian revolution and its leadership. Another was that much had happened between the two events in the Islamic world by way of a reawakening of its traditions which made the theocratic constitution perhaps the only option for a Muslim state. Professor De Vries here discusses the centrality of theocracy in the Islamic tradition which makes it not just appealing but almost imperative to many Islamic nations of the world today.

Bert De Vries who has done extensive research in the history of the Middle East is currently professor and chairman of the Department of History at Calvin College.

We in the West assume that secular political systems in which matters relating to the state are kept distinct from those relating to the Church are normal. We have tended to view those instances of the influence of religion on politics that still occur as vestiges of Medieval practices that will eventually wither in the face of modern progress. In view of this the role of Islamic religion in Middle Eastern political systems had been either ignored or undervalued by Westerners over the past century. Either the secularist assumption was applied to the Islamic world without attention to the facts or Islam was dismissed as a curious but irrelevant and irksome hurdle to political progress. This line of thinking has made it difficult to comprehend recent events in which the reassertion of Islam as a political force was a factor. In the recent Iranian revolution much was made of the corruption and cruelty of the Shah's regime, the bitterness and old age of Khomeini and the symbolism of the return of the veil. In addition to these superficial factors the religious dimension was seldom discussed, and then often as a mere cover for social discontent and left-wing movements. The possibility of a revolution to reverse the trend of secularization and re-establish the traditional role of religion in the political system was given scant attention or ignored altogether. It has been difficult to believe that an entire nation would let its religious conviction provide the moving force behind a political revolution.

The fact is that, for people outside the Western tradition, religion and politics have always been two sides of the same coin. This is particularly true of people in the Islamic cultural sphere. From their point of view political systems that exclude religion from politics appear strange and unworkable. The introduction of such systems into the Islamic world was therefore unsettling and considerable cause for puzzlement and unrest. In fact, acceptance of secular political methods was often seen as a mark of the decline not only of local autonomy, but of the Islamic religion as well. Hence it is not surprising that religious revival movements have worked energetically at the reinsertion of Islam into politics. From the point of view of many serious and traditional Muslims this is seen not as a slide backwards, but simply as a return to normal.

This difference in perspective comes from a marked difference in historical experience. Europe in the Middle Ages shared with Islam the assumption that religion and politics went together. The working out of this principle in the assignment of political functions to both priests and kings provided fodder for much debate and military conflict in the period. Europe, however, gradually moved away from that assumption over a period of more than five hundred years through a series of intellectual movements: Renaissance, Reformation, Enlightenment, Political Revolutions. While these changes in political outlook were taking place in the West, Islamic political theory continued unaltered. When change came, it was not gradual and internal, but abrupt and external; it came from Europe under the conditions of

European control of the Islamic world from 1750-1950. It came not in the form of gradual discovery to which adjustments in practice could be made over a long time span, it came rather as a blow from which recovery was essential.

In order to understand the role of religion in current Islamic politics, the above observations suggest three separate historical phases: I. The Medieval Background. II. The European Challenge, 1750-1950. III. Islamic Resurgence, 1950-1980.

I. The Medieval Background

From the outset of his prophetic ministry Mohammed assumed that religion was pervasive in all aspects of life. No act was so minute, so insignificant, so private as to be hidden from God's sight. Every act, therefore, done in God's presence, was a religious act, done in response to Him. Religion was an affair of the market place as well as of the mosque. To those of us accustomed to seeing activities related to the church as especially religious, while the rest of life remains more or less secular, one of the biggest surprises is the visibility of Islam in practice. While an alien visitor to New York City might go for weeks before discovering that its citizens engage in religious activities at all, the religious impact on such a visitor to a city like Cairo or Damascus is almost instantaneous. He cannot escape the call to prayer reverberating over traffic noise, the minarets still competing for skyline with high-rises, the devout kneeling in prayer on bustling sidewalks, the name of God invoked repeatedly in ordinary conversation. Religion is life and all of life is religious. (In stressing this we sometimes go overboard in a tendency to see Muslims as categorically different from Westerners of Christian background. It is then asserted that no matter what effort is made, the differences are too great to achieve understanding. It is important to remember, then, that Muslims are human: they laugh at jokes, cry from pain, find candy sweet and children cute, love the gleam of gold, are tempted by the corruption of power and capable of benevolence to the needy. It is in the context of this shared humanity that differences in culture, religion and politics should be understood, respected and appreciated.)

In the light of this pervasiveness of religion in all aspects of life, the view that politics is inseparable from religion is automatic. The Meccan merchants opposed Mohammed's preaching because they perceived it as a threat to their political hegemony while the tribes of Medina invited him to arbitrate intertribal disputes. Given the revivalist nature of Mohammed's early preaching these responses would be somewhat similar to expecting Billy Graham to become a candidate for the presidency on the strength of his Crusades.

This equation of the political leader with the religious revivalist was by no means a new idea, rather it fit into a Middle Eastern tradition that was millennia old and had been shared by virtually all peoples of the region. For the ancient Egyptians "god" and "king" were one and the same. The ancient Babylonians saw their "king" as the human servant of the "god" who was the real ruler of the realm. The Hittite king was both the chief general on imperialistic military campaigns in summer and the chief priest on the snowed-in Anatolian plateau in winter. This basic pattern in the so-called naturalistic polytheisms of the Near East survived the Hellenization of the region after Alexander's conquests and was still the norm in the religion of Arabia at the time of Mohammed.

That this pattern was also typical of the Judaism and Christianity with which Mohammed was familiar is less clear to Western Christians who equate their own religion with the separation of Church and State. All are familiar, of course, with the theocratic concept underlying both the Mosaic and Davidic forms of Israelite government. The teaching of Jesus, however, appeared to set a different precedent for Christianity: Unlike Mohammed in Medina, Jesus refused to be drawn into the Roman-Jewish political quarrels; his denial of the sword to Peter stands in stark contrast to Mohammed's sanctioning of attacks on Meccan caravans. Much is often made of the fact that the Christian Church existed outside the formal structure of the Roman state for the three hundred years before Constantine, while the Muslim community was immediately political. Although these events gave the Christian Church much more potential for political quiescence, in actuality it did not turn out that way, especially in the East. After the emperors had converted to Christianity and made it the official and exclusive religion they became the real power above the bishops in the religio-political system of the Byzantine Empire known as caesaro-papism. Eastern Christians knew that religious heresy meant higher taxes as well as the Meccan merchants knew that following Mohammed would eat into their profits.

Hence, the concept of theocracy suggested itself to Mohammed as normal from all directions. That it became particularly intense in Islam may be due to the sense of the pervasiveness of the deity in pre-Islamic Arabian polytheism combined with a sense of the majesty of the deity in imperial Byzantine Christianity.

As the Islamic theocracy developed from the tribal confederacy ruled by Mohammed from Medina to the world empire ruled by the Abbasid monarchs from Baghdad the basic concepts of that theocracy were refined and defined in theory and practice to the point that a commonly understood and agreed upon religio-political body of doctrine came into existence. As a result the theocracy acquired its distinctly Islamic character. A brief explanation of these basic concepts is necessary to fathom the role of Islam in modern politics.

1. The Power of God

Whereas in Christianity the outstanding attribute of God that affects human destiny most deeply is His redeeming grace, in Islam it is His power. This power inheres not only in the initial act of creation but is manifest constantly in the application of His will in the natural and human realms.

The proper response of both man and nature to this power is *islam,* "submission." This submission is not simply a fatalistic bowing under a superior force, it is rather a fitting into the harmonious totality and unity of God's creation; it is entering into the only possible state of well-being.

This concept of God's rule over creation is applied specifically to His rule over human society in the state. God expresses His will directly and clearly to man in the organized structure of the body politic. In this respect the Islamic view of the state differs from the Christian in two significant ways:

First, it is more simple because the distinction between the spiritual and political realms (as set forth in Augustine's *City of God*) is practically non-existent. Within the realm of Islam the believer can be confident that the state is God's sphere of operation.

Second, it is more optimistic because as in all of creation the condition of harmony possible in the state through *islam* is not tainted by a concept of man's fallen nature. Even if seldom realized in practice, the well-being of the state is an attainable goal.

2. The Law of God

The assumption that God communicates His will directly to human society implies the existence of divine law revealed to man. That divine communication took place in history through a series of prophetic ministries culminating in that of Mohammed and the canonization of his messages in the Koran.

The Koran is particularly suitable as a source of divine law for two reasons. First, there is remarkable agreement throughout the Islamic world that it is the literal, divinely inspired word of God. There has been far less dispute on this point than there has been over the Bible in the Christian community. Second, the content of the Koran emphasizes practical directions for the life of the community. Especially as Mohammed became involved in the management of the affairs of Medina did his messages deal with the day to day problems that this community faced. It was therefore relatively easy to develop from the Koran a universally applicable set of rules that provided uniform standards of conduct acceptable throughout the Islamic world as the will of God.

As time passed and the setting shifted from the desert of Arabia to the urban centers of Damascus and Baghdad those situations not covered in the Koran could be informed by the numerous traditions — stories about and sayings attributed to the prophet by his companions — involving Mohammed. When these failed to shed light on a situation the principle of analogy was invoked to tie the new circumstance into the sphere of the divine revealed will.

The study of the Koran itself, the authentication of traditions and the application of the principle of analogy required considerable scholarly activity and debate in order to achieve assurance and agreement that the laws derived from these really did reflect God's will. The end product of this scholarly activity was the establishment of the several schools of law that divide both the Sunni and the Shi'ite communities into separate (though very similar) "rites."

The body of religious law is called the *"Shari'a,"* the "street" or way of Islam. Whereas the Christian world adopted the secular laws of pagan Rome as the basis for political system, in Islam the *Shari'a* became the law of the state. In the sense that the law represents the will of God, while the ruler is merely its administrator, the law stands above the state. In this sense it is perhaps more apropos to characterize Islamic politics as "nomocratic" rather than "theocratic."

3. The Community

It is obvious from the above that the criterion for membership in the political community is religious. The Islamic nation formed in the lifetime of Mohammed and expanded under his successors grew as converts were gained to the new faith. Of the various terms for "nation" used in the Koran without apparent preference the one that became predominant and is still used today is *umma*. In addition to the religious qualification for membership two outstanding qualities of the *umma* are unity and equality.

Because God is one, it was a foregone conclusion that the nation be one. Consequently, the new Islamic community cut across Arabian tribal lines and age old political and cultural barriers like those between Byzantium and Persia to form a single political entity. Any subsequent divisions of that political unit were artificial departures from the ideal.

Before the awesome power of God even differences between king and pauper become insignificant. In theory all were equal before Him. Politically, this means that all are subject to the law equally. This sense of equality provided political impetus for the leveling of status between Arab conqueror and the conquered converts. It also gave even the lowest subjects of the realm the solace that before God he and the most autocratic of Caliphs were equal. This quality gives Islam a built-in motive for the correction of social and political injustices.

In its geographic extent the nation is *Dar al-Islam*, "The House of Islam." This is the realm in which Islam has become politically predominant and/or the religion of the majority, the area in which through its citizens God is in charge. In this region it is possible to establish the government on the basis of the *Shari'a*. In the Middle Ages *Dar al-Islam* was synonymous with the extent of the Islamic conquest. Two aspects of geographic community are significant.

While "The House of Islam" was the realm of peace, the rest of the world was the realm of war, *Dar al-Harb*. Just as in contemporary Christian Europe it was not legitimate to wage war among fellow Christians, while crusades against heretics and Muslims were considered sanctioned by God, the Islamic community distinguished between just and unjust wars on religious grounds. Ironically, it was fair to be at war with Christian Byzantium and Europe while Christians within "The House of Islam" were not only tolerated but given legal status based on their own religious perspective as well. With respect to Christians, Jews and Zoroastrians it was sufficient for Islam to be in control in the House of Islam, and not necessary that Muslims be the exclusive residents.

4. Theocratic Institutions.

a. The Caliphate.

The role of the prophet as the political leader of the community was unique in the sense that he was so clearly singled out by God, but also in the sense that he was selected for a special, one time task. This special authority was extended in its administrative aspect (but not in its revelational aspect) to the office of caliph — the "successor" of the prophet of God. Because no provision for such an office was made by Mohammed, the community was forced to work out its nature after his death. Hence it developed gradually on the basis of tribal, Byzantine and Persian models of rulership. The actual form of the caliph's rule varied from that of the approachable leader who received his authority from the consensus and respect of his subjects to the distant potentate whose succession was hereditary and who was removed from the people by a bureaucratic barrier. Between the ninth and thirteenth centuries the office declined until finally it was reduced to a mere symbol while the real ruler became known as the *sultan* ("the one in charge"). Even so, the office survived as a symbol of Islamic political unity and the succession of authority from the prophet under the patronage of the Ottoman sultans until World War I.

The earliest religio-political rift in Islam was a dispute over the succession of the fifth caliph. One group felt that the caliph should be appointed from among the Meccan aristocracy, and opted for Mu'awiya, the founder of the Umayyad dynasty. Another group argued for hereditary succession, which would make one of the sons of 'Ali, the fourth caliph and son-in-law of Mohammed, the next caliph. The party *(shi'a)* of Ali lost, while Mu'awiya established the mainstream *(sunna)* line of caliphs. Thus the basic division between Shi'ism and Sunnism developed. The Shi'ites have refused to recognize the caliphs except 'Ali and see as legitimate only the blood line of 'Ali. These religio-political leaders (titled *Imam*) existed as political revolutionaries until the twelfth Imam disappeared (in occultation). While the return of the twelfth Imam is awaited the various Shi'ite communities are under the leadership of learned men who advise the communities on his behalf by means of their political-theological wisdom. Such are the Ayatollahs of Iran, for example.

b. The *'Ulemā* (Learned men)

As was observed earlier, a considerable amount of scholarly activity was necessary to develop the *Shari'a*. This activity, ranging from grammar, lexicography and textual criticism to law and theology, was the work of the *'Ulemā*, "scientist-theologians." The *'Ulemā* were to Islamic theology what medieval scholastics like Aquinas were to Roman Catholic theology. However, while the sphere of the scholastics was limited to university and church, the *'Ulemā* played a considerable role in the political life of the Islamic community. Three aspects of this role are worthy of mention.

First, the 'Ulemā were never a formally organized body. This means that they never function from their own political structure. There was no formal process of promotion by means of which one became an 'alīm (singular for 'ulemā); instead, one earned that stature by the consensus respect granted by the community for one's scholarly depth and skill. It was this informal authority, however, that enabled them to be real influences on the administrations of Caliphs, Sultans and Shahs.

It was as interpreters of the law especially that the 'Ulemā played a significant role. While the Caliph was merely the administrator of the law, the 'Ulemā were called on for proper interpretation, and as such acted as a check on the acquisition of random legal power by the caliphs. As such they were (informally) both the guardians of the theocracy against secularization and the protectors of the legal rights of the subjects against whimsical rulers. The 'Ulemā survived a major challenge from the traditional pre-Islamic Persian (and therefore secular) bureaucratic professionals who almost succeeded in isolating them from the Caliph's court at Baghdad.

Finally, in the late Middle Ages, to ward off the above challenge, as well as challenges from the Islamic philosophers and the European Crusaders, the 'Ulemā became traditionalist and conservative. To preserve the theological-legal tradition formal mosque schools were developed as a means of passing on the body of knowledge and preserving the status of the 'Ulemā. These institutions of learning have tended to survive into the twentieth century rather oblivious of or threatened by the new science brought by the West.

The above has been a brief and very simplified summary of traditional concepts of Islamic theocracy that are significant for understanding the role of Islam in current politics. Before moving on to the era of European control it is necessary to observe that theocracy did not always work out ideally in practice before this European phase. This is important because one may get the impression that the above ideals worked perfectly before 1750; this impression in turn may lead to the mistaken conclusion that all the ills suffered by Islam politically since 1750 are to be attributed to Europe and the West.

Already inherent in what was said above is the fact of the continual accomodation of the ruling institution to the actual situation, so that Arabic, Byzantine, Persian and Turkish phases can be distinguished. This is perhaps a strength in the sense that it enabled Islam to survive and absorb numerous political challenges. It, however, also results from the failure of Islam to develop a uniquely defined ruling institution. This weakness has been particularly crucial in face of the Western political challenge.

Also inherent in the above is the almost immediate failure of the ideal of unity. Although the rift remained informal until much later, if the Shi'ite civil war is taken as the indicator, real unity lasted less than a half century. By the nineteenth century the Islamic world had become so splintered by inner dissension as well as external attacks that politically irreparable diversity was normal.

Lastly, the institutions of Caliphate and 'Ulemā tended toward rigidity and formality in the late Middle Ages. Perhaps it is the product of public discouragement with the human frailty displayed in these theocratic institutions that the Sufi mystical orders flourished: In the face of the failure of the formal political structure to provide a meaningful experience of God in the life of the citizens, Sufi mysticism offered an alternate way that was direct, experiential and emotionally satisfying. After mysticism gained theological respectability, it became possible to be Muslim with minimal political involvement. Even though mysticism has played a major role in the survival of Islam from major non-Islamic challenges such as the Mongol invasions, the Islam that survived on the eve of the European influx was politically much more quietist than Islam had been a millennium earlier.

II. The European Challenge, 1750-1950.

In the two centuries from 1750-1950 almost the entire Islamic world from Indonesia to Morocco experienced European political control, "imperialism," of one form or another. Although in only few instances did this mean the total loss of independence, and in one case it even meant liberation from Muslim overlords (the Arabs in World War I), in each case it meant dependence on a European power. This dependence on the various European nations was a tremendous challenge to the traditional theocratic concepts of Islamic politics. For the first time almost the entire Islamic world was under the control of non-Islamic political powers which represented the very Christian West with which Medieval Islam had been in successful confrontation on the frontiers of Spain and in the Crusades. This non-Muslim force did not break down and disintegrate as the Mongols had, but rather it settled in and sought to change existing structures. It introduced secular political principles of liberalism and nationalism with an attitude of superiority that assumed that the European knew all while the "native" was without political understanding.

The result in much of the Islamic world was a sense of shocked inferiority and loss of confidence in the theocratic tradition: Is God really in charge? Is He without authority even in the heart of *Dar al-Islam?* The result was a floundering inability to cope with the reality of the political present and a growing resentment (often coupled with admiration for Western power and success) that made *independence* from the West the overriding political passion in the first half of the Twentieth Century.

III. Islamic Resurgence, 1950-1980.

As happens in so many revolutionary movements, when independence finally came, as it did in much of the Islamic world in the 1950's and 1960's, political leaders had been so busy with the struggle that theorizing had taken a second seat. Many of the newly independent states were left with Islam still the popular religion, while the political structure was mostly based on European non-Islamic models. What we have seen in the past thirty years is a slow process of political modernization in which to an increasing degree traditional principles of Islamic politics are being integrated with the political structures installed by and copied from the European nations in the previous century. Although the outcome of this process is still very unclear and many faceted, the following factors should help give some explanation of the political changes that have taken place in the past several decades:

A. *Renewed Confidence.*

After more than a century of domination by European powers there is a growing feeling among the Islamic peoples that their states can not only go it alone, but stand up to the West as well. Some of the key events in this return of confidence are worth mentioning. Nasser's neutralism of the fifties (mistaken for pro-communism by Western policymakers) announced to the world that it was possible for a non-Western nation to escape the side-choosing pressures imposed by U.S.-U.S.S.R. Cold War politics. The successful Algerian revolution showed that even the most intensely colonized could overthrow their European masters, given enough fervor, self-sacrifice and national pride. Even the limited successes in the initial battles of the October War (1973) were enough to erase the shame of repeated military humiliations suffered by Israel's neighbors. Coupled with this the spectacular success of the oil embargo (coincident with OPEC price hikes) brought sudden economic and political power especially to Islamic nations like Saudi Arabia and Iran. That this renewed confidence is tinged with the bitter memory of the imperialist exploitation of the past was illustrated by the enthusiastic reception of Yasir Arafat of the PLO at the U.N. General Assembly meeting in 1974 and is, of course, also a strong factor in Iran's anti-American behavior today.

B. *The Islamic Alternative.*

When the traditional Middle Eastern dynasties (the Ottomans of Turkey and the Arab World and the Qajars of Iran) were disbanded at the beginning of this century, the newly formed nations had little choice but to accept secular governments on the European model installed under European supervisions. With few exceptions (Saudi-Arabia) this meant the adoption of democratic constitutions most often in the form of constitutional monarchies (Egypt, Jordan, Iraq, Iran). These new democratic forms had little chance of success for a variety of reasons. In almost every instance they became associated with the continued European control, so that the final expulsion of the Europeans was often accompanied with political revolution as well (Egypt and Iraq in the fifties). In addition the fledgling monarchs tended to see the elected branches of their governments as competitors for political power; the result was frequent conflict rather than cooperation, and usually the elected branches became less than effective in the process (this was especially true in Iran under the Pahlavis). Finally in almost every instance the majority of the population was left out of the democratic process due to lack of education and the survival of traditional socio-economic gradations. The political parties of the 1930's were usually controlled by a relatively small number of wealthy landowning "party bosses."

It is not surprising that when real independence came after World War II that in many instances (Egypt, Syria, Iraq) these old constitutions were abandoned as corrupt, unfair and ineffective (exceptions were Lebanon, which until its tragic civil war was often touted as the only successful democracy in the Arab World, and Iran and Jordan, where practically all power had become concentrated in the hands of army backed monarchs). Again the models adopted by revolutionary leaders were secular and turned out to be one party systems that emphasized the nationalization of resources and industry under the label "socialism." Because of the survival of traditional social structures and ethno-religious groupings as bases for the distribution of real political power the term "socialism" is a mistake if it is understood in its European sense.

It is these so-called "left wing" regimes that have often been associated with communism, especially because these regimes have not been afraid to accept soviet military and economic assistance. However, to date, largely because of the continued strength of the Islamic religion, communism has not been a viable alternative in the Islamic world. Although there is currently some theoretical investigation into the possible compatibility of Marxism and Islam, communism has traditionally been seen as an atheist and therefore alien political system. Even at the height of Soviet presence in Egypt and Iraq the communist party has remained outlawed in those countries.

In the atmosphere of religious revival and in keeping with the renewed confidence in political self-identity, the theocratic Islamic political model has become an attractive alternative to secular forms of government. In particular it suggests itself as a viable option to the choice between democracy and communism that the duality of Free World-Soviet politics has tended to force on the rest of the world.

To many serious Muslims the life of Islam is not complete unless it is manifest in an Islamic community in the political sense as it was in the Middle Ages. It was such sentiment that underlay the Indian-Pakistani split and the foundation of the Islamic theocratic state of Pakistan. For many other Muslims Pakistan has been the symbol of the political-theocratic renewal of Islam.

What perhaps explains the new emphasis on Islam is that in some Arab countries and in Iran there is growing popular involvement and awareness. Whereas in the politics of the 1920's and 1930's entire rural populations could remain nearly ignorant of national party activities, the behavior of political leaders and the formation of national policies, today vastly improved communication, transportation, public education and economic improvement has informed and involved populations of even the most remote villages. This has brought into the political field a' majority of traditional religious convictions that can outvote and outdemonstrate the more secular educated and urban citizenry. It is not surprising that this new group on the political scene is exhibiting a measure of fundamentalist resentment against those who appear to have abandoned Islam while having hoarded the national produce at the same time.

It is with these developments in mind that the current formation of the Islamic republic of Iran may be seen as a phase in a trend toward theocracy.

C. The Reality of the Nation-State.

All attempts at a return to Islamic theocracy have had to accomodate themselves to the existence of the modern nations. The various national divisions themselves represent secular and non-religious concepts; such as, geography, language, self-determination and popular soverignty. These are in fact in conflict with the Islamic notion of political community strictly in terms of united religious allegiance to God.

The possibility that the trend toward theocracy will lead to a pan-Islamic political unity does not exist today. This concept was discussed in the 19th century when the traditional Islamic empires were still nominally intact, but even then the idea had little appeal. Today, after several decades of separate independence, individual patriotism and national identity have become as strong as among the variety of European nations.

There is, of course, potential for greater cooperation among Islamic nations on the basis of shared Islamic political ideals, as, for example, in the meetings of the Islamic Congress and voting as a block in the United Nations. Even on this level, however, there is still too much diversity of practice and opinion on the role of Islam to make cooperation very effective. The possibility of real cooperation between Iran and Saudi Arabia, for example, is hampered not only by very different foreign and economic policies, but also by religious differences, such as the Shi'ite-Sunni split and the exclusiveness of Wahhabism.

Islam, therefore, may have to accomodate itself to political systems within the boundaries of existing nation-states. With the exception of Turkey and Lebanon, which have secular constitutions, most countries in which Muslims predominate include some reference to Islam in their constitution. Pakistan, one of the most theocratic, blends a confession of belief in the sovereignty of God over the entire universe with the democratic concept of the will of the people. Others, like Jordan's state simply that Islam is the religion of the state and that the law is based on the *Shari'a* if Muslims are involved. The extent to which these theocratic elements will be observed, even in a so-called secular nation like Turkey will depend on the strength and sincerity of the popular Islamic religious revival and the ability of political leaders to cope with that.

Conclusion

This has been an imperfect and superficial attempt to give meaning to the religious dimension of national politics in the Islamic world today. The essayist does not intend to say that the so-called Islamic Resurgence will last (a prophet he is not), or that it is even properly Islamic at all (that depends on the variation of Islam to which one adheres), but he does intend to say that Islam is a political factor to be reckoned with in some parts of the Islamic world.

The survey has dwelled on the Middle Ages because it is assumed that is what the reader is least familiar with; it has drawn most of its information from the region of the Middle East because that is what the author is most familiar with. It should be stressed that the political situation is really quite different for Muslims who live in situations of religious minority, as those in the Soviet Union, China and India and (in much smaller numbers) the United States. For them the practice of religion has become largely a private matter, a situation far removed from the theocratic character of Islam in the Middle Ages.

Selected Bibliography

Abu-Lughod, Ibrahim, "Retreat from the Secular Path? Islamic Dilemmas of Arab Politics." *The Review of Politics* (1966): 447-476.

Akhavi, Shahrough, *Religion and Politics in Contemporary Iran.* Albany: State University of New York Press, 1980.

Arberry, A. J., trans. *The Koran Interpreted.* Toronto: The Macmillan Company, 1969.

Aruri, Naseer H., "Nationalism and Religion in the Arab World: Allies or Enemies." *The Muslim World* (Oct. 1977): 266-279.

Binder, Leonard, *Iran: Political Development in a Changing Society.* Berkeley and Los Angeles: University of California Press, 1962.

Cragg, Kenneth, *The House of Islam.* 2nd ed. Encino and Belmont, California: Dickenson Publishing Company, Inc., 1975.

Gibb, H. A. R., *Mohammedanism.* 2nd ed. New York: Oxford University Press, 1962.

Hourani, Albert, *Arabic Thought in the Liberal Age.* New York: Oxford University Press, 1970.

Lewis, Bernard, "The Return of Islam." *Commentary* (Jan. 1976): 39-49.

Nasr, Seyyed Hossein, *Ideals and Realities of Islam.* London: George Allen & Unwin Ltd., 1966.

Rahman, Fazlur, *Islam.* London: Weidenfeld and Nicolson, 1966.

Sharabi, Hisham, "The Transformation of Ideology in the Arab World." *The Middle East Journal* (Fall, 1965): 471-486.

Smith, Wilfred C., *Islam in Modern History.* Princeton: Princeton University Press, 1957.

Von Grunebaum, G. E., *Modern Islam: The Search for Cultural Identity.* Berkeley and Los Angeles: University of California Press, 1962.

_____, ed. *Unity and Variety in Muslim Civilization.* Chicago: The University of Chicago Press, 1955.

Watt, W. Montgomery, *Islamic Political Thought: The Basic Concepts.* Islamic Surveys, no. 6. Edinburgh: Edinburgh University Press, 1968.

VI

THE ISLAMIC WORLD AND THE WEST TODAY

C. Ernest Dawn

The confrontation between the United States and Iran on the hostage issue in a way typifies the tense relationship between the West and much of the Islamic world. Professor Dawn describes here the involvement of the Euro-American West in the Islamic countries of the Near East in this century, particularly since World War I which is the root cause of this tension. He also describes how the political forces at work in the Islamic world, while lacking unity of ideology, purpose or program, are nevertheless using their anti-imperialism (directed chiefly against the West) and their common Islamic heritage as rallying points.

Ernest Dawn, veteran specialist in modern Arab history, has been an inspiration for generations of younger scholars in Middle Eastern culture and history. The author of **From Ottomanism to Nationalism: Essays on the Origins of Arab Nationalism** *and many articles on Arab history, he is currently professor of history at University of Illinois, Urbana-Champaign.*

Since the Iranian revolution in early 1979, Islam or the Islamic world has been presented in the world news media as a vigorous entity or force. This intensified attention to the Islamic world coincides with the culmination of a counter-movement composed of scholars who have been vigorously denying that Islam is an entity or that it is meaningful to speak of "the Islamic world." There is a large area of territory extending continuously across Asia and Africa which is inhabited by a predominately Muslim population. Surely, there can be no objection to calling this territorial region the Islamic world. But problems immediately arise. Those Euro-Americans who have concerned themselves with the lands inhabited by Muslims have throughout history thought of Islam as an entity in contradistinction to another entity, the West, which is the Euro-American world. For over a century now, Euro-Americans generally have believed Islam to be radically different from the West or from other religions, notably Christianity. Most frequently, Euro-Americans have believed that "modernity" is the product of the "West" and that the Islamic world cannot be truly modern until Islam is radically reformed. Some have even gone so far as to say that Islam cannot reform. Another strand in the Euro-American view is that Islam intrinsically commands and receives a stronger allegiance from its adherents than does Christianity and other religions and that Islam, unlike Christianity, is necessarily insistent on worldly success, on earthly power and glory, for the believers. None of these opinions are self-evidently true, nor can it be said that scholarship has resulted in unanimity with respect to the ontological status of either Islam or the West. But Muslims do share common beliefs which distinguish them from non-Muslims, and during the past hundred years or so the inhabitants of the Islamic world have reacted in similar fashion to the Euro-American world.

Muslim jurists and theologians have unanimously agreed that God is one, that Mohammed is the seal of God's prophets, that the law is divine revelation, and that the state exists only to execute God's law, the *sharī'ah*. They further agree that the community of believers is one and that ideally a single state should govern the entire community of the faithful. The ideal of the universal state, however, has never been realized. The majority of Muslims, the Sunnites, came to adopt the view that kingship is based entirely on acquisition. They accept the division of the community among numerous temporal sovereignties and they accord legitimacy to any ruler who enforces the *sharī'ah*. A substantial minority, the Shi'ites, came to regard all historical states as illegitimate. To the Shi'ites, temporal sovereignty belongs only to the divinely appointed ruler. To the most important of the Shi'ites, the Twelvers, the ruler, the Hidden Imam, is absent, to return in the fullness of time. Meanwhile, the community must obey the *sharī'ah*.

In both Sunnite and Shi'ite doctrine it is the *sharī'ah* which governs the life of the faithful and which provides the focal point for the allegiance and unity of the community of the faithful. The *sharī'ah* reached perfect form in essentials in the golden age of the Prophet and the blessed ancestors or of the Prophet and the visible imams. Moreover, Sunnite and Shi'ite doctrine have been at one in the belief that the *sharī'ah*, God's law, is in the sole custody of the learned men, the *ulamā*. This doctrine ultimately was accepted by the historical

Muslim states, Sunnite and Shi'ite. Thus, the state did not legislate. Instead, the state enforced the *sharī'ah* which the authoritative scholars expounded. In both Sunnite and Shi'ite states the *ulamā* constituted a body with a high degree of autonomy. The state appointed scholars to judgeships and other offices with religious functions, but eminence in scholarship to a great degree was dependent on the consensus of the *ulamā* and of the people, not on the monarch or his officials. The *ulamā* thus provided the judges, the religious functionaries, and the teachers for both the subjects and the rulers. In Sunnite lands, such as the Ottoman territories, there was little tension between state and *ulamā*. In Twelver Shi'ite Persia, on the contrary, the *ulamā* never wholeheartedly accepted the state.

Despite the Muslim attachment to the ideal of a universal Islamic state, Muslims have accepted the political division of the community and rule by monarchs whose claim is essentially no more than the right of conquest and possession. But such states may be accepted only if they apply the *sharī'ah* as preserved by the *ulamā*. The unity of the community and its territories thus is maintained by the *sharī'ah*, not the rule of a universal monarch. Muslim rulers, to be legitimate, must also defend their people and territory against non-Muslim encroachment, at the least, and should expand the domain of Islam at the expense of the infidels.

Until the end of the sixteenth century the Muslim rulers in the Near East met their obligations with glorious victories. The faithful had no reason to fear or to respect their most dangerous and prominent neighbors, the Christian Europeans. But in the latter part of the sixteenth century Christian Russia conquered the Muslims of the Volga. One century later, the tide began to run strongly against the abode of Islam. The Ottomans lost Hungary to Austria. By the end of the eighteenth century something clearly was wrong. Moghul India had passed under British rule. Russia had inflicted humiliating defeats on Ottoman armies and had annexed the Muslim Crimea. The nineteenth century was a disaster. Rebellious Christians in the Balkans gained successively autonomy and independence as a result of Russian victories and European pressures on the Ottomans. European commissions investigated Ottoman treatment of Christian subjects and suggested or imposed special administrative arrangements. Russia conquered the Transcaucasian area and central Asia. France occupied Algeria, Tunisia, and Morocco; Britain Cyprus and Egypt; Italy Libya. Nevertheless, both the Ottoman Empire and Persia throughout the nineteenth century remained independent sovereign states in full possession of most of their territories which were inhabited by Muslim majorities. But by this time the threat of the Christian West in Muslim eyes was at least as much internal as it was external.

By the end of the eighteenth century, the Islamic governments had come to believe that the infidel Franks and Russians must be resisted with their own weapons. Sultans and viziers began to recast the military and then the administration along European lines. The Europeanizing impulse strengthened as the century progressed. European, and later American, military advisors and a variety of experts were brought in to investigate, write reports, train, and reform. State schools were established to educate the necessary personnel for the military and the bureaucracy. Student missions went to Europe for training. All this required knowledge of a European language, usually French. Before long, the bureaucrats and soldiers had greater acquaintance with European learning than with the higher Islamic culture that their ancestors had imbibed in the educational institutions of the *ulamā*. They also began to dress in European style, to adopt European manners and tastes. By midcentury, some bureaucrats and ex-bureaucrats had begun to imitate European literature, to write novels and plays in the Frankish fashion which dealt with some of the social themes that concerned the Europeans.

The West also intruded increasingly as the world economy developed. European manufactures, when cheaper than the native products, were imported, sometimes displacing in part or entirely local manufactures. European markets for primary products, and occasionally manufactures, stimulated local production. The number of foreign merchants, who had special legal status under the capitulations, increased. There was need for port facilities, roads, railroads, and telegraph systems. Europeans came in to provide the technical expertise. To attract foreign capital, the rulers granted concessions and contracted foreign loans. Public debt to foreigners led to foreign fiscal authorities, officials or commissions of the public debt, both in Egypt and the Ottoman Empire, the former in Persia.

Europeanized officers and officials and foreigners in positions of privilege and authority were perhaps less troublesome to Muslim sensibilities than the stress that Europe's new position in the world placed on fundamental Islamic concepts. Christian and liberal Europe insisted that Islam's treatment of non-Muslims, native as well as foreign, was a species of antiquated barbarism. Under pressure, the Ottoman government and its Egyptian dependency formally proclaimed the legal equality of Muslim and non-Muslim, adopted European penal and commercial codes, and created new courts to be staffed by personnel trained in European law, not the *sharī'ah*. Persian rulers did not go so far, but they did attempt to bring the courts under royal control and to meet European objections to Islamic law and judicial procedure.

The culture and ways of the West became visible in the Islamic world in the persons of the foreign businessmen and officials, much more importantly in the native soldiers, officials, businessmen, and intellectuals. The masses of the towns and countryside, however, were hardly touched. More importantly, the *ulamā* remained to a great degree free from the new cultural influences, for the religious schools and the mosques remained under the *ulamā*, relatively free of state control. This cultural dualism separating the ruling and religious institutions from each other did not, as a general rule, lead to sharp political antagonism between the two main divisions of the Islamic state structure. Despite some resentment of Frankified ways, the *ulamā* rarely formed a group adamantly opposed to a government or its policies. After all, they had been left in control of the religious educational system and of worship. Moreover, the most important part of the *sharī'ah* which historically was enforced by the state, family law, continued to be applied in courts staffed by *ulamā*. In politics, the *ulamā* behaved, as they had before, more or less in the same fashion as the Westernized soldiers and officials.

The *ulamā* were very much members of the political classes of the Islamic states. Along with the soldiers and officials, they staffed the state, directed its policies, and enjoyed the material benefits at the disposal of the state. As in all political societies, competition for office was the rule, and the political classes arrayed themselves into two groups, the government and the opposition. In the words of a fourteenth century Arab poet, which were thought to be apposite by an Arab Ottoman statesman of the early twentieth century, "Half the people are enemies of the one who has charge of the government. This, if he is just."[1] Members of the *ulamā* were rivals with each other for position in the religious institution, just as the soldiers and officials were rivals with each other in their sphere. Political groups were formed across the line separating the soldiers and officials from the *ulamā*. Every political grouping had members from both sections who had rivals in their own arenas. Thus in the Ottoman Empire and in Egypt, there was never any clear political confrontation between the state and the *ulamā*. Instead, the *ulamā* were to be found in every political party and no government ever lacked its own following among the *ulamā*. In Twelver Shi'ite Persia, where religious belief was less accepting of the state, the *ulamā* came closer to forming a body which was antagonistic to the state, but the general tendency was the same as elsewhere in the Near East. Twice, in 1891-1892 and in 1905-1906, the Persian *ulamā* almost united in opposition to the monarchy, but in both cases they had allies from among the secular magnates, and in both cases the clerical unity soon dissolved as members of the *ulamā* returned to their old political habits. By this time, moreover, many persons whose ancestors had been prominent *ulamā* had changed their career lines. They acquired the new Western learning and embarked on careers as officials or men of letters.

Just as there was no political contradiction between the ruling and the religious institutions, there was no ideological dichotomy by the end of the nineteenth century. The soldiers and officials were just as vocal in their loyalty as the *ulamā* and, despite their adoption of some Frankish ways, just as vehement in their rejection of the infidel West. If we can judge their inner feelings from the pamphlets and books and the newspaper and magazine articles which they published, and from the speeches which they made, they were filled with resentment of the West and regarded it as the enemy which must be repulsed at all costs.

The Westernizing reformers sought to strengthen the Islamic states' defenses against the Western threat. This was the aim of even the legal reforms, the proclaimed guarantees of security and equality for all, Muslim and non-Muslim, the new law codes and the state courts. To some slight degree, perhaps, the legal reforms were concessions to Christian Europe's pressures, designed to gain diplomatic support, but it is certain that the reformists genuinely believed that freedom, equality, and security were the sources of Western patriotism and thus of Western greatness, power, and glory.

Implicitly, and before long explicitly, the reformists, at least the intellectuals, found their culture and themselves to be wanting in comparison to the Christian West, which they perceived as having left Islam and the East far behind. This injury to the reformists' self-view created an urgent need to catch up with the West, even to surpass it and to restore Islam to its rightful position in the world. The reformists were possessed of a burning drive to become the full equal, at least, of the alien West, not merely to ward it off and preserve the independence and integrity of the Islamic East.

The Islamic reformists have suffered the common experience of human individuals and groups, communities and societies, who have perceived the self as lacking, deprived, or inadequate in comparison to another. As is the universal case, the Islamic reformists have sought deliverance from the unbearable pain of the shameful present condition. The pain may be lessened by looking to the future. Hope for the future is instilled by, perhaps it requires, confidence in oneself. The earliest reformists had such confidence in themselves, their culture, and their religion. They looked forward to surpassing the West once the requisites of modernity had been borrowed. But they also felt the need to reassure themselves of their own adequacy and vitality. So they asserted that the Islamic *sharī'ah* was the perfect way of life in spiritual, i.e., cultural matters, that the Islamic East was spiritually superior to the West, which was ahead only in material things.

Soon, however, the reformists' confidence in their present state was shaken, as the perceived gap widened instead of closing. Many devoted themselves to frenzied affirmations that the materialism of the West did not and could not bring the human happiness that Islam did. To a greater number this approach was unsatisfactory. To these people, the painful present could not be accepted as adequate and needing only a few materialistic reforms, and consequently the present culture could not instill confidence and hope for the future. As so many others in all parts of the earth have done, they turned to the past for self-assurance and hope. Fortunately, the Islamic East did have a glorious past, as even some of the Franks acknowledged. It could be, and was, asserted that the Islamic East was the source of the Christian West's progress. The explanation of Islam's past glory and of the West's modernity was found to be God's gift to the faithful of the first and only rational religion, Islam. The explanation for the Islamic world's present backwardness was the deviation of the Muslims from the true Islam of the ancestors. Thus the past provided assurance of the adequacy of Islam and the means of deliverance from the unbearable present. Return to true Islam was the medicine which would cure the disease.

Those who have found self-assurance in the rationality of true Islam and hope in the prospect of returning to it have not been able to agree on the exact nature of the true Islam of the ancestors. To some it has meant consultative monarchy, rational administration, due process of law; others have added intellectual freedom. Others still have insisted on parliamentary government. And some have insisted on full equality for women. Ultimately, true Islam came to be viewed as the original and pure socialism. But whatever difference there has been over details, there has been unanimous insistence on the need to realize true Islam in this world, on the denial of Western superiority, on restoring Islam to its rightful position in the world, equality with or superiority to the only dangerous neighbor, the Christian West.

Those who have been most agitated about the West have not been aiming at the West alone. In the Islamic world, as elsewhere, those who compete for position and rewards, material and immaterial, are also serving the higher cause of community and society. The continuing debate over the nature of and the remedy for the Islamic predicament has been a part of the internal competition for office and position. The most telling point that a competitor can make is that the rivals have failed or are unable to defend Islam and the East against the alien West. Pressures from the West have always weakened a government and provided opportunity for the opposition. Lacking overt pressure, any economic crisis or internal disturbance, or, in the absence of either, the general malaise, can be attributed to the West and their puppets in the state and society. Charges that the internal competitor is the instrument of the external enemy, in short a traitor, are not necessarily a mere political tactic. In fact, those who make the charges give every appearance of being sincerely convinced of their truth. They seem to be possessed by the belief that they alone are totally committed to the defense of their community and state, that they alone are willing to die to expel the foreign enemy.

Competition for offices and ideological debate are the essential elements in the political process in all polities, not just those of the Islamic Near East. Western observers, however, have generally believed that Near Eastern and Western politics are radically different. Those who hold these views usually have ignored the upheavals which have occurred in the West. Yet, it may be that Near Eastern politics have been characterized by more frequent outbursts of violence and sudden changes of regime than Western politics have been.

It is possible, but far from certain, that economic conditions in the Near East make the political contest much more intense than in the West. It is doubtful that material rewards have been distributed much more inequitably in the Near East than in any other region, but it is certain that in the last century or two the Near East has had far fewer material goods than the Euro-American world to distribute among the populace. In the distribution of what there is, the state has been the chief allocator. It has settled the ownership of property, it has provided employment and incomes for the great majority of those with a higher education and for many ordinary laborers, it has provided opportunity and assistance to men of business. For those who seek improvement, politics is not the most important thing; it's the only thing.

In Near Eastern social, economic, and political activities, direct personal contacts, rivalries and alliances, are far more important than they are in the Western world in the twentieth century. The social horizon of the masses is the family and the neighborhood. Family and neighborhood are still important to the life of the more advantaged. In general, employment, finding and obtaining a means of livelihood, depends on personal ties. Maintenance or improvement of one's position requires establishing a symbiosis with another who has more. The resultant symbiotic group then establishes a similar relationship to other groups. The symbiotic ties are always personal. Thus villagers, townsmen, and nomads form themselves into factions or clans, and different groups relate to other groups through ties among their leaders. Even when one leaves his place of origin, to find a job and settle anew, the ties go with him. The established ties facilitate the move and resettlement. The move and resettlement establishes additional ties.

The Near Eastern state reflects its society. Officials and civil servants, including teachers in the state schools, are recruited and assigned on the basis of personal ties. Many come from families of established leading position, either locally or in the state structure. Many originate in less privileged circumstances, but they possess advantages above the average. Virtually all, however, are recruited as a result of membership in a network of personal connections which extends from the locality to the upper echelons of the state structure. In the state structure they make new connections, enter new networks. Assignment, promotion, and discipline are in the sole control of the higher central authority. The chief of state, whether king, president, or head of the revolutionary command council, legally the final authority, decides all major personnel questions, but he must direct the system as a whole through his assistants in the upper echelons. Each of these has his own network of connections throughout the system whose members at lower levels and in the provinces can and do approach him. The various networks are competitive. Frequently, government action is blocked, in both the central bureaucracy and the provinces, as rival connections collide. The connections and networks are fragile. Members can defect and realign with others suddenly, with or without warning. Thus it is not possible for the legal supreme authority to be sure of the reliability of the bureaucracy or the armed forces.

Tensions within the state structure, which reflect the tensions within the leadership of the society, need resolution. Frequently resolution is accomplished by a reshuffle of the personnel of the supreme authority, the bureaucracy, or the armed forces. Sometimes a military coup takes place. Sometimes the disaffected utilize their followings in society at large by organizing popular demonstration or uprising. If the unity of the government and the reliability of the armed forces are maintained, popular action can be handled. But if the state structure is stalemated by internal conflict, popular action can effect a change of government, even the supplantation of a regime.

The degree to which popular attitudes and actions with respect to a government are conditioned by perceptions independent of personal ties, even contrary to personal ties, cannot be determined. It is almost certain that no popular demonstration or uprising in the Near East has occurred which has not had ties with members of the highest and most advantaged members of the society. Yet personal networks are fragile and unstable. In all societies conflict among close friends or associates, even among kinsmen, takes place. Perhaps such instability is more intense in societies like the Near Eastern where material rewards per capita are substantially less than in the Euro-American world. Those who perceive themselves as deprived or who have unrealized expectations perhaps have only a weak loyalty to their patrons. Defection from one's acknowledged leader and patron should be more common when deprivation occurs or expectations are not met. Defection is likely to appear much more justified when one's troubles are perceived to be the result of the leader's capitulation to the foreigner.

Political leaders in the Islamic Near East, government and opposition alike, have been unanimous in setting the goal of government as independence from the West. They may have been aiming too high in their insistence that the Islamic East must overtake or surpass the West. Human history has not yet produced agreement on the causes of human inequality, within or among human groups, but surely important among the conditions which have determined the position of the Islamic world relative to the Euro-American world is the latter's possession of superior natural resources. Whatever the case may be, thus far no government in the Near East has been able to satisfy all members of its polity that independence of and equality with the West has been achieved.

The Near East in fact did not fare too poorly in the nineteenth century. The Ottoman Empire lost its European provinces, whose populations were religiously and linguistically different from the rest of the Empire. Egypt and north Africa came under European control, and southern Arabia felt the presence of the British, but the Ottomans had never really ruled in these areas. Russian troops occupied parts of Persia after 1909. Despite these real encroachments of European imperialism, both the Ottoman Empire and Persia in 1914 were independent states which retained legal sovereignity over large territories which were free of foreign troops.

The relative freedom of the Near East from imperialism in its pure form did not convince its inhabitants that they were not the victims of Western imperialism. Instead, they changed the definition of imperialism. In doing so they were assisted, as they had been before, by ideas which had become popular in the West. The notion that foreign economic activities were to the sole profit of the foreigners and a mere handful of local puppets had become commonplace by the end of the nineteenth century, as had the belief that the Islamic world's economic backwardness was the result of foreign economic control. By 1914, full Marxist interpretations were current in Turkish in the Ottoman Empire, among the Turks of Russia, and most likely similar theories were circulating among Iranians. In the aftermath of World War I these Marxist ideas came to seem peculiarly applicable to many Muslims.

At the end of World War I Western troops occupied the Ottoman territories and Persia. Imperial Russia had been supplanted by Bolshevik Russia which proclaimed war on imperialism in the world at large. Russian Muslims adapted Bolshevik theory to their own ends. The notion of a revolution of the proletariat against imperialism instilled hope and enthusiasm for the struggle. But as the Muslims saw it, the true proletariat in the struggle against imperialism were the Islamic nations, and the Russian Bolsheviks, like the anti-Bolshevik Russians, were a part of the enemy. The Russian Muslims called for and looked forward to the proletarian nations of the world rising against Western imperialism, and restoring Islamic unity. The Russian Muslims did not succeed, and the exponents of these ideas were ultimately liquidated. But the call was heard among non-Russian Muslims, at least in Turkey. In all parts of the Near East, most of the politically active believed that they were engaged in a life-and-death struggle with Western imperialism.

In Turkey and Iran the crisis resulted in new governments supplanting the old. Both governments succeeded in expelling the foreign imperialists. Almost certainly their success in this endeavor contributed greatly to the hold that the two leaders, Kemal Ataturk and Reza Shah Pahlavi, had on their governments. Both interpreted their mandates as being to eliminate foreign influence and to develop a fully independent national life, economically and culturally as well as politically. The world political situation favored them until World War II, for the great powers paid them little attention. Success against the foreigner undoubtedly contributed to the two leaders' popularity, which appears to have been great. Nevertheless, both used repression, which was rather great in the case of Reza Shah.

Both Ataturk and Reza attempted national reconstructions which lessened the importance of Islam. Each sought to modernize by adopting the elements of modernity from the center of modernity, the West. But they insisted, and their economic and educational policies embodied their insistence, that this was a purely national development, not just imitating the foreigner. As Islamic sentiment was a source of opposition to Westernization, they sought to create new nationalisms. The Kemalists officially disestablished Islam and based their regime on a purely secular Turkish nationalism. They did not, however, as events were later to demonstrate, eliminate Islam among the masses or the classes. Reza also adopted an Iranian nationalism. Under this cover he reduced the importance of the *ulamā*, notably by excluding them from the judiciary, but he did not eliminate Islam from Iranianism. By implication, the Iranian nation was more important than Islam as the basis of social, political, and cultural life, but the explicit transition to a Kemalist secularism was never made.

The Arab countries did not fare so well as did Iran and Turkey. The events of the war had destroyed Ottomanism everywhere, and political activists now were the representatives and soldiers of Arab nationalism, or of Egyptian or some other local patriotism. But the imperialists were not defeated. The Europeans kept their positions in northern Africa, Egypt, and Arabia, and Britain and France took over Iraq, Syria and Lebanon, and Palestine as mandates. Arab popular demonstrations and insurrections could not drive the imperialists out, but Arab resistance denied Britain and France the cooperation of an effective portion of the Arab leadership and forced the British and French to resort to military and administrative measures which were harmful to their budgets and their reputations.

Among the Arabs, the slogan was Arab freedom and unity. Even

Pharaonic nationalist Egypt ultimately responded; there were echos in Lebanon where the most popular notion was a confederation of religious confessions. Rarely were independent governments in power, and political energy was absorbed in the struggle for liberation. But the question of Islam was not neglected. The ideologist most favored by the nationalist leadership was an advocate of a secular Arab nationalism. Yet it is clear that the original Arabism in which Islam was inseparable from the Arab nation survived in full vigor. No attempt was made to displace religious family law. Most importantly, secularist intellectuals, even in Egypt, received a poor hearing and bad treatment from the *ulamā* and the political leaders. By 1939, both Christian and Muslim Arabs were expounding theories of Arab nationalism which gave an important place to Islam.

By the end of World War II, all Arab countries from Libya to Iraq were independent except for Palestine. But the British remained in Palestine and in Iraq and Egypt under treaties. The British, with the approval of the Americans, wished to extend the treaty system. Many Arab statesmen favored the idea. But Arab politics and the Arab attitude to the West had not changed. Foreign treaties were attacked as imperialism. The Arabs, the political slogans said, should unite, liberate the Arab lands still under foreign control, and go forward on their own. The governments of Egypt and Iraq, unable to rid themselves of the British treaties, were shaken. When the British left Palestine and the Arabs lost the war with Israel, the dam broke. A succession of military coups occurred, and the old generation of nationalist leaders was eliminated. The new contestants and holders of power proclaimed themselves to be mobilizing the Arab nation against imperialism. Increasingly, the United States was painted as the leader of imperialism and as the creator of Israel. Alliance with the United States, American economic activities, notably oil concessions, even American economic assistance, were all depicted as subjecting the Arab nation to imperialism. The Soviet Union, which had been of more practical assistance to the infant Israel than the United States, found willing Arab recipients of Soviet military and economic assistance. By the early 60's, Egypt, Syria, Iraq, Algeria, and the Yeman were ruled by governments based on armies which used a common ideology.

The new Arab regimes, which Libya joined in 1969, have been rivals with each other, but their ideologies have common features. Like their predecessors, the radical Arab regimes exhort the Arab people to struggle to liberate themselves from the shameful present and reachieve the glorious past in the future. Socialism, they have discovered, is Islamic or Arab in origin, and to it the Arabs must return. The cause of Arab decline, the great enemy of the Arabs is "capitalist imperialism," whose center is the United States, which has achieved its purposes through Arab "capitalist feudalist" stooges. The Arab socialists have supplanted the puppets of "imperialism" in the "progressive" Arab countries, but they still rule in the "reactionary" countries as the tools of "imperialism." In addition, "capitalist imperialism" continues to possess a bridgehead in the Arab homeland in Israel. The Arabs, they say, are among the proletarian nations of the world, now called the Third World, who will defeat imperialism on a world scale, and then realize their greatness through their own indigenous socialism. The Soviet bloc is not a member of the Third World, but it is an ally in the struggle.

The outcome of World War II ended the relative insulation of Turkey and Iran from the great powers. Both came under Soviet pressure at the end of the war. Both accepted American diplomatic support and then American military and economic assistance. The Turkish political classes appear to have been nearly unanimous in support of the new policy, and there was substantial support for it among the Iranian political leadership, but Iran was divided.

Reza Shah had been deposed by Britain and the Soviet Union in 1941. Under his son and successor, Mohammed Reza, the magnates and *ulamā* regained much lost ground. Elements which had been especially embittered by Reza's repression were convinced that the British were still running the country. Dr. Mussaddiq led a great popular movement against the British which inevitably threatened the shah. But Musaddiq created expectations which he could not satisfy in the face of the Western world's economic retaliation. Musaddiq lost support and was turned out by the shah, who had some assistance from the CIA, the importance of which has been greatly exaggerated. Musaddiq and most of his followers saw Britain as the enemy; many of his followers were also fearful of the Soviet Union. Thus a substantial portion of the Musaddiqist nationalists had no hostility to the United States. Instead, they hoped to gain American assistance. Mohammed Reza remained the symbol of internal tyranny to them, but they did not oppose his alignment with the United States.

By 1950, it was clear that the Kemalists had not irrevocably fixed the relation between Islam and Turkism. Some very important Turks, some of them heroes of the war of national liberation, had never accepted Ataturk's rejection, as they saw it, of the Islamic past. By

1950, they had won control of the Turkish Republic. The secularist laws were relaxed. The Turkish masses remained Muslim in faith. The religious leaders, limited to the conduct of religious services, had not been greatly affected by the Kemalist reforms. With the initiation of two-party politics, the parliamentary system did not work as had been envisaged. By 1960, the Cyprus question had inflamed Turkish politics. The Army then made itself the guardian of the republic.

Turkey has not been able to reach an agreed solution to its internal conflicts, despite the continuing vitality of the parliamentary regime under the guardianship of the armed forces. The situation has been made more difficult by the continuation of the Cyprus conflict. The behavior of the American ally with respect to the Cyprus problem has been unsatisfactory to every shade of opinion. Perhaps well into the 70's, no major party questioned the American connection. But the heirs of Ataturk appear to have been becoming cooler toward the ally. In part this may be the result of the fact that the more religiously oriented party has been in power through much of the life of the Turco-American alliance. The Kemalists during this period have expressed deep concern over the possibility of a religious restoration. The period has also seen the growth of leftist groups who explicitly identify the United States with imperialism and with religious and political reaction.

By this time, Mohammed Reza had been identified in the minds of many Iranians as the tool of American capitalist imperialism in its exploitation of the Iranian people and of Islam. The years 1960-1962 saw the reawakening and the final frustration of hope among the Musaddiqist nationalists. The shah finally decided on royal absolutism and launched the White Revolution. The dissidents determined on resistance. They were joined by important members of the *ulamā*, notably Khomeini. The demonstrations and uprisings were crushed by the Army. Khomeini and the *mullas* had attacked the shah as the tool of American imperialism who was betraying Islam for his master. The opposition was suppressed, but it survived underground and in exile. Mohammed Reza himself spoke as the leader of the Iranian nation in its march to recover its lost greatness, to become one of the great powers of the world, truly independent, free of the vices of the West. The general economic growth, assertions of great power status, the assumption of the guardianship of security in the Persian Gulf and Indian Ocean, and the "oil takeover" aroused enormous enthusiasm and created great expectations. But by the mid-70's these expectations were dashed as inflation grew by leaps and bounds and, so it seemed to countless Iranians, the foreigners still took the lion's share of Iran's wealth. In these circumstances, the cabinet lost its unity, discontent among the members of the state structure grew, the Musaddiqist nationalists became more successful and established a working relationship with the embittered *ulamā*.

Today, as at the beginning of the century, the Islamic world appears to be mobilized for a great struggle against Western imperialism. The center, the heart and the brain, of imperialism is perceived to be the United States. The words of a Russian Muslim Bolshevik seem to apply to the present Muslim attitude as well as they did when he wrote them in 1921: "During the course of the last century the whole of the Muslim world was exploited by West European imperialism and served as the material base of its economy. . . . The majority of Muslims always felt this battle to be a political conflict, that is to say as a battle against Islam as a whole. Moreover, the reverse would have been impossible, for in the eyes of Muslims, the Muslim world forms an indivisible whole, without distinction, nationality, or tribe."[2] The sentiment of Islamic unity is beyond question widely dispersed and deeply rooted, strengthened, if not created, by confrontation with the West. Furthermore, the feeling of hostility to the West, a sense of being the victims of unfair exploitation by the West, is not confined to Muslims in the Near East. For over a century, Christian Arabs have shared this sentiment and have rallied to their Muslim compatriots, even to the extent of glorifying Islam as the mark of Arab greatness, of finding affirmation of the self in Islam's past greatness.

Whether there is emerging a true Islamic unity is very much in doubt. Before the Western onslaught there was no agreement among Muslims about what Islam means in detail. Political unity was acknowledged to be unnecessary or unachievable. The political division has survived, strengthened by the adoption of ethnic or territorial nationalisms, most of which have an Islamic rationale. Nor is there today any agreement on what Islam means. Those who zealously speak in the name of Islam today advocate disparate things which range from the enforcement of the Koranic penal prescriptions to a socialist state in which the Prophet's birthday is a national holiday. Perhaps anti-imperialism may prove to be a firmer bond than Islam. Even secularist Turks are now finding anti-imperialism attractive.

But neither anti-imperialism nor Islam is likely to unify the Near East. In every country of the region, as is true elsewhere, immediate interests and concerns have priority. The West may be the great enemy on high, but the immediate problem to be taken care of is the man next door. Those who rule, regardless of the slogans which they use in the contest for office, still have to face objective realities. The region bristles with arms, all imported from the Euro-American world and unobtainable anywhere else. Oil is abundant, but it is consumable chiefly in the industrial countries. So governments do what they cannot avoid. Radical Arab governments denounce the United States and imperialism, but they sell oil, for the right price, and they buy American goods and expertise when the cost-benefit ratio is favorable. The alien West will surely remain in some fashion in the Islamic East for the indefinite future. But, as Arab poet and Arab statesman have agreed, no government in human history, even when it is just, has ever succeeded in pleasing all the people. Those who perceive themselves as deprived will surely point to their government's alien associates. Capitalist imperialist powers, headed by the United States, today are perhaps the most popular villians. But, as Sadat's Egypt has shown, and as radical Iraq recently has been suggesting, the socialist Soviet ally of the proletarian nations can also become the focus of the conflict.

Notes

[1]Yūsuf al-Hakīm, *Dhikrayāt al-hakīm*, vol. I: *sūrīyah wa al-'ahd al-'uthmāni* [Al-Hakim's Memoirs, Vol I: Syria and the Ottoman Era] (Beirut: al-Matba'ah al-Kāthūlīkīyah, 1966), p. 136, quoting Ibn al-Wardi.

[2]Sultan Galiev, "The Methods of Antireligious Propaganda Among the Muslims," *Muslim National Communism in the Soviet Union: A Revolutionary Strategy for the Colonial World*, by Alexandre A. Bennigsen and S. Enders Wimbush (Chicago and London: University of Chicago Press, 1979), p. 147.

Bibliography

Algar, Hamid, *Religion and State in Iran, 1785-1906: the Role of the Ulama in the Qajar Period.* Berkeley: University of California Press, 1970.

Bennigsen, Alexandre A., and S. Enders Wimbush, *Muslim National Communism in the Soviet Union: A Revolutionary Strategy for the Colonial World.* Chicago: University of Chicago Press, 1979.

Berkes, Niyazi, *The Development of Secularism in Turkey.* Montreal: McGill University Press, 1964.

Cleveland, William L., *The Making of an Arab Nationalist: Ottomanism and Arabism in the Life and Thought of Sati 'al-Husri.* Princeton: Princeton University Press, 1971.

Cottam, Richard W., *Nationalism in Iran.* Pittsburg: Pittsburg University Press, [1964].

Dawn, C. Ernest, *From Ottomanism to Arabism: Essays on the Origins of Arab Nationalism.* Urbana: University of Illinois Press, 1973.

Gibb, Hamilton A. R., *Modern Trends in Islam.* Chicago: University of Chicago Press, 1947.

Haim, Sylvia G., ed. *Arab Nationalism: An Anthology.* Berkeley: University of California Press, 1962.

Hourani, Albert H., *Arabic Thought in the Liberal Age.* London, New York, and Toronto: Oxford University Press, 1962.

Ismael, Tariq Y., *The Arab Left: The Transformation of Contemporary Arab Nationalism.* Syracuse, New York: Syracuse University Press, 1976.

Keddie, Nikkie R.,ed. *Scholars, Saints, and Sufis: Muslim Religious Institutions Since 1500.* Berkeley and Los Angeles: University of California Press, 1972.

Khadduri, Majid, *Political Trends in the Arab World: The Role of Ideas in Politics.* Baltimore and London: The John Hopkins Press, 1970.

Kushner, David, *The Rise of Turkish Nationalism, 1876-1908.* Totowa, New Jersey: Frank Cass, 1977.

Mardin, Serif, *The Genesis of Young Ottoman Thought: A Study in the Modernization of Turkish Political Ideas.* Princeton: Princeton University Press, 1962.

Mitchell, Richard P., *The Society of Muslim Brothers.* Royal Institute of International Affairs Middle Eastern Monographs No. 9. London: Oxford University Press, 1968.

Smith, Wilfred Cantwell, *Islam in Modern History.* Princeton: Princeton University Press, 1957.

von Grunebaum, Gustave E., *Modern Islam: The Search for Cultural Identity.* Berkeley: University of California Press, 1962.

VII

THE POLITICAL ECONOMY OF MIDDLE EASTERN OIL AND THE ISLAMIC REVIVAL

Karim Pakravan

The revival of Islamic religious nationalism in the Middle East and the Near East will significantly affect — it already has — relations between Muslim countries of these regions and the rest of the world. A most immediate and tangible result of the Islamic revival is a disturbance in the international oil market which has already unsettled the economies of many countries. Dr. Pakravan here describes the factors that led to this disturbance, the role of Islamic nationalism in it, and its impact on the main "actors" on the stage of the International oil market — OPEC, multinational oil companies and governments of oil consuming countries — upon whose fortunes will depend the material welfare of the world.

Karim Pakravan has worked extensively on the economics of international energy markets and on Middle Eastern economies, both as a researcher and a consultant. He is currently continuing his research and teaching in the United States, at the Hoover Institution.

The purpose of this paper is to analyze the effects of the Islamic revival and the Iranian revolution on the future trends in the world petroleum market. It will be shown that long term oil policies that have resulted from this revival are a continuation of existing trends, trends that are closely related to regional economic and institutional issues. The Islamic revival crystallized these tendencies and accelerated these trends, while also introducing some strong but, hopefully, short term destabilizing tendencies and greater uncertainty.

The first energy crisis of the early seventies forced the industrialized nations to face the harsh realities of the emergence of a new order on the world petroleum market. The governments of these countries and the multinational oil firms who had dominated this market for decades now had to make room for a third actor, the oil exporting countries, represented collectively and efficiently by the Organization of Petroleum Exporting Countries (OPEC). The emergence of this new force was due to the conjunction of several forces, both political and economic: the unquenchable thirst of industrialized countries for crude oil in the 50's and 60's; the dwindling of their own oil and energy resources and/or limitations put on their use; and the concentration of most of the world's oil reserves in a handful of Islamic Middle Eastern and African countries, all of them underdeveloped.

The concentration of production of oil in underdeveloped areas, unable to produce it without the help of Western technology, the concentration of its consumption in the industrialized countries and the reliance of these countries on oil as the main energy source not only made oil the biggest industry and the most important traded commodity but also one of the major economic and political issues in international relations.

A non-negligible factor in the issues related to oil was that of Islam. While not all members of OPEC were Muslim countries, and while most of them agreed tacitly not to introduce ideological or political issues in the decision-making process of this organization, Islamic solidarity played an important role in determining the oil policies of Arab countries vis a vis Europe and the U.S.A., mainly in relation to the Arab-Israeli conflict.

However, the policy of the Shah's regime in Iran was not to mix oil and politics and to maintain a steady flow of oil to all customers, including Israel and South Africa. The Iranian revolution of 1978-1979 and the advent of a fundamendalist Islamic regime in Iran sounded the end of this policy. Not only production was cut, thus precipitating the advent of the long-brewing second energy crisis, but also Iran joined enthusiastically the ranks of those who wanted to use the oil weapon for the advancement of their struggle against Western imperialism.

Let us begin by looking at the main actors of the international petroleum market — the multinational firms, the governments of the major oil consuming countries and the OPEC.

I. The Actors

1. *The Multinational Oil Firms*

Traditionally, the international oil industry is divided into two groups: The Seven Sisters (B. P., Exxon, Shell, Gulf, Texaco, Mobil, Socal) and the other international companies. Much of the discussion has been about the extent of the control of the oil industry by the Seven Sisters (also known as the Majors). Each of them is one of the largest firms in the world, with a high degree of vertical integration. In addition, before the early 1950's, all of the foreign oil operations were controlled by one or several of these firms.

The question is: How much effect do these firms have in the world petroleum market and how this effect has changed and is changing over time. A brief historical survey will be helpful in understanding the role of these large oil companies.

While the oil industry started in 1859 in the U.S.A., the granting of the first Middle Eastern oil concession in 1901 can be looked upon as the true beginning of the multinational oil industry. This concession was granted by the Persian government to William Knox d'Arcy, who after several years of unsuccessful efforts, struck oil in 1908 at Masjed-Soleyman. In 1914, under the influence of Winston Churchill, who was seeking long term oil supplies for the Royal Navy, the British government acquired a major interest in this concession, leading to the formation of the Anglo-Persian Oil Company (APOC).[1]

At the same time (1907) another important group was formed by British and Dutch capital: Royal Dutch Shell. On the other side of the Atlantic, the divestiture of the giant Standard Oil group in 1911 led to the formation of another group of giants: Esso, Mobil, Socal. These five firms, plus Texaco and Gulf formed the group dubbed as "The Seven Sisters" by Enrico Mattei in the 1950's.

By the mid-twenties, the fear of depletion of the oil reserves in the U.S. pushed the U.S. government to adopt an aggressive policy in order for U.S. oil companies to acquire a share in the Middle Eastern oil resources from the British. The first result of this policy was the purchase of 23.75 percent of the shares of the Turkish Petroleum Company (TPC) by American oil companies in 1928. In exchange, the American participants were compelled to agree not to seek concessions within an area circled by a red line, including the former Ottoman Empire, except through the TPC.

Thus started the era of cooperation of the majors: Exxon, Socal, Mobil, Gulf, Texaco, BP, and Shell, who by a complex network of agreements, both implicit and explicit, acquired an almost absolute control of the international oil markets.

The main problems for the Seven Sisters (or the majors) were:

1) Fixing quotas.
2) Establishing adjustment mechanisms for over-and-under trading by partners in the international oil cartel.
3) Fixing prices and sale conditions.
4) Dealing with outsiders.

These problems were dealt with in the Achnacarry Agreement (or the "As Is" agreement [1928]), which was later complemented by the Memorandum for European Markets (1930), the Heads of Agreement of Distribution (1932) and the Draft Memorandum of Principles (1934).

By these agreements, a complex structure of international and national cartels was set to control all international oil operations, from production to marketing. Even though by the 1950's, the entrance of so-called "independent" and consumer government-owned oil companies changed the picture to a large extent, the majors retained a large degree of control on the international petroleum market, through implicit and explicit collusion.[3]

The extent of control of Middle Eastern oil by the "Seven Sisters" even as late as the mid-1960's is evident from the following table.

Interrelationships Between the Major Oil Companies in 1966 (Percentage share holding)[4]

	Abu Dhabi Marine Company	Kuwait Oil Co.	Iran Consortium	IPC	ARAMCO
BP	66.2/3	50	40	23.75	
Mobil			7	11.875	10
Socal			7		30
Texaco			7		30
Exxon			7	11.875	30
Gulf			7	13.75	
Shell		50	14	23.75	
CFP	33 1/3		6		
TOTAL	100	100	95	95	100

Yet it must be noted that starting in the 1950's, the situation began to change. Faced with rising demands which they were unable to fulfill through their own production, many so-called "independent" and government-owned companies in the consuming countries started to enter the international oil market in order to add to their oil reserves. By offering better terms to oil producing countries in the form of joint ventures, contractual agreements or production sharing (as opposed to the regime of concessions granted before 1950 that characterized the majors) they managed to obtain a market share and gradually increase it, at the expense of the majors. Between 1953 and 1972, 350 new firms thus entered the international oil market. Among these entrants, 15 were large U.S. oil companies with assets totalling $20 billion by 1972, 20 were medium-sized firms, 25 were non-U.S. private firms, and 15 were non-U.S. government firms. The following four tables show how these new entrants effected a decline of the share of the majors in all aspects of the international oil industry.[5]

Table 1.
Summary of Changes in Concentration of the Foreign Oil Industry By Division, 1953 and 1972

Division of the Industry	1953 "Seven Largest" Companies Combined (Percent)	1953 All Other Companies Combined (Percent)	1972 "Seven Largest" Companies Combined (Percent)	1972 All Other Companies Combined (Percent)
Area of Operation	64	36	24	76
Proven Reserves	92	8	67	33
Production	78	13	71	29
Refining Capacity	73	27	49	51
Tanker Capacity	29	71	19	81
Product Marketing	72	28	54	46

Table 2.
Summary of changes in Concentration of the Foreign Oil Industry By Division, 1953 and 1972

	1953 Majors	1953 Others	1972 Majors	1972 Others
Production (in TBD)	4422	632	22200	7811
Percentage Production	87	13	74	26
Reserves (in billion bbls)	72084	6735	350,853	158,374
Percentage Reserves	92	8	69	31
Refining Capacity (TBD)	3090	1389	17416	17732
Percentage Refining	73	27	50	50
Tanker Fleet (1000 DWT)	9841	24682	42827	176,063
Percentage Tanker Fleet	28.6	71.4	19.5	80.5

Table 3.

Growth of the "Seven Largest" and of All Other Oil Companies, Between 1953 and 1972, by Division of the Foreign Oil Industry

(Average Annual Compound Rates)

Division	"Seven Largest" Companies (Percent)	All Other Companies (Percent)
Proven Reserves	9	19
Average Daily Production	9	15
Refining Capacity	8	15
Tanker Capacity	8	11
Products Marketed	13	17

Table 4.

Reserves-Production Ratio

	1953	1972
Major	45	43
All Others	30	55

While it is clear from these tables that the degree of competition in the international petroleum industry increased significantly since the 1950's we must also consider other factors that help maintain the influence of the "Seven Sisters" relatively undiminished. They are:

1) Throughout the post-1954 period, the "Seven Sisters" retained their control of the international petroleum market, though less and less successfully, by the use of the following instruments:

    a) Control of supply: An important example of this is the Aggregated Programmed Quantity Agreement between the Iran Consortium members.

    b) Control of marketing, with the active support of U.S. government bodies. An outstanding example of this support was the effort by the U.S. National Security Council and President Truman to cripple the antitrust suit brought by the Federal Trade Commission in 1952 against the oil majors.

c) Exclusion of outsiders through suppression of discoveries; government pressure on "independent producers"; boycotts against the nationalistic measures of oil producing country governments (e.g., boycott of Iranian oil following the 1951 nationalization); pressure on foreign oil consuming countries, oil companies and contributions to political parties (e.g., Italy).

2) While the share of reserves controlled by the majors has significantly declined, it remains that because of their early entry in the international oil operations they own what one could label the choice pieces of the world's reserves (i.e., the largest and/or lowest cost fields).

3) There are significant pressures from the consuming countries' governments to encourage cooperation among oil companies in developing their foreign operations, which is in itself a restraint on competition, both on producer and consumer alike.

4) Within a given oil producing country:

a) The number of operators is restricted.

b) The operators dispose of substantial production potential elsewhere.

c) Operators are closely linked to each other by global joint shareholding.

5) In general, given the complexity of the international petroleum market and the very close interdependence between the various parties, there is finally a symbiotic relationship between oil producing country governments, the Seven Sisters, the so-called independents and the consuming country governments.

Therefore, the competition on the operators' side is very restricted and the host governments' possibility of playing them against each other is very limited.

For all these reasons we arrive at the conclusion that while the degree of competition has increased in the international petroleum industry, it is still extremely concentrated, and that any future entry of new firms will be affected by the following factors:

1) There are very few good prospects left: As far as oil producing areas are concerned, the industry is entering an irreversible increasing

cost phase and the large and increasing amounts of capital necessary to develop new capacity will act as a restraint on new entry.

2) The trend seems to be for multinational companies to act more and more as contractors for exploration and development; such contracts are often associated with long term sale agreements. Parallelly, national companies in oil producing nations are taking over an increasing share of upstream operations, but the expansion of their activities is limited by the near monopoly that multinationals have on the technology of the oil industry.

2. Oil Consuming Countries' Governments

The second set of actors in the international petroleum market are the governments of the major industrialized nations, who have played an increasingly important role in this market ever since World War II. These governments intervened in several manners in the field of oil: In the first place, they provided the administrative and legal framework which made life easier for the major multinational oil corporations, protecting them from antitrust laws, competition and other rules that are supposed to provide the framework of economic activity in the Western countries; in the second place, they provided them with the political (and sometimes military) backing necessary to face successfully the challenges of oil producing countries which were struggling for an increase in their control over their natural wealth; and finally in many cases, they entered directly in the international market through partly or wholly owned, vertically integrated oil companies.

However, one observes important variations and sometimes competition between the governments of these countries, especially between the U.S. and European ones:

a) The U.S. government has been reluctant to enter directly into the petroleum industry operations. Even at the height of World War II, the oil industry had torpedoed the idea of a direct U.S. government participation in ARAMCO, calling it a "fascist" measure that would lead to statism and maybe socialism. The European governments have always held the opposite view and have aggressively competed with the majors for control of crude oil supplies.

b) The U.S. government has, on the other hand, consistently advocated a hardline oil policy, backing the U.S. multinational firms with the full power of its diplomatic machine, with the threat of the use of force always looming in the background.

These introductory remarks will lead us now to examine more in detail the role of the industrialized countries' governments in the international petroleum market.

1) The 1950's and 1960's: Confrontation and Competition

The 1950's opened with the Iranian nationalization crisis, which pitted the Anglo-Iranian Oil Company (later called British Petroleum) against the government of Dr. Mossadeq (the Iranian Prime Minister). The British government, which was also a major shareholder in AIOC, enforced with a naval blockade an embargo against Iranian oil, which had been unilaterally nationalized by the Iranian government. Eventually the crisis was solved in 1953 by the ouster of the Mossadeq government (with some help from the CIA), the return to power of a more "reasonable" Shah, and the 1954 Consortium agreement, which created a joint company whose shares were held by BP (40%), Shell (14%), the five U.S. majors (7% each), Compagnie Francaise de Petroles (8%) and a U.S. consortium of independents (5%), formed for the exploitation of Iranian oil resources. Interestingly enough, the five U.S. majors, awash in crude oil, were unwilling to participate in the Consortium and did so only after a great deal of pressure from the U.S. government and formal assurances from the administration that they would be immune from antitrust action.

By the late 50's, the Italian state-owned oil company, AGIP, rose to challenge the supremacy of the majors by entering into a joint venture deal with Iran, the first of its kind, giving a 75-25 profits split to the advantage of Iran. This came in the age of the rise of the independent crude-hungry oil companies, and it was quickly followed by other contracts of this type between government-owned firms and producer countries.

In the mid-sixties, ERAP, a French government-controlled oil company, started a new type of contract: the service contract. By contrast to the aggressiveness of the European governments in gaining control of crude oil sources by offering more and more advantageous conditions to the producing countries, the U.S. government remained aloof, leaving the conduct of its international oil policy to the U.S. majors.

2) The 1970's: Cooperation

In the 1970's, the governments' role shifted considerably. The main reasons for this shift were:

a) The rise of OPEC as a major force in the world petroleum market.

b) The parallel decline in the power of the majors, reduced in most cases to service contracts and long term purchases of crude.
c) The worsening of the energy crisis.

These three factors led to a greater degree of cooperation between the oil consuming national governments (witness the formation of the International Energy Agency in 1974) in order to coordinate oil policies, especially in times of crisis. They also led to some efforts, although fruitless, on the part of these governments to present a united front in negotiations with OPEC. At the same time the multinational oil firms which seemed to have become the agents of OPEC rather than of their own governments were beginning to be considered as adversaries rather than as agents by the U.S. government, this point of view being reinforced by the fact that their profits seemed to be positively correlated to the intensity of the energy crisis. In addition, the 1970's witnessed petroleum becoming a basic issue in high level international negotiations among the OECD group. In these negotiations the trend seems to be that of increasing cooperation among these governments and to a certain extent between these governments and OPEC members, taken individually or collectively.

Let us now turn to the third actor: The petroleum exporting countries, represented by OPEC.

3. The Organization of Petroleum Exporting Countries

OPEC was formed in 1960 by the five leading oil exporters, Saudi Arabia, Kuwait, Iran, Iraq and Venezuela, in an effort to prevent any further declines in the posted price of oil. Despite the fact that both the multinationals and the oil consuming nations' governments refused to recognize its existence as the representative of oil exporting nations until 1970, OPEC was not altogether unsuccessful in the first decade following its formation. A non-negligible achievement was the fact that it resisted successfully any further decline in posted prices despite the rapid rise of world oil reserves and capacity. Furthermore, the spirit of cooperation on petroleum matters for the advancement of what was perceived as a common cause was created, and this spirit survived and was strengthened despite strong political and ideological differences. Over the years, most oil exporting nations of the Third World joined OPEC.

As a result, OPEC controlled by 1970 over half of the world's production and reserves. The rapid growth of world demand (averaging over 7 percent per annum in the 60's), the decline in the rate of additions to reserves in the late sixties, and the adoption of policies detrimental to the development of native energy resources in the industrialized nations led to the gradual increase of OPEC's monopoly power over the world's petroleum, a power that has been felt strongly ever since the early seventies and that has made OPEC into the third main actor in the international petroleum market.

Having now briefly examined the actors, let us turn to the issues in the world petroleum market in the 70's, from the point of view of the oil exporting countries, issues that have dominated the political relations within the area and between it and the rest of the world, issues that have become increasingly intermingled with militant nationalism and the Islamic revival.

II. The Issues

Introduction

For most countries of the Third World, finding sufficient funds for financing economic development has been a major challenge. While the existence of a steady flow of oil income did remove the financial bottleneck for most oil producing nations in the 1950's and 1960's, their natural resource remained under the control of giant multinational oil companies which controlled to a large extent every aspect of the upstream, midstream and downstream operations of the international oil industry. Thus, the steady flow of oil revenues, while allowing to finance on a continual basis the large scale development programs of the oil producers, permitted them little control over the flow of oil, or its price. In effect, the economic, political and technical factors discussed in the previous sections denied them the much coveted sovereignty over their oil resources. But, why was the issue of sovereignty so important? After all, these countries did benefit from the operations of the multinationals. The answer to this question can be found in economics: while from a purely political point of view, sovereignty over national resources is important and does play a role in the objectives of the state, economics dictate an "optimal" time path of production for oil, a time path that is closely related to the country's objectives and the physical, technical and institutional constraints it faces. There is *a priori* no reason for the multinationals to have the same objectives and/or to face the same set of constraints as the country in which they operate. Therefore, the production time patterns they will choose will in general be different from those chosen by the country (had the latter the means to exploit its own resources).

One important area in which this difference can be seen is "conservation": while the oil producing state, which is uncertain about its prospects once its oil has run out, will prefer to increase the life of its oil reserves, the multinationals whose objectives are global and who always face the threat of nationalization, will not have an incentive to do so. In other words, the issue of sovereignty goes beyond its political context into the realm of political economy.

The emergence of OPEC as a unified cartel in the early seventies set the stage for the takeover from the multinationals. The key word was "participation," or takeover of oil operations by national companies. This process was completed by the mid-seventies and with its completion the multinationals changed from concession holders to service contractors and long term purchasers of oil. They found the new order to be agreeable to their aims and adapted very quickly to their new role, to the extent that they started being considered with distrust by their erstwhile patrons, i.e., the governments of industrialized nations, who on some occasions accused them of acting as OPEC agents in enacting the cartel's policies and strengthening it at the expense of the consumers.

Issues of the Seventies

The price explosion of 1973-1974 and the ensuing rise in revenues of the oil producing nations focused attention on a new issue (absorption of excess oil revenues), while reviving an existing one (conservation). The quantum jump in oil revenues faced the oil producers with the problem of absorbing them in their economic development and growth process, a challenge which they met by rushing headlong into hasty upward revisions of their development plans, leading to a quantum jump in their expenditures on everything, from large scale development projects to weapon systems and imports of consumer goods and services. The goal of reaching the developed stage in less than half a generation seemed finally at hand. However, this "goldrush" economic approach failed spectacularly: by the mid-seventies, less than two years after the first price explosion, this failure could be seen in a stagnation of real GNP, a galloping inflation, an increased inequality in the distribution of income, corruption, increased dependence on the Western industrialized nations and a multitude of unsolved social problems. This failure led to the strengthening of the view that with the present high levels of prices and the inability of the Middle Eastern economies to absorb continuously a high level of oil revenues, production should be cut back. However, any large scale cutback in production would undoubtedly affect adversely the Western economies; therefore the industrialized world should engage in a program of energy conservation and development of alternative energy resources. In other words, the energy and revenue needs of oil producing nations did not warrant keeping production at such a high level.

The aspirations of the Middle Eastern oil producing countries for a more balanced economic and social development and economic independence from the industrial powers found a new ally: Islam, whose language could be more easily understood by the masses of uneducated but deeply religious people than the more complex modern political and economic brand of reasoning.

The Islamic Revival

The economic development and growth process made possible in the Middle East by a sustained and rising flow of oil revenues in the 50's and 60's was accompanied by increasing Westernization and a parallel decline of religious and traditional values. Islam was seen by the decision makers as a backward force that impeded development. The only way to meet the assault of the dynamic Western civilization was to absorb its values over the shortest period of time and thus be able to answer its challenge. Thus the driving force was modernization — economic, political and cultural.

Modernization was pervasive in the ideology of the state in the Middle East, whether it be Arab Socialism, Pahlavism, or Ataturk's Etatism. By the end of the 60's, the failure of economic development plans to achieve their perceived goals, i.e., economic growth, elimination of poverty, unemployment and social injustice, and economic independence from the West, and the progressively strong penetration of what was seen as corrupt Western values led to increased unrest in most of the Middle Eastern societies, unrest that gradually found a vehicle in Islam, the only political language that was free to a certain extent of political repression and which could readily be understood by the uneducated, traditional and deeply religious masses. Thus Islam transformed the issues we discussed above — sovereignty, absorption and conservation — to conflict between Islam and the West. Iran was an extreme case in point. The new Islamic militancy saw the increasing economic difficulties of the mid-seventies as the result of an economic, political and cultural penetration of Western imperialism, whose goals of domination were carried out by the corrupt governments and Westernized elites. Islam provided not only the spiritual values that allowed the East to resist the West, but presented also an alternative model of political and economic development based upon social justice and freedom from want.

In this context, oil was seen as the instrument of economic and social development and as a potent weapon against a Western world for whom this precious resource was vital.

The above analysis, which is obviously confined to an economic context, will provide us the framework for projecting the effect of the Islamic revival on future oil policies of Middle Eastern countries. However, we need one more element to complete this framework: the international petroleum market in the mid-seventies, to which we now turn.

The International Petroleum Market Revisited

The international petroleum market in the mid-seventies was, as said before, dominated by three forces: OPEC, the multinationals and the oil consuming nations' governments. This section will be devoted to a brief analysis of the nature of OPEC, and its relationships with the other actors in this period and the effect of the Iranian crisis on the international petroleum market.

1) OPEC — The Cartel's Mechanism

To the average U.S. consumer, OPEC is a cartel bent on squeezing the last drop of blood out of the Western economies. Does such an image fit the reality? To start with, let us say that the oil resources of the world were exploited for decades by multinational oil companies whose first aim was to defend their own interests (and sometimes those of the consumer in their home countries) with very little interference by the oil producing nations. In this framework OPEC can then be understood as an instrument for reassertion of national sovereignty over their natural resources by these nations.

OPEC does not function as a cartel in the traditional sense, as it does not impose production quotas on its members. Its main function is to determine at regular intervals the posted price of the basic crude (or Arabian Marker). It also has a less known function, and that is to set maximum allowable quality and freight price differentials, based on differences in gravity, sulfur content and location of crude. The effect of this very complex pricing system that is determined by the posted price and its effects on world petroleum consumption will determine OPEC's global output, while on the other hand the price differentials will determine the market shares of the different OPEC members, whose reserves obviously differ both in quality and distance from markets.

How does such a system work? Cartel theory tells us that the members of any cartel have an incentive to cheat by practicing price chiseling in order to increase their market share at the expense of other cartel members, and therefore, unless there is a strong enforcement system within the cartel, it will tend to break down. In other words, a cartel will survive only if its members are willing to play the game, and in order for them to do so, the incentive of keeping the cartel together must be greater than the incentive to cheat.

It is my belief that OPEC functions as what we could call a "dominant duopoly": the pricing decisions are made by two leaders acting in explicit or implicit collusion, i.e., Iran and Saudi Arabia, while the other members are acting as price takers. Together, these two countries control almost 50 percent of OPEC production and reserves, thus playing a determining role in the pricing decisions. No other single OPEC country can match either of these two countries in these aspects. Yet, neither Iran nor Saudi Arabia has the power to singly control the market, therefore the cartel could break if one of the two leaders decides to follow an independent course.

In other words, as long as the leaders of the cartel act in a collusive fashion, all its members, both price fixers and price takers, will benefit from it in terms of their long run stream of revenues.

Furthermore, given the fact that only two cartel members have to make the pricing decisions, its policing costs are much lower than if all cartel members had to be controlled. This is possible because, apart from the leaders, all other cartel members react passively to the price.

The following table shows the market shares of the cartel members in the past 6 years. We can see that: a) Iran and Saudi Arabia control close to 50% of the total shares, and b) shares have remained remarkably stable.

	1973	74	75	76	77	78	79
Saudi Arabia	.24	.28	.26	.28	.29	.26	.27
Iran	.19	.19	.20	.19	.18	.19	.13
Iraq	.06	.06	.08	.07	.07	..05	.11
Kuwait	.10	.08	.08	.06	.06	.07	.07
Venezuela	.11	.09	.09	.08	.07	.07	.08
U.A.E.	.05	.06	.06	.06	.07	.06	.06
Libya	.07	.05	.05	.06	.07	.07	.07
Others	.17	.19	.18	.20	.19	.19	.21

The effectiveness of this pricing scheme and cartel control was closely related to the international oil marketing mechanism. The early 70's witnessed a gradual takeover of oil operations by the producing governments and the shift of the "majors" from concessionaires to service contractors and long term purchasers of oil. The spot market remained a residual market, where oil producing governments, oil companies and brokers would sell the oil not marketed through long term contracts. This meant that in general the spot price was very close to the posted (or market) price, even slightly lower. Only in periods of crisis, when buyers built up their stocks as a precautionary and speculative measure, did the spot price rise significantly above the market price.

The stability of the international petroleum market was something much desired by all the parties. The producing nations, while maximizing their revenues through the existence of the cartel, could forecast their vitally important oil revenues; the oil consuming nations could count on a steady, if increasingly expensive, flow of oil imports, while evolving a national and international conservation policy based upon conservation and development of alternative energy sources; the oil companies, who profited anyway, could forecast their cash flow stream with reasonable accuracy.

Therefore, basically, we can state that the OPEC cartel worked because of stabilizing forces, both internal and external.

However, against this background of apparent stability, some long term trends were at work.

2) The Second Energy Crisis and the Iranian Revolution

OPEC, by the mid-seventies, was an important factor in the international petroleum market. However, both this market and OPEC were threatened by a number of political and economic forces, the main ones being:

(a) Because of the increased militancy of OPEC countries in their dealings with the oil companies, the majors, now reduced to service contractors and long term purchasers, significantly reduced their level of investments in exploration and development in OPEC countries (witness the long and fruitless negotiations between Iran and the Consortium).

(b) The ineffectiveness of energy conservation policies in the major industrial countries resulted in the continuation of the trend of increased oil consumption.

(c) The oil producing countries, worried about the falling level of their oil reserves and the incapacity of their economies to absorb rising oil revenues in a productive manner, embarked on a long term conservation policy which entailed reductions in planned capacity increases, or actual production cuts.

(d) The increased political tensions in the Middle East due to the impasse of the Arab-Israeli negotiations and the uncertain future of Iran cast further shadows on the already troubled international oil market.

The halt of Iranian oil operations — amounting to nearly 5 million barrels a day — caused by strikes and disruptions in the fall of 1978 and winter of 1979 caused the small worldwide surplus capacity (of about 2 million barrels per day) to be wiped out very quickly. The depletion of reserves, along with the fact that the fall is traditionally the fuel stockpiling season, caused a rush on the spot markets, raising the spot price of oil to unheard-of levels in the winter of 1979.

The gradual return of post-revolutionary Iranian oil production to the oil markets in the spring and summer of 1979 did not mean a return to normalcy, and that for several reasons:

(a) Iran's production did not exceed 4 million daily barrels.

(b) Iran took over completely all its oil operations, selling oil only on a medium term (9 months) contract basis to individual oil companies.

(c) The political unrest in Iran, accompanied by strikes and sabotage, aggravated by purges of politically "nonreliable" personnel from the oil industry and technical problems, caused frequent interruptions of the Iranian oil production.

(d) The new rulers of Iran, bent on eradicating all vestiges of "imperialism" in their international relations and "Westernization" at home, called for drastic cuts of oil production. While most experts (even the "Westernized" types) agreed that there should be a cut in oil production, Khomeini's regime envisaged an almost total one.

Such a chaotic situation, coupled with the inability of the totally ruined Iranian economy to absorb any oil revenues, led to the pursuance of an erratic and short-term oriented oil policy whose basis was the diversion of oil from contract sales to the spot market, where prices of up to U.S. $40 per barrel could be obtained (as opposed to a maximum posted price of U.S. $23.50 in 1979).

This policy was in fact a breach of OPEC internal discipline. As stated before, Iran, as one of the two "leaders" (in a cartel theory sense) of OPEC, played a crucial role in determining its stability. Its *de facto* withdrawal from the OPEC collective policy-making mechanism caused the other cartel members to follow suit, as the policing of the cartel, which depended crucially on Iran, could not be effective anymore. The increased reliance of OPEC member countries on the spot market for the sale of their crude and refined products means in effect a disruption of the stability of market shares system that ruled OPEC throughout the seventies. This breakdown of discipline within OPEC and the increasing degree of anarchy on the international petroleum markets pose a major threat to the very existence of OPEC, as these seriously undermine its effectiveness as a cartel.

III. Future Prospects

It is obviously very difficult to forecast with any degree of precision the future trends in the international petroleum market. We can nevertheless indicate some possible trends that are directly linked to the resurgence of nationalism in the form of an Islamic revival. This revival, as we have seen, affects the political economy of oil in two different manners: internally, it affects OPEC and externally it will determine the attitude of the oil producing nations of the Middle East towards the industrialized countries.

The Islamic Revival and OPEC

As we mentioned before, the main strengths of OPEC and reasons for its strong performance as a cartel lay in two factors: firstly the fact that OPEC was a single purpose association, based upon the collective defense of petroleum related interests and in which politics did not play an essential role; secondly the internal decision making was made by explicit or implicit collusion between Saudi Arabia and Iran, with other OPEC nations reacting passively to their decisions.

The Iranian revolution, which resulted in a very fanatical version of pan-Islamism, presented for the first time a real threat to OPEC's very existence. OPEC, as a showcase of a political cooperation between petroleum exporting countries and a major element in the prestige of the member nations' regimes, was obviously an obstacle to the pan-Islamic and radical plans of the Khomeini regime. In addition, OPEC was an institution ready to cooperate with the West in order to maintain stability for the sake of reforming the world economic order, at least to its own benefit, rather than shattering it. This also went against the deep hatred of Khomeini for everything Western. Therefore, Iran was to weaken OPEC rather than to reinforce it. Iran's actions ever since the change of regime prove this, especially its behavior since the Caracas meeting of December, 1979. While Iran obviously lacks the power to carry its politicies in OPEC, as its moves are being countered by Saudi Arabia, its moves have certainly reinforced the hardliners group in OPEC, a fact that has a strong destabilizing effect on the world petroleum market.

Economic and Institutional Aspects

However, the survival of the present Iranian regime and its ideology are still very much in doubt, and therefore it is quite likely that radical pan-Islamism will subside within the medium term, leaving the more fundamental institutional and economic aspects of the present crisis as the main determinants of the future trends in the international petroleum market. These institutional and economic aspects are:

(a) The realization by the oil producing countries of the limited absorptive capacity of their economies, leading to the need to cut back production, especially in the light of recent price increases,

(b) The nationalistic and anti-imperialistic movements within these nations, calling for a reduction or total elimination of Western economic penetration in the area,

(c) The destabilizing threat of these tendencies on the present regimes of Middle Eastern oil producing countries, and

(d) The inability of industrialized nations to develop a consistent energy policy, based upon energy conservation, development of alternative energy sources and encouragement of non-OPEC oil and gas production.

These aspects will undoubtedly affect decisively the future trends in the international petroleum market, and while it is difficult to choose between a large number of equally possible scenarios, we can present what seems to be the best and the worst cases.

Best Possible Case: The efforts at developing a national energy policy in industrialized countries will be successful and these countries, therefore, will reduce their demand for imported oil. This will lead to a gradual decline in OPEC production over the next two decades. At the same time, alternative renewable energy sources will be developed, replacing a declining global production of oil. However, for most of the transition-out-of-oil period, the world petroleum market will remain on a precarious "razor edge" equilibrium, an equilibrium that could be disrupted by any of a number of political and economic crises.

Worst Possible Case: While OPEC cuts back its production by 10 to

25 percent, excess demand will continue to grow both in the industrialized countries and the Eastern bloc, leading to an economic, political and possibly military confrontation in the Middle East in which OPEC will be shattered as its members will be forced to choose sides.

In conclusion, let me note that the Islamic revival of the mid and late seventies, seen as an attempt to translate into a more easily understandable political language the nationalistic and anti-imperialistic aspirations of the Middle Eastern nations, does not represent a fundamental change of direction in the politics of the area, especially the oil politics, except in the relation between the new Iranian regime and OPEC. This new situation in which OPEC is seen as an obstacle to Iran's pan-Islamism, is dangerous for OPEC and by extension, for the stability of the international petroleum market.

In the near future we probably will see the translation of these nationalistic and anti-imperialistic aspirations into a reduced (in relative and/or absolute terms) flow of oil from OPEC to the industrialized nations, a reduction that could cause a succession of energy crises leading to international conflict, unless patterns of energy use and production change drastically in the industrialized nations.

Footnotes

[1] Known since 1954 as British Petroleum.

[2] Known today as Exxon.

[3] There is evidence that as late as 1971, disputes between members of the "Seven Sisters" were referred to two high level committees for solution. For details see J. Blair, *The Control of Oil.* New York: Vintage Books, 1976.

[4] Taken from E. T. Penrose, *The Large International Firm in Developing Countries — The International Petroleum Industry.* London: Allen and Unwin, 1966.

[5] All tables taken from N. Jacoby, *Multinational Oil.* New York: Macmillan, 1974.

Bibliography

Adelman, M. A., *The World Petroleum Market*. Baltimore: John Hopkins Press, 1972.

Allen, L., *OPEC Oil*. Cambridge: Oelgeschlager, Gunn and Hain, 1980.

Blair, J., *The Control of Oil*. New York: Vintage Books, 1976.

Fesharaki, F., *The Development of the Iranian Oil Industry*. New York: Praeger, 1979.

Ghadar, F., *Evolution of OPEC Strategy*. Lexington, 1977.

Jacoby, N., *Multinational Oil*. McMillan, 1974.

Levy, W., "The Year the Locust Hath Eaten: Oil Policy and OPEC Development Projects," *Foreign Affairs*, v. 57, no. 2, Winter 78/79.

Longrigg, S., *Oil in the Middle East*. Oxford University Press, 1968.

Penrose, E., *The Large International Firm in Developing Countries: The International Petroleum Industry*. MIT Press, 1963.

Odell, P., *Oil and World Power*. Penguin, 1974.

Sampson, A., *The Seven Sisters*. New York, 1975.

Schurr, S., *Middle Eastern Oil and the Western World*. American Elsevier, 1971.

VIII

THE ISLAMIC WORLD, ISRAEL, AND THE UNITED STATES

Frank Tachau

> Since the First World War the growing impact of the Zionist movement in Europe and America and the increasing Jewish population of Palestine had much to do with the West's relationship with the Muslim peoples of the Middle East. Since 1948, however, the creation of Israel as a new state, the rise of the United States as the leader of the Western world, and the emergence of Russia as a superpower contesting against the West added new twists to this relationship. Israel and the Muslim Middle East became a chief center of superpower political/military rivalry. The way this rivalry is played out is determined in a large measure by public opinion in the United States. Professor Tachau here attempts to correct some of the misconceptions that help to distort American public opinion and consequently American foreign policy towards the Middle East.
>
> Frank Tachau, long time teacher of Middle Eastern politics and author of several works in this field, is currently professor and chairman of the Political Science Department at the University of Illinois, Chicago Circle.

Perhaps no current political problem is more fraught with emotion than the Arab-Israeli conflict. It is also one of the most intractable. Consider the ingredients:

At the heart of the conflict is the clash of two nationalist movements, Zionist and Palestinian Arab, both of which lay claim to a remarkably small but highly symbolic territory.

Associated with this clash of nationalist movements are large numbers of displaced persons on both sides: the bulk of the Jewish population of Israel consists of refugees from and survivors of the European holocaust of the 1930's and 1940's on the one hand, and refugees from Arab and other Muslim states of the Middle East and

North Africa on the other; while hundreds of thousands of Palestinian Arabs who fled their homes as the result of the warfare of 1948 and 1967 remain scattered in surrounding Arab countries (Lebanon, Jordan, and Syria particularly) as well as in other more distant countries (in the Arabian peninsula, Egypt, and even the United States).

The Territory at the heart of the conflict is part of deeply embedded and very ancient religious scripture and tradition: it is the promised land of the Old Testament; the land in which Jesus lived and the Christian religion was born; and the site of some of the most significant religious experiences of Muhammad, the Prophet of Islam.

The conflict has continued uninterruptedly for over thirty years now, and has spawned at least four outbreaks of full-fledged warfare (in 1948-1949, 1956, 1967, and 1973).

The conflict has increasingly threatened to involve the superpowers: Soviet pilots flying combat missions for the Egyptian Air Force during the so-called war of attrition in the summer of 1970; activation of large scale military re-supply operations during the 1973 war from the Soviet Union to Syria and Egypt, from the United States to Israel; military alerts and preparations for intervention by both the United States and the Soviet Union in 1973; and stationing of U.S. personnel in surveillance stations in the Sinai Peninsula to monitor the Israeli-Egyptian disengagement agreements of the mid-1970's.

The emergence of control of world oil supplies as a political weapon in the hands of the Arabs to pressure Western supporters of Israel (particularly the United States) to adopt more conciliatory policies toward the Palestinian Arabs.

It should therefore occasion little surprise that with the winding down of the war in Viet Nam, American policy-makers should pay increasing attention to the Arab-Israeli conflict. The culmination was the personal involvement of President Carter in the negotiations leading to the conclusion of the first formal treaty of peace between Israel and any of its Arab enemies, the Israeli-Egyptian peace treaty signed in a memorable ceremony on the White House lawn in March of 1979.

Given the strong emotions and the evident dangers, it is disheartening to note that the American public impresses foreign observers as both misinformed and disinterested in the conflict. Consider the following account by the Acting Managing Editor of New Outlook, a leading English-language Israeli journal espousing a highly dovish approach to the problem:[1]

> Two p.m. in the afternoon is usually soap opera time in America. Yet that was the time set aside for the historic signing of the Israeli-Egyptian peace treaty on the White House lawn. Why was 2 p.m. chosen? Because 2 p.m. Washington time equals 9 p.m. Egyptian and Israeli time, prime time, when the greatest psychological impact could be made on the two peoples most directly involved in this historic event.
>
> Since I was just beginning a visit to America, I made sure to set aside time to be near a television set at the appointed hour. But how many Americans did the same?
>
> The following day's television rating showed where the average American's allegiances lie. A record audience set aside 9 p.m. Washington time in order to watch the final game of the N.C.A.A. collegiate basketball championships. And the names on everyone's lips the next day were not Anwar Sadat, Menahem Begin, and Jimmy Carter, but rather Larry Bird and "Magic" Johnson, the two heroes of the basketball game. . . .
>
> So basketball takes precedence over the historic signing of a peace treaty between Israel and Egypt. And not only because basketball is more fun. It's also more clearcut. Michigan State faces Indiana. The game will only last for so long. One side wins, and the other side loses. While the Middle East conflict is so complex. There is no apparent time-limit for the game, and when one aspect of the problem is resolved, there seem to be so many others left to be faced.

Apathy among Americans towards international politics has long been deplored. It is certainly understandable in the light of the frustrating and demoralizing experiences of the Viet Nam war. Misinformation, however, is perhaps more dangerous. Unfortunately, there is a great deal of misinformation regarding the Arab-Israeli conflict. In the face of evidence of unsteadiness at the helm of state, and increasing threats to vital American interests (revolution in Iran,

Soviet invasion of Afghanistan, upheaval in Mecca, attacks on American embassies in Pakistan and Libya, and continuing uncertainties regarding oil supplies to the U. S. and its allies), it is more important than ever that a well informed public be prepared to provide some balance by helping to define the limits of foreign policy. Perhaps the best way to contribute here is to examine some of the common misconceptions concerning the relationships among Islam, the Arabs, and Israel and their implications for American interests and policy.

Misconception I: All Arabs are Muslims; all Muslims are Arab.
This misconception is wrong on both counts. In fact, the Muslim world encompasses hundreds of millions of people from the Atlantic shores of North Africa, along the southern and eastern shores of the Mediterranean, all across central and southern Asia and into the western Pacific. Arabs constitute only about 20% of this vast agglomeration of people. The most populous Muslim countries (e.g., Indonesia, Bangladesh, Pakistan) are both non-Arab and located well beyond the limits of the Middle East. Both the Soviet Union and India have Muslim minorities whose numbers in each case exceed the most populous single Arab country (Egypt). Even in the Middle East, the most populous country is Turkey whose population is also distinctly non-Arab. Significantly, Islam has also been making headway among the black people of sub-Saharan Africa.

Nor is it true that all Arabs are Muslims. At one time, there were sizable Jewish minorities in many Arab countries (e.g., Morocco, Algeria, Tunisia, Egypt, Syria, Iraq, Yemen), and some of these remain today. Significant Christian minorities have survived also, for example in Egypt, where the Coptic church (perhaps the oldest in Christendom) accounts for some 10% of the population. In Lebanon, the Christian population accounts for close to half the population; indeed, one of the main issues of the civil war of 1975-1976 (which continues to simmer today) was the allocation of political power between Christian and Muslim elements. There are also significant Christian minorities in Syria and among the Palestinian and Israeli Arabs.

While neither all Muslims are Arab, nor all Arabs Muslims, it remains true that Islam has played a central role in Arab culture. Islam, after all, was born among Arabs. Its founder, the Prophet Muhammad, was an Arab (a member of the leading tribe of Mecca at that). The language of the Koran, the word of God as revealed to the Prophet, is Arabic. Indeed, to this day, it is a tenet of Islam that because the language of God is Arabic, the Koran cannot be translated. (Accordingly, an English version was published under the title "The Meaning of the Glorious Koran."[2]) It was under the leadership of the Arabs that Islam enjoyed its first great earthly successes. In turn, it was Islam which provided the Arabs with their greatest earthly glory, specifically the conquest of the Fertile Crescent, North Africa, and the Iberian Peninsula (in fact, the Arabization of these lands and their inhabitants dates from these conquests during, roughly, the first century of Islam).

On the other hand, the central importance of Islam for the Arabs should not be misconstrued to mean that Islam is a purely Arab creation or that it lacks salience for non-Arab Muslims. Suffice it to note that with the rise of the Abbassid Empire in the middle of the eighth century A.D., Arab political and cultural dominance of the world of Islam began to fade. Iranians, Indians, and others in turn made major contributions to the further development of the religion and culture. In our own day, the revolution in Iran provides powerful evidence of the close identification of national consciousness among non-Arabs with one or another of the many extant branches of Islam.

Misconception II: Islam is obscurantist, primitive, and uncivilized.

In fact, Islam is one of the three great monotheistic religions of the world (the other two being Judaism and Christianity). It is culturally and theologically closer to western religion and culture than perhaps any other culture or religion. While the sociological roots of Islam clearly were nurtured in the pre-Islamic society of the Arabian peninsula, its theological origins are predominantly rooted in the Old and New Testaments. In fact, such scriptures as the Pentateuch or Torah, the Psalms, and the Evangel or Gospel are specifically cited in the Koran. According to H.A.R. Gibb, "All these scriptures were written revelations, and all alike are to be believed and accepted, since they all confirm one another and the Koran in particular not only confirms earlier scriptures, but, as the final revelation, clears up all uncertainties and is the repository of perfect Truth."[3] Hostility toward Jews and Christians is based not so much on differences in beliefs as it is on the charge that these pre-Islamic "People of the Book" either rejected or corrupted the word of God, thus in fact necessitating the prophecy of Muhammad.

Far from being inherently obscurantist, primitive, or uncivilized,

Islam in fact enjoyed an exceptionally high level of culture and civilization at various times and in a variety of places. A number of illustrious empires emerged over the centuries (the Umayyad based first in Damascus, later in Spain; the Abbassids with their capital in Baghdad; the Mughals of India; the Iranian Safavids; the Seljukid Turks and later the Ottomans, whose empire finally collapsed as recently as World War I; these to name but a few). Most notably, from the Western perspective, it was under the aegis of Islam that the classical learning of ancient Greece was preserved during the European Dark Ages, to be passed back to modern Europe in the Renaissance. In fact, modern English bears a good deal of evidence of this influence in the form of scientific terms clearly reminiscent of their Arabic origin (e.g., algebra).

Given these cultural and religious ties, how are we to explain the negative images which have persisted for so long? The answer to this question is important, for these negative images have had a major impact on the Arab-Israeli conflict.

The explanation is most usefully broken down into several component elements. It begins with one important theological difference between Islam and Christianity. This lies in the Koranic rejection of the divinity of Jesus. The religion of the Koran is uncomprisingly and emphatically monotheistic. It rejects both the polytheism of pre-Islamic Arabia and the trinitarian creed of western Christianity. Sura 112 of the Koran, for example, declares: "Say: He is God alone: God the eternal! He begetteth not, and He is not begotten; and there is none like unto Him."[4] More explicitly, Sura 9 chastises Christians in the following terms: ". . . the Christians say, 'The Messiah is a son of God.' Such the sayings in their mouths! They resemble the saying of the Infidels of old! God do battle with them! How are they misguided! They take their teachers, and their monks, and the Messiah, son of Mary, for Lords beside God, though bidden to worship one God only. There is no God but He! Far from His glory be what they associate with Him!"[5] Despite other, friendly references to Christians in the Koran, it is undoubtedly such pointed rejections of fundamental beliefs which helped give rise to the Christian image of Muhammad as Anti-Christ.

A second element underlying the negative image of Islam in the West inheres in the historical record of the relations between the world of Islam and western Christian Europe. It is a record replete with hostility and conflict. When Muslim Arab warriors first burst forth from the Arabian Peninsula in the seventh century A.D., the lands they conquered in the Fertile Crescent were wrested from the Christian Byzantine Empire. Muslim conquest of Iberia was never accepted by the Spanish Catholics; indeed, a 700-year-long war of attrition followed, culminating in the ejection of the last remnants of the Muslims late in the fifteenth century. The Portuguese voyages of exploration around the continent of Africa were initially motivated at least partly by the desire to carry the Christian crusade against the hated Muslims to their home territory, specifically by establishing an alliance with the fabled Christian ruler Prester John rumored to rule over an extensive kingdom in eastern Africa. Among the first victims of the extension of Portuguese power into the Indian Ocean were Arab seafarers who had played a critical role in the spice trade between farther Asia and Mediterranean Europe. That trade itself had begun as one of the results of the Western Crusades of the Middle Ages, which, it will be recalled, succeeded to the extent of establishing Latin mini-states in the Holy Land.

Ironically, just as the Portuguese were turning the tables on their Muslim antagonists in Iberia and at sea, another Muslim power was overwhelming the last bastion of Eastern Christianity and threatening the heart of Europe from the East. Every Western school child of the first half of the 20th century will recall the date of 1453. That was the year the Byzantine Empire finally gasped its last breath at the hands of the Ottoman Turks, who captured the city of Constantinople in that year. Not only did western history texts incorrectly trace the decline of trade between the Mediterranean and the East to this event, but the memory lingers on in other more visible forms: American politicians seeking election have been heard, even in recent years, to persist in calling the city by its archaic name of Constantinople, rather than Istanbul, its official name since the Turkish conquest over 500 years ago! Moreover, the Turkish conquest of Byzantium was followed in short order by the appearance of a powerful Ottoman army before the city of Vienna, that glittering capital of central European culture and civilization. Small wonder that, in the words of one scholar, Islam was more thoroughly feared and hated throughout Europe than any other political or cultural force prior to the rise of Communism.

This hostility was mutual, though not as intense on the Muslim side. Christians and Jews are portrayed in the Koran as recalcitrant and wrong-headed people who rejected or distorted the word of God as proclaimed by a series of prophets. They are, however, not beyond hope of redemption. So long as they accept Muhammad's message, they are to be accepted as full-fledged believers in Islam. In practice, so long as Jews and Christians (collectively referred to as People of the Book) accepted the supremacy of Islam, they were left in peace to practice their religions as they saw fit. Thus, sizable communities of Jews and Christians survived within the realm of Islam over the years. Jews in particular thrived from time to time (particularly in Muslim Spain between the 7th and 15th centuries A.D.) where Muslim tolerance was especially benevolent. But the Koran also preached continuing conflict and even warfare against those who remained outside the Muslim realm (the realm of War, as opposed to the realm of Peace within).

The ultimate point of Muslim belief, of course, was that inasmuch as Muhammad had brought the final word of God to mankind, the community of faithful believers in the world must ultimately prevail over infidels, liars, and those who have gone astray. Thus, so long as Muslim armies prevailed in conflict with non-Muslim foes, and so long as Muslim communities were free of alien, non-Muslim rule, the affairs of this world could be perceived as in harmony with God's plan for mankind. In terms of the relations between Middle Eastern Muslim communities and Christian Europe, then, so long as the Muslims remained on the offensive and Europe on the defensive, this Muslim world view was confirmed, or at least not seriously contradicted. This was, in fact, the nature of the relations between Europe and the Middle East for virtually all of history up to the eighteenth century, with the exception of the relatively brief and limited interlude of the medieval Crusades, and the slow ebbing of the Muslim tide in Iberia.

With the failure of a second siege of Vienna by Ottoman armies late in the seventeenth century, however, the tide began running ever more strongly against the Muslims. Throughout the eighteenth century, the Ottoman Empire lost territories north and east of the Black Sea to the Russians. At the end of the eighteenth century, the forces of Napoleon landed in Egypt, very near the heart of the Muslim world, bringing Arab Muslims under non-Muslim rule for the first time since the Crusades, and significantly bringing large numbers of Arabs face to face with the powerful political and economic forces of modern Europe for the first time. (Ibrahim Abu Lughod details the manner in which Napoleon tried to propagandize the Egyptian Arabs with the ideals of the French Revolution, bringing along French scholars familiar with the Arabic language, only to discover that there was no Arabic equivalent for the European concept of Parliament).[6] Simultaneously, the British displaced the Muslim rulers of India, the Dutch imposed their rule on Muslim Indonesia, and Russia began extending its sway over the Muslim peoples of Central Asia. By the end of World War I, with the collapse of the independent Ottoman Empire, hardly a single Muslim community remained free of alien non-Muslim domination. The community of the faithful, which believed that it alone was in possession of the true word of God, had been overwhelmed by the superior military, political, and economic power of Christian Europe. Reality had come into sharp conflict with the Muslim world view.

Muslim attempts to come to terms with these distasteful developments continue to this day. In a sense, the revolution in Iran is but the latest example. Elsewhere in this volume, Professor Nasr has dealt with this question in more detail. Suffice it to say here that it is this clash between the Muslim world view and historical reality which explains the tremendous popular response to every successful act of defiance against the West by any Muslim political figure (e.g., Nasser's nationalization of the Suez Canal in 1956). So also with the apparent popularity of overt rejections of Western modes and artifacts (e.g., movie films, free public mingling of the sexes). Use of the oil weapon and the apparent success of Arab arms in the 1973 Arab-Israeli war are further highly significant examples.

In fact, the entire Arab-Israeli dispute should be understood in the context we have just described. Israel is, in fact, a particularly painful thorn in the side of Arab Muslims. This is so for two reasons: first, because it is a non-Muslim entity physically located near the heart of both the Arab and the Muslim world, and includes within it (at least since 1967) one of the holy shrines of Islam (the Dome of the Rock of Jerusalem); and second, because it is a Jewish entity, the first time that Muslims have been bested in battle and even come under the domination of that other People of the Book.

Misconception III: Israel is an alien Western implantation in the midst of the Muslim Middle East; it is the handmaiden of Western imperialism.

This misconception stems largely from opponents of Israel and has led to a variety of other misconceptions and distortions, some of them of extreme form. Underlying these notions is a basic denial of the legitimacy of statehood as a form of political expression for the Jewish people. Zionism and its success in establishing the State of Israel is, in this view, squarely blamed on the Western world. It is argued that Palestinian Arabs in essence have been made to pay the price for the guilty conscience of the West resulting from the Nazi holocaust of World War II. Moreover, the Zionist founders of Israel are labeled as western colonialists whose status is as illegitimate as that of European colons in Algeria or white settlers in southern Africa. In its extreme form, this perspective led to the U. N. resolution labeling Zionism as a form of racism.

In fact, Zionism emerged long before the Nazi holocaust. As a poltical movement, it was clearly a response to the development of romantic nationalist movements in Western Europe during the nineteenth century. Pogroms in Russia late in the nineteenth century underlined the basic insecurity of the extensive Jewish communities concentrated in eastern Europe, while the Dreyfus affair in France jolted such emancipated Jews as Theodor Herzl out of the complacent expectation that the future of western Jewry lay in assimilation. The European holocaust of the 1930's and 1940's exceeded even the most pessimistic assumptions of Zionists, but it emphatically reinforced their basic arguments: Jews could not expect to attain safety as a community except in a society, and preferably a state, of their own.

There is no question that Zionism was immensely strengthened by the support of Great Britain, specifically as expressed in the Balfour Declaration of 1917. Nor can it be doubted that at least part of the British motivation consisted of strategic considerations based on imperialist interests (specifically, a desire to attain a territorial buffer to the east of the Suez Canal). Moreover, the notion of a friendly population ensconced in a strategic area was a further attraction for the British. On the other hand, so long as the British had ultimate control, the nature of the inhabitants of the territory was necessarily a secondary concern for them. Thus, the British responded to Arab opposition to Zionism by increasingly placing obstacles in the way of the entrenchment and expansion of the burgeoning Jewish community in the mandated territory of Palestine. The culmination came with British refusal to admit refugees fleeing the Nazi holocaust to Palestine. Clearly, by the 1930's, the British had concluded that the interests of the Empire would best be served by a Palestinian Arab state with the Zionists relegated to the status of a minority community. Thus, in the aftermath of World War II, far from being brought into existence with the help of British imperialism, the state of Israel emerged in the wake of organized Jewish violence *against* British rule.

Nor is it accurate to label Zionism as a form of racism. Unlike colonialist settlers, Zionists did not migrate to Palestine to seek personal fortunes through exploitation of indigenous populations or natural resources. On the contrary, they were determined to establish a viable community of their own, specifically by working the soil with their own hands, explicitly rejecting the option of hiring others to work for them. While they may have been insensitive to the needs and demands of the existing Arab community, that is quite another matter. So also, the question of whether the Zionist program was reconcilable with the political interests of the Palestinian Arab community is debatable. But if in fact the goals and ambitions of the two communities were or are incompatible, this does not mean that one or the other is racist.

It should also be noted that the common image of Israel as a society made up exclusively of Jewish emigrants from Europe is a misperception. In fact, over half the Jewish population of the state is of non-European origin, and the bulk of these people migrated from nearby Arab countries. Nor do these people accept another common notion: that Jews in Arab countries fared well prior to the emergence of the state of Israel. Indeed, like their European counterparts, they moved en masse to Israel precisely to escape what they perceived to be oppression in the lands of their birth. Albert Memmi, a Tunisian Jew by birth, though strongly supportive of national liberation movements among colonized peoples, has written bitterly of the living conditions of Jews in the slums of North Africa, of the choices available to them under both French colonization and national liberation, and, in turn, of the relative indifference of French and other Western communities to their fate. Accordingly, he defines Zionism and migration to Israel as a legitimate — though not inevitable — option:[7]

> ... Whereas for the vast majority of Moslems there was only one, obvious solution, the liberation and reconstruction of themselves, it was impossible to rally all colonized Jews to one, single undertaking. Although they wanted to see an end to colonization, they hesitated as to what aftermath they wanted.... Three ... solutions ... were adopted to an equal extent, because they corresponded to three equally strong requirements: keeping a European option open ...; continuing to associate one's destiny with the country of one's birth, with which one is actually in closest harmony (if the experiment had been feasible, it would certainly have been legitimate); and re-creating a more complete Jewish existence by returning to the sources and conquering the national dimension, which, for the

Jews of the Maghreb, was a way of liquidating their own colonial oppression. When all is said and done, I do not believe that political morals can condemn any given attitude. No one solution could be found to an essentially ambiguous condition. It is clear, however, that the one which would run exactly parallel to the self-retrieval of the colonized Moslems, namely, the genuine and specific rebirth of the Maghreb Jews, would consist of their national reconstruction and affirmation; in other words, the State of Israel.

Misconception IV: Israeli and Jewish interests control U. S. foreign policy on the Middle East and interfere with the rational pursuit of vital U. S. interests in the Arab world.

At its worst, this misconception suggests that Israel is in fact an embarrassment to the United States which prevents the active pursuit and consolidation of true American interests in the region. The existence of a powerful pro-Israeli lobby in the United States, allegedly based on Jewish money and Jewish votes, especially in the urban-industrial states which loom large in Presidential elections, is held responsible for this state of affairs.

It is true that Israel has enjoyed an unusually favorable image in American public opinion. The reasons are not far to seek, nor are they as sinister as this misconception would lead one to believe. One may begin from the link between Jews and the prophecies of the Old Testament, a link that is especially vivid with regard to the Holy Land, a link which is particularly significant in that part of American culture that is derived from the tradition of the Puritans. One may cite, further, the character of Israel's genuinely democratic political system, an all too rare phenomenon even in the world that emerged from the Second World War. One may note traditional American sympathy for peoples and societies burdened by persecution and oppression and seeking national liberation and independence. The fact that Israel was created out of a widely diverse group of immigrants fleeing unfriendly countries and that Israeli society embodied a bold pioneering spirit not unlike another aspect of the American tradition undoubtedly contributes further to the favorable image. Finally, the Nazi holocaust of World War II undeniably evoked basic sympathy among Americans.[8] Clearly, the generally favorable American image of Israel resulting from these factors has provided opportunities for organized Jewish groups to play on a basically sympathetic public opinion and to bring pressure to bear on policy makers. But this is a far cry from sinister allegations of secret influence and control.

In the first place, the existence of basic public sympathy and well organized interest groups in the United States has not dissuaded the American government from pursuing policies which are not only pro-Arab, but even clearly inimical to Israeli interests. Numerous examples may be cited. During the six months between the adoption of the U. N. partition resolution in November 1947 and the declaration of Israeli independence in May 1948, for instance, the U. S. government systematically sought to weaken if not nullify the impact of the resolution. Nor did the Eisenhower Administration shrink from voting for a U. N. resolution condemning Israel during the 1956 war even in the face of the impending Presidential election. In the tense weeks preceding the 1967 war, the U. S. government seemed to vacillate in the face of what appeared to Israel as a mortal threat from Egyptian troops in Sinai and Nasser's declared blockade of the Gulf of Aqaba, a body of water which Washington had explicitly recognized as international. And in October 1973, the U. S. made it clear, both explicitly and implicitly, that it would not tolerate a decisive Israeli military victory west of Suez, where Israeli forces were poised to the rear of an entire Egyptian army. In short, pro-Israeli pressure groups in the U. S. do play a role (not unlike the role of pro-Irish, pro-Greek, pro-Italian, pro-Polish, and other groups), but within the context of American policy-makers' perceptions of U.S. interests.[9]

Secondly, it is manifestly absurd to assume that America's problems in the Middle East would disappear if Israel did not exist. To cite but one example, it has been suggested that the arms deal between Egypt and the Soviet Union in 1955 was triggered by a massive Israeli raid on the Gaza strip. In fact, this dramatic move on the part of Nasser was most likely undertaken in response to heavy-handed attempts by the Eisenhower Administration to extend the cold war into the Arab world, specifically by drawing Iraq into the Western alliance system by means of the Baghdad Pact. Such a decisive bolstering of a conservative Arab regime ruling a country traditionally a rival to Egypt even under the best of circumstances was a challenge Nasser could not afford to overlook. And this had nothing whatsoever to do with Israel. Indeed, quite the reverse, it was the introduction of Soviet arms into the Middle East which emphasized the utility of Israeli arms for the U. S.; in the face of Israeli military power, anti-American leaders such as Nasser clearly were less free to pursue policies of aggrandizement at the expense of more conservative Arab regimes. This realization undoubtedly contributed to the growing collaboration between the American and Israeli governments. That collaboration in turn provided the motive for Nasser's successor to abandon the Soviet connection and seek to substitute an American connection for it, simultaneously creating a favorable context both for renewed U. S. influence in the Middle East and for a possible long-term Arab-Israeli peace settlement. In short, while Israel's presence in the midst of the Arab world clearly has been an important factor, its absence would not have automatically either enhanced American interests nor guaranteed greater stability among the Arabs.

Misconception V: A. Israelis are intransigent and bent on expansion at the expense of the Arabs; B. Arabs are bent on sweeping Israel into the sea.

In a remarkable book published in the mid-1970's, we find the transcript of a dialogue between a prominent Israeli journalist and writer, Amos Elon, and a young Egyptian scholar, the daughter of a diplomat and wife of a high echelon official, Sana Hassan. Groping for a basis of common understanding in the wake of the October 1973 war, before the dramatic Sadat visit to Jerusalem in 1977, the protagonists give expression to the mutually antagonistic stereotypes which prevail among Arabs and Israelis. Speaking for the Israeli perspective, Amos Elon charges:[10]

> In the past twenty years a vast literature of downright racism calling for genocide has been published in Egypt and Lebanon, often by government-owned publishing houses. You probably know that this racism has penetrated even school textbooks for Arab children. When the Israeli army entered the Gaza Strip in 1967, they found dozens of such textbooks issued by the Egyptian Ministry of Education. In tone and content, even in their graphic illustration, these textbooks resembled the worst Nazi propaganda during World War II. (p. 17)

From the other side of the fence, Sana Hassan confides:

> When I grew up in Cairo in the fifties and sixties, the word "Zionist" was a dirty word which was muttered under one's breath, like "sweat" or "sex" in a

Victorian household. And "Israel" wasn't a word at all. We heard only of "occupied Palestine." We referred to your government as the "gangster regime of Tel Aviv." (p. 97)

Or again, Elon speaks of Israeli stereotypes of Arabs:

> In Israel we often go from one extreme to another. If we don't view you as monstrous Nazi devils, we tend to look at you as subhuman or irrelevant. The Hebrew colloquialism for a shoddy, sloppy job is *avodah aravit* — "Arab work." When you want to tell a man, "Don't be a fool," or "Don't be devious," you tell him, "*al tehive aravi*" — "Don't be an Arab." (p. 10)

In a more lurid vein:

> I grew up with stories of horrible mutilations of the sexual organs of Jews in remote settlements entrapped by Arab rioters. Of decapitated corpses, bandied around by mobs running amuck in the streets. (p. 101)

In short, the two counterpart misconceptions cited above represent fearful stereotypes held by each of the antagonists regarding its opposite. Both ignore a high degree of political heterogeneity in the opposing camp, ranging from extreme doves to aggressive hawks on the Israeli side, and from radical and fiery ideologues to pragmatic realists on the Arab side. The dramatic breakthrough of the Sadat visit to Jerusalem in November of 1977, and the subsequent painful negotiation of a formal peace treaty between Egypt and Israel give ground for hope that perhaps the worst is behind us. Such hope must be tempered by the realization that the parties to the conflict have hardly even begun negotiating on the most difficult and critical issues of all: the political future of the West Bank, the Gaza Strip, and Jerusalem.

Perhaps the final word should be that of an anonymous Middle Eastern humorist, though hopefully he will not turn out to be prophetic:

> A scorpion wanted to cross a river and asked the frog to ferry him across. "How can I?" said the frog. "You'll sting me and I'll die." "Nonsense," said the scorpion, "If you die, we both drown." On the strength of this convincing argument the frog started

across the river with the scorpion on his back. Suddenly, the scorpion stung the frog. Its dying words were: "Why — why did you do it? Now we both die." "My dear," said the scorpion, drowning, "This is the Middle East . . ."[11]

Footnotes

1. *New Outlook*, XXIII, 5 July/Aug. 1979, p. 11.

2. *The Meaning of the Glorious Koran.* New York: Mentor Books, 1953.

3. H. A. R. Gibb, *Mohammedanism.* 2nd edition. New York: Oxford University Press, 1962, pp. 59-60.

4. *The Koran.* Translated by J. M. Rodwell. London: J. M. Dent and Sons, 1909. p. 29.

5. *Ibid.*, p. 474.

6. Ibrahim Abu Lughod, *Arab Rediscovery of Europe.* Princeton: Princeton University Press, 1963.

7. Albert Memmi, *Jews and Arabs.* Chicago: J. Philip O'Hara, 1975. p. 45.

8. For a summary of these factors in the general context of American-Israeli relations see Nadav Safran, *Israel, The Embattled Ally.* Cambridge, Mass.:Harvard University Press, 1978. pp. 571-3.

9. For the parameters of American foreign policy-making system with particular application to the Arab-Israeli dispute during the years from 1967 to 1976 see W. B. Quandt, *Decade of Decisions.* Berkeley: University of California Press, 1977. Chapter 1.

10. Amos Elon and Sana Hassan, *Between Enemies*. New York: Random House, 1974. The passages that follow are taken from the above book. Page numbers as indicated.

11. *Ibid.*, p. 135.

IX

THE ARABIAN PENINSULA AND THE ISLAMIC "REVIVAL"

Manfred W. Wenner

As the birthplace of Muslim religion the Arabian Peninsula holds a central position in Islamic history and culture. In the peninsula itself Saudi Arabia and its ruling family play a central role as hosts and protectors of Islam's holiest shrines and the pilgrims who flock to them every day of the year. In addition, Arabia has also been the springboard of various Muslim reform/revival movements in the past. Most recently, the takeover of the Grand Mosque of Mecca by a fervent group brought world attention to the peninsula. In view of all these it must be asked whether Arabia plays a special role in the current militancy in the Islamic world. Professor Wenner addresses this question.

Manfred W. Wenner, born in Switzerland and educated in Europe, Lebanon and the United States, has held a variety of positions — foreign policy analyst of the U.S. Congress, journalist and professor at several universities. Currently serving in the Department of Political Science at Northern Illinois University, Wenner is the author of **Modern Yemen, 1918-66** and several other monographs and articles on Middle Eastern subjects and comparative politics.

In a paper which seeks to treat a subject of this sort, it is necessary to begin by defining what one means by "revival" as applied to the practice of Islam in the Middle East in general, and in the Arabian Peninsula in particular. This is especially important when one recalls the special place which the Saudi state has claimed for itself within the Islamic world, and the previous politico-religious history of that state.

There are at least two possible meanings for "revival" in the Arabian context. One is to refer to an increase in the power, prosperity, and international respect paid to the Muslim states in general (and perhaps Saudi Arabia in particular). If this is what is meant we must accept that such a "revival" took place in all those states which are petroleum exporters, but that this is not necessarily the case for those that are not (compare Kuwait with North Yemen, for example). Alternatively, "revival" can also mean an intensification of the role of Islam in public life and in the hearts of men. In this sense also a "revival" occured in at least some states of the peninsula, notably in Saudi Arabia.

The problem with the word "revival" is that in the English language it carries the connotation that what one is referring to is/was either moribund or already dead. This is not the case with Islam in general, and certainly not in the Arabian Peninsula. I doubt that any writer in the last century, writing about the peninsula, could have written that Islam was moribund or in retreat. Indeed, until the takeover of South Yemen by the current Marxist regime, most writers would have agreed that Islam was, if anything, on the ascent. And, even there, Islam is recognized and its pervasive role accepted.

It must be understood, therefore, that when we use the term "revival," in the Arabian context we are not referring to any basic change in the status of Islam there but to a change in the attitudes and modes of expression used by the intellectual, economic, and political elites of the countries in question. It is, in a word, now more fashionable to use Muslim terms, expressions, and referents in daily speech. It can also be said, I believe, that there has been little, if any, change in the orientation of the mass of the population — the devout masses, if you will. What changes that came about have taken place among the technocratic elite, the economic policy makers, the political uppercrust, some parts of the social elite, and among specific Islamic sect members.

ISLAM IN THE ARABIAN PENINSULA

Surprising though it may seem in view of the origins of the Islamic faith, and the Wahhābī movement, the Arabian Peninsula remains host to an amazingly numerous variety of Islamic schools of thought. Although Arabia is the original home of Islam and as such put its stamp on the new faith — many of the social ideas of seventh century Arabia make up an important element of the thought, principles and value system of Islam — this does not mean that the whole of the peninsula immediately accepted the new faith — either then or now. Furthermore, it does not mean that those areas which accepted the faith accepted the same version of the faith. In fact, if one considers the relatively small population of the peninsula and its immense territory, the variety of Islamic beliefs and practices is surprisingly large. There are many areas of the peninsula where the adherence to Islamic principles is superficial at best, while in others it is close to non-existent.

It is difficult to be precise concerning many characteristics of the population of Arabia. Few countries have undertaken population censuses which are reliable. Saudi Arabia has never had a modern census; while the far smaller states of Bahrain and (North) Yemen have had accurate censuses which even permit reliable demographic analyses, there is nevertheless no data whatsoever on the relative numbers and strength of religious groupings. The subject of one's religious beliefs in Arabia is extremely sensitive — for personal as well as political reasons.

The personal aspect is due to the fact that some Shi'a Muslims practice *taqiyya*, or dissimulation, i.e., claiming to belong to one faith to protect oneself against real or imagined discrimination due to one's real faith. Furthermore, precise knowledge concerning relative numbers of adherents to the differing schools of Islamic law could have very real political consequences; while it may be an exaggeration to suggest that bitter disputes over relative sectarian strength of the kind which Lebanon experienced could erupt in Arabia, there is little doubt that such relative strength has played a role in Yemeni politics since 1962, and in the Eastern Province of Saudi Arabia in 1979.

With these caveats in mind, it is still possible to make some general statements concerning religious preferences in the Arabian Peninsula, i.e., which sect or school of law predominates where, and what effect this has had in the social, economic and political arenas.

Sunni Islam in Arabia

Sunni or "orthodox" Islam has developed four schools of legal thought; basically the four schools differ on the relative weight to be given to ways of coping with new situations, and in their interpretation of some elements of the basics of all Islamic thought, i.e., the Quran, the life of Muhammad, etc. The four schools grew up in the second and third centuries after Muhammad, and each Muslim at least in theory adheres to the principles and interpretations of one of the four. Each predominates in certain areas, usually for reasons of chance rather than any systematic program of expansion by the followers of a particular school. Yet, one must immediately add that where which school predominates may, nevertheless, have an important impact upon the socio-political characteristics of the area. The four schools are:

1. Maliki: Today predominant in north and west Africa as well as Upper Egypt, it is found on the Arabian Peninsula primarily in the Gulf state of Kuwait. Nevertheless, some judges trained in Maliki law practice in the Eastern Province of Saudi Arabia, where they act as judges for the Shi'a population of this region. It is precisely this discrepancy which has led to some of the disputes which have occured in the Eastern Province recently.

2. Hanafi: The Hanafi school was adopted and propagated by the Ottoman Empire during its heyday. As a result, it still is influential in those areas where the Empire was dominant for long periods. On the peninsula, this essentially restricts its influence to the Hijaz in the western part of the Saudi Arabian state, and in some limited areas of the north and east.

3. Shafi'i: Although outside the peninsula it is found only in Lower Egypt, its influences in southwestern Arabia is quite significant. It is dominant in the southern and lowland areas of North Yemen, as well as throughout South Yemen. In North Yemen, its political role is very great, since the Shafi'i portion of the population has historically been associated with movements for the reform of the traditional economic and social structure of Yemen.

4. Hanbali: By all odds the most important school of Islamic law in the peninsula today is the Hanbali, which is also considered the most conservative. Founded considerably later than the other three (9th century AD), it is opposed to the use of reasoning by logic or analogy, and restricts its sources to the Quran and the Sunna. Although influential for a while in Iraq (the birthplace of its founder), it was not until the 18th century that it became really powerful.

In the mid-18th century, in central Arabia, one Muhammad ibn Abd al-Wahhāb was born into a family of jurists. Exposed to various ideological strains as part of his legal education, he opted for what we might today call a "strict constructionist" view: he opposed the various innovations and changes which had taken place over the centuries since Muhammad's death, and argued vehemently for a return to the practice of Islam as it had been around Muhammad's time.

Unable to obtain a following for his ideas among his family, or for that matter in his home town, he found a friend, a protector, and an ally in Muhammad al-Sa'ud, the chief of Dariyah, a small town in central Arabia. The alliance between religious prophet and "secular" leader proved propitious: together they began a religious campaign to purify Islam and conquer Arabia. And, in order to solidify the relationship, the two families began to intermarry. Together, they managed to alter the course of history as well as the Islamic faith — at least in the Arabian Peninsula.

After about 150 years, towards the latter part of which period the fortunes of the two families tended to wane as they came in conflict with the territorial interests of the Ottoman Empire, the scion of the House of Sa'ud began to re-establish the family's hegemony: Abd al-Aziz al-Sa'ud, usually known as Ibn Sa'ud, began in the early years of the 20th century a campaign which was to lead to the creation of the modern state of Saudi Arabia, in 1932. In establishing the Saudi state, Ibn Sa'ud brought together peoples with a variety of religious, political and economic interests; and territories with a variety of geographical features. Though it may be argued that today there is a substantial interest among these varied peoples and territories for retaining their mutual affiliation, it must also be said that this feeling is not necessarily universal.

The Eastern Province, which contains the largest petroleum deposits known today, clearly dominates the domestic scene economically. On the other hand, the Najd, in which the administrative capital (Riyadh) is located, is the ancestral home of both the Saudi family as well as the family of the Shaykh (Abd al-Wahhāb). It therefore dominates the administrative arena. Further west, the old Hijaz (like the Najd, now subdivided into newer districts) contains the two holy cities of Mecca and Madina. As a result, it dominates the field of religious affairs, a factor which is, as we have seen, of immense importance to the Saudi state. Last but not necessarily least of the traditional sections is Asir. Though neither rich in economic, religious, or administrative terms, it is by all odds agriculturally the most important part of the kingdom. Without Asir, the state lacks all but the most rudimentary of agricultural resources (a few oases in the east). But, perhaps of even greater significance is the fact that Asir provides an important buffer area against the peoples of the southwestern corner of the peninsula — more numerous, more aggressive, more secular, and above all, more poor than the Saudis.

Shi'a Islam in Arabia

Although united on a few basic principles, the Shi'a Muslims of the world are themselves divided into a number of different, sometimes mutually antagonistic, groups.

Foremost among the distinctions between the Sunni and Shi'a is the status of Ali, Prophet Muhammad's son-in-law and cousin (he married the Prophet's favorite daughter Fatima). After Muhammad's death in 632 AD, there arose the problem of a new head of the Islamic community. Although some favored Ali from the very outset (the Shi'at Ali, or Party of Ali), they eventually accepted the community's choice, Muhammad's father-in-law. The first four of these successors, called caliphs (from the Arabic *khalifah*) were accepted by the entire community; Ali, who acceded in 656, was the last of this group. His accession, however, was the result of the premature death of his predecessor, whose murder was attributed to Ali's followers. Unhappiness over this caliph's murder created a climate of dissent in which one of his relatives proclaimed himself caliph in opposition to Ali. Thus started the first great schism in the Muslim community — between the Sunnis who accepted his claim, and the Shi'a, who argued that the descendants of Ali had a pre-emptive right to the office.

Although this split was originally a genealogical one, it rapidly developed theological and metaphysical bases as well. Today, it may be legitimately argued that these latter distinctions are far more important than the original and more limited one. The claim of the Shi'a to special position for the descendants of Ali, through his two sons Hasan and Husayn (who also became martyrs to the cause), involved mystical doctrines which imputed hidden, divinely inspired powers to Ali's descendants as a result of his marriage to Fatima. However, though this belief is central to most Shi'a, this does not mean that there is agreement on *which* descendants of Ali and Fatima possess this mystical and divine charisma. As a result, the Shi'a, like the Sunni, are divided into a number of different sects. Taken in order, they are:

1. The Zaydis: Often known as the "Fivers," the Zaydis accept the first five imams, i.e., Ali, Hasan, Husayn, ali Zayn al-Abidin, and then Zayd, who was killed at Kufa (Iraq) in the year 740. Since Zayd died fighting for specific principles (which are considered important by the Zaydis), and his place and time of death are known and accepted, the Zaydi position on many matters of faith and practice are not far removed from those accepted by the Sunni. In fact, the similarities are

so great that the Zaydis are often known as the "fifth school" of Sunni Islam. In their view, for example, the descendants of Ali have their special claim as a result of Ali's special qualities — of leadership, intelligence, and ability — and not (at least solely) as a result of the blood relationship to Muhammad. Therefore, the Zaydis reject many of the beliefs and practices of other Shi'a.

2. The Ismailis: Known as the "Seveners," their last recognized imam is Isma'il, who died around 760 under strange circumstances; he is expected to reappear at some unknown time in the future as the saviour of the (Muslim) world. In the interim, the leadership of the major part of the Ismailis has (hereditarily) devolved to the Aga Khan.

3. The Ja'afaris: Known as the "Twelvers," their last legitimate imam is Muhammad al-Muntazar, who disappeared under mysterious circumstances around 878; he is expected by the Ja'afaris to return as the savior. There is no hereditary family which has been recognized as the interim leaders of the community.

For the purpose of this paper, and any discussion of the Islamic "revival" in Arabia, what is of greater importance is the location of these groupings:

a. The Zaydis: The Zaydis are found only in the central and northern uplands of North Yemen; some one thousand years ago, they established themselves there and, despite some efforts to expand their political influence, they have not been able to effectively spread outside the mountains of Asir and Yemen. Because of their political role in Yemen, a brief analysis of their current status is in order.

Zaydi doctrine *explicitly* requires a living imam; it does not permit "hidden imams" (Mahdis), and in fact the imam must be politically as well as religiously active in order for him to be accepted by the adherents of Zaydi doctrine. It is for this reason that the Zaydis present a notable contrast to developments elsewhere in the peninsula and the Muslim world. This is the situation: the last unopposed Islam of Yemen, Ahmad, died in 1962; his son was accepted as successor but shortly thereafter was deposed from his secular position (King of Yemen) upon which he fled into the northern mountains to lead a counter-revolution. But he did not succeed. In ill-health, and not particularly effective or popular, he has now disappeared from public view to all intents and purposes. He is *not* in Yemen, though Zaydi doctrine demands it; and he is *not* recognized by the majority of Zaydis, though that is required. No other candidate has stepped forward to lay claim to the imamate, either. In essence, then, we have here a Muslim community which has for more than a thousand years required a living, active imam which has lost such in the past two decades, and, most important of all, which has made *no effort to reinstitute the imamate, or see to it that the imamate is in some way retained.* Yemen seems to be, then, an example of a modern Muslim community which is, if anything, retreating from its adherence to its traditions.

To make this point, however, is not to say that there is no interest in Islam among the Zaydis, nor that the Zaydis are not motivated at least to some degree by the same concerns as other Muslims. Yemen was governed by Zaydi imams for far too long for that to be the case (though among the northern tribes of Yemen Islam has always sat very lightly upon even older tribal traditions of government and civil and criminal codes). It does seem clear, though, that the zeal which has characterized other groups is notably lacking in Yemen — among both Zaydi and Shafi'i alike (much to the distress of the Saudis, as will be shown below).

b. The Isma'ilis: Except for small splinter groups as in Yemen, the great majority of Isma'ilis are found either in Iran or further east. While it may be that there are remnants of the tribes which were Isma'ili more than two centuries ago (and related to the Isma'ili groups in Yemen, of which there used to be far more than today), it seems fair to report that the Isma'ilis are not a significant factor in Islamic affairs in Arabia today.

c. The Ja'afirs: Unquestionably, the most important Shi'a group in Arabia today are the Ja'afari's or the "Twelvers". And, it is among the Ja'afaris that the major movement has developed in the past few years; today this is associated in the popular mind with Iran and the role of Ayatullah Ruhollah Khomeini.

In the peninsula, the numbers and influence of the Shi'a is open to debate; this is basically because the Saudi government has for so long denied their existence and little or no interest in them has been shown by Western scholars. They seemed to be irrelevant; so it was that when the Khomeini revolution of Iran touched off convulsions among the Ja'afaris in Arabia, we were largely uninformed about their numbers, their location, their grievances, their influence, their economic position, or their political goals.

As already indicated, statistics in Saudi Arabia are unreliable; it is certain, however, that a great number of the Ja'afaris are in the Eastern Province, which has an estimated population of about 900,000, of which it is estimated that about one-third are Shi'a. Qatif, one of the Province's major agricultural oases, with an estimated population of near 50,000, is widely believed to be the major center of the Shi'a population. In support of this, one can cite the large-scale riots which shook the city in late 1979, leaving as many as one hundred dead, with additional hundreds injured, and further hundreds arrested by the Saudis.

THE ISLAMIC REVIVAL IN SAUDI ARABIA

Since the so-called Islamic "revival" in the peninsula has had its greatest impact in Saudi Arabia while passing most if not all of the other states by, and in view of the American interest and concern with the affairs of that country because of its petroleum deposits and strategic location, the remainder of this paper will concentrate upon developments concerning that country.

For an understanding of the importance of Islam to Saudi Arabia, one should recall a few things: (1) the Islamic faith had its origins in Mecca and Madina; (2) Mecca and Madina are two of the most holy places in Islam, and the Islamic rite of pilgrimage, which is one of the cornerstones of the faith, urges at least one trip to these cities during a Muslim's lifetime; and, (3) the strong association between the Saudi family/government and the Wahhābī movement. These factors have made Islam the central fact of life to most Saudis. On the other side, being the guardians of the holy places of Islam, the Saudis enjoy a special status within the world of Islam. Proportionate to their status, more is expected also of the Saudi government and its ruling family than of others, and when these expectations are not fulfilled, there is a greater sense betrayal than might otherwise be. Recent events would seem to bear this out. There appears to be a feeling among significant elements within the Kingdom to the effect that the ruling family has wavered in its support and implementation of Wahhābī doctrines, and that many members of the elite classes are hypocritical in their public support of these doctrines (in contrast to their private betrayal).

Although the Wahhābī reform movement is central to an understanding of the role of Islam in Saudi Arabia today, one must not forget a number of other movements which have existed for the same purpose — elsewhere as well as in Arabia itself. Foremost among these is, of course, the Muslim Brotherhood (or Muslim Brethren). Founded in Egypt in the late 1920's by Hasan al-Banna, its aims and general inclinations are in many respects very different from those of the Wahhābīs [e.g. a greater concern with social justice, active participation in commercial ventures, political organization along Western lines ("cell-type" organizational structure), and the like]. Although the Brotherhood became by far the most well-organized, largest, and, best-known of these Islamic organizations, it did not always enjoy the blessing of authorities at home; in fact, from time to time many of its members were forced into exile. Such members nearly always saw Saudi Arabia as a place of refuge, and many thus moved to the Hijaz.

On the other hand, one should also add that the Brotherhood was not, and is not, a monolithic entity; it suffered doctrinal divisions along a number of lines, with some members considerably more militant and some others considerably more secular in their outlook than others. In their basic motivation they in a general way follow the pattern of many of the Islamic movements which have surfaced in the Muslim world during the past two centuries, most of which, if not all, arose to meet the challenge of the multifaceted and overpowering impact of the West in the political, economic, social, and most especially religious life of the Islamic peoples. While in some areas these movements focused on military action, most of those which had long-term impact interested themselves in such things as the revitalization of the Muslim orders (e.g. the Naqshbandi), and the formation of a variety of "revitalization" movements in other areas (e.g. the Sanussi Brotherhood in North Africa, the Ahmadiyya movement in India, etc.).

With the spread of secular education, it may be suggested that secular efforts became more prominent and widespread, i.e., the formation of organizations with secular goals. This was especially true during the period of Western dominance in Islamic countries. It seems that the Western educated Muslim elite chose Western-based methods to deal with the West. But as the Western political (though not necessarily economic) presence waned, and some of the older traditions resurfaced, older methods for dealing with the West re-appeared. Clearly, the most logical, the most widespread, the most easily accepted, and the most easily understood of such organizations received their inspiration from Islamic traditions. Regardless of the methods they use, Western or traditional Islamic, some of these organizations focus on political change while others concentrate on religious renewal.

Political Organizations

In the case of Saudi Arabia it is only since the 1960's that any of these movements obtained any significant following, although even before the 1960's some clandestine movements operated there. It may seem odd, but in some ways it was the Yemeni Revolution of 1962 which materially changed much of Saudi politics, including the individuals and groups seeking to effect change; this was because the Yemeni revolution was the first successful overturning of a traditional regime by individuals committed to republican and modernizing ideas. And, when Saudi Arabia supported the traditional regime in its efforts to regain power, Yemen's leader (Abdullah al-Sallal) announced the formation of the first of many organizations dedicated to change in the *whole* peninsula — the "Republic of the Arabian Peninsula" movement. This movement was short-lived, however.

Most of its successor organizations were similarly short-lived and no detailed coverage of them seems necessary here. There are, on the other hand, many organizations which have been founded in the more recent past which seek to bring about extensive political, economic and social change, along Western lines. Parallel to them there arose also organizations with their chief focus on the re-establishment of Islamic regimes in the peninsula (and elsewhere). Both these groups of organizations seek revolutionary change — the former according to Western principles and the latter according to Islamic principles.

The most well-known among the latter (though this does not imply widespread support or popularity) are: (1) the Federation of the Peoples of the Arabian Peninsula; (2) the Saudi Arabian National Liberation Front, which is affiliated with (3) the Committee for the Defense of the Rights of the Saudi People; (4) the Peoples Democratic Party (a fusion of former Baathists and Nasirites); (5) the Popular Front for the Liberation of the Arabian Peninsula; (6) the Popular Democratic Front in Saudi Arabia, as well as a number of regional liberation fronts for such areas as Asir and the Najd.

The basis of support of all these groups was an unstable and often shifting "alliance" between many of the foreigners working in Saudi Arabia (e.g. Egyptians, Sudanese, Yemenis, Palestinians, etc.) and those commercial and intellectual elements in the country which saw the Saudi regime as "anachronistic" and utterly tied to "imperialist" powers, as well as a few external elements sympathetic to these generally leftist perceptions. As far as is known, none of these groups ever obtained a sufficiently large following — domestically or externally — to seriously erode the bases of the Saudi state, family, or government.

Religious Organizations

The "new" element in the history of opposition to the Saudi regime is opposition based upon religious principles. Insofar as the government of Saudi Arabia is concerned, as well as the whole world is concerned, the watershed was the attack on the Ka'aba in Mecca — the holiest shrine in the Islamic world.

The date of the seizure of the Grand Mosque in Mecca is a clue to the nature of the movement: it was 1 Muharram 1400 (20 November 1979); in other words, it was the first day of a new century in the Muslim calendar. In Islam, no less than Christendom, the beginning of a century marks a turning point which has often been used by religious reformers to mark the beginning of the end. Though this writer believes that the definitive account of this incident remains to be written at some point in the future, there are sufficient independent accounts to reconstruct at least a blurred picture of who participated and for what reason.

The leadership was in the hands of two individuals, Juhayman al-Utaybi, (whose name indicates his tribal affiliation, the Utaybah), and Muhammad al-Qahtani, who apparently stems from the Jizan region. Both were former students of Islamic law and theology, and appear to have believed, and convinced others to similarly believe, that the Mahdi had arrived, and that the Saudi government was both lax and immoral in its inability and/or unwillingness to properly promote the faith. It is, however, interesting to note that the two tribes to which the leaders belonged have participated in rebellions against the Saudi clan and its leadership, most notably the Utaybah in the early 1930's. The point, of course, is that it is in the interest of the Saudi government to promote accounts which attribute religious fanaticism as the motive for the attack, rather than political grievances against the royal family and its activities in the Kingdom. In the case of the former motive, the government can suggest that its association with the Wahhābī movement guarantees that it will honor and defend the faith at all costs (supported, of course, by the *ulamā* — the religious scholars).

The latter motive is far more difficult for the government either to accept or deal with: it implies a level of political repression and unwillingness to accept the participation of others in important decision-making which the Saudi royal family would find both extremely distasteful as well as dangerous to its continued dominance of the state and the sources of its economic strength (oil).

All this is not to indicate that the writer believes that the sole motive for the attack on the Grand Mosque was political; it is, rather to suggest that just because the successful Khomeini Revolution in Iran had a religious thrust, we should not assume that all other opposition movements to the *status quo* are also Islamic in origin or goals.

In fact the religious motive is more plausible in view of the activities of the Muslim Brotherhood which had markedly increased in the peninsula in recent years — perhaps an indication of the Brotherhood's belief that the Saudi authorities had become lax. For example, in North Yemen, the Brotherhood engaged in the type of violence more traditionally associated with the "Left": the dynamiting of the tombs of local *walis* (saints), and public demands for more stringent controls on behavior patterns believed to be immoral or conducive to a decline in public morality (e.g. the institution of "traditional" Shari'a punishments, prohibition of co-education in institutions of higher education such as the University of Sana, and the like). Even in Saudi Arabia, which has supported these demands in Yemen (much to the dismay and evident unwillingness of the Yemenis), the Brotherhood engaged in protest actions against what it perceived to be laxity in Saudi policy, e.g. removing the power to make arrests from the "religious police," permitting public television broadcasts which showed men and women interacting, etc.

Having treated the above movements in two separate categories — political organizations and religious organizations — I must immediately add that this distinction is arbitrary, to make the situation comprehensible to the Western mind which is used to such distinctions. In actuality these organizations themselves do not make such distinctions, nor does the Islamic society around them. Surely, the agitation of the Shi'a in the Eastern Province, and the Wahhābī unrest among the Utaybah, the Qahtani and others is not exactly the same phenomenon, but there are definitely important points of commonality. The most obvious are dissatisfaction, bitterness, frustration, and a certain amount of disappointment with the quality and morality of the administrative and governmental practices of the Saudi ruling elite. The reports of clandestine Khomeini tapes being spread throughout the Eastern Province is consistent with the clandestine activities of individuals such as Juhayman al-Utaybi, not to mention the more "modern" foes of the current government and elite.

CONCLUSIONS

There is, I believe, little doubt that Islam in the broadest sense of the term has become more militant that it is resisting Western encroachments and erosions of its traditional spheres of influence and power — both in the private and public lives of its followers. But, "militant Islam" does not mean "Islamic revival." The first term implies greater power, greater activity, more forcefulness, and greater awareness of global perspective — all of which are characteristics of much of the Islamic world today (but not all!). The latter term, on the other hand, implies that Islam was in the process of dying, of being superceded, when suddenly it has undergone a rejuvenation for unknown and largely unspecified reasons. Accepting this latter view is, I believe, a mistake.

In the first place, such acceptance would contribute to reducing traditional Islam to an historical curiosity from the point of view of the West. Second, it would contribute to greater hostility, making Islam a dedicated opponent of all social, economic and political policies which are of "Western" origins. And third, perhaps most important, it would cause the West to see Islam as a monolithic and unified phenomenon, which must then be countered by a similarly monolithic response. This last point needs to be emphasized, that there is no monolithic Islam, and that everything that happened in the Islamic world cannot be considered as part of a centrally guided larger movement. Many of these events/movements may have received inspiration from an Islamic source but they are largely responses to local conditions. While the new "militant" Islam is indeed a social, economic and political force in the contemporary world it is important to realize that Islam is also being used as a cover to protect social or political movements which might otherwise be easily detected and suppressed. The Iranian revolution is a case in point.

Similarly, militant Islam serves as a rallying point for people with grievances against their temporal authorities — as is the case of the Shi'a community in the Eastern Province of Saudi Arabia; and it is the cement that holds together ethnically and culturally diverse societies in many parts of Asia and Africa in so far as they offer a common front against the "secularization" and "Westernization" of their peoples. This Islam is also used as a springboard for the activities of groups such as the one that took over the grand Mosque in Mecca. While we may consider all these as aspects of a newly militant Islam we should not ignore the immediate social, political and economic circumstances surrounding them which may have as much or even more to do with these as militancy in Islam.

Selected Bibliography

Articles

Dekmejian, R. Hrair, "The Anatomy of Islamic Revival: Legitimacy Crisis, Ethnic Conflict, and the Search for Islamic Alternatives," *Middle East Journal*, vol. 34 (1980), pages 1-12.

Humphreys, R. Stephen, "Islam and Political Values in Saudi Arabia, Egypt and Syria," *Middle East Journal*, vol. 33 (1979), pages 1-19.

Lewis, Bernard, "The Return of Islam," *Commentary*, vol. 61 (1976), pages 39-49.

Rahman, Fazlur, "Islamic Modernization: Its Scope, Method and Alternatives," *International Journal of Middle East Studies*, vol. 1 (1970), pages 317-333.

Books

Holden, David, *Farewell to Arabia*. New York, 1966.

Hopwood, Derek, ed., *The Arabian Peninsula: Society and Politics*. London, 1972.

Howarth, David, *A Desert King: Ibn Saud and His Arabia*. New York, 1964.

Jansen, G. H., *Militant Islam*. New York, 1979.

Kramer, Martin, *Political Islam*. Washington, DC, 1980.

Philby, H. St. J., *Saudi Arabia*. London, 1955.

Smith, Wilfred C., *Islam In Modern History*. New York, 1957.

X

ISLAMIC REVIVAL IN EGYPT AND GREATER SYRIA

Ibrahim Ibrahim

> *Egypt and Greater Syria (Syria, Jordan, Lebanon and Palestine) have been in the center of the Arab-Israeli conflict, the most difficult and unsolvable international problem since the Second World War. In it, this problem contains ingredients for high grade explosions of global proportions as well as potential for any number of minor conflicts any one of which could trigger a chain reaction leading to a major war. While much has been written in the world press about the most obvious issues and the most visible actors in this Middle Eastern theater the world knows very little about the myriads of movements behind the scenes that make up the whole drama. Professor Ibrahim identifies the most significant among these movements which are linked in one way or another to developments in the Islamic world.*
>
> *Ibrahim Ibrahim who has done extensive work in the history and culture of the Arab nations is currently Research Professor, Center for Contemporary Arab Studies, Georgetown University.*

Religious revival or resurgence, is not something new in the Islamic world; there have been Islamic movements protesting — sometimes rebelling — against despotism of governments or other injustices throughout history. The re-emergence of such movements in recent times can, therefore, be seen partly, as a historical continuation of those 'protest' or reform movements. It can also be seen as by-products of a multi-faceted crisis in contemporary Islamic countries.

In Egypt, for instance, the Muslim Brothers, a well-organized and perhaps the most powerful movement in the Muslim world, was founded in the late 1920's; it grew rapidly in the thirties and became a mass movement in the 1940's. As a movement and an ideology, it is a by-product of the intellectual, social, economic, and political crisis that modern Egypt has been facing since the turn of this century. In order to appraise and understand this movement we have to set it back into its historical context.

Until the turn of the 18th century, Egyptian society was living under an Islamic civilization which embraced and provided guidelines for every sphere of life. In the sphere of law, for instance, the *shari'a*, Islamic law, was the 'regulative principle' of society. Islamic law, a combination of natural and positive law in the West, is derived from the Koran but embodies custom, too. For Muslims it governs not only religious rituals but also social, economic and political matters. Indeed, there can be no political community without Islamic law; and the *caliphate*, the Islamic state, is needed to implement the commands of God on earth. Thus, the Christian Bible's "render unto Caesar the things that are Caesar's and under God the things that are God's" is in contradistinction with Islamic doctrine. For Islam combines both the temporal and the sacred.

In the field of education, the Azhar and the religious schools were the sole centers of learning. The classical Arabo-Islamic culture was the only recognized culture. And finally the *ulamā*, men of religion, were not only the revered men of learning but also the mouthpiece of the *umma*, the political community; the people looked up to them as their leaders in their relations with the ruler.

From the beginning of the nineteenth century and henceforward, a change, a transformation in many aspects of life began to take place that resulted in the disruption of the prevailing culture and outlook. This was due to the impact of Westernization, a process instigated by the rulers of Egypt and the Ottoman Empire in the 19th Century. The European positivist laws which they introduced weakened the hold of the *shari'a*, which was the instrument by which the social ethic of Islam was consolidated. But the most profound effect resulted from the educational policy, which the rulers of Egypt throughout the 19th Century pursued. By the establishment of modern schools on Western models and by sending educational missions to Europe, they — consciously or unconsciously — not only opened society to new modes of thought and ideas and thus demonstrated the superiority of Europe and the need to conform to its civilization, but also created gradually a new non-traditional intelligentsia: civil servants, technicians, jurists and journalists, a social stratum which was not guided by the rule of tradition.

Thus by the end of the 19th Century, Egyptian society was no longer the traditional Islamic society with its uniform institutions, culture and outlook, but a disrupted society which revealed the contradictions that influences from outside as well as from within created. In it one found the Old existing beside and competing with the New: the modern judge of the secular civil courts beside the traditional *qadi* (Muslim judge) at the *shari'a* Islamic court; the *'alem* (learned man of religion) of the *Azhar* (the ancient and most revered university in Cairo) beside the professor at the secular institutes — that is to say, there was really a schism in society.

The rise and development of the Muslim Brothers is the best proof for the disruption of the Egyptian society which became, because of the continuing Westernization, polarized into two communities: the modernists and the traditionalists, each of these two groups living in its own world. Thus, while the Westernizers found themselves at universities, expounding their views in the press and furthering the process of modernization, the traditionalists were still gathering at the *Azhar*, frequenting the *salafiyya*, circle of Rashid Rida, a leading Muslim scholar, and contributing to his periodical, *al-manar*, as well as to other Islamic-oriented reviews such as *al-fath*. With the continued advancement of Westernization, the gap between these became wider and wider. For the more the Westernizers proceeded and gained momentum, the more violent became the reaction of the Traditionalists. It was no mere coincidence, therefore, that by the end of the 1920's, new Islamic societies had been set up. Thus, *jam'iyyat al-shubban al-muslimin*, the society of Muslim Youth, was set up in 1927 under the board of directors constituted of some well-known Muslim conservatives such as Abdul Hamid Sa'id of the *watani* party (Nationalist Party), Sheikh Abdul 'Aziz Shawish, a student of the famous Muslim reformer, Jamal al-Din al-Afghani and Muhhib al-Din al-Khatib, a prominent member of the *salafiyya* (fundamentalist) movement, and the publisher of *al-fath*, a conservative paper, which carried its attacks throughout the 1920's against the modernizers.

In 1928 the Muslim Brothers was founded by Hasan al-Banna who had been frequenting these Islamic circles. He himself comes from the prototype of a traditional Muslim family and had been educated at the religious schools and later at *Dar al-'ulum*, an exclusively Islamic teachers' college specializing in theology, Muslim jurisprudence and classical Arabic literature. The movement started as a puritan social movement with the aim of purifying the alien and "corrupted" Westernized society and preaching the return to Islamic morals and ethics. Unlike the benevolent Muslim societies, however, the Muslim

Brothers had, from the very beginning, a social and political color. The fact that the leader Hassan al-Banna himself came from a "lower middle class" family (his father was a watchmaker) and he addressed himself primarily to the poor is revealing. The very first members of the movement came from the very same social and cultural background — graduates of the religious institutes, who were extremely poor but also "unspoiled" by Western learning and way of life. Apart from the fact that al-Banna saw in this group the stuff of the virtuous Muslim society, there was undoubtedly a social solidarity in his reasoning. It is significant also that the movement was born in the provincial town of *al-Isma'iliyya* on the Suez Canal, a town that symbolizes both the social and political problems of Egypt of the time. For one thing, the presence of the foreigners: the English army, the Suez Canal Company, and the privileged European community on the one hand, and the miseries of the Egyptian workers on the other, left their impact on his mind. Indeed *al-Isma'iliyya* must have inspired and generated many things that contributed to the creation of the Muslim Brothers movement.

Until the mid-1930's, Hasan al-Banna and the movement remained on the periphery of Egyptian social and political life; however, it grew rapidly in the late 1930's and became a mass movement in the 1940's. Many factors were behind this growth. One was the structure of Egyptian society: the majority of Egyptians were still traditionally oriented and Islam for this majority was its *raison d'etre*, in the best sense of the word. By preaching a simple Islam, al-Banna found a favorable response from the broadest stratum of society. Another reason was this: the movement came at a time when, thanks to the process of Westernization, the *Sufi* orders, which could have absorbed a large number from this stratum, were entering a phase of decline. In other words the decline of the *Sufi* orders was to the advantage of the Muslim Brothers, for those classes from which in the past the orders would have drawn their members turned instead to the movement of the Muslim Brothers. In it they found the spiritual compensations which they were yearning for and an outlet for activity; it offered also opportunity for organized social intercourse, which the *zawiya* (*Sufi* gathering club) of the orders used to offer. It is very interesting that al-Banna himself was acquainted with the orders and had been, at one time, an initiate in the well-known *hasifiyya* order, and hence he knew how to use his charisma to attract the masses to his movement.

In spite of all these, the growth of the Muslim Brothers and its emergence as a mass political movement should be attributed to socio-political factors: the economic and political crisis, and the growth of the urban lower middle classes and proletariats. The crisis arose as a result of the corruption in the political parties and the failure of the *wafd* (the leading middle-class party) to continue as the party of the common man. The negative attitude of the *ulamā*, men of religion, the *azhar*, and the Western-educated elite toward this crisis also turned many people away from them and to the Brotherhood. In addition the emergence of conflicting ideologies such as Fascism, Nazism and Communism in the West and the outbreak of World War II intensified the politicization of the young, educated Egyptians. Western ideas which were hitherto held in high esteem because of the influence of Westernized exponents like Taha Husayn, the celebrated Egyptian man of letters and historian, could no longer pass without questioning.

The political and social views of the Muslim Brothers matured during the 1940's as the society's need to respond to this growing crisis arose. The Brotherhood's response was to present Islam as a comprehensive ideology to redress the ills of Egypt and revive the hopes of the disillusioned students, workers and the lower middle classes. The Islam the Brotherhood presented was imbued with puritan and moralistic values which applied to these groups. This was a major reason for the movement's success. Indeed, it restored to the disillusioned Egyptian hope for a better life and rendered him relief from corruption and hardships.

For the Muslim Brothers, Islam offered a total philosophy which explained this world and the next and regulated human life in its totality. It was the true and complete doctrine that established a true concept of God and being. It followed, then, that there could be no division between spiritual and temporal powers as in Christianity and Buddhism. For this very reason any exclusion of Islam from public life would be in opposition to the order of the universe, i.e., to the will of God. This would certainly lead to crisis which could not be overcome except by acceptance of the *shari'a*, Islamic law, as the regulative principle. Once the *shari'a* was restored, social justice and political freedom, i.e., the Muslim virtuous society, would fully materialize.

For the Brothers, Islamic order rested on three general principles: justice of the ruler, obedience of the ruled, and the *shura* (consultation). The obedience of the ruled to their ruler sprang from the fact that the ruler was just and the true guardian of the *shari'a*. He would lose, however, this right and consequently his authority, if he neglected the *shari'a*. Seen in this light, the ruler had no absolute rights and was dependent on the will of the community which elected him. Because of this, the Muslim Brothers rejected the hereditary principle for that would be contrary to the principle of election. The *shura*, for the Brothers, was one of the most important principles of Islamic order; they meant by it the right of the people to elect, control, and if need be, depose the ruler.

The *shari'a*, therefore, was supremely important to the Brothers; it was to them not only the kernel of Islam itself but also a means of self-identification. The need for self-identification has always been the problem of all alienated men. In the case of the Muslim Brothers, their alienation was serious and very deep indeed. For, on the one hand, they were socially and politically alienated from the privileged Westernized ruling class; on the other, they were alienated from the new culture and outlook of the Westernized intelligentsia, whose habits and predominance were felt at the very heart of modern Egypt.

For the Brothers the *New* was imposed from without and hence was alien: it could not correspond to the spirit of the people, that is to say, to the "traditional" sector of Egyptian society, from which they sprang. The spirit of the people meant for them Islam: Islam was conceived not only — and here lay the crux of the matter — as a social, political and ethical system, but also as the total world-view. In it, they found not only their spiritual comfort, but also their originality, their distinctiveness from others, i.e., Westernizers, conservatives and revolutionaries alike. It was indeed a complete and full estrangement from Western ideas, institutions and habits.

This romantic nostalgia for the past, for an idealized puritan and happy life, was undoubtedly one of the profound stimuli behind the growth of the Muslim Brothers. And the insistence on the return to Islam, to the roots, was actually an endeavor to restore to Muslims self-esteem and respect in their own cultural heritage and traditions.

By the late 1940's, the Muslim Brothers could boast of their mass following; indeed they were able to attract quite a large number of the salaried, professional, lower and middle classes as well as some army officers. Through these officers they established an alliance with the Free Officers Movement, which eventually staged a successful *coup d'etat* against the monarchy in 1952 under the leadership of the late President Gamal Abdel al-Nasser. But the leaders of the 1952 revolution saw the rebirth of Egypt in the continuous modernization of its social, political, and economic institutions based on Western models. For Nasser and his colleagues, the Brothers' Islamic doctrines could no longer meet problems of the modern world. No wonder then that, after a very short period of cooperation with the new government, the Muslim Brothers started challenging Nasser's policies. In 1954 when they revolted and tried to assassinate him, Nasser hanged their leaders and ruthlessly suppressed the movement without encountering any outcry from the majority of Egyptians.

Nasser was able, during the 1950's and 1960's, to gain popular support partly due to his charisma and partly because of his struggle against colonialism (the tripartite Anglo-French-Israeli invasion of the Suez Canal in 1956). His adoption of a higher cause such as Arab nationalism and his role as initiator and leader of the non-aligned Third World movement enhanced his status. Today, Sadat's Egypt is different from Nasser's; this is so not because compared to Nasser Sadat lacks charisma, but because the problems and difficulties Egypt now faces are far more acute and urgent. The economic situation of the 1970's, as proved by the riots of 1979, was grave. At present the economic crisis caused by explosions in both demography and education seems almost insurmountable. Sadat's Egypt is witnessing an unprecedented demographic expansion; a mass migration is taking place from the countryside into the urban centers. Cairo, for instance, grew from almost four million inhabitants in 1960 to eight million in 1979. Coupled with this is the tremendous growth of the student body; there are millions of high school and university graduates every year, in a country where the rate of unemployment is almost the highest in the world. It is to be remembered that the majority of students come from the traditional Muslim-oriented, under-privileged classes: lower middle class, peasants and urban proletariat, that is to say, potential material for the Muslim Brothers who have made a comeback since Nasser's suppression. Unemployment and other social and economic dislocations can intensify the feeling of uprootedness and eventually lead to alienation. This is what is happening in Egypt today. Neither in the economic field, nor in the political arena, has the government been successful, in spite of the widely publicized promises that a pact with Israel and alignment with the West, particularly the United States, would bring about employment and economic prosperity.

Arabic culture and Islam were always a major concern of the intellectual and ruling elite of Egypt. It is true that while Islam as dogma, as a political bond and regulative principle, has lost its hold over the minds of this elite, it has, however, retained its power as a social and moral factor. The national heritage is considered to be the Islamic culture and the Arab-Islamic heroes are the heroes of the common man in Egypt. Politically Egypt since the 1930's was becoming aware of its role as a leading Arab country, seeking leadership and cooperation with other sister Arab states. This tendency was furthered and promoted by the *Azhar*, the leading Islamic center of learning, and by a group of enlightened, prominent Muslim Egyptians who supported the Arab cause in Palestine, Syria and North Africa. With the creation of the Arab League in 1945, Cairo became its seat and Egypt was acknowledged as the leader of the Arab world, a role she assumed with enthusiasm.

The movement of the Muslim Brothers is very much in support of Arab cooperation and Arab unity. The Egyptian government's involvement in the Palestine question and its struggle against Zionism and Israel are, therefore, in tune with Egyptian public opinion in general, and, in particular, with the Brothers who participated in the war of 1948. For the Muslim Brothers, Palestine is the heart and central issue of the matter. Zionism for them is an extension of Western colonialism, whose object had been to humiliate the Arabs and defeat Islam. A return to the rule of Islam, to the virtuous Muslim society, was thus envisaged as the only way for the Arab and Muslim communities to withstand Zionist conquest and Western imperialism.

Palestine is at the heart of Arab politics; it is so for radicals, conservatives, and moderates; secular and religious people; movements and governments. Nasser's success in assuming the leadership of the Arabs was due to his steadfast stand against Israel and Zionism. President Sadat inherited this leadership from Nasser without having his predecessor's charisma or cunning. Misjudging the 'organic' and historical relationship of Egypt with its neighboring Arab countries, the economic, political, and cultural bonds between Egypt and the Arabs, and the psychological and religious importance of Palestine for the majority of his own countrymen, President Sadat went on his visit to Jerusalem, the visit which ended with his signing a peace treaty with Israel, a treaty that not only alienated the rights of the Palestinians to their homeland but also radically altered the inter-Arab state system and jeopardized the leading position of Egypt in the Arab and Muslim worlds as indeed in most countries of the Third World.

If President Sadat had known prior to his visit to Jerusalem of the coming of a successful uprising in Iran under the banner of Ayatollah Khomeini, he might have changed his mind about the visit and his policy. But "ifs" cannot help explain history; Sadat's visit did take place and in its aftermath the Camp David accord and peace treaty with Israel were signed and a new alignment with the United States was declared. This new Egyptian orientation coincided with that popular uprising in Iran, a rich neighboring Muslim country, that successfully brought about the overthrow of the Shah. The return of a triumphant Muslim fundamentalist Khomeini to Teheran, replacing an unpopular Shah Mohammed Reza Pahlevi, sent shock waves in the Islamic world but the fact that the Shah was received in Egypt as the guest of President Sadat inflamed a number of zealots in Cairo, especially after Khomeini and the Iranian leadership not only reversed the Shah's policy toward Israel and the West but also declared their condemnation and enmity for Sadat's peace treaty and their unlimited support of the Palestinian movement.

Peace with Israel and the break with sister Arab countries, in particular Saudi Arabia, the traditional patron of the Muslim Brothers, is bound to engender opposition to Sadat from the majority of Egyptian Muslims. Indeed the Muslim Brothers have already started to voice their strong opposition to his policies. They publicly condemned the Camp David accord and the peace treaty with Israel. Consequently the movement of the Muslim Brothers is a potential threat to President Sadat's regime, especially since that regime is unsuccessful in solving Egypt's difficult problems. Frequent changes in the government (for example, in the offices of prime minister and foreign minister) and Sadat's attacks against the leadership of the Coptic Christian minority are indications of growing tension within Egypt.

In spite of many similarities between Egypt and its neighbor Greater Syria (Syria, Lebanon, Jordan and Palestine) there are some differences that have important bearings on the political process in the latter region. One lies in the partition of Syria in the wake of World War I, a fact that proved to be disastrous in that it reduced the four ensuing entitites to a state of precariousness and chronic instability. Another important difference between Greater Syria and Egypt is that the former is a mixed society. To be sure Islam is the majority, but Christians and some heterodox Muslim sects compose an important part of Syrian society. It is no mere coincidence, therefore, that ideas of secular nationalism, such as pan-Arab nationalism and Syrian nationalism originated in Syria and found many leaders and followers not only among Christians but also among Muslims. The trend of secular nationalism is the reason why Islam, while it is held in high esteem by the leaders of Arab nationalism in greater Syria, cannot find a militant movement comparable to that of the Muslim Brothers in Egypt. It is true, however, that the coming of Zionism into the Middle East and the creation of Israel in Palestine on biblical grounds helped promote some criticism about the failure of Arab nationalism. The Muslim Brothers who were already active in Syria under the leadership of Mustapha el-Siba'i, did gain some momentum as a result of this but in terms of influence and following they never came close to their counterparts in Egypt. For from the 1950's onwards Syria was increasingly becoming the land of secular movements and parties. Recently there have been, however, some reports of the re-emergence of Muslim movements in Syria, as a challenge to President Assad's regime. Like all authoritarian governments President Assad's rule is bound to encounter opposition from other political groups, and the fact that he himself comes from the Alawites, a depressed Muslim minority, is a matter of grievance to members of the Sunni Muslim majority. On the other hand, Syria has been not only aware and conscious of its mixed population but also solidly wedded to the idea of secular nationalism. An Islamic movement similar to that of the Muslim Brothers in Egypt is highly unlikely to succeed in Syria.

One Islamic movement similar to that of the Egyptian Muslim Brothers (*Hizb al-Tahrir al-Islami*, Party for the Liberation of Islam) was founded in Jordan (the West Bank) in the early 1950's by Sheikh Takieddin Nabhani, a *shari'a* court judge from Palestine. Like the Muslim Brothers, the movement called for the return to Islamic virtues and the establishment of a caliphate as the only means of resurrection and recovery of Palestine. It attracted followers mainly in the countryside and provincial towns, among school teachers, government clerks, artisans and so on. However, it failed to attract the Damascenes, Beirutis, and in Jordan itself, it came to a halt partly due to Government vigilance and partly because it did not appeal to members of the intelligentsia and salaried middle class. In other words, it remained a small, weak lower middle-class movement, suffering from its provincial origin and could not, therefore, compete with the secular nationalism of either the Ba'th or the Arab nationalists.

It is true that the Iranian revolution had a tremendous impact on most peoples in the Middle East, particularly those Palestinian Muslims experiencing daily life under harsh Israeli occupation on the West Bank. Khomeini's unequivocal support of the Palestinian revolution and Palestinian rights might serve as inspiration among some Muslim groups in the West Bank as well as among Shi'ites in Southern Lebanon. But it is a stubborn fact that more than any other Arab people, the Palestinians are strongly committed to a concept of nationalism and secular socialist ideas. This was the case since the turn of the century, when they encountered at first Zionism and then British occupation. In 1918 (November) a Muslim-Christian association was founded which later became the Palestine national movement, and in 1935 another Palestine Arab party was started with Christians as Vice President and Secretary.

At present the leadership of the Palestine Liberation Organization is fully aware of the need for national unity; its emphasis is on the overriding importance of a united front based on the devotion to a Palestinian nationhood. It is composed of such devout Muslims as Yasser Arafat, but also of Christian guerilla leaders such as the Marxist George Habash and radical leftist, Nayef Hawatmeh. Thus, the PLO cannot afford to grant Islam an overriding role in the Palestinian movement, and its only ultimate objective is a democratic, secular state in Palestine that would comprise Jewish, Christian and Muslim citizens.

Lebanon is a mosaic of minorities; therefore, neither Islam nor Christianity could be stressed. From its emergence as a state in 1920, a compromise between Muslims and Christians had to be reached, as happened in the national pact of 1942 in which the two leading communities recognized that due to its multiplicity of religions and sects, Lebanon does not lend itself to fundamentalist movements of any kind. To be sure, there are certain Muslim groups that are amenable to manipulation, especially the Shi'a population in Southern Lebanon who could be influenced by Islamic ideals, given the rise of Khomeini in Iran. By and large, however, Lebanese Muslims are more attracted to Arabism, and their political aspirations are identical with those of Pan-Arabism. While it must be acknowledged that Lebanon has been the scene of a series of religious wars, the most savage of which is the ongoing civil war, these wars are more examples of social and political strife than religious conflict. The Lebanese Muslims are fighting against the predominance of the Christian Maronites not on the grounds of their being Christians per se, but on the basis of Muslim grievances. In other words, the war that is being waged there is not to replace the political system by an Islamic order, but to reform it in a secular direction.

In conclusion, like many regions of the Third World, Egypt and Greater Syria are passing through a revolutionary phase, in their case caused in part by the pressures of Zionism and the depressing reality of the Palestinian people. Other causes can be found in the crisis of legitimacy, the absence of political participation, and the excesses of coercion, all of which contribute to instability. But above all, economic difficulties, unemployment, social and economic dislocation, and cultural alienation could pave the way for fundamentalist Islamic movements, especially in Egypt of today. In Greater Syria, however, militant Islamic movements are unlikely to succeed in competition with the already existing and ever growing secular nationalism and secular political parties.

Selected Reading List

Abdel-Malek, A., *Egypte Societe Militaire*. Paris, 1962.

Ahmad, J. M., *The Intellectual Origins of Egyptian Nationalism*. Oxford University Press, 1960.

Antonius, George, *The Arab Awakening*. Reprint, Khayats, Beirut, 1938.

Berque, Jacques, *Egypt, Imperialism and Revolution*. London: Faber & Faber, 1972.

_____, *The Arabs: Their History and Future*. London, 1960.

Gibb, H. A. R., *Modern Trends in Islam*. University of Chicago Press, 1947.

_____, *Islam, A Historical Survey*. Oxford University Press, 1975.

Grunebaum, G. E. von, *Modern Islam, The Search for Cultural Identity*. New York: Vintage Books, 1974.

Hourani, A. H., *Arabic Thought in the Liberal Age*. Oxford University Press, 1962.

_____, *Minorities in the Arab World*. London, 1947.

_____, *Syria and Lebanon*. O.U.P., 1954.

Jansen, GH., *Militant Islam*. London: Pan Books, 1979.

Karpat, K. H., (Ed.), *Political and Social Thought in the Contemporary Middle East*. New York: Praeger, 1968.

Khadduri, Majid, *Political Trends in the Arab World*. John Hopkins Press, 1970.

Mitchell, R. P., *The Society of the Muslim Brothers*. O.U.P., 1969.

Rosenthal, E. I. J., *Islam in the Modern National State.* Cambridge University Press, 1965.

Smith, W. C., *Islam in Modern History.* London, 1957.

Smith, D. E., *Religion and Political Development.* Boston, 1970.

Sayigh, Rosemary, *Palestinians: From Peasants to Revolutionaries.* London: Zed Press, 1979.

Said, Edward W., *The Question of Palestine.* New York: Times Books, 1979.

Schacht, J., *Introduction to Islamic Law.* O.U.P., 1964.

XI

SHI'I SOCIAL THOUGHT AND PRAXIS IN RECENT IRANIAN HISTORY

Shahrough Akhavi

> The Iranian revolution, led by the Muslim clergy, and the Islamic republic they erected represent ideologies, events and institutions that have no direct parallel in Islamic history. That the resurgence of the Shi'ite version of Islam is chiefly responsible for the developments in Iran is fairly clear to those who follow the world press. But, it is not as easy, for outsiders, to obtain knowledge about the various factors and forces that are within and without this Shi'ite movement that determined the course and outcome of the Iranian revolution, let alone analyze correctly their relative significance in terms of past events and future prospects. Professor Akhavi here identifies the various actors in the Iranian Drama and analyzes their roles from an historical and sociological perspective.
>
> Shahrough Akhavi, author of **Religion and Politics in Contemporary Iran: Clergy-State Relations in the Pahlavi Period** and several articles on similar Iranian topics, has had academic experiences in the Near East and Europe and is currently a professor in the Department of Government and International Relations at the University of South Carolina.

Preliminary Remarks

Developments in the last few years in Iran have led to the convening of numerous conferences on the "Islamic revival". More and more, participants at such meetings are coming to the conclusion that if revival means "giving life back to", this confounds the issue. For "Islam" had not been dead, and only modernizing elites or scholars entangled in the "Project Camelot" syndrome could have thought otherwise.

Resurgence would seem a better word. But, if we can agree upon the premise of a religious resurgence in Iran in the 1980's, we must not forget that very deep stirrings among Iranian religious thinkers and activists existed in the late forties to late fifties, the early sixties, the late sixties and early seventies, and the late seventies. We should be perfectly clear in advance that these considerations do not imply unanimity of views or ranks; nor do they mean that the clergy was the vanguard and the lay intellectuals the opportunist allies of the former; more, no imputation should be made that the "high religion" doctrine of the scholars *(ulamā)* caused the mobilization of the masses.

Perhaps a major feature of the Iranian revolution is that upper-ranking members of the professional clergy by and large continued their highly intellectualized discourse among themselves and their students in the period of 1975-1978. In the meanwhile the lay intellectuals (doctors, lawyers, professors, architects, economists, engineers, journalists, bureaucrats, students) continued *their* discourse in *their* circles. Ayatullah Khumayni's ability to bridge, *to some extent*, the gap between *ulamā* and lay intellectuals was based upon his charismatic authority, his use of dramaturgical symbolism and rhetorical argumentation. The substantive issues between clergy and non-clerical intellectuals continue to loom large. But, once again one must not exaggerate and suggest that such issues are insuperably complex[1]. After all, the common point of departure for the clergy and the secularists is the emphatic repudiation of *zulm* (oppression).

The Genesis and Development of Shi'i Resurgence: 1945-1958

The clergy's resurgence after WW II was led by Ayatullah Sayyid Muhammad Husayn Burujirdi, the leader of Qumm between 1946 and 1961 (when he died). Qumm was — and continues to be — the center of the Iranian religious institution and Burujirdi sought to raise it to the eminence enjoyed in the Sunni Islamic world by al-Azhar in Egypt.

Now, Burujirdi's efforts to invigorate Shi'ism in Iran did not consist of the modernization of the curriculum of the theological seminaries *(madrasahs)*; nor did it amount to bold innovations in administration and organizational matters.[2] Instead, his tenure can be characterized as one during which the state acknowledged the clergy's continuing interest in public morality; worship (especially the construction, upkeep and refurbishing of mosques); anti-leftist propaganda *(tabligh)*; dialogue with Sunni Islamic leaders; increasing enrollments in the madrasahs; anti-Baha'ism; admonitions against the clergy's trafficking in politics; and redoubling efforts to enshrine *fia* as the cornerstone of Islamic education.[3]

Burujirdi enjoyed deference of such magnitude among his colleagues and the Iranian masses in general that he was endowed with the title of *marja'-yi mutlaq-i taqlid.* This title meant that (theoretically at least) he was considered the sole source of emulation on the part of Shi'i adepts, each of whom is required by the faith to follow a living *mujtahid* in matters of religious belief and practice.

The enrollment of religious studies students in the *madrasahs* increased dramatically during the 1950's, a pattern that stood in marked contrast to the Riza Shah and WW II periods. The resurgence of Shi'ism had a great deal to do with the government's willingness to make concessions to the clergy on questions of: (1) alcoholism, gambling and easy living; (2) greater stress upon sermons and homiletics in public broadcasting and television; (3) pressure upon the press to delete "anti-Shi'i" articles; (4) women's rights; (5) vigilance in observing Shi'i days of mourning, fasting and similar commemorations; (6) more intensive and frequent consultation on the part of the government leaders with the clergy.

Left almost untouched were social organization, finance, curriculum reform, social theory, ideology, political authority and its exercise, and constitutionalism. In the 1950's any rare instance of clergy assertiveness in these areas either had no wider impact or else redounded adversely against innovators. The classic example of an innovator who came under the regime's censure and opprobrium was Ayatullah Sayyid Mahmud Taliqani (d. 1979), co-founder (with Muhandis Mihdi Bazargan) of the Freedom Movement. Imprisoned by the regime, Taliqani's new edition, in 1954, of the classic constitutionalist treatise of 1909 written by Ayatullah Agha Shaykh Muhammad Husayn al-Na'ini (d. 1936) and entitled *Tanbih al-Ummah wa Tanzih al-Millah* symbolized his liberal position on political rule.

As against the Burujirdi "mainstream" faction of the *ulamā*, one must mention the political activism of Ayatullah Sayyid Abu al-Qasim al-Kashani (d. 1962). This individual, supported by such popular preachers as Hujjat al-Islam Muhammad Taqi Falsafi, represented the archtype of the politically "engagé" clergyman. Ranged against him, on the left and in the camp of the nationalist Prime Minister Muhammad Musaddiq were individuals such as Ayatullah Sayyid Abu al-Fazl al-Musavi al-Zanjani. Finally, outside the ranks of the clergy proper, but sometimes receiving at least the tactical support of individuals in the *ulamā* stratum such as Kashani and Falsafi, was the militant fundamentalist movement known as the Fida'iyan-i Islam. This organization, utilizing assassination tactics to realize its aim of returning to a "pure Islam", was established in 1945. In particular, its ties to the *mujtahids* (most of whom disapproved of it) was through Kashani, who nevertheless obstructed their wishes to share in political power and thereby caused them to break with him in March 1951.

The complex relationships involving Burujirdi, Kashani, Zanjani, and the Fida'iyan highlight for us the fact that the clergy was not a monolithic social force. In the denouement between the Shah and Dr. Musaddiq in August 1953, Zanjani and his supporters lost out and were imprisoned; Kashani was thoroughly discredited and promptly sank into obscurity; and what had remained of the Fida'iyan was systematically crushed. This permitted Burujirdi, with his solid ties to the important Tehran-based *mujtahid*, Ayatullah Sayyid Muhammad al-Musavi al-Bihbihani (d. 1965?), to establish a dominant role in the next eight years. He entered into an alignment with the Court that was to last for about five of these eight years. In this period, he and his supporters attacked the left and maintained a studied silence on issues which had historically excited the clergy — namely, foreign influence in the country. Such influence was represented in the midfifties by Iran's adherence to the Western sponsored defense alliance (Baghdad Pact) and Iran's dealing with the Consortium of oil companies after the overthrow of the Musaddiq movement.

State Suppression of Clergy Opposition, 1959-1963

Between 1959-1963 serious problems began to arise between the government and the clergy. More and more in the previous year the *ulamā* came to feel that the Shah and his government were reneging on their tacit agreement to maintain close communications and consultations with the clergy on various matters of public policy. Dr. Mussaddiq's National Front (a coalition of political parties and personalities that survived his downfall) increased its agitation against some of the same issues that had come to excite the clergy, without, nevertheless, having significant contact with the *ulamā* apart from Ayatullah Taliqani. The regime sought to depict clerical opposition to the Shah's "White Revolution" as rooted in opportunistic and reactionary motives.[4] Yet, such charges were recognized both in the religious institution and among many secularists for what they truly were, that is, polemics for the sake of discrediting one's opponents.

Ayatullah Burujirdi's death in March of 1961 disconcerted the clergy and emboldened the Shah's government to push forward with its programs and policies. About this time, though, a group of modernist *ulamā* and lay supporters of a stronger clergy role in social affairs came together under the leadership of Ayatullah Shaykh Murtaza Mutahhari (d. 1979). In many significant respects, the activities of this group comprised the first truly meaningful reform effort in the 20th century among Iranian clergymen. That the movement was overdue, may be gathered from Mutahhari's ironic comment in 1961 that things had reached such a pass in Iranian Shi'ism that soon people would be saying that its latest reformer (Shaykh Murtaza Ansari "al-Mujaddid" [d. 1864]) lived a hundred years ago!⁵

Now, the clergy as a whole challenged various facets of the Shah's behavior and principles. These included arbitrary rule by decree and disregard for constitutionalism. The *ulamā* remonstrated against the government for its land reform law because it disregarded the sanctity of private property as underwritten by the Qur'an, and it was feared that its provisions would be used against the clergy to declass its members. The enfranchisement of women was anathematized by the clergy, who saw in it the potential corruption of Iranian womanhood, the disruption of traditional family life and the buying off of women through the extension to them of meaningless suffrage. The clergy attacked the Literacy Corps as an instrument designed to replace the rural preachers and therefore eliminate at one blow whatever exemplars of Islamic piety were considered to exist in the villages of Iran.

But Mutahhari's group was primarily interested in matters that were intrinsic to the religious institution. While its members were also involved in the general protest movement of the early sixties, their concentration was the reform of Iranian Shi'i thought and organization.

Limitations of space forbid even a brief exposition of Shi'i juristic theory of the state and political authority, anchored as they are in the doctrines of the imamate and of *valayat* (the rule of the *imams* and allegiance to such rule). However, it may be said here that Shi'is believe that only the Imam has the right to rule the community. In the absence of the Imam (the last of the line of twelve such preternatural souls having miraculously disappeared from terrestrial life in 874 A.D.), can rule by temporal authorities be legitimate? In a minimal sense, Shi'is answer in the affirmative, although such rulers must be considered to be implementing the laws of the Ja'fari (Twelver Imami) rite of Islam.⁶

Meanwhile, the clergy constitute themselves collectively as *al-wukala' al-'amm* (the General Agency) — i.e., the deputies of the Imam. While they do not have the authority to exercise rule in his absence according to classic Shi'i doctrine, they do have the right and duty to ensure that laws not be inimical to the injunctions of the faith.

Such being the case, there is at least some room in Shi'i social thought for the clergy to play a socio-political role in society. The Iranian *ulamā* have participated in politics on an ongoing basis in Iranian history. Even in the Safavid period (1501-1722), when the Safavid Shahs were successfully claiming lineal descent from the Imam, the clergy accepted incumbencies in state administration.[7] In the Qajar period (1785-1925) their behavior turned increasingly to protest against what they saw as the violation of the Imam's justice.[8] In the Pahlavi period (1925-1979), after some thirty years of virtual elimination from socio-political participation, they made increasingly forceful arguments about the need to get politically involved. And one eminent *mujtahid* — Ayatullah Sayyid Ruhullah al-Musavi Khumayni — has argued trenchantly and forcefully that even the classic doctrine urged clergy rule in the absence of the Imam.[9]

We now return, after this digression, to the efforts of the reform movement known as the Monthly Religious Society. The activities of this group consisted in monthly lectures and roundtables and lasted from 1960 to early 1963. The participants in the movement argued in favor of a socially active clergy and a Shi'ism to which believers had responsibilities surpassing mere private worship. Revitalization of Iranian Shi'ism involved for them a broad range of innovations. Among these may be listed the following:[10]

1. Curriculum reform in the *madrasahs*. This in particular meant more frequent and more challenging courses in *tafsir* (commentaries on the Qur'an); *ma'rifat al-rijal* (biography); *tarikh* (history); *'aqa'id* (ideologies).

2. A dynamic interpretation of such principles as *taqva* (piety). Accordingly, the faithful were invited to insist upon righteous behavior from their leaders, including political rulers.

3. A view that religion and politics had common goals — a line of thinking that was inevitable, given the three principles of the faith that these reformers felt lent themselves to "political" matters: *al-amr bi al-ma'ruf wa al-nahy 'an al-munkar* (commanding the good and forbidding evil); *jihad* (holy war); *khums* (a 20% tax on annual income).

4. Rationalization of the financial administration and organization of the religious institution.

5. Dividing *marja'iyat* (the principle of emulating a *mujtahid*) so as to obviate pressures for the emergence of a sole *marja'-i taqlid*, in light

of the complexities of law in the modern period; and given the improbability of one individual mastering the knowledge necessary for providing model solutions to any and every problem.

6. Constituting a collective body of *mujtahids* with the authority to issue *fatvas* (authoritative opinions in matters of Islamic law) on any issue of public policy or interest. This seemed an attempt to activate the provisions of Article Two of the Constitution of 1906/1907, entailing the creation of a five-member council of high-ranking clergymen with the power of judicial review.

7. Urging that the clerical leadership provide exemplary guidance for youth — not only on the level of ethical conduct but also in terms of committing itself to the need for public and social mobilization, interest articulation, recruitment of cadres, inculcation of political consciousness, etc.

8. The delegation of the Imam's authority being a *sine qua non* of any Shi'i society, it was argued that only those who have shown outstanding achievement as to piety, justice and administration were the rightful legatees of such authority. Secular rulers, including those of the 20th century, had sinned and shown their inability to imitate the traditions of the prophet as befits the task of him to whom the *imams'* authority is delegated. Therefore, doctrinal grounds are established implicitly for rule by the clergy *('ula al-amr minkum* — those in authority among you) as the only social stratum with the potential to avoid sinful behavior.

The government's suppression of this reform movement occured simultaneously with its violent reaction against the clergy's participation in the 1962-1963 demonstrations. It is clear that, given the range of demands set forth by the movement, the regime greatly feared its success. It was determined not to permit a social and political role to the *ulamā* because of their likely ability, if the need arose, to mobilize masses in support of their own views. The bottom line of these reform demands, as the government saw them, was independent organizational capability. It therefore came as no surprise that the regime, in crushing the political opposition, also stifled the religious reform efforts.

This does not mean that religion was uprooted; not at all. Many of the Westernized intellectuals, for whom religion continued to provide symbolic significance, turned toward *'irfan* and *tasawwuf* (gnosis and sufism respectively). The leading example of an individual who was attracted toward mysticism was Seyyed Hossein Nasr.

Now, Sufism has always been suspect in Qumm, although *'irfan* has been tolerated. Rarely at least, *mujtahids* (including Ayatullah Khumayni at one point) have instructed in this subject. Non-*mujtahids* of the stature of 'Allamah Muhammad Husayn Taba'taba'i, have also been able to hold forth in the bastion of Iranian Shi'ism itself, the holy city of Qumm.

The principal difference between the *ulamā* and those Westernized intellectuals who nevertheless decried the West's "materialism" and opted for mysticism is the latter's insistence upon intuition and anti-rational symbolism.[11] The variant of mysticism followed by individuals such as Nasr represents a self-consciously elitist and highly cosmopolitan reflective orientation. For the clergy, it seems to be a sort of intellectual escapism from the social reality of daily deprivations faced by the masses. The willingness of the Court to underwrite *Sufism* and parade it as the genuine spiritual heritage of Iran also offended the *ulamā*, who regarded it as an effort to distort what they held was true Shi'ism.

Lay Intellectuals and the Husayniyah Irshad

Engineer Mihdi Bazargan and Dr. 'Ali Shari'ati (d. 1977) have probably been the two most outstanding examples of laymen with non-Sufi affinities of a revitalized Shi'ism. Of the two men, Shari'ati has had more far-reaching impact upon Iranian society. Little is reliably known of his early childhood and youth, apart from the fact that he came from a clergy background. His father, Ustad Muhammad Taqi Shari'ati, for many years was a respected professor of Islamic sciences in the Mashhad area in Northeast Iran. Father and son were arrested in 1957 for activities under the aegis of the National Front. Shari'ati was permitted to travel to Europe in 1960 and earned a doctorate in sociology at the Sorbonne. While in France, he met with Frantz Fanon, Jean-Paul Sartre and the sociologist, Georges Gurevich. He became radicalized on third world issues to the point of seeking common ground with Afro-Asian and Latin American intellectuals. He reportedly assisted in the composition of articles for the Algerian nationalist paper, *al-Mujahid*, during this time.

In 1964 he returned to Iran upon the death of his sister but was promptly arrested at the Turkish frontier and imprisoned. Six months later, he was released and, after several months of teaching in rural schools in the Mashhad region, he was invited to accept a faculty position at Mashhad University. During his stint there he introduced a course on the sociology of Islam, which rapidly became a highly popular class; in fact, it is speculated that his dismissal was related to the fact that he was too successful as a teacher. Nonetheless the regime permitted him to affiliate with a group of learned men, some of whom had participated in the sessions of the now defunct Monthly Religious Society. Thus was born the Husayniyah Irshad.[12] Shari'ati's participation in anti-regime activities during his years of study in France, and especially his role in the publication of the newsletter of the European branch of the National Front, *Iran-i Azad (Free Iran)*, during 1962-1964 left its mark on the student movement. Thus, it is difficult to know why the government equivocated so much about him: jailing him in the fifties, permitting him to go abroad in 1960, arresting him upon his return in 1964, releasing him six months later, permitting him to join the Husayniyah Irshad circle, arresting him in the summer of 1973, and releasing him again 18 months later. Perhaps pressure on the part of European intellectuals helped. But another reason may have been the government's desire to split the ranks of the religious opposition. It already favored mystical orientations to Islam. And now, in Shari'ati it found an individual with critical things to say about certain "mainstream" *ulamā*, especially but not only, about Ayatullah Sayyid Hadi Milani of Mashhad (d. 1975). one of the *maraji'-yi taqlid* of Iran.

It has been broadly hinted that Shari'ati's final arrest in 1973 was linked to the increasing emergence in Iranian protest politics of the Mujahidin-i Khalq (an urban-based Islamic guerrilla movement with ties to certain clergymen, notably Ayatullah Taliqani).[13] Yet, his release from prison in 1975 came at a time when the Mujahidin had certainly not ceased their guerrilla actions. Nevertheless, after another 18 months of virtual house arrest with severely restricted rights to have visitors, he was permitted to leave for Europe around early Spring, 1977. Just two months later friends and relatives found his dead body near London under circumstances that were highly suspicious. It is widely believed that he was murdered under orders of the security apparatus, SAVAK.

Shari'ati encountered problems with the *ulamā* almost from the beginning of the activities of the Husayniyah Irshad in 1965. His father's background and library brought Shari'ati into contact with the religious sciences at an early age; moreover, the young Shari'ati had attended lessons in his father's *madrasah* up to the intermediate cycle. He was therefore familiar with the discourse of the *ulamā*. Yet, the latter wished to dispute with this person who was urging a new approach to Shi'ism. And, in this process of disputation some technical "errors" on his part were alleged. Among the most commonly cited of his miscues, in the view of the clergy, were:

1. In a 1968 volume on the prophet, Shari'ati is alleged to have suggested that *shura* (a collegial decision-making body) was the appropriate way of selecting the leader of the *ummah* (Islamic community); whereas the Shi'ah have always held that the *vasayat* (bequeathal) and *valayat* (delegated authority) of the prophet flow to Imam 'Ali and his issue (i.e., the twelve *imams*).[14]

2. He used Sunni sources (the history of Tabari and the biography of ibn Hishsham) in discussing the life of the prophet; whereas sound Shi'i sources exist and should be utilized to avoid error.[15]

3. He declared that the forbidden fruit in the Garden of Eden was symbolic of knowledge; whereas Shi'ah have long held this to be a Christian view with no foundation in the Islamic tradition.[16]

4. He used the word *ijma'* to mean majority opinion; whereas Shi'i *ulamā* understand it to be a technical concept describing agreement by the learned men of the religious law on the basis of which they can issue a *fatva*.[17]

5. He claimed that the prophet was so happy to see his followers praying at the time of his illness that, upon getting up from bed and joining them, he placed himself beside Abu Bakr, rather than taking over the duties of leading the prayer.[18]

6. He regarded Buddha, Confucius and other great historical personalities as prophets; whereas no Muslim could call an individual a prophet who lacked a divine religion.[19]

A full exposition and critique of Shari'ati's thought would be beyond the limits of this essay. The most that can be done here is to outline his major points and to suggest those junctures where he had new things to say. Among the distinctive aspects of his writing and lecturing was his vigorous attack against those members of the clergy whom he regarded to be betraying their calling. To be sure, he had good things to say about the "true" *ulamā*, but on numerous occasions he vehemently attacked those individuals masquerading in the garb of the clergy but in fact bent on doing mischief. "We know the political past and social role of those who drag scientific inquiry and philosophical and historical criticism into the gutter . . . ."[20] In one of his most important works entitled *What Is To Be Done?* he excoriates traditionalist clergymen for their shortsightedness, abdication of responsiblity and implicit cooperation with *zulm*. A favorite term that he used was *ulama'-yi qishri* (hidebound clergymen), whose only interest, as Shari'ati saw it, was the mindless repetition of lessons in *fiq* (jurisprudence).²¹

Shari'ati placed enormous emphasis upon man's responsibility. In his essay, *The Responsibility of Being a Shi'i*, he said: "Everyone, whatever his level of scientific thinking or school or sect to which he belongs, must face this question: what responsibilities does my belief impose upon me?"²² The responsibility of the Shi'i is to insist upon man as a being who makes choices and who acts. Shari'ati emphatically rejected historical determinism if what is meant by that concept is that man does not make his own history through his conscious decisions.²³

Shari'ati's plans for religious education in Iran were radical. They involved a major shift of attention away from the staple of the *madrasahs: fiq* and *usul* (principles of jurisprudence); and a redirection of emphasis to sociology, history and biography. The names of Western scientists such as Einstein, Jung, Planck, Marx studded his model curriculum for the Husayniyah Irshad. Now, the references, in themselves, to such thinkers were not new, since the more recent generation of *madrasah* professors (including Ayatullah Nasir Makarim Shirazi)²⁴ have illustrated their lectures by using their names. What made Shari'ati's approach unique was the thorough analysis of people such as Marx or Sartre as progenitors of schools of thought.²⁵

Another feature of Shari'ati's pedagogy was his explicit concern for the philosophy of history as an integral part of one's *maktab* (belief system). Attention to this concept led him to and through considerations of causal sequences, motor forces of social change, historicist arguments about universal history, and the like. And ontologically, his position was that the basis of social reality is what he termed *tawhid* (lit. monotheism). Now, again, *tawhid* is not anything new for the *ulamā* since, quite obviously, it is absolutely central to Islam and the clergy's articulation of the faith. But Shari'ati insisted that *tawhid* for him meant something the clergy had never stressed in the past: the unity of God, nature and man. The concrescence of God, nature and man is an expression of what Shari'ati considered, in his major work, *The Sociology of Islam*, to be "the embracing of the entire world in a unity." And, he rejected the possibility of contradictions in the relationship between the three elements of his ontology.²⁶

A final aspect of Shari'ati's thinking worth citing is his preference for activism and dynamic orientation to the faith. Refusing to lie back and passively await the return of the Imam, Shari'ati held up the model of Abu Zarr Ghaffari, an early partisan of Imam 'Ali, for emulation. *Shi'ah* had for too long bemoaned their fate, he complained. Cathartic release from the sufferings of centuries at the hands of oppressors could not simply be gained from the reciting of the lives of Shi'i martyrs *(rawzah khvani)* or enactment of passion plays *(ta'ziyah)*. The time had come to stop lamentations and futile talk and to start acting. Unless the *Shi'ah* could engage in social action, the Imam would not consider them worthy and would continue to withhold his presence.[27] Ineluctably, he led himself to thinly disguised political criticisms of the regime. This criticism was couched in Aesopian language, to be sure, but on rare occasions he would deliver such statements as "... we are in dire need, [being] *more painfully than at any other time* ... sacrificed to captivity, ignorance and abjectness."[28]

The Role of Ayatullah Khumayni

The Shi'i resurgence in Iran has had its roots in three movements. The first is the Monthly Religious Society; the second is the Husayniyah Irshad; the third is Ayatullah Khumayni and his followers among the clergy: the *ulamā*, the *fuzalā* (clerics of intermediate rank), and the *tullab* (*madrasah* students). It is possible that certain individuals among the clergy have played a part in the events and intellectual currents of Iran during the 1960's and 1970's apart from the three movements abovementioned. But, oversimplified as this scheme may be, it perhaps does not distort reality greatly.

Ayatullah Khumayni's political opposition in the early 1960's was not the only social action at that time involving the clergy. It was, however, by far the most salient example of political protest. On the laymen's side there was, of course, the movement led by Shari'ati. But there seems to have been no relationship established between the two men. Between 1963 and 1978 Khumayni was in exile in the 'atabat (Shi'i Shrines) in Iraq. But, distance was not the problem, it appears: both individuals proceeded on their autonomous, but nonetheless similar, paths. In general, it may be said that Shariati's thought and behavior had greater influence among lay intellectuals; whereas Khumayni's impact was more decisive among the professional cadres of the religious institution. Each mobilized support among the partisans of the other, however. Shari'ati, the younger man, with his background in the National Front, probably esteemed Khumayni, but the latter may not have been enthusiastic over the activities of a person who was a member of the secular stratum of society, although himself not a secularist.

At the time of Khumayni's protest against the Shah's "White Revolution" the remaining *maraji'-yi taqlid* (Gulpaygani, Mar'ashi Najafi, Shari'atmadari, Khvansari, Milani) in Iran had remained relatively quietist. Khumayni's speeches in the Madrasah-yi Fayziyah of Qumm — the town's most important — against the government were in the tradition of the *mujtahids'* protests in the 19th and 20th centuries. The essential criticisms that he made were against the Shah's autocracy, corruption, social inequity and injustice, foreign domination, the regime's enfranchisement of women and the Family Protection Law, and the government's land tenure policies.

Yet, it was not until 1971 that he began to raise the question of the incompatibilities of Islam and monarchy.[29] And, it took him until 1978 to commence advocating the overthrow of the monarchical system and, pursuant to it, the end of the incumbent dynasty.[30]

Seeking doctrinal justification for the clergy exercising rule in the absence of the Imam, Khumayni begins his book, *Islamic Government*, by unequivocally declaring that logical proof is not necessary for the principle of *valayat-i faqih* (rule exercised by an eminent *mujtahid* in the absence of the Imam) [p. 6]. He argues in terms that will recall to the reader the language of those who struggle and seek justice. Unhappily for Shi'ism, in his view, false Muslims have infiltrated the *madrasahs* and other institutions of the faith; and, in the employ of imperialists, they have conveyed a distorted version of Islam, an Islam devoid of its "distinctive revolutionary character" *(khassiyat-i inqilabi)* and its manifest political and social dimensions. (pp. 7-8).

Khumayni's position on the role played by *mujtahids* in Iran during his years of exile is critical. He accuses them of contenting themselves with writing practical treatises — the *Risalah-yi Tawzih al-Masa'il* — on technical questions of worship and private morality. Rebukingly, he says that the ratio of verses in the Qur'an dealing with social issues to those covering matters of worship is 100 or more to one. (p. 9). The view that the proper role of the clergy is to sit in a corner of a mosque in Najaf or Qumm and read ordinances pertaining to menstruation and childbirth is a ludicrous distortion promoted by imperialists and their domestic agents, he holds. (p. 23). Khumayni thereupon expounds an argument on the concept of *valayat*, stating that the prophet designated a successor ('Ali) not so that he could codify ordinances of the faith but in order that he could implement laws and administer an

Islamic government. The successor of the prophet of God must, and was intended to, do far more than simply make pronouncements regarding ordinances *(bayyan-i ahkam)*; rather, the essential thing is to implement laws *(ijra' al-qanun)* and administer *(idarah)* government. (pp. 20 ff.)[31]

A doctrine of revolution exists in Islam, he asserts in a section of the book that focuses upon the appropriation of rule from the *imams* by their enemies. The *Shi'ah* have a duty, therefore, to make revolution against all those, including contemporary descendants of the enemies of 'Ali, who made it impossible for the *imams* to establish the *valayat* of the prophet. (pp. 39-41). Not long afterward, Khumayni cites a tradition from Imam Riza (the eighth *imam*) concerning the need to obey "those in authority among you" *('ula al-amr minkum)*, in keeping with the verse from the Qur'an: "O Ye who believe, obey God, obey the prophet and those in authority among you." The *hadith* (saying attributed to the Imam) suggests three reasons: (1) the believers will err in the absence of a proof *(hujjah)* of God (i.e., the Imam); (2) the community will become divided; (3) the religion will collapse from the onslaught of its enemies. (pp. 45-48).

It follows, then, for Ayatullah Khumayni, that efforts must be bent to insure the application of *valayat*. Since the Imam has disappeared and will only return to usher in the golden age, what must the Shi'i community do in the meantime? Khumayni posits that the Qur'an and the *sunnah* (traditions of the prophet's behavior) indicate that the ruler of the community must meet two qualifications: (a) eminence in knowledge of the Islamic law; (b) possession of the highest commitment to justice. Now, God has chosen not to designate for the *Shi'ah* any particular person to establish an Islamic government in the era of the occultation of the Imam. But yet, since there must be an Islamic government, *Shi'ah* must and can justifiably find candidates among the *ulamā*. "If they unite, they can establish a government of universal justice on earth." [sic!][32] (p. 63). This is the juncture at which Ayatullah Khumayni returns to the theme of *valayat-i faqih:*

> If a suitable individual endowed with these two qualities (knowledge and justice) should rise up and establish a government, he will have the very *valayat* of the prophet(s) as to the administration of society; and it will be incumbent upon all the people to obey him. (p. 63).

There follow some one hundred pages in which Ayatullah Khumayni cites verses from the Qur'an and *hadiths* attributed to the prophet and the *imams*. The references are meant to show that the eminent *mujtahids* of the age justly can claim *valayat.* During the argument, he several times has to face certain intricate problems, such as that posed by a more authoritative source [e.g., ibn Babuyah (d. 991)] transmitting a weaker version of a *hadith* and a less authoritative source [e.g., Shaykh Mufid (d. 1022)] citing a stronger version of the same *hadith.* Although it is impossible here to focus more closely on the details of his argument, it may be said that *Islamic Government* is more than a revolutionary tract arguing in favor of the overthrow of a system and its replacement by another. Its author, a learned man of the law, exerts himself to substantiate his arguments from classic sources of the *shari'ah* as befits his calling as a *marja'-i taqlid.*

The remainder of the book is dedicated to exhorting the clergy to protest, if not physically — because of the apparent power of the bureaucratic state in 1971 — then at least verbally. At one point, the author says that subjecting oneself to *zulm* is worse than *zulm* itself. (p. 158). And, as if wishing to illustrate his discussion with more contemporary developments, he cites the burning of al-Aqsa Mosque in Jerusalem in 1969 as an example of oppression in recent times. Khumayni accuses the Iranian government of having engineered a publicity campaign for voluntary contributions from the masses to help reconstruct the damaged structure but pocketing most of these funds. Moreover, the repair of the mosque itself was not in Islam's best interests, according to Khumayni, because it thereby erased "the traces of Israel's crime." (p. 161).

Somewhat later, Khumayni sounds a good deal like the reformers of the Monthly Religious Society, Murtaza Mutahhari and Muhammad Ibrahim Ayati, in their essays on *al-amr bi al-ma'ruf wa al-nahy 'an al-munkar.* Echoing their words, written in 1960, he here complains that Iranians have virtually forgotten the powerful force of this principle of the faith and have "placed it within a narrow compass . . . ." (p. 163). In short, they have contented themselves with applying the principle to individual acts of transgression by private persons, rather than employing it in a broad range of public policy issues. As long as the clergy play with words they will forfeit their true role. The *ulamā* must, of course, not ignore matters of worship *('ibadat).* "But the important things are the political, economic and legal questions of Islam." (p. 173). And, it will not do for the clergy to dissimulate their belief *(taqiyah)* according to the technically permissible practice of the oppressed *Shi'ah* in history. *Taqiyah,* Khumayni writes, is valid in the present period only if it permits its practitioner to penetrate the regime and thus lay the groundwork for revolution against it. (pp. 200-201).

He concludes by urging his audience to expel the royalist clergy from their posts; to purge the *madrasahs* of *ulamā* collaborators; and to "establish new legal, financial, economic, cultural and political institutions." (pp. 199 ff., and at 204). To fail to do these things would be tantamount to nothing less than "the defeat of the Mahdi, Imam-i Zaman." (p. 202).

Clergy Relations With The Left In The 1970's

In the 1970's the left in the main was comprised of the Tudah (Communist Party — pro-Moscow), the Mujahidin-i Khalq and the Fida'iyan-i Khalq. Of the three the first has a much longer record, having been constituted in 1941.[33] But, virtually all observers agree that it participated little in the developments culminating in the 1978-1979 revolution. Its former Secretary-General, Iraj Eskandari, in late 1978 welcomed "the fact that the religious movement is performing currently an important role in mobilizing the democratic and national forces. . . ."

> The situation would be different if the matter concerned the creation of a theocratic state. But as far as we know, the Iranian religious leaders have not called at all for anything of the sort.[34]

To be sure, December, 1978, was a time when the revolution had not yet reached its climax. But Iskandari must have known about Ayatullah Khumayni's book, *Islamic Government*, and his perfervid appeals to bring about an Islamic government (i.e., a theocratic state).

Of greater political significance than the Tudah — at least in the short and medium runs — is the orientation of the Mujahidin-i Khalq. Several clergymen had unsuccessfully interceded on behalf of five members of the Mujahidin in 1972 with the intent of saving them from the regime's plan to execute them. It was rumored that several of the *maraji'-yi taqlid* were involved in this abortive effort, and we know that Ayatullah Taliqani was exiled for his role in this affair and related events of protest.[35]

The Mujahidin's relations with Taliqani derived from their having come into existence as an offshoot of the Nihzat-i Azadi-yi Iran (The Freedom Movement of Iran) — of which Taliqani, as already noted above, had been co-founder with Mihdi Bazargan in the early 1960's. It therefore might be expected of the Mujahidin that they would entertain a pro-Shi'i perspective. In 1979, a brochure published by this organization, declared:

> After years of extensive study into Islamic history and Shi'i ideology, our organization has reached the firm conclusion that Islam, especially Shi'ism, will play a major role in inspiring the masses to join the revolution. It will do so because Shi'ism, particularly [Imam] Husayn's historic act of resistance, has both a revolutionary message and a special place in our popular culture.[36]

We have little reliable information on the ongoing relations between the Mujahidin and the clergy. In general, it may be surmised that such relations — if they existed — were, and continue to be, fragile and irregular. After the departure of the Shah and return of Ayatullah Khumayni to Iran (February, 1979), the regime attacked the Mujahidin as part of an overall anti-leftist campaign. Bazargan, the Prime Minister, called those adhering to the left "SAVAK agents". And Khumayni has denied that the left played any constructive role at all in the revolution. With the death of Ayatullah Taliqani in September, 1979, the Mujahidin appear to have lost the only potential important ally among the clergy. And even during his lifetime, toward the end, Taliqani turned against the left.

Asked about his organization's role during the revolution, a Mujahidin spokesman declared in August, 1979: "We were a vanguard organization, and we offered a correct analysis. . . . But we did not operate under our own name. We worked in secret."[37] Although the movement had suffered a split in 1975 that led to the emergence of a strongly Marxist faction, the "loyalist" non-Marxist Mujahidin in 1979 did not boycott the referendum on the Islamic Republic in March of that year. On the other hand, both the Tudah and the Fida'iyan-i Khalq did boycott it on the grounds that the manner of posing the question prejudiced the outcome in favor of a "yes" vote. Though the Mujahidin (non-Marxist) did not oppose the referendum, Ayatullah Taliqani attacked the leftist parties in a speech in July in which he pointedly failed to differentiate among any of its factions.[38] In this way, the leaders of the Islamic republic of Iran have condemned the Tudah, the Fida'iyan-i Khalq, the original (non-Marxist) Mujahidin and its Marxist faction (known as Paykar) as being all of a piece.

Before the 1975 split, the Mujahidin spoke in these terms about the relationship between Marxism and Islam:

> Of course, Marxism and Islam are not identical. Nevertheless, Islam is definitely closer to Marxism than to Pahlavism [from Pahlavi, the name of the fallen dynasty]. Islam and Marxism teach the same lessons for they fight against injustice.[39]

It is fair to say that the Mujahidin continue to adhere to such a view; whereas the Paykar faction is definitely anti-religious. A serious problem arose for Ayatullah Taliqani when his son declared his adherance to Paykar,[39] and this was no doubt an incentive for his attacks during the spring and summer of 1979 against the left. The Tudah Party has been more circumspect than Paykar regarding Islam. It has considered Shi'ism as too important a cultural phenomenon to combat head on. Thus, Ihsan Tabari, the veteran Iranian Marxist-Leninst, has recently written in the Party's newspaper (published outside Iran):[40]

> The history of the Tudah shows that people with deep religious convictions have been party members. Moreover, some of the founders of our party were religious. All this is proof of the Party's principled attitude toward Islam. The Tudah has consistently cooperated with progressive religious elements . . . such as Ayatullah Khumayni and Ayatullah Shari'atmadari . . . in the spirit of the teachings of Muhammad, 'Ali and Husayn.

The Fida'iyan (like Paykar) does not disguise its anti-religious orientation. In a recent interview with a spokesman for the Fida'iyan, the latter spoke about the movement's assessment of Ayatullah Khumayni:[41]

> His support comes from the upper sections of the traditional bourgeoisie [sic]. His outlook just consists of Islam and nothing else. And his reliance on religion leads him to confuse a popular with an anti-popular line. Each of the two factions thinks that Islam can solve their problems. There are revolutionaries in the committees [formed by the regime], and there are SAVAK agents.

The splintering of the left into further factions and their realignment in the 1977-1980 period has produced two tendencies: one has called for the consolidation of gains; the other has urged permanent revolution and the overthrow of what it regards to be a "petit bourgeois" regime of clerics and middle class secular nationalists, replacing it with the dictatorship of the proletariat.[42] It may reasonably be expected that continuous evolution and crystallization of views will occur in the Iranian left in the next one or two years. Whether this process will lead to more coherent ties to the *ulamā* is difficult to predict with any assurance.

Conclusions

While emphasis in this discussion has been on the role of a resurgent Shi'ism in the 1978-1979 Iranian revolution it is not meant to imply that the revolution was an exclusively religious phenomenon. Yet, there is no question that the efforts of the clergy for nearly three decades (1950-1980) to reinvigorate the religious institution had much to do with the revolution and its outcome. Although the various religious leaders and the religiously-oriented lay intellectuals differed in their approaches and emphases, it is clear that Iranian Shi'ism was the rallying point for all of them; furthermore, those active in Shi'i movements during this time, seemed to have as their common foe the secularization of society under the aegis of the state.

The sociologist Max Weber considered social action to consist of an event, together with the meaning attributed by individuals to that event. And for Weber such social action derives from the *ideal and material* interests of the actors as they perceive them. The Iranian revolution may be seen in these terms. The clergy and their supporters alone did not make the revolution. But, the symbolic discourse and praxis of the *ulamā* and their lay supporters were absolutely crucial for its success.

Shi'ism, it has often been suggested, provides a sharper cutting edge than Sunnism for social protest and political activism. This has to do with such doctrinal principles as the imamate, *valayat,* and *ijtihad* (mental exercise by legal specialists to render interpretations on points of law). It also has to do with the financial autonomy of the religious institution from the state; and finally, it stems to a large degree from the vocabulary and dramaturgical elements familiar to practitioners of the faith. Sunni Islam differs in these respects.

Iranian Shi'ism is, therefore, in some respects, *sui generis*. It would be an error to make generalizations on the Muslim world as a whole based on the Iranian experience. Yet, as the other essays in this volume show, movements of Islamic revival are taking place in almost every Muslim country in the world. While there is no way to foretell what kind of configurations such movements will take in the future, we do know that organizational and ideological ties that exist between Iranian Shi'ism and Sunni Islam elsewhere will make such configurations almost inevitable. At the very least it can be assumed that the Iranian revolution will influence religiously inspired social action and protest in other parts of the Islamic world. Scholars and policy makers will need to accustom themselves to a new paradigm concerning social change, therefore. Similarly Muslim clergy who have not filled such decision-making roles in the past will have to be ready to assume such roles. Whether or not Ayatullah Khumayni's vision of an Islamic government under the principle of *valayat-i faqih* will be supported by all segments of Iranian society is another question, however. Only history will answer that. Similarly, whether or not such Islamic governments will rise to power in other Muslim countries will depend on many factors, some of them as yet unknown.

Footnotes

[1] Perhaps the gap dividing the religious fundamentalists (the Fida'iyan-i Islam) and the lay circles *is* insuperable. Of course, the fundamentalists must not be confused with the leaders of "high religion" — whom we can identify as the ranking *mujtahids* of the country.

[2] Assessments of the contributions of Ayatullah Burujirdi to Iranian Shi'ism appeared in the panegyric written by 'Ali Davani, *Zindigani-yi Ayatullah Burujirdi* (Qumm: Hikmat, 1340 H. Sh./1961); for a more even-handed appraisal, consult Murtaza Mutahhari, "Mazaya va Khadamat-i Marhum Ayatullah Burujirdi," *Bahsi dar Barah-yi Marja'iyat va Ruhaniyat* (Tehran: n. p. 1341/1962).

[3] For the period between 1945-1958 see Shahrough Akhavi, *Religion And Politics in Contemporary Iran: Clergy-State Relations in the Pahlavi Period* (Albany: State University of New York Press, 1980), pp. 63-90.

[4] See the articles attacking the clergy in *Ittila'at* (Tehran) for the following dates in 1963: 15, 16, 18 Isfand 1341 H. Sh.; 13, 15 Murdad 1342 H. Sh.

[5] Mutahhari, "Mushkil-i Asasi Dar Sazman-i Ruhaniyat," in *Bahsi dar Barah-yi Marja'iyat va Ruhaniyat,* pp. 118 ff.

[6] As Bernard Lewis points out, the Islamic doctrine of revolution is based on the legitimacy of same in the event that the ruler is impious (cf. tyrannical). The Qur'anic injunction that "there is no duty of obedience in sin" suggests the potential of violent social protest against the ruler. But, as Lewis additionally points out, no criterion of sinfulness was generated by the Islamic community upon which all could agree; and no machinery to impose sanctions against a sinning ruler was devised in the historical development of Islam. See Lewis, "Islamic Concepts of Revolution," in *Revolution in the Middle East,* ed. P. J. Vatikiotis (London: Allen & Unwin, 1972) p. 33. Yet, the Shi'i clergy has behaved in such a way in the history of modern Iran that

they have a greater sense of confidence concerning *zulm*, including their ability to detect it.

⁷V. V. Minorsky, *Tadhkirah al-Muluk*. E. J. W. Gibb Memorial Publications, N. S. Vol. XVI (London: Luzac, 1943), pp. 42, 78-79, 111, 146-47.

⁸Hamid Algar, *Religion and State in Iran, 1785-1906* (Berkeley: University of California Press, 1969), *passim;* Nikki R. Keddie, *Religion and Rebellion in Iran: The Tobacco Protest of 1891-1892* (London: Frank Cass, 1966), *passim*. The literature on the Qajar period is growing rapidly, with many excellent contributions in the form of monographs and essays too numerous to list here.

⁹On the Pahlavi period, see Hamid Algar, "The Oppositional Role of the *Ulamā* in Twentieth Century Iran," in *Scholars, Saints and Sufis: Muslim Religious Institutions Since 1500*, ed. Nikki Keddie (Berkeley: University of California Press, 1971), pp. 231-55; Michael M. J. Fischer, *Iran: From Religious Dispute to Revolution* (Cambridge: Harvard University, 1980). Akhavi, *Religion and Politics in Contemporary Iran*. Keddie, *Iran: Politics, Religion and Society* (London: Frank Cass, 1980). M. Bonine and N. Keddie, eds. *Modern Iran* (Albany: State University of New York Press, 1981), including the two essays by Mangol Bayat-Philipp on 'Ali Shari'ati and the reform tradition in modern Iranian Shi'ism. On Shari'ati and Khumayni, see below in the text.

¹⁰On these extremely important issues, see 'Allamah Muhammad Husayn Taba'taba'i, et. al., *Bahsi dar Barah-yi Marja'iyat va Ruhaniyyat;* and the three volume compendium collectively entitled *Guftar-i Mah dar Namayandan-i Rah-i Rast-i Din,* 3 Vols. (Tehran: Sadduq, 1339-1341 H. Sh./1960-1963.

¹¹"The contrast with the *ulamā* . . . becomes striking . . . For the *ulamā,* gnosis is not a different realm of experience but only a deeper level of comprehension. . . . Above all, the *ulamā* are less interested in the self than in society." Fischer, *Iran,* p. 146. For some of Nasr's large corpus of writings, consult his *Sufi Essays* (Albany: State University of New York Press, 1972); *Islam and the Plight of Modern Man* (New York: Longmans, Green, 1975); *The Encounter of Man and Nature* (London: Allen and Unwin, 1968); *Science and Civilization in Islam* (Cambridge: Harvard University Press, 1968).

¹²For information on Shari'ati, see the following: *Yadnamah-yi Mujahid-i Shahid Dr. 'Ali Shari'ati,* a special issue of the journal, *Fajr,* published by the Anjuman-i Islami-yi Danishjuyan-i Hawzah-yi Oklahoma, Vol II, no. 5 (Shahrivar 1356 H. Sh./1977); *Hijrat va*

Shahadat-i Abu Zarr-i Zaman: Mujahid Dr. 'Ali Shari'ati, a memorandum issued by one of the Iranian Islamic Societies of University Students in the United States, n.d.; *Asnadi bar Shahadat-i Ustad 'Ali Shari'ati* (Tehran: n.p., n.d.); and Translator's Foreword by Hamid Algar to his translations of Shari'ati's excerpted writings entitled *On the Sociology of Islam* (Berkeley: Mizan Press, 1979), pp. 5-7; and the anonymous sketch in *ibid.*, pp. 3-34.

[13] *Asnadi*, p. 24.

[14] Shari'ati, "Az Hijrat Ta Vafat," in *Muhammad, Khatam-i Payambaran*, Vol. I (Tehran: Husayniyah Irshad, 1347 H. Sh./1968), p. 345 ff. In fact Shari'ati was somewhat remiss with his language, but he is right in his claim that he was not trying to say *shura* is a model solution for designating the leader of the *ummah;* rather that, given that the discussion that immediately preceded was about the weaknesses and defects of Western democracy, he was trying to make the point that the companions of the prophet were more successful in their application of democratic principles than Western leaders today in countries where large inequities exist.

[15] He replied that he used Sunni sources for a variety of reasons: (1) he wanted to utilize primary sources as much as possible; (2) he felt that as a comparative historical sociologist he had a duty to his profession to utilize all available materials; (3) he hoped that his example would lead Sunni scholars to utilize Shi'i sources; (4) using a source for reference does not mean wholesale transfer of the analysis to be found in that source to one's own writing. See Shari'ati's defense in the proceedings of a roundtable at the Husayniyah Irshad entitled *Pasukh bi Su'alat va Intiqadat* (Tehran: Husayniyah Irshad, 1971), pp. 3 ff., 37 ff., pp. 91-93.

[16] See the polemic launched against Shari'ati by Ayatullah Shaykh Nasir Makarim Shirazi, "Aya Hukumat-i Islami bar Pay-i Shura Ast?" in *Darsha'i az Maktab-i Islam*, Vol. XIII, no. 1 (1392 H.Q./1972), pp. 76-78; and Shari'ati's response in "Namah'i az Dr. 'Ali Shari'ati bi Agha-yi Nasir Makarim," *Haft Namah az Mujahid-i Shahid Dr. 'Ali Shari'ati* (Tehran: Intisharat-i Abu Zarr, 1356 H. Sh./1977), p. 28. Shari'ati's word was "awareness" *(agahi)*. One wonders whether Makarim was discomfited partly because he saw lurking in Shari'ati's identification of the fruit with knowledge the seeds of an incipient eulogy for Prometheus and the Prometheus legend.

[17] Makarim, "Aya Hukumat-i Islami," pp. 76-78; Shari'ati, "Namah'i," p. 33.

[18] Shari'ati, "Pasukh", pp. 43-45. Shari'ati says that in relating this *hadith* (which Makarim alleged was not sound), he did not mean to imply that Muhammad was thereby investing Abu Bakr with the succession (caliphate). Muhammad's behavior can simply be described in everyday human terms as the behavior of a person delighted with what he sees immediately before him. The smile on his face had no further or future implications for the rule over the *ummah*. See also *ibid.*, pp. 77-84, 114 ff.

[19] Shari'ati, "Sima-yi Muhammad," in *Muhammad, Khatam-i Payambaran*, I, p. 459 ff. Shari'ati was using the term prophet from the point of view of the Weberian tradition of comparative historical sociology, of course.

[20] Shari'ati, "Namah'i," p. 30. Recently, there have been attempts to conflate the differences between Shari'ati and the traditional clergy. This is the course followed by Hamid Algar in a paper he presented to the Conference on the Islamic Revival, University of Chicago, 28-31 May 1980. Shari'ati, himself, notes that he is not an inveterate critic of the clergy. See his long statement in rebuttal to a complaint that he was anti-clerical in *Pasukh bi Su'alat*, pp. 121-131.

[21] Shari'ati, *Chih Bayad Kard?* (Tehran: Husayniyah Irshad, n.d.), p. 15.

[22] Shari'ati, "Mas'uliyat-i Shi'ah Budan," in *Shi'ah* (Tehran: Husayniyah Irshad, 1350 H. Sh./1971), p. 229.

[23] Shari'ati, *Jabr-i Tarikh* (Tehran: n. p., 1354 H. Sh./1975), *passim*. He wishes to make a distinction between the French *déterminisme historique* and the Farsi phrase *jabr-i tarikh*. The former suggests that man is bounded by the corporeal realities of his existence — he must eat, he cannot dispense with the force of certain natural laws, etc. In that sense, man is "determined" by circumstances beyond his control. But in every other respect, he is free to choose. However, he argues, Iranians have used the phrase *jabr-i tarikh* in so literal a sense that they mean by it that man is a mere plaything of historical events in the making of which he does not exercise any free will. This version of historical determinism Shari'ati repudiates utterly in favor of a view of man as a responsible, choosing individual. The theme is to be found virtually everywhere in his writings. For an explicit rejection of Marxism on these grounds, consult his *Insan, Marksizm, Islam* (Qumm: n. p., 1355 H. Sh./1976), *passim.*

[24] On Ayatullah Makarim's teaching style and content, see Fischer, *Iran*, pp. 66-73.

[25] On the curriculum Shari'ati proposed, as well as an analysis of his

thought in its larger context, see Akhavi, *Religion and Politics,* pp. 156-158, and 144 et. seq. Further research on Shari'ati continues and will be published in the near future. These efforts include the essay by Bayat-Philipp (fn. 9 *supra*) and a paper to be published by Syndikat, Frankfurt (in German) on the topic of "Shari'ati's Political Ideas," by Shahrough Akhavi. This paper will be part of a series of papers presented as proceedings of the Seminar on the History and Politics of Religious Movements in Iran held under the auspices of the Berlin Institute for Comparative Social Research of the Free University of Berlin in September 1980. An American, English-language volume is also contemplated under the editorship of Nikki Keddie. Additionally, Hamid Algar is working on a history of the Iranian revolution and will focus much of his attention on Shari'ati. Mention should also be made of 'Ali Shari'ati, *Marxism And Other Western Fallacies: An Islamic Critique,* Tr. R. Campbell (Berkeley: Mizan Press, 1980).

[26] Shari'ati, *Islamshinasi* (Tehran: Husayniyah Irshad, n. d.), pp. 47-53.

[27] Shari'ati, *Intizar-i Mazhab-i I'tiraz* (Tehran: Husayniyah Irshad, 1350 H. Sh./1971), *passim.*

[28] Shari'ati, *Shahadat* (Tehran: Husayniyah Irshad, 1351 H. Sh./1972), pp. 69-70. Emphasis supplied.

[29] Ruhullah al-Musavi Khumayni, *Hukumat-i Islami* (Najaf: n. p. 1391 H. Q./1971), pp. 12, 55-57. Some thirty years earlier he had argued that the clergy were not against monarchy but only against erring and sinning monarchs; and he came perilously close to the long-held Sunni view that it was better to have a bad government than none at all. See his *Kashf al-Asrar* (Tehran: n. p. 1363 H. Q./1943), pp. 187 ff.

[30] Akhavi, *Religion and Politics,* pp. 163-171, esp. 167.

[31] Khumayni points to the following features of the *shari'ah* (Islamic law) which he feels establishes without doubt that social and political issues are integral to Shi'i Islam: (1) regulations concerning finance; (2) regulations concerning defense of the community; (3) regulations concerning the administration of justice *(ihqaq-i huquq)* [pp. 34-39].

[32] "... *hukumat-i 'adl-i 'umumi dar 'alam*..." What is surprising about this phrase that Khumayni uses is that "a government of universal justice on earth" is historically associated with that which the Imam will establish upon his return.

[33] Sepehr Zabih, *The Communist Movement in Iran* (Berkeley: University of California Press, 1966); George Lenczowski, *Russia and the West in Iran* (Ithaca, N. Y.: Cornell University Press, 1948);

Ervand Abrahamian, "Communism and Communalism in Iran," *International Journal of Middle East Studies*, I, 1 (January 1970), pp. 291-316.

[34] Reported in *al-Nida'* (Beirut), 17 December 1978, cited in *Middle East Research and Information Project Report* [hereafter MERIP], No. 87 (May 1980), p. 30.

[35] Akhavi, *Religion and Politics*, pp. 162, 235. The names of the religious leaders in Shiraz who sent a telegram of protest against the pending executions to Ayatullah Milani in Mashhad were Ayatullah Majd al-Din Mahallati — who had been active in the 1963 disturbances — and Ayatullah Muhammad Ja'far Tahiri.

[36] Cited in Ervand Abrahamian, "The Guerilla Movement in Iran, 1963-1977," *MERIP Report*, No. 86 (March/April 1980), p. 10.

[37] Fred Halliday, "Interviews," *MERIP Report*, No. 86 (March/April 1980), p. 17.

[38] *Ibid.*, p. 19.

[39] The account of the split within the Mujahidin ranks is in Abrahamian, "The Guerilla Movement," where this citation is also to be found on p. 11.

[40] Cited in "Tudah: 'Socialism and Islam,' " *MERIP Report*, No. 87 (May 1980), p. 29.

[41] Halliday, "Interviews," p. 18.

[42] Abrahamian, "The Guerilla Movement," p. 14.

Bibliography

Abrahamian, Ervand, "Communism and Communalism in Iran," International Journal of Middle East Studies [IJMES], I, 4 (1970). pp. 291-316.

_____, "The Guerilla Movement, 1963-1977," *MERIP Report*, No. 86 (March/April 1980). pp. 3-15.

Akhavi, Shahrough, *Religion and Politics in Contemporary Iran: Clergy-State Relations in the Pahlavi Period.* Albany: State University of New York Press, 1980.

Algar, Hamid, "The Oppositional Role of the *Ulama* in Twentieth Century Iran," *Scholars, Saints and Sufis*, ed. Nikki Keddie. Berkeley: University of California Press, 1971. pp. 231-255.

_____, *Religion and State in Iran, 1785-1906.* Berkeley: University of California Press, 1969.

Arjomand, Said Amir, "Political Action and Legitimate Domination in Shi'ite Iran: Fourteenth to Eighteenth Centuries A. D," *Archives européenes de sociologie.* XX, 1 (1979). pp. 59-109.

Avery, Peter, *Modern Iran.* New York: Praeger, 1967.

Bill, James A, "The Pattern of Elite Politics in Iran," *Political Elites in the Middle East.* ed. George Lenczowski. Washington, D.C.: American Enterprise Institute for Public Policy Research, 1975. pp. 17-40.

_____, *The Politics of Iran.* Columbus, Ohio: Bobbs-Merrill, 1972.

Binder, Leonard, *Iran.* Berkeley: University of California Press, 1961.

_____ "The Proofs of Islam," *Studies in Honor of H. A. R. Gibb.* ed. George Makdisi. Leiden: E. J. Brill, 1965. pp. 118-140.

Cottam, Richard, *Nationalism in Iran.* 2nd ed. Pittsburgh: University of Pittsburgh Press, 1980.

Eliash, Joseph, "The Ithna Ashari Juristic Theory of Political and Legal Authority," *Studia Islamica.* XXIX (1969), pp. 17-30.

_____, "Misconceptions Regarding the Juridical Status of the Iranian *Ulamā*," *IJMES.* X, 1 (1979). pp. 9-25.

Fischer, Michael M. J., *Iran: From Religious Dispute to Revolution.* Cambridge: Harvard University Press, 1980.

_____, "Persian Society: Transition and Strain," *Twentieth Century Iran.* ed. H. Amirsadeghi and R. W. Ferrier. London: Heinemann, 1977.

Graham, Robert, *Iran: The Illusion of Power.* London: Croom Helm, 1978.

Ha'iri, Abdul-Hadi, *Shi'ism and Constitutionalism: A Study of the Life and Views of Mirza Muhammad Husayn Na'ini, A Shi'i Mujtahid of Iran.* Leiden: E. J. Brill, 1975.

Halliday, Fred, "Interviews," *MERIP Report.* No. 86 (March/April 1980). pp. 16-21.

_____, *Iran: Dictatorship and Revolution.* London: Penguin, 1979.

Keddie, Nikki, *Iran: Politics, Religion And Society*. London: Frank Cass, 1980.

_____, *An Islamic Response to Imperialism: Political and Religious Writings of Sayyid Jamal al-Din "al-Afghani."* Berkeley: University of California Press, 1968.

_____, and M. Bonine, eds. *Modern Iran*. Albany: State University of New York Press, 1981.

_____, "The Origins of the Religious-Radical Alliance in Iran," *Past and Present*, XXXIV (1966). pp. 70-80.

_____, "Religion and Irreligion in Early Iranian Nationalism," *Comparative Studies in Society and History*. IV, 3 (1962). pp. 265-295.

_____, *Religion and Rebellion in Iran: The Tobacco Protest of 1891-1892*. London: Frank Cass, 1966.

_____, "The Roots of the Ulama's Power in Modern Iran," *Studia Islamica*. XXIX (1969). pp. 31-53.

_____, *Sayyid Jamal al-Din "al-Afghani:" A Political Biography*. Berkeley: University of California Press, 1968.

Lambton, Ann K. S., *Landlord and Peasant in Persia*. 2nd ed. London: Oxford University Press, 1969.

_____, *The Persian Land Reform*. London: Oxford University Press, 1966.

_____ "Quis Custodiet Custodes?" *Studia Islamica*. V (1955). pp. 125-148; VI (1956). pp. 125-146.

_____, "A Reconsideration of the Position of *Marja' Taqlid* and the Religious Institution," *Studia Islamica*. XX (1964). pp. 115-135.

Millward, William G., "Aspects of Modernism in Shi'a Islam," *Studia Islamica*. XXXVII (1973). pp. 111-128.

Nasr, Seyyed Hossein, *An Introduction to Islamic Cosmological Doctrines*. Cambridge: Harvard University Press, 1968.

_____, *Islam and the Plight of Modern Man*. New York: Longmans, Green, 1975.

_____, *Science and Civilization in Islam*. Cambridge: Harvard University Press, 1968.

Shari'ati, Ali, *On the Sociology of Islam.* Tr. Hamid Algar. Berkeley: Mizan Press, 1979.

_____, *Marxism and Other Western Fallacies: An Islamic Critique.* Tr. R. Campbell. Berkeley: Mizan Press, 1980.

Taba'taba'i, Muhammad Husayn, *Shi'ite Islam.* Tr. Seyyed Hossein Nasr. Albany: State University of New York Press, 1975.

Yann, Richard, *Le Shi'isme en Iran.* Paris, 1980.

Zonis, Marvin, *The Political Elite of Iran.* Princeton: Princeton University Press, 1971.

_____, "The Political Elite of Iran: A Second Stratum?" *Political Elites and Political Development in the Middle East.* ed. Frank Tachau. Cambridge: Schenkman: 1975. pp. 193-216.

XII

THE SCOURGING OF THE SHAH

Russ Braley

Just months before the Iranian revolution President Jimmy Carter stood in Teheran and toasted the Shah of Iran as a close friend of the United States and a rock of stability in the Near East. Yet in a short while this rock of stability was swept away in a revolution whose apparent engineers came right out of the medieval Muslim madrasa, not from a modern leftist guerilla training camp. Everyone who should have known better seems to have been caught off guard by the revolution — the Shah, the SAVAK, the CIA, the U.S. State Department, the world press. There must be much more to the revolution than what we know so far; the pieces simply don't fit together. A national debate over "Who Lost Iran?" may not serve any useful purpose at this point, but we must get to the bottom of this affair to know what exactly happened, if for nothing else. Mr. Russ Braley attempted to do this. His investigations produced this report which provides a plausible explanation to what happened but at the same time casts a shadow of doubt on the faithfulness of the U.S. Government, the intelligence of the SAVAK and the CIA, the wisdom of the Shah and the credibility of the American media. There are indeed serious indictments in this report. Mr. Braley's conclusions are presented here not as final judgments but as serious questions to those who are bound by duty and ethics to give responsible answers and in the interest of open discussion on an event that touched the lives of all of us, perhaps more than any other in recent years.

Russ Braley was foreign correspondent for the **New York Daily News** *from 1955 to 1975, reporting on such events as the Hungarian revolution in 1956, the building of the Berlin Wall in 1961, the Middle East Six Day War in 1967, the "Prague Spring" in Czechoslovakia in 1968, Jordan's civil war in 1970, the Middle East October War in 1973 and the summit conferences and foreign ministers' conferences of the period. In November 1978 he reported on the Iranian revolution. He is presently United Nations correspondent of the* **New York Daily News.**

Iran is difficult for Americans to understand, so I would like to stop off first in a country we know a little better, West Germany.

Almost 13 years ago, on June 2, 1967, Iranian students studying at universities in West Germany traveled to West Berlin, where the Shah was on a one-day visit. They joined their colleagues studying there and staged a riot.

They distributed paper-bag masks and six-foot staves, which made sure there would be a violent clash with the police, although the police were popular in West Berlin.

The Iranians were backed up by thousands of German students, mostly from the Free University, which was subsidized by American foundations. The young Germans had become quite radical.

Young West Germans didn't really have anything to revolt against. They were at peace, had a working democracy and unprecedented prosperity, and they had no sense of guilt over World War II, which had subdued their parents politically for a time. But they had psychological grievances.

The young Germans felt guilt over the abandonment of East Germans. They had wounded pride: the enduring Berlin Wall meant to them that Germans were not trustworthy enough to have their own nation.

They turned radical in the atmosphere of the 1960's, following the example of young Americans, who had started a wave of civil disobedience in 1964 at Berkeley with Mario Savio's Free Speech movement, and who were getting ready to march on the Pentagon behind Norman Mailer protesting the Vietnam war.

The Berlin students resented the Vietnam war, partly because it had made Washington forget the Berlin Wall entirely, and they had romanticized Ho Chi Minh, Che Guevara and their own rediscovered Rosa Luxemburg. They were studying the third-way communism of Professor Theodor Adorno of Frankfurt University, which was related vaguely to the ideas of Professor Herbert Marcuse in California, Marcuse being a born Berliner.

Mostly, though, it was the Berlin Wall that had made them radical. The passive acceptance of the Western nations, especially the United States, of the Berlin Wall in 1961 was a kind of national insult as well as a trauma. About 1964, many Berlin students turned to studying Marxism-Leninism in the hope of playing a modifying role on what looked like the winning side in both Berlin and Vietnam.

The West German radical youth movement was loosely organized in the APO, the German acronym for "opposition outside parliament." It had a naive slogan authorizing "violence against property but not against persons."

The anti-Shah riot changed that. During the riot, a young German rioter, Benno Ohnesorg, was killed by a shot from a high ranking police officer, who immediately resigned.

In a follow-up demonstration, a row of girls in tight white T-shirts marched to City Hall, the fronts of their T-shirts lettered to spell out the name of the mayor, Heinrich Albertz. When they turned around in unison, their backs spelled out "resign," with an exclamation point at the end.

To everyone's surprise, Albertz, a pacifist pastor who only recently had inherited the job from Willy Brandt, did resign. It was a striking success for the young radicals, and it cost only one life.

The girl who played the exclamation point was Gudrun Ensslin. A year later she, Andreas Baader and two others set fire to two department stores in Frankfurt, protesting obscene consumerism. The Hamburg columnist Ulrike Meinhof attended their trial, and the first contacts were made for what became in 1970 the Baader-Meinhof Gang, or Red Army Faction, *(Rote Armee Fraktion)* as they called themselves.

The Red Army Faction inspired extremism in a number of ancillary organizations and underground newspapers. One group was called the June 2 Movement, in honor of Benno Ohnesorg.

Over the next decade, the groups killed, maimed and kidnaped judges, prosecutors, police officers, U.S. Army officers and soldiers and some of their own members who tried to defect.

After a series of attacks in the late 1970's, including the murders of a leading national banker and a leading industrialist, the sleepy capital of Bonn was turned into an armed camp, with barbed wire barricades and troops carrying machine pistols.

When the Red Army Faction leaders were caught and jailed, terrorists working with the Palestine Liberation Organization tried to free them by hijacking aircraft to Entebbe and Mogadishu. The Israelis and West Germans broke up these two hijackings, and most of the Red Army Faction leaders committed suicide in prison. Their sympathizers dispute this and say they were murdered.

Before that anti-Shah riot, about all the German students knew about Iran was what they read in Der Spiegel magazine, which was a kind of bible to German students in the mid-1960's, and which was virulently anti-Shah. Its publisher, Rudolf Augstein, became a hero to students when he was jailed temporarily for publishing NATO defense plans. The government of Konrad Adenauer, which jailed him, was not very despotic. Der Spiegel also had lionized some of the Red Army

Faction people, such as the attorney Horst Mahler, who helped lead the 1967 Berlin riot and defended Ulrike Meinhof along with some intellectuals, including the Nobel Prize-winning novelist Heinrich Boell.

The Berlin anti-Shah riot of 1967 is both instructive and a little bit deceptive as a starting point for looking at the Shah and Iran. In Iran, terrorist cells began operating about 1968, using tactics very much like those of the Red Army Faction in West Germany and later by the Red Brigades in Italy. International contacts were made between all of these groups, and both the German radicals and Iranian revolutionaries traveled to Syria to study guerrilla methods with Al Fatah, the Popular Front for the Liberation of Palestine and the Popular Democratic Front — all factions of the Palestine Liberation Organization. This collusion between international terrorist groups had something to do with the resurgence of terrorism in Turkey, some of it believed directed by the Turkish Communist Party's exile headquarters, which is, surprisingly, in West Berlin (not East Berlin), in the Kreuzberg district where many Turkish guest-workers live.

What is deceptive about the Berlin riot, and this applies to Iranian students who became apparent Marxists in American and French universities, is that it led almost everyone in the West watching the Iranian situation to expect a Marxist revolt there in terms recognizable to the Western mind.

No one expected, in the years following 1967, that the Ayatollah Ruhollah Khomeini would in 1978 hijack a revolution prepared for a dozen years by ideological Marxists of one shade or another.

I have made this stopover in Germany on the way to Iran because Americans can understand Germans, with a little effort, although we have not had their experience of living divided, within vulnerable borders, with a 2,000-year history of dominating or being dominated. It eases the transition eastward to a country with a 7,000-year history (according to art relics), from ideology to theology, to a people who had a part in inventing civilization and who have been invaded and occupied by Arabs, Mongols, Turks, Russians, Englishmen and, according to the Islamic revolutionaries, Americans.

Iran is going to be harder to understand. Neither the State Department nor the CIA foresaw that Khomeini would take over in 1979, nor did such experts as Professor James A. Bill of the University of Texas and Professor George Lenczowski of the University of California, who both wrote in Foreign Affairs. The first who realized what was happening were the Israelis, who got their diplomatic personnel out of

Iran by early November 1978. The Israelis pay close attention to the Muslim countries, and Washington does not always listen to their information.

It is no disgrace that we all were fooled — so were many Iranians. The leaders of Iran's National Front opposition thought they could ride to power on Khomeini's coattails, unaware that they were riding a tiger.

Professors Bill and Lenczowski, both leaders of Middle East study groups, take diametrically opposite views of the Shah. Bill sees the Shah as villainous and ruthless, lion and fox. His assessment loses some force when set alongside some of his other judgments: his report that the Shah "in the early 1970's instituted a reign of repression so severe that it *spawned* a terrorist network" (my italics) — in fact, as we have seen, a wave of terrorism started before 1970 in free West Germany, Iran and also in non-repressive Jordan, where it became a civil war in 1970, and the Shah's crackdown responded to it rather than spawned it; his suggestion that the National Front could become the backbone of a new government in Iran, which it could not, and his belief that the Shah had "a very sophisticated public relations organization" in the United States — and we see no sign of it.

By contrast, Professor Lenczowski saw the Shah's Iran as an authoritarian state but not totalitarian. He mentioned a "campaign of the American news media against the Shah" operating in 1976. Lenczowski noted that, far from having a slick public relations, the Shah was a sucker for interviews with "Western news commentators who specialized in provocative and insulting questions addressed to the monarch, encouraging adverse publicity and correspondingly *emboldening the opposition."* (My italics.) That may have been a reference to a "60 Minutes" interview on CBS in 1976. Mike Wallace pressed the Shah on reports of tortures in which political prisoners were forced to watch their wives raped and had bottles shoved up their rectums. The Shah interrupted him sardonically to say, "Broken bottles," and then went on to deny condoning torture. (Part of that Wallace interview was repeated recently on "60 Minutes", and it came out differently, without the "broken bottles". They do a lot of editing on that program.)

Since we are only beginning to learn about the Iranian context, and don't know who is right about the Shah, and since all accusations against him were made by persons who are considered irrational when they accuse people other than the Shah, the reaction of the American media last November was all the more dismaying.

Mohammad Reza Pahlavi arrived in New York secretly, yellow with jaundice, his lymph nodes swollen with cancer, and Khomeini's organized followers, behaving in the guise of a mob, seized about 62 American hostages at the U.S. Embassy in Tehran — and the media turned on the Shah, not on Khomeini.

Every night network television started out with a report on the mobs around the U.S. embassy in Tehran, then a report on the oil situation, and then moved to a standup: a reporter outside the New York hospital asking how soon could we be rid of the Shah, and was he really sick?

In my newspaper, *The Daily News*, and others, columnist after columnist heaped vilification on the Shah, although few if any of them had been to Iran. Newspapers competed in compiling the money the Shah allegedly had stolen. I think the *Chicago Tribune* won with about $10 billion. We printed lists of the Shah's assets, and it seemed to bother no one that the listed assets were mostly in Iran, or in places like the Pahlavi foundation in New York, which the new Iranian regime already had taken over. We were in one of our pack-journalism frenzies.

The American correspondents in Iran did a good job, progressively better as they learned more about the place, but editors in the United States ordered and used stories on the basis of their preconceptions. The news story was handicapped because in 1975, when we finally lost the Vietnam war, the American public stopped the world and got off. There are only about a quarter as many American correspondents overseas as there were in 1969. News play on the Iran story was dismal; the oil story came first, and we lost the oil anyhow.

When the hostages were seized, the first public figure off the mark was, as always, Andrew Young, who compared the Shah with Adolf Eichmann, with the disclaimer he had learned as an apprentice diplomat, "in the Iranian view." Young was defending a position he had taken earlier, that Khomeini might be a saint.

Next was the millionaire investment broker and foreign policy expert George Ball, who had been eased out of the State Department in 1966 by Lyndon Johnson. Ball advised the Carter administration in the fall of 1978 to dump the Shah. After the hostages were seized, Ball returned to NBC television to acknowledge that he had been right all along and to lay blame for the mess on Henry Kissinger.

No wonder that, by the end of last November, an ABC television poll showed that 79% of Americans favored making sure that the Shah left the United States as soon as the doctors could pull the drainage tubes from his abdomen. On television, only David Brinkley on NBC said the Shah should be offered asylum here.

The figures 79% to 21% proved irresistible to Senator Edward Kennedy, whose presidential campaign was flagging. Kennedy charged the Shah with running "one of the most repressive regimes in history" and stealing "umpteen billions of dollars from Iran."

There was a public backlash, but Kennedy's campaign men were confident that his view would prevail in the long run.

Now, if we understand little of Iran, we ought to understand politics in the United States and politics in the media. Kennedy, Young, Ball, Mike Wallace, the networks and many newspaper columnists have staked out a position on the Shah, and they have a vested interest in proving him guilty to preserve their credibility.

The scourging of the Shah became inevitable, for American domestic political reasons that have nothing to do with whether his rule was good or bad.

All this reminds me of 1963, and a series of articles by David Halberstam in the New York Times condemning South Vietnamese President Ngo Dinh Diem and his alleged persecution of Buddhists. Diem's sister-in-law, Madame Nhu, made a remark about Buddhists barbequeing themselves, trying to speak in what she thought was the American idiom — much like the Shah's "broken bottles" remark.

All of the major newspapers and the two news weeklies carried a quote from an anonymous phrasemaker about Diem's family: "There has been no family like it since the Borgias."

The upshot of the American media campaign against Diem — not organized, just a mindless campaign — was a famous message, "The Cable of August 24" from the State Department ordering a coup. After stalling by Vietnamese generals, it occurred, killing Diem and his brother. Six months later, almost unnoticed, Diem's other brother was executed at the demand of the Buddhist monk Thich Tri Quang, whom we had sheltered in our embassy in Saigon.

To make the parallel more uncanny, that fatal cable was signed by the then-acting secretary of state, George Ball.

Diem was a thoroughly decent man, and his loss practically doomed any effort the United States could make thereafter in Vietnam.

If the United States follows its established pattern, the Shah will not get a hearing for a long time, even after his death, his case having been decided in advance by the media, self-serving public figures and our need for relations with Iran.

The Shah's sophisticated public relations operation in the United States is not in evidence. It didn't exist in Iran, either.

After I had been a week in Tehran in November, 1978, I asked an American embassy councillor, "Why doesn't this government explain to its people what it is doing?"

The councillor smote his desk with his fist and said, "That's a damn good question. I ask it all the time, and I've never gotten an answer."

Iranian state television news and programming was too offensive to have been the product of incompetence. It had to be sabotage. I mentioned this to an European diplomat, who said the only genuine Communist he had discovered in Tehran worked in television programming.

The Shah had a case, although, disdaining the media, he did not deign to present it. When he did try to present his case, in an interview with David Frost in Panama, nobody would buy the full interview. ABC bought a small section, naturally including the section with a grilling on alleged torture in Iran and the number of people killed in the revolution. Nothing whatever about the other dramatic episodes in a rule longer than 35 years. And even that segment did not entirely please Frank Reynolds, the program moderator, who asked Frost why he had taken it so easy on the Shah. Frost explained he was trying to draw him out, apologizing for being courteous and trying to get the Shah's story.

When the Shah was born, Iran was an oriental, medieval nation, almost entirely illiterate, with literacy being a privilege of the wellborn, living under the degenerate Qajar dynasty. Travelers entering Tehran after dusk had to know the password.

The Shah's father, a remarkable soldier, ruled only 15 years before the British exiled him to South Africa and took over part of the country with the Soviets during World War II.

From that unpromising beginning, the Shah, who was a working king, raised literacy to almost 50%, partly emancipated women, distributed land — both "his own" and the church's — tried to internationalize the outlook of the geographically pivotal and threatened nation, allied Iran with the West against Soviet-style Communism and began creating an infrastructure that almost brought Iran into the 20th century. His periodic attempts at liberalization always were met by confrontation, as though there were no spirit of compromise in the country.

He also built, to preserve Iran's independence and unity, a modern military force of over a half million men. It is a mistake to say that the

Shah's army "proved useless" to him in the end. For decades it did what an army is supposed to do — it deterred. Henry Kissinger remarked in his memoirs that the Shah always was informed of American plans in Middle East crises. The existence of the Shah's army probably kept Iraq out of the Six Day War in 1967, the civil war against King Hussein of Jordan in 1970 and the October War in 1973. It probably delayed for years the Soviet move into Afghanistan. In 1978 the Shah did not lose his army; he lost his ally.

Along the way the Shah was deposed twice, survived at least two assassination attempts, had two prime ministers murdered and subdued major riots in 1952, 1963 and 1978.

He could not do without a security service, or SAVAK, even though its members would be tough cops, reflecting Iran's rough heritage and the cultural values of the region.

To people in the West, the most inexcusable charge against the Shah has been that of "systematic SAVAK torture of political prisoners."

This charge has been so skillfully spread — for its Western consumers and especially starting in the late 1960's — that anyone who says, "But wait a minute . . ." is going to be accused of condoning torture. Well, I don't condone torture, by anyone, under any circumstances.

Still, I will say, wait a minute. If I am not an expert on Iran, I know the media; I know what it bites on. So do the Shah's opponents. Their mode of speech is hyperbole, but some of them are intelligent, sophisticated in a unique oriental-occidental manner, and they know the United States and the West much better than we know them, thanks to the Shah's sending them by the tens of thousands to the West to study.

You may have wondered why other countries in the region, which have more torture, don't also revolt, a point mentioned by Professor Lenczowski. The torture issue is a bigger deal in the West that it is in Iran, where pain and punishment are so much a part of the culture that the country's biggest religious holiday, Ashura, features parades of penitents whipping themselves with chain whips.

The American hostages in the embassy were subjected to mental torture for many months. One of them has had convulsions. Many Iranians approve of this, although the Americans involved have done nothing to injure Iran. The Iranians simply view torture differently partly because they assume that the next bunch in power also will practice it when they take over police stations. Knowledgable Iranians tell me that SAVAK was not at all entirely disbanded; part of it continues to work, but now for Khomeini, as SAVAMA.

The Shah, in his interview with David Frost and elsewhere, concedes that torture occurred, as it still occurs throughout that area of the world, and that he had been unable to stop it entirely.

Because of the effective anti-Shah publicity over the years, Amnesty International has kept an eagle eye on Iran, and it has found torture cases going back 16 years, that is, to the first Khomeini-inspired riots over the emancipation of women and special status for American businessmen that led to Khomeini's being sent into exile. Compared with other countries in the region, Amnesty International has not had too much difficulty getting into Iran or visiting where they wanted to visit.

Amnesty International's annual report of 1978, covering June, 1977, to June, 1978, said, "Some allegations of torture have been received during the last year, but Amnesty International has not been able to substantiate them." It found that two political prisoners had been executed, one after conviction for the murder of a translator at the U.S. embassy, and the other a major general convicted of espionage. In most nations, these would not be considered political-prisoner cases.

In neighboring Iraq, during the same period, Amnesty International found that "torture allegations are frequent, and almost all those who are arrested are reported to be tortured (in Iraq). The bodies of those who are executed, when returned to their families, frequently bear the marks of torture, and deaths under torture are reported." Amnesty International received a list of political executions in Iraq of 200 Kurds, seven Communists, 21 military men and one Jordanian. Amnesty International cannot get information in other neighboring countries, such as Saudi Arabia and Afghanistan.

As the revolution burgeoned in late November, 1978, Amnesty International sent a team to visit six Iranian cities and towns, and it charged in a special report added to its annual report, "Political prisoners still were being tortured and treated cruelly by police and SAVAK agents," without giving details or numbers. I was in Iran at that time, a period of breakdown when the Shah was concentrating on getting troops into the oil fields, when the information ministry had been destroyed by a mob, and I doubt that Tehran had contact or control over police everywhere.

By comparison with the above reports, in the first year after the Shah fell, news agencies reported about 700 executions in Iran, mostly political, by no means all of them SAVAK or police, and some of the defendants appeared on television after obvious beatings. Khomeini's contribution to the region's torture history was to bring it into the open, where everyone could enjoy it, with public floggings in the Caspian Sea towns and at least one case of stoning adulterers to death.

Neither of the two last Amnesty International reports is entirely typical, because when the Carter administration took office in 1977 under the banner of human rights, the State Department insisted that the Shah do something about the torture charges. The Shah's absolutism was not total, and he depended on a lot of people ranging from his oil ministers to his police leaders, but he did do something about it.

We recall that Iran experienced between 1971 and 1976 what Professor Bill called a wave of repression, and which I will call an underground war between terrorists and police, that actually started in 1968. At the beginning of this period the Shah's regime stopped publishing telephone books and took sensitive targets for terrorists, such as the Israeli embassy, off street maps of the city, in order to make things more difficult for terrorists who came into Tehran from outside the country. During that period, given the macho cultural context of Iran, SAVAK appears not to have been entirely opposed to the spreading of torture stories — the stories themselves were a weapon: of intimidation in a war of intimidation on both sides. During that period, several American Army officers were assassinated, and also some American businessmen. Our media reported these stories, but not the killings of little-known Iranians by terrorists.

As the Carter administration took office, the International Red Cross also made inspections in Iran, visiting prisons to check on the treatment of prisoners. Unlike Amnesty International, the Red Cross does not publicly accuse or publish such reports (it was investigating three other Western-oriented countries at the same time). It gives the reports to the man in charge, in Iran's case, to the Shah.

When the militants took over the U.S. embassy in Tehran, they found the Red Cross reports, and at the beginning of this year published selected figures from them that indicated a high percentage of mistreated prisoners in 1977, perhaps higher than in, say, U.S. prisons.

This lent important credibility to their cause, because for 35 years such reports had been vague and unspecific. The International Red Cross is one of the most reliable organizations in the world.

But — last January 9 the International Red Cross held a press conference to say, in effect, that the figures were taken out of context and misrepresented the confidential Red Cross report.

The Red Cross, it turned out, had visited 18 penal institutions in Iran in April and May, 1977 and found scars and other evidence to support prisoners' charges of mistreatment in all but two of the detention centers.

The Red Cross reported that to the Shah, and then made a follow-up inspection of the prisons in October, 1977. They found no new evidence of mistreatment. On a third inspection, in April and May of 1978, they found a drop in complaints of physical mistreatment and a notable improvement in medical care provided to prisoners.

My interpretation of the Red Cross experience is that, when the Carter administration convinced the Shah that the reports of torture and prison mistreatment — however organized the reports may have been — had to be answered, and that he had to divert his attention from other matters and respond to it, he did respond vigorously. That, in turn, put another obligation on President Carter to give him at least moral support in the trial he was facing in 1978. In May, 1978, the time of third Red Cross report, the Shah's attention was very much taken up with local and world economics, which were getting out of hand, and by direct threats to the region's stability which were exacerbated by America's disinterest in foreign affairs in that period. A coup in Pakistan had overthrown Zulfikar Ali Bhutto, with whom the Shah had worked out some cooperation, and he found he had little influence with the new boss, Mohammed Zia ul-Haq. In Afghanistan, things were worse than that: the Soviets had moved in overtly with the coup of Nur Mohammed Taraki that overthrew President Mohammed Daud and killed him along with his family and advisers. The Americans were making ineffectual responses to both of these events, to the dismay of the Shah, and the American media was reporting Nur Taraki's assurances that he was not a Communist.

Washington appeared more interested in how prison reform was going, a subject that probably didn't seem the top priority to the Shah, as it didn't to most Iranians.

How much is true and how much is systematic propaganda in the torture charges? I believe the exaggeration is in the same degree as the revolution's casualties, the next point to be considered.

Ten months after the Shah left Iran, Western correspondents there could not get any specific charges against him. So in November, 1979, the Associated Press asked Iran's foreign ministry when it would get around to specific charges against the Shah. The spokesman, Ibrahim Mokkale, replied, "Isn't 60,000 dead enough?"

President Abolhassan Bani-Sadr, then finance minister, said the Shah killed 65,000 during the revolution alone.

The Shah then was in Mexico, and the Iranian embassy in Mexico City announced that he had been charged with killing 365,995 persons, evidently believing that Mexicans are especially gullible.

While I was in Iran I tried to sort out such figures and the Shah's responsibility for them.

It required starting with the beginning of the revolution on January 8, 1978, when a letter appeared in a daily newspaper attacking Khomeini as a homosexual and an agent of the British.

Iran's press, while restricted and forbidden to criticize the Shah, was not as tightly controlled at that time as most Americans assume. It played a role in the revolution, especially with charges of widespread corruption, which were true, until censorship was clamped down in November, causing a total newspaper strike. Such a strike is impossible in a totalitarian country.

The letter attacking Khomeini was blamed on SAVAK by most Iranians, and that seems logical. But it could have been a provocation, considering some of the other devious revolutionary ploys that have surfaced since then. I'm thinking, for example, of a tape of the Shah, allegedly ordering his generals to keep shooting after he left to promote a civil war, which was reported in this country and then found, by voice prints, to be a fake.

The insulting letter caused a demonstration in Qom on January 9, 1978. Reuters agency reported it first from Tehran: the government said demonstrators attacked a police post, and five rioters were killed and nine wounded. But Reuters led the story off with a report from dissidents who had telephoned to say that 20 were killed and 200 wounded — by the police, implying doubt of the government figures. Professor Bill, in Foreign Affairs, said that "troops" killed "dozens" and wounded hundreds. CBS television much later called it the "slaughter" at Qom.

Forty days later, the mourning period for those killed at Qom, a worse riot broke out in Tabriz, which was a hotbed of political factions, some with connections outside the country. Then riots occurred every 40 days, directed from the network of mosques throughout the country.

On August 29, 1978, arsonists poured gasoline in the exits of the Rex Cinema in Abadan, and at least 377 persons were burned to death.

This is the only casualty figure of the revolution that seems to be proved by photographs.

The clergy had been campaigning against Western movies, so it was logical to assume that Islamic fanatics had been the arsonists. In Tehran, the revolutionary students charged it was a SAVAK job, a provocation to discredit the *mullahs* (exploiting the clerics' anti-movie campaign). That did not appear to make sense, as the Shah was desperately trying to quiet things down, not whip up emotion.

Nevertheless, ten days after the Rex Cinema fire, the Tehran University revolutionaries organized a mass demonstration at Jaleh Square to charge that SAVAK had burned the Rex Cinema in Abadan as an excuse to crack down on the Islamic clergy. Aside from being implausible, there was no such crackdown on the clergy.

The September 8 riot in Jaleh Square ended in severe casualties. The army, equipped to fight a war and having no crowd-control equipment or training, opened fire with West German-designed G-3 assault rifles, which have a tremendous rate of fire, sending off streams of bullets.

The government at first said 58 were killed and 205 wounded, then raised the dead figure to "nearly 100" as more wounded died, the Associated Press reported. United Press International got a figure of 95 dead from a government official. Both wire services reported that witnesses at the scene estimated 200 to 300 died. Since witnesses seldom underestimate, most correspondents in Tehran concluded that 100 to 200 people were killed.

The opposition was calling reporters in town to say that 3,000 died, which reporters in Tehran discredited. The speed and unanimity of the reports suggested that the figure was an organizational figure, perhaps agreed on before the riot. Cameras abound in Tehran, and photos were produced, but no photos exist showing such a world-record slaughter.

The students, undaunted, set teams to work compiling names of the dead, with a list finally totalling more than 3,900.

Thereafter, in Iran's revolutionary mythology, "4,000 died in Martyrs' Square," the new name for Jaleh Square.

Der Spiegel magazine, the Shah's old friend in Germany, used the 4,000 figure without reservation, and by last December the New York Times had inched up to a figure of "over 1,000." This is that 100-200 we spoke of.

About two months after the Jaleh Square riot and massacre, I discussed the revolution's casualty figures with the National Front, which was considered by much of the media to be the only alternative government.

An American embassy official remarked that I would find the National Front leaders, "Uh, kind of underwhelming," which I took to be normal State Department arrogance. This official was right.

I had been present when the Front's leader, Karim Sanjaby, and his spokesman, Dariush Forehar, were arrested in Sanjaby's comfortable villa in north Tehran as they were preparing to issue a public call for the Shah's abdictation. (They were released, unbeaten, some days afterward.) They had just returned from a meeting in France with Khomeini, and their call, while flamboyant, contained some legalisms that could have been used later to provide a defense if the Shah had defeated the revolution.

National Front headquarters, off an alley in downtown Tehran, was in a small apartment house. Inside, it looked like the museum of a failed local labor union. Forehar's office was decorated with photos and drawings of the Front's revered leader, Mohammed Mossadeq, the charismic, weeping and fainting prime minister of the early 1950's who ousted the Shah temporarily, nationalized the oil industry and invited the Communist Tudeh party into the government.

The half-dozen Front people I talked with behind drawn window blinds — they didn't know whether SAVAK watched the house or not, or seem to care — included a young physician who ran his own clinic and a former army colonel. The conversation was difficult to keep steered to any point.

The colonel, who spoke French, was the most interesting. He said he had been close to the Shah, an officer of the imperial guard. When the Shah accepted a medal and a general's rank in Britain's Royal Air Force (in the 1950's), the colonel had suggested mutiny to some of his fellows, and was booted out of the army and jailed — for two years, I think he said. When he got out of jail he got a law degree and defended Khomeini on the Shah's 1963 expulsion order, he said.

The colonel was impatient with most of my questions, dealing with authoritarianism, torture, police brutality, corruption. Yes, yes, the colonel said, but the real issue was his kowtowing to the British, who had deposed his father, couldn't I see that? The Shah's real crime was that he was the lackey of foreigners.

The physician's main contribution, in good English, was that Iran wanted no alliance with industrialized nations. It wanted to join the Third World, where it would be a leader, probably *the* leader.

All of my discussion partners insisted that the figure of 4,000 dead in Jaleh Square was correct. I asked if any evidence, perhaps photographs, could be found.

"Four thousand is correct," the physician assured me. "Why, only yesterday the army killed 200 in the bazaar."

"The town is full of reporters," I said, "and not all of them are in the pay of the Shah. My hotel is near the Bazaar. If 200 people had been killed in the heart of Tehran yesterday, surely we all would have heard of it. Someone would have checked it out."

"Well, if not 200 dead, then 200 wounded," he said.

In fact, shots had been fired in the bazaar the day before, and two persons were seen to have dropped to the ground, either hit or hitting the dirt. There was a lot of firing into the air at the period.

At a show trial in Tehran in December, 1979, Iranian army officers were formally charged with killing 6,000 in Jaleh Square.

I don't mean to minimize the real reports of heavy casualties. Many hundreds, perhaps several thousands, were killed in the last month of the revolution, *after the Shah had left Iran* to avoid such a slaughter, and Khomeini returned to unseat Shahpour Bakhtiar, the National Front man who had been installed by American intervention. The rest of the National Front refused to join Bakhtiar. On February 12, 1979, almost a month after the Shah left Iran, Iranian television reported 400 killed in Tehran that day alone, and there were clashes all over the country as the revolution's guns came out of hiding.

My attempt to check figures leaves me not too far from the Shah's estimate to Frost that fewer than 1,000 were killed in the revolution while he was in Iran.

And I question whether the Shah is responsible for any of them.

By November, 1978, Khomeini, who was in France, was calling for "shaheed," or Islamic sacrifice, from tape casettes played in many of the tens of thousands of mosques throughout Iran, and perhaps before that period, Khomeini called for "rivers of blood," and promised eternal life in paradise for those who would sacrifice themselves. Rather large numbers of men put on their white funeral shrouds and ran into the army's guns.

The Shah did not sit down and decide that people would die; Khomeini did, and his call was open-ended; how many died was of no consequence. Even some of Khomeini's Arab allies at the United Nations say he is a man obsessed with vengeance.

'The leftist groups that prepared the revolution could recruit cells of men and women for high-risk sabotage and assassinations, but they could not find masses willing to revolt. '

Only Khomeini could deliver sacrificial masses, in concert with some of the multilingual, sophisticated revolutionaries the Shah had helped create with his unprecedented subsidies to hundreds of thousands of gifted Iranians to study abroad.

Some Iranians believe that Khomeini could not have pulled it off without the contribution of a secular Islamic prophet, Ali Shariati.

Shariati was arrested in the 1950's as a Mossadeq supporter, yet he later studied under a Shah scholarship at the Sorbonne, where Bani-Sadr also studied. In Paris, Shariati met Franz Fanon, the Third World apostle of Marxism and vengeance from Martinique, who participated in Algeria's revolt against France and wrote the revolutionary guidebook, "The Wretched of the Earth." Shariati also met Jean Paul Sartre and leading French Communists.

In the early 1970's Shariati was lecturing in Iranian cities, rejecting Marxism while offering to reform Islam that offended the traditional clergy. Among those said to have been influenced by Shariati was Dr. Ibrahim Yazdi, the American physician from Houston, Texas, who served as Prime Minister Mehdi Bazargan's first foreign minister.

What the clergy did like in Shariati's teaching was his condemnation of the West for eroding the moral worth of Islam, and he stressed "shaheed," the belief that those who die in a holy undertaking live forever. He may also have invented the technique of spreading the word to illiterates with tape cassettes.

Shariati died of undetermined causes in London in 1977. His followers charge that SAVAK murdered him, but if so, Scotland Yard must have covered it up.

In Khomeini's charges against the United States, there are irritating grains of truth, of which we could make pearls if we were oysters. The ayatollah charges that the United States created the Shah, that the Shah served us faithfully for 37 years, that "America, mother of corruption," destroyed moral values in Iran.

Our contribution to destroying moral values in Iran, and elsewhere, including at home, began in the 1960's, coinciding with the wave of students from Iran that the Shah sent to study.

The Iranian students were intrigued by our student revolt against the Vietnam war, and to see on television the assassinations of our leaders. They also suffered culture shock. Just as we are sometimes shocked by such spectacles as Ashura penitents or the sacrifice of a camel, they were appalled by American violence, crime, drug use, pornography, anti-patriotism, permissiveness in sexual and other affairs — all blasphemous to Islam.

An American cultural item of significance to Iranians three years before the revolution was the best-selling novel, "The Crash of '79," by Paul Erdman, in which the Shah is described by name as the new Hitler and a rapist who radioactively contaminates the Persian Gulf Oil in a misfired attempt at conquest. Erdman was hard-pressed to come up with another best-seller to follow the one he had written in jail after his conviction for running a Swiss bank in a manner injurious to its customers, by a presumably despotic Swiss court. His straightforward slander of the Shah was not only acclaimed by book critics, but also promoted by gossip columnists with the unlikely story that Kissinger, a friend of the Shah, had pronounced the book the inside dope on what would happen next in the Gulf area. (Erdman's prophecy was 180° off target.)

Iranians with whom I discussed the book were most impressed by the critics' approval of it. They assumed that the novel represented the American opinion of the Shah.

Considering American contributions to the revolution, it was out of place for the Carter administration to substitute evangelism for policy when the upheaval came in Iran.

In early December, 1978, the United States turned down a request for Mace, because it could not be flown into Iran without being detected, and we were disengaging from the Shah. Instead of help, the Washington news corps reported that the President expressed the belief in private conversations that the Shah's chances of surviving as king were only 50-50. The crucial religious holidays were coming up, and the Shah's supporters were hoping that if he could get through them, he would keep power. Carter's failure to deny vigorously the reports gave great encouragement to the revolutionaries, as did Washington's wavering throughout the autumn.

Probably only the Shah knows to what degree he was willing to fight to preserve the throne. Those who saw him in the autumn of 1978 reported he was subdued and shaken by the increasing scope and violence of the riots and resigned to constitutional reforms that would reduce his power. He was reported dismayed and apparently surprised at media revelations of the scale of corruption that had developed in the government and military since oil prices began soaring in 1974, injured at the desertion of his middle-class following, distrustful of the Americans who were backing away from him and baffled that "Islamic Marxism" could have an appeal.

Washington's concerns in the winter of 1978-1979 appeared to be the preservation of the President's image as a champion of human rights and the prevention of disruption in the oil fields, rather than the prospect of losing Iran permanently. The United States urged the Shah not to fight, but to leave the country in the hope that it would end the oil strike, which had been organized in part by Mehdi Bazargan. (He had announced he would not join Khomeini in leading his country back into the middle ages, and then did so).

Given American contributions to his overthrow, the United States owed the Shah an offer of asylum, and the media needed a look at the evidence before pronouncing sentence on him. If the Shah had been given asylum at the time of his fall, the U.S. would have had to close its embassy and resign itself to doing without Iranian oil for a time. By reneging on our debt to the Shah, we lost the oil anyway, had our embassy personnel taken hostage, and, as Khomeini put it, had our noses rubbed in the dirt.

If the United States had fully backed the Shah in the autumn of 1978 — which nobody in media dared suggest — as it had fully backed King Hussein of Jordan in 1970, he may have had to kill many thousands, perhaps more than Hussein's army did. When I returned from Jordan's civil war to Beirut in Black September, 1970, a State Department expert there told me that "Hussein will never live down the carnage. He will be known as the Butcher of Amman until he falls." The mysterious East once again proved the experts wrong.

As I was writing this paper, Mike Wallace, on "60 Minutes," presented on March 2 a devastating picture of the Shah and SAVAK, with two torture cases and massive charges against the Shah and the CIA. I could devote another paper to the manipulations in that broadcast, but here I will concentrate on one:

Like the revolutionaries, Wallace found that SAVAK set the Rex Cinema fire in Abadan, although he threw in the word, "allegedly." He did not mention any possible alternative, so his audience must assume that SAVAK is the only suspect. Wallace even pointed out the man he implied was responsible, an escaped police official from Qom and Abadan, who he said was living under an assumed name in Fresno, California. In solving this case, Wallace even found a new motive for SAVAK: they were trying to "kill or capture several key agents of the Khomeini revolution" who were inside the theater. Considering the anti-movie campaign of Khomeini supporters, which had rubbed off on all of the "houses of Satan," it was a curious place for them to be. There is no background in Wallace's presentation: it is socko-whammo American journalism — and the most expensive journalism in the world.

Here is some background: after the Jaleh Square riot, when the false figure of 4,000 dead was adopted (for perhaps 100 to 200 killed), the real casualties at the Rex Cinema had been dwarfed, so to speak, and Jaleh Square, not the Rex Cinema, became the centerpiece atrocity of the revolution.

Then on November 5, 1978, two months after Jaleh Square — with the Rex Cinema temporarily out of mind — mobs came out of the bazaars in Tehran and demolished liquor stores, because Islam forbids alcohol, and banks, because it forbids usury. None of the liquor stores or banks was burned, but almost all of Tehran's cinemas were burned, dozens of them, and nobody asked if anyone was inside them. The Park Hotel was over a cinema, and it caught fire. Foreign guests were rescued from the roof by a building crane.

That seemed to be a rather strong indication that Islamic extremists also set the Rex Cinema fire.

The Carter administration had asked CBS to delay the "60 Minutes" broadcast, and it was held back one week, giving CBS more time to check its facts. The media generally assumed that Carter asked for the delay because of the New Hampshire primary, since its message was in line with Kennedy's views. So, going after Carter's "attempt at censorship," other television stations repeated the CBS report days later, and in New York the popular Channel 11 repeated, with pictures, that CBS had "implied" that SAVAK set the Rex Cinema fire. The suggestion that the broadcasts would encourage the militants in Tehran to feel they were winning was not raised in television reports I could monitor.

If the British Broadcasting Company had made a program using the same materials used in "60 Minutes," it would have been backgrounded. A BBC program also would have been disturbing, but would leave the viewer's mind with something to work on, because that would have been BBC's aim. The CBS show left the mind stunned, reeling — because that was the show's aim.

Andrew Young, writing in his guest column in the New York Times, said the CBS show that depicted torture in Iran under the Shah "not only delayed my family's Sunday dinner but ruined everyone's appetite." Young obviously believed it, as he was predisposed to do.

"60 Minutes" has an awesome power over tens of millions of Americans, and it is so successful that it can spend as much as it wants chasing down a story. If Wallace has real and credible evidence that SAVAK set the fire, he owes it to the audience to show the evidence.

If he has no evidence, then the show went far beyond slander into a manipulation of history that some of the greatest despots could be proud of.

Americans are susceptible to the word "revolution," which has a pleasant association with our country's founding. But most of the Third World revolutions have little in common with our revolution 200 years ago.

There are some legitimate revolutions, but most recent revolutions are pure power struggles: someone has power; someone else wants it. Tactics have become sophisticated. Tyrants have not been overthrown by revolutions recently. Idi Amin was overthrown by the invading army of Tanzania. French troops overthrew the Emperor Bokassa in the Central African Republic. No revolt overthrew Hitler.

In Iran's revolution, much of the anti-Shah propaganda was aimed at the United States, because to depose the Shah required that he be separated from his principal support. Iraq is not our ally, so we are not receiving a regular dose of reports on tyranny in Iraq.

Let me answer a question in advance. Why would anyone want to defend the Shah of Iran, an authoritarian, second-generation monarch and apparently inept politician, since he lost his kingdom to a revolution that had widespread, if hysterical, support, who died unwanted by all his friends, in lonely exile.

Several reasons.

The continuing development of jackel-pack journalism, in which the media becomes unanimous — who can buck "60 Minutes"? — and scornful of dissent, drops all its rules of accuracy and decorum in its eagerness to get on the winning side and kick a loser, is a menace to the media itself and to the country.

To much of the world, the Shah is a symbol of American treachery, not too strong a word. Even out there in the revolutionary world some of the old values still apply, and the biggest charges against us are that we are faithless and irresolute. Having helped bring down the Shah, the State Department advised against admitting him to the United States, holding out hope that maybe he could come later, and when he was admitted for medical treatment, told him "not to linger." That made him unacceptable anywhere, since his closest ally had rejected him.

The Shah also is a symbol of American popular indifference to, or rejection of, the rest of the world. That his fall can have cataclysmic consequences is a matter of indifference to Americans as we move on to whatever is new — we're a busy people — without a look back.

If a unanimous, one-sided view of the Shah is encouraged, as it will be by the United Nations commission's work, and possibly by Congressional committees seeking political gain once the hostages are freed (if they are freed), and the other side of the question is intimidated into silence by the media pack, then another distorted judgment will become part of the load of misconceptions the Americans carry around the world where we are doing no one any good.

Bibliography

Amnesty International Report 1978. London: Amnesty International Publications, 1979.

Bill, James A., "Iran and the Crisis on 1978", *Foreign Affairs,* Winter 1978/79, vol. 57, no. 2.

"David Frost Interviews the Shah", Transcript, ABC Television, January 17, 1980.

Der Baader Meinhoff Report, Aus den Akten des Bundeskriminalamtes, der "Sonderkommission, Bonn" und dem Bundesamt fuer Verfassungsschutz. Mainz, West Germany: Hase und Koehler Verlag, 1972.

Fanon, Franz, *The Wretched of the Earth.* New York: Grove Press, 1963.

Glubb, Sir John, *Soldiers of Fortune — The Story of the Mamlukes.* New York: Stein and Day, 1973.

Hurewitz, J. C., *The Persian Gulf After Iran's Revolution, Headline Series 244.* New York: Foreign Policy Association, 1979.

The Iran File, 60 Minutes. vol. XII, no. 25, CBS Television, March 2, 1980.

Laqueur, Walter Z., ed., *The Middle East in Transition.* New York: Praeger, 1958.

Lenczowski, George, "The Arc of Crisis", *Foreign Affairs,* Spring 1979, vol. 57, no. 4.

"The Mantle of the Prophet" (by staff members), *The Economist.* London, 23-29 February 1980, vol. 274-7121.

Pahlavi, Mohammed Reza, *Mission for My Country.* New York: McGraw-Hill, 1961.

Sanghvi, Ramesh, *The Shah of Iran.* New York: Stein and Day, 1969.

XIII

RELIGION AND ATHEISM AMONG SOVIET MUSLIMS

Alexandre Benningsen

Why did the Soviet Union invade Afghanistan? One view is that the answer to this question lies, perhaps, more in the Muslim territories of the USSR than in Afghanistan or any other country outside of Russia. Those who hold this view consider that the invasion was, in large measure, intended to hold in check the Islamic revival in the Soviet Union which might otherwise have linked up with similar movements in Iran, Iraq and other Muslim countries of the Near East, using Afghanistan as a meeting ground. Although this much could be inferred from journalistic reports from Afghanistan and the Soviet Union itself it was difficult to learn about the internal developments among Soviet Muslims that, at least in part, prompted the Kremlin to take such a drastic step. Therefore I requested Professor Benningsen who knows, perhaps more than any other Westerner, the Muslim communities of the Soviet Union to address this question.

Alexandre Benningsen who has published numerous works on Soviet Islam is currently Director of Studies at the École des Hautes Études en Sciences Sociales, Paris, (Chair of History of non-Arabic Islam) and Visiting Professor in the Department of History, University of Chicago.

The Soviet Union is a Communist state and Marxism-Leninism is its official ideology that is supposed to rule all aspects of its public and private life. Atheism and an uncompromising hostility to all religions — considered as obstacles to the building of a new and better Communist World — are integral and essential elements of the Marxist *Weltanschaung* especially and even more so in its fanatical Leninist version, for it must not be forgotten that whilst still an emigre Lenin had proclaimed that he would tolerate "no little god whatsoever" *(nikakogo bejenki)* amongst his followers. There is no doubt that

Lenin's pathological hatred of religion gives a *sui generis* flavor to Marxism as applied throughout USSR, Muslim territories included. Islam, as any other religion, is classified as an obnoxious survival of a pre-socialist era, having no place, as such, in the Communist society. It must disappear. The only debatable point is the manner of its disappearance. Optimists in the ranks of Marxist doctrinaires in the USSR consider that, Islam deprived of its social basis, will die a natural death. Pessimists find that this death is too remote and that the process must be hastened by administrative or police measures. Vigilant pessimists have always predominated in the Soviet Union. Hence violent persecutions of Islam started before 1928 and lasted until the War. Suspended between 1942 and 1953 and replaced by the so-called "Scientific propaganda", the anti-Islamic campaign was resumed with accrued violence in 1954 and lasted until 1964, that is for ten years.

Statistics demonstrate the results of this 40 years long effort:

Number of mosques before 1917 25,000
Number of mosques in 1964 300
                                                    (approximately)
Number of religious schools before 1917..................14,500
(mektep and medresseh)
Number of religious schools in 1964..........................1
                                                    (Mir-i Arab of Bukhara)
Number of Muslim clerics before 1917 47,000
Number of Muslim clerics in 1964 1,000
                                                    (maximum)

Since 1964, the administrative oppression has been replaced once more by the "scientific propaganda of atheism". However, during the last 9 years some new mosques (approximately a dozen) have been put into service; also, a second medresseh has been created in Tashkent ("Imam Ismail al-Bukhari").

No *Shariyat* courts are left in USSR, no *waqfs*, no religious publications (except one quarterly journal published in Tashkent and meant for foreign consumption).

Nevertheless, and in spite of the immense propaganda effort aimed at its destruction and after half a century of anti-religious pressure, Islam as religion is still alive in the USSR and instead of describing the death agony of the religious *"perezhitki"*, the Soviet sources are reluctantly acknowledging that a "certain religious revival" is taking place in all the Muslim territories of the Soviet Union.

I shall endeavor to analyse the scope of this revival as well as its possible implications for the Soviet Union. The revival itself is manifested in the exceptional tenacity of Muslim believers and in the fervent manner in which the "Five Pillars of Faith" are practiced by them.

A. Believers and Unbelievers

Several recent Soviet sociological surveys effected in various Muslim territories (Central Asia, Northern Caucasus, Azerbayjan) divide Soviet "Muslims" (this term, commonly used in the USSR, designates individuals belonging to an historically Islamic nationality) into the following five categories:

1. *"The fanatical believers"* or believers by *"personal conviction"*, who observe the maximum of religious rites and customs, are intolerant toward non-believers and indulge in active propaganda of their faith. They are generally members of the older generation (over 45 years of age), with a high proportion of women.
Average — 13% of the population.

2. *"The believers by tradition"* who observe religious rites and conform to religious customs but are relatively tolerant and do not attempt to force their faith on the non-believers.
Average — 15% of the population.

3. *"The wavers between belief and atheism"* who observe certain rites and conform to certain religious customs but try to hide their attachment to Islam whilst refusing to declare that they are "atheists".

4. The *"non-believers"* who do not believe in God (or pretend not to believe) but nevertheless observe certain religious rites and ceremonies and conform to customs, either through tradition or by nationalism, or else under the compulsion of the social environment.
Average — 39% of the population.

5. The *"atheists"* who proclaim themselves as such and do not practice religious rites but who, nevertheless, in the majority of cases observe, either in compliance with the tradition or under pressure, the three essential religious prescriptions: circumcision, religious marriage and religious burial in special Muslim cemetaries.
Average — 20% of the population.

It should be remembered that the official proportion of "atheists" among the Russians, formerly Christian, is of 80%. And it should also be kept in mind that with some rare exceptions, there are no *absolute* atheists among the Muslims. In Islam, total unbelief is synonymous with total stupidity, not a romantic rebellion against God, nor a mark of superior intellect and philosophy. Indeed, in all Turkic languages the word *"dinsiz"* (atheist) is an insult. It is significant that Muslim religious leaders in the Soviet Union do not acknowledge the existence of atheists among Soviet Muslims. In 1978, the Great Mufti of Tashkent, Zia ut-Din Babakhanov declared *(Radio Moscow,* April 5, in Turkish) that the number of "Muslims" in USSR is "over 40 million", a figure which practically corresponds to the total Islamic population of the Union. Another religious leader, the *imam-khatib* of the "Sheikh Zeinutdin" mosque of Tashkent reduced even more the number of atheists, by limiting the appellation to those who openly and officially proclaim their breach from Islam:

> "A Muslim who does not perform the prescriptions of the Kuran, who does not fast and does not accomplish the five daily prayers, still cannot be considered as an unbeliever. A real non-Muslim would be someone who declares publicly, speaking to the believers in a mosque, that he does not recognize the prescriptions of God."

In other terms, an *absolute atheist* is an individual who not only rejects God, but also breaks completely with his community. This is a dramatic decision and, as a rule, the renegades live outside their national territory, in a non-Muslim milieu and marry Russians.

B. The Five Pillars of Faith

According to the Islamic law, a believer is supposed to perform certain acts which constitute what is known as the Five Pillars of Faith *(arkan ud-Din).* In the conditions prevailing in the Soviet Union, compliance with this obligation is either impossible or else must be restricted to a certain minimum.

a) *The zakat* — obligatory alms destined to assist the poor — is forbidden by Soviet law. Muslim believers circumvent this interdiction by paying the *sadaqa,* the voluntary contribution of the believers (and also of many non-believers) to aid the mosques.

b) The *Hajj* (pilgrimage to Mekka) has become impossible since 1920, after the closing of the borders of the USSR. Officially re-introduced in 1945, it is limited to one or two chartered flights every year, for the benefit of some 30 to 60 selected pilgrims, generally executives of the Spiritual Directorates.

The pilgrimage to the Shia holy places in Iran and Iraq has been sporadically permitted since the Second World War. There have been no such pilgrimages in the last four years.

The believers use the pilgrimage to the *local holy places* as a substitute for the impossible *hajj*. There are several thousand such holy places (generally tombs of Sufi Saints) in Central Asia and the Caucasus visited every year by thousands of pilgrims. They are being constantly closed by the Soviet authorities and periodically reopened by the believers.

c) The *Sawm* — fast during the month of Ramadhan — is not officially prohibited but difficult to observe because of the conditions of work in the cities. Muslim religious authorities now admit that the faithful are allowed to fast on the first, the fifteenth and the last day of Ramadhan only. This mitigated fast remains today the *most popular* of the five pillars of Faith, especially in the countryside. The great majority of the believers and of the "waverers", and a certain proportion of "non-believers" and even some of the "atheists" observe it, because it has acquired a "national" ("Uzbek" or "Tatar") character. The Ramadhan fasting, especially painful in Summer is a practice of which Muslims are especially proud, an ascetic experience which differentiates them from Russians who drink alcohol and eat pork.

d) The *Salat* — private prayer to be said five times a day — is a practice still observed in rural areas by a minority of the population. In the cities, the percentage is even lower. Often the believers say only two prayers: one at dawn and one at sunset.

e) The *Shahada* — The profession of belief in One God and the recognition that Mohammed is His Prophet is made by the believer in the secret of his heart and thus escapes detection. It seems, therefore, that at present, in the Soviet Union, this secret *Shahada* remains the only obligatory pillar of Faith that is observed without any restriction.

Friday is a working day in the Soviet Muslim Republics and the congregational prayers on Friday are attended by a relatively small number of aged believers. By contrast, great Muslim festivals, especially the *Aīd al-Fitr* celebrating the end of the Ramadhan fast, the *Aīd al-Kebir* or Feast of Sacrifice on the first day of the month of Dhu'l Hijja and the Shia festival of *Ashura* commemorating the martyrdom of Imam Husain on the tenth of the month of Muharrem are increasingly observed by many thousands of both believers and non-believers. These festivals are considered as part of the national tradition.

In addition to the "Five Pillars" Muslims in the Soviet Union observe a set of "Family Rites" as part of their Islamic heritage. Three such essential religious rites in the life of a Muslim are observed by the immense majority of the population — believers and non-believers alike — including official atheists and members of the Communist Party.

a) *Circumcision*, which is not compulsory in Islam, is practiced by some 90 to 95% of the population. Atheists and non-believers practice it because of its "national" significance. As the saying goes, "A non-circumcized cannot be an Uzbek (or a Turkmen, or a Tatar...)." Sometimes, circumcision is semi-symbolic. Preaching in the Summer of 1975, the *Imam* of the Kizyl Orda mosque declared:

> "It is not necessary to accomplish completely the ritual of circumcision. It is sufficient to touch the sex of the boy with a razor and let some blood to *perform the national tradition of the Kazakhs.*"

b) *Religious marriage*, a simplified ceremony in Islam, is observed by a very large proportion of Muslims: 95% according to certain sources.

c) *Religious burial* — in special Muslim cemeteries; observed in practically 100% of cases. Even the high ranking members of the Communist Party and the Godless militants are finally buried as "Muslim believers."

These three basic family rites are deemed part of the "national way of life" and as such are observed by those who no longer practice religion and adopt officially an attitude of indifference to all forms of religious expression but who refuse to break with their community. It must be noted that the strict observance of these rites makes it difficult, if not impossible, the biological symbiosis between Muslims and Russians.

Various marriage customs, of non-religious origin but sanctified by many centuries of tradition, make the cohabitation between Muslims and Russians even more difficult. Such are for instance: the strict sexual morality of the Muslim Society with compulsory sexual segregation, early marriage of girls, various matrimonial taboos (endogamic or exogamic), payment for the bride *(kalym)* and even polygamy as well as several other less observed customs such as the *levirate* or the *kaytarma* (the obligation for the bridegroom to remain in the family of his bride), etc. etc. Finally, Muslim Society is still a traditional community, where the clanic and tribal relationship, with its complicated structure remains very active and where the elder generation (the *aqsaqals* or "white beards") has kept its prestige and authority.

To sum up: Now more than ever Islam is part of the national background of the USSR Muslims. The intellectuals of the younger generation are more respectful of their national traditions (including their ancestors' religion) and more interested in same than the generations of their parents and grand parents. As a consequence, religion is practiced today more extensively than it was thirty or forty years ago.

Explanation of the religious survival

It is certain that Islamic rites and customs are preserved at all the levels of the population of the USSR Muslim territories both by the believers and the non-believers because they represent the most treasured patrimony of the national culture. Nevertheless, it is obvious that without an organized *"religious establishment"*, these rites and customs would have rapidly lost their religious meaning so that the population would have relapsed into superstition, ignorance and shamanism. Although for over half a century the Soviet Government made great efforts to destroy it, this "religious establishment" still exists in the USSR. Thanks to its unrelenting activity, Islam in the USSR is still alive and orthodox though "simplified" and intellectually restricted.

This Islam which is alive and orthodox has also two aspects in the Soviet Union. They are:

I. The "Official" Islam

During the Second World War, Sunni and Shia Muslims of the USSR were endowed with an official Administration which has no parallel throughout the Muslim World. Sunnis who form the vast majority of Islamic peoples being highly decentralized and having no "clergy" have hence no need for an "ecclesiastical establishment." The Shi'ites also do not have a well defined religious administration.

The territory of the Soviet Union is geographically divided between four Spiritual Directorates, each of which is administered by an Executive Committee, elected by a regional Congress of the believers and composed of both clergy and laymen. It is presided by a *Mufti* (or a Shia *Sheikh ul-Islam* in Transcaucasia) nominated by the Executive Committee and approved by the Soviet authorities. The official relations between the Spiritual Directorates and the Soviet Government are regulated by the *Council of the Religious Affairs* attached to the Council of Ministers of the USSR and, at the Republican level, by its branches.

a) *The Spiritual Directorate of Central Asia and Kazakhstan*
Sunni of Hanafi rite.
Founded at the first congress of the Muslims of Central Asia and Kazakhstan, convened in Tashkent on October 20, 1943.
Seat: Tashkent, Uzbekistan SSR
Chairman: Great *Mufti* Zia ud-Din Babakhanov

b) *The Spiritual Directorate of the Muslims of European Russia and Siberia.*
Sunni of Hanafi rite.
Seat: Ufa, Bashkir ASSR.
Founded in 1783 by Catherine II.
Chairman: *Mufti* Abd al-Bary Issaev (since 1974)

c) *The Spiritual Directorate of the Northern Caucasus and Daghestan*
Sunni of Shafe'i rite.
Seat: Makhach-Kala (before 1974, Buynaksk), Daghestan ASSR.
Chairman: *Mufti* Mahmud Gekkiev.

The authority of this Directorate covers all the Autonomous Republics and regions of Northern Caucasus (except Abkhazia which comes under the Directorate of Baku) and the territories *(krais)* of Stavropol and Krasnodar.

d) *The Spiritual Directorate of the Transcaucasian Muslims*
Mixed: Shia of Ja'fari rite and Sunni of Hanafi rite.
Seat: Baku, Azerbayjan SSR
Chairman: the Shia *Sheikh ul-Islam* Mir Kazanfer Akbar Oglu (since 1978)
Vice-Chairmen: the Sunni *mufti* Haji Ismail Ahmedov (since 1976) and the Shia *akhund* Haji Alla-Shukur Pashaiev (since 1978)
The authority of this Directorate covers all the Shia communities of the Soviet Union and the Sunni Communities of Transcaucasia.

Because of the importance of Central Asia where live 75% of the USSR Muslims and because of the personality of its Chairman, the *mufti* Zia ud-Din Babakhanov, the Tashkent Board has a leading position. It is the only one to possess a real publishing activity. Furthermore the only two official *medressehs* of the USSR are established on its territory. However, the other Boards are autonomous, not only as administrations but also in canonical matters. As a consequence, there exist great differences between the Boards, in particular between the more progressive and modernist Boards of Tashkent and Ufa and the more conservative Caucasians.

The four Spiritual Boards are empowered by the Soviet Government to exercise their control over all public and private lives of Muslim believers. All the "working" mosques are placed under their responsibility. Under the Soviet legislation, any religious activity outside the working mosques is illegal and strictly forbidden. All Muslim clerics must be nominated and remunerated by the Boards.

"Unregistered" clerics performing religious rites are branded as "antisocial parasites" and hunted down as criminals. It is the Spiritual Boards and their executives that, alone, are entitled to represent Islam vis-a-vis the Soviet authorities and only members of the Boards may represent Soviet Islam abroad. These Boards and the "working" mosques have as sole means of support the voluntary and generous contributions *(sadaqa)* of the believers. They are prosperous and the "registered clerics" are well paid. The Boards cannot use the money they receive for social activities: the Soviet State alone is supposed to take care of this. Since according to the constitutions of all the Republics "the mosque and the church are separated from the State" the Boards are forbidden to exercise political activity, except, of course, insofar as such activity would express the support of the Soviet Government or constitute propaganda aimed at the Muslim World abroad. No intellectual activity is authorized either outside or within the "working mosques". Serious theological debates are discouraged and missionary activity is considered unlawful. No preaching outside the mosque is allowed and there are no religious publications except a quarterly journal published by the Tashkent Spiritual Board *(The Muslims of the Soviet East)* in Arabic, English, French and Uzbek (in Arabic script and therefore not for domestic use). "School is separated from the mosque" according to the constitutions so that no religious education is provided for children. On the other hand, atheism is being taught in all Soviet schools to children, as soon as they are four years old.

The "registered clerics" belonging to the "Official Islam" are not numerous: one to two thousand. This group is composed of executives of the four Directorates and of the staff of the working mosques: *imam-khatibs* and their assistants, *mutevvalis, muezzins, kadis, mudarris*. Obviously, the number of "registered clerics" is barely sufficient to accomplish the religious ceremonies within the few surviving mosques and, of course, absolutely insufficient to perform the domestic rites outside the mosques. However, their real role is not so much to run the houses of prayer as to maintain the existence of a kind of "Reserve General Staff" of highly trained *ulemās*, destined to guarantee the preservation of purity and integrity of traditional Islam. The majority of "registered clerics" are young Soviet intellectuals who, before joining the religious establishment had completed their studies in regular Soviet schools and universities and later graduated from the two Central Asian *medressehs*. Some of them are finishing their religious education abroad in Egypt (Al-Azhar), Morocco (Qarawiyin) and Lybia (Al-Baidha). Their intellectual and cultural level is good, often excellent. In the case of Central Asian *ulemās*, their "professional standard" may be considered as higher than that of the pre-revolutionary *mollahs*, their predecessors.

The religious leadership appears as perfectly loyal toward the Soviet regime and it recommends the same loyalty to the believers. Official clerics never emit a single protest against the anti-religious propaganda, much less against the atheistic character of the Soviet society, never criticize the policy of the Communist Party or denounce Marxism as opposed to Islam. They even accept that believers should become members of the Komsomol or of the Communist Party, the only condition being that in the secret of their heart they remain loyal to the dogmas of Islam.

Official religious leaders act as precious allies of the Soviet *Agitprop*. While broadcasting for the Muslim World abroad or in the course of their frequent visits to foreign countries, Soviet religious dignitaries maintain a line of absolute loyalism towards the Soviet regime, proclaiming at every possible occasion, whatever the evidence to the contrary, that in the USSR Muslim believers are free and happy. The same intense, though rather crude, pro-Soviet and anti-imperialist propaganda is being conducted by Muslim leaders when foreign delegations visit Central Asian Republics. It is being particularly stressed at the occasion of international congresses organized in Central Asia by the Spiritual Directorate of Tashkent.

At the same time, from the standpoint of the dogma, the leaders of the Official Islam in the USSR appear as perfectly orthodox. They have never accepted any compromise between Islam and Marxism.

II. The "Non Official", Underground Islam

The "parallel", non-official Islam — more powerful and more dynamic than the Official Islam — is based on the Sufi brotherhoods *(tariqa)*. The *tariqas* are secret societies, outlawed by the Soviet authorities, but in practice operating almost in the open, especially in Northern Caucasus. The adept *(murid)* is accepted into the brotherhood after a ritual of initiation and remains under the control of his master *(murshid* or *sheikh).* Throughout his life he must follow a complicated and compulsory spiritual rule in which permanent prayers, invocations and litanies — loud or silent *(zikr)* — are accompanied by specific breathing and physical movements, and play an important part in the preparation of other adepts for a state of intense mental concentration. The *tariqas* represent perfectly structured hierarchical organizations, endowed with iron discipline, certainly stronger than that of the Communist party.

Two *tariqas* dominate Soviet Islam: the *Naqshbandiya*, an old Turkestani order, founded in the XIVth century in Bukhara and introduced into Northern Caucasus in the late XVIIIth century; and the *Qadiriya*, a Baghdad order founded in the XIIth century. Both orders have a long tradition of resistance to the Russian conquests in the Caucasus, in the Middle Volga and in Central Asia; in particular, the century long "Holy War" waged by the North Caucasian Mountaineers was directed by Naqshbandiya adepts.

Naqshbandiya has branches both in the Central and Northern Caucasus. Qadiriya, first introduced into Northern Caucasus in the late XIXth century, was brought to Central Asia after the Second World War by the deported Caucasian Mountaineers.

There are still two other old Sufi brotherhoods in Central Asia: the Qubrawiya (mainly in Turkmenistan) and the Yasawiya (Kazakhstan, Kirghizia, Northern Uzbekistan); both originated in the Turkestan and both are mystical orders, more interested in spiritual progress than in politics. However, under the Soviet regime, the Yasawiya has branched out into a highly politicized radical "sub-order": the *tariqa* of the "Hairy Ishans" in Kirghizia.

Though outlawed by the Soviets, the Sufi orders are not small secret "chapels" but mass organizations and this in spite of their clandestine character. According to recent Soviet sociological surveys, in certain areas, especially in Northern Caucasus, "more than half of the believers belong to Sufi brotherhoods". This would represent a fantastic number of hundreds of thousands of Sufi adepts for the Caucasus alone, certainly more than before 1917.

The organization of the present day brotherhoods is a curious blend of the traditional and the new. The innovations which have been introduced aim to give the brotherhoods greater protection against the Soviet police and to implant them more deeply within the popular masses. Sufi orders tend to limit the recruitment of their adepts to specific clans. This provides the *tariqa* with a greater degree of secrecy since adepts are bound by a double loyalty: to brotherhood and to clan. They have also begun to accept a large number of women as adepts and even as leaders (sheikhs). Finally, the membership of the *tariqa* has become much younger than before and is increasingly drawn from the Soviet intelligentsia.

The Underground Sufi Islam is more dynamic than the skeleton Official Islam. Thousands of Sufi adepts perform the prescribed religious ceremonies *outside* the working mosques. They run their own clandestine religious schools where Arabic is taught and have their own network of underground houses of prayer.

Of particular importance is the constant active counter-propaganda which the Sufi orders mount, often victoriously, against the official Soviet, anti-religous *agitprop* which is dull and bureaucratic. The *tariqa* thus exercise a deep influence on public opinion and are responsible for the high proportion of practicing believers among the Muslim populations of the USSR, especially in Northern Caucasus, where Sufi brotherhoods dominate much of the private and collective life of the Muslims.

In spite of the efforts of the Soviet authorities in that direction, Official Islamic leadership has always refused to condemn the Parallel Islam as heretical or unorthodox. On the other hand, the leaders of the Sufi Islam always refrained from attacking the Official Directorates for their submissiveness to the Soviet authorities. Both faces of the Islam are part of the same realm so that some of the better informed Soviet observers express their doubts as to the existence of contradiction between the official clerics and the Sufi adepts. Certain specialists even go so far as to hint at a secret alliance between the two.

The Soviet Government considers Sufi Islam as a declared enemy. Sufi *tariqas* are accused of being "anti-socialist", "anti-Russian" and "reactionary". Ever since 1928 members of brotherhoods had been arrested, deported and executed. After the Second World War the bulk of anti-Islamic propaganda was aimed mainly at Sufism. In Northern Caucasus, numerous leaders and adepts were tried and sentenced to severe punishment for "anti-socialist" behavior.

In spite of all this, Soviet authorities have neither succeeded to infiltrate the *tariqas* nor to neutralize their activity. It is certainly thanks to the Sufi orders that Islam in the Soviet Union remains a living popular creed.

C. Present Religious Revival and the Future of Islam in the USSR

We may forecast a threefold evolution of the Soviet Muslim community during the coming twenty years. As a matter of fact this development is already in progress and there is no evidence that some new obstacle can modify it:

1) *Demographic explosion*

It started in all the Muslim territories after the Second World War and it is still going on.

In 1979 the Muslim Community of the USSR numbered some 44 million. It is estimated that by the turn of the century the number of Muslims will be between 70 and 85 million in a total Soviet population of 320 million, i.e. one out of every four Soviet citizens will be a Muslim. Even more significant is the steady "nationalization" of all the Muslim republics due to the very rapid growth of Muslims as compared to the very low increase of Russians and of the other Slavs. The relative numerical predominance of the Russians has been steadily falling and by the turn of our century it will sink into insignificance. In some areas (for instance in Azerbayjan) Russian communities are decreasing in absolute numbers. Russians and other Europeans leave Muslim territories because of the growing Muslim competition for jobs and because of the unbearable psychological pressure due to Muslim xenophobia.

Percentage of Russians in Muslim republics

	1939	1970	1979
Uzbekistan	13.5%	12.5%	10.8%
Kazakhstan	42.7%	42.4%	40.8%
Azerbayjan	13.6%	10.0%	7.9%
Kirghizia	30.2%	29.2%	25.9%
Tajikistan	13.3%	11.9%	10.4%
Turkmenistan	17.3%	14.5%	12.6%

By the turn of the century, Russian colonies within Muslim republics will be greatly reduced. The big cities in particular will have a Muslim majority and Muslims will dominate local administration and local Communist Parties. There is no evidence whatsoever that xenophobia which nowadays characterizes relations between Muslims and Russians in Central Asia or the Caucasian Republics will be then replaced by a climate of friendship and brotherhood. Sixty years of Soviet regime did nothing to develop the spirit of understanding and cooperation between the two communities.

2) *The Increasingly Strong Consciousness of Muslim Identity*

The numerical growth and the qualitative development of native intelligentsia in the Muslim Republics of the USSR produced one unexpected consequence. Instead of growing more Marxist and "sovietisized", this intelligentsia rediscovers its national patrimony, the bequest of a thousand year history thoroughly impregnated by Islam. It is easy to predict the final outcome of the conflict between the twelve centuries old glorious Muslim culture and the sixty years old Marxist bureaucratic anti-culture forced upon the Muslims by the hated and despised aliens. Islam is already victorious. As a result, we find in all the Muslim territories of the USSR a growing sense of religious kinship among the new intelligentsia. The term "Muslim" is currently used to designate nationality. In Central Asia and in the Caucasus one often hears the following sentence: "I am a Communist and therefore an Atheist, but of course I am a Muslim".

The supra-national awareness of belonging to the Muslim *Umma* — the "Community of the believers" — is stronger today than it was thirty or forty years ago. It does not suppress the awareness of belonging to a more limited nation, Uzbek or Tatar, Checken or Kirghiz but gives it another dimension, that of religious/cultural brotherhood. It also stresses and reinforces the existing sense of alienation from the non-Muslims, especially from the Russians.

3) *The Switch to Conservatism*

The predominance of conservative Sufism over the liberal "Official" Islam reflects the general trend of the Muslim world — the switch toward conservatism which accompanies the fundamentalist revival of the *Dar ul-Islam*. In the Soviet Islam the movement is not basically different from the evolution of the Muslim World abroad but because the modernist pressure of secularization has been more brutal and because it has been imposed from above, by aliens (Russians), the Soviet Muslim fundamentalism takes on a xenophobic coloring.

Though the trend of Soviet Islam towards conservatism is similar to trends in Turkey, Iran or the Arab countries, it still is — or rather was — a purely local phenomenon. This may change with the beginning of the "Holy War" waged against the Soviet Union by the Afghan *mojahedeen*. The border separating the Soviet Central Asia from Afghanistan is a thousand miles long; uncensored exchange of ideas, information and probably individuals is already taking place. If the resistance of the Afghan *mojahedeen* goes on — as it probably will —

its impact on the evolution of the Soviet Muslim territories may be dramatic.

Bibliography

I. Soviet sources

a. *Monographs:* Our main source for the analysis of Islam in the USSR remains the Soviet non-periodical and periodical anti-religious literature, very abundant, published in Moscow, in the republican and regional capitals of Muslim territories, and in all languages of the USSR. The intellectual level of this literature is, as a rule, exceptionally low. There are, however, some few exceptions. Two Soviet sociologists have recently published four works of high standard in Russian:

Ashirov, Nugman, *Islam i Natsii* (Islam and the Nations). Moscow: Politizdat, 1975, 144 pp.

_____ , *Evolutsiia Islama v SSSR* (The Evolution of Islam in USSR). Moscow: Politizdat, 1978, 153 pp.

_____ , *Musul'manskaia Propoved.* Moscow: Politizdat, 1978, 80 pp.

Saidbekov, T. S., *Islam i Obshchestvo* (Islam and the Society). Moscow: "Nauka", 1978, 254 pp.

b. *Periodicals:* The periodical anti-religious literature is represented by two journals:

Nauka i Religiia (Science and Religion), Moscow, monthly (lower level); and *Voprosy Nauchnogo Ateizma* (Problems of Scientific Atheism), Moscow, Quarterly (higher level).

In each issue of this last periodical there is at least one, often two or more, important articles on Islam.

Of special interest is, of course, the quarterly published by the Muslim Spiritual Directorate of Central Asia and Kazakhstan, *Muslims of the Soviet East,* in English, French, Arabic and Uzbek (in Arabic script).

II. Sources in Western languages

There are but very few monographs or articles on the subject in Western languages:

Bennigsen, A., & Chantel Lemercier-Quelquejay, *Islam in the Soviet Union*. London-New York: Pall-Mall, F. Praeger, 1967. Especially Chapters 9 ("Communism and the Muslim Religion") and 12 ("Islam as a Religion").

Bennigsen, A., "Islam in the Soviet Union, the Religious Factor and Nationality Problem in the Soviet Union", in B. R. Bociurkiv & John Strong (Eds.), *Religion and Atheism in the USSR and Eastern Europe*. Toronto: University of Toronto Press, 1975.

Bennigsen, A., & S. E. Wimbush, "Muslim Religious Dissent in the USSR", in Richard T. DeGeorge & James P. Scaulan (Eds.) *Marxism and Religion in Eastern Europe*. Dordrecht-Boston: R. Reidel, 1976.

Bennigsen, A., & Ch. Lemercier-Quelquejay, "Muslim Religious Conservatism and Dissent in the USSR", in *Religion in the Communist Lands*. Keston College, London, vol. 6, no. 3, 1978.

Bennigsen, A., & Ch. Lemercier-Quelquejay, "Official Islam in USSR", in *Religion in the Communist Lands*. Keston College, forthcoming. *vol.* 7, 1979.

Bennigsen, A., & S. E. Wimbush, *Muslim National Communism in the Soviet Union*. Chicago: University of Chicago Press, 1979. Especially Appendix C, Sultan Galiev, "The Methods of Anti-Religious Propaganda Among the Muslims".

Bracker, Hans, *Kommunismus und Weltreligionen Asiens; zur Religions und Asienspolitik der Sovjetunion*, I, Kommunismus und Islam, 2 vols. Tubingen: J.C.B. Mohr, 1969-1971.

Rodinson, Maxime, "Problématique de l'etude des rapports entre l'Islam et le Communisme", *Correspondance d'Orient*. Brussels, 1961. vol. 5

XIV

RELIGION AND ETHNIC CONSCIOUSNESS AMONG TURKS IN THE SOVIET UNION

Ilhan Başgöz

Muslims in the Soviet Union had to face ideological conflicts which religious groups in all Communist countries had to confront. In addition, the majority of Soviet Muslims who are of Turkish descent had to bear the brunt of the historical enmity between Christian Russians and Ottoman-Turkish Muslims. Their problems, therefore, was compounded by an ethnic rivalry the roots of which can be traced to the late Middle Ages. However, since the Stalin era both the Soviet regime and the Turkish Muslim leadership have come to realize that the ethnic nationalism of the various Turkish groups could be channeled in a constructive manner for mutual benefit. Professor Basgoz here describes this process of accomodation and its results.

Ilhan Başgöz, renowned for his extensive researches in the folklore of Central Asia, is currently professor in the Department of Uralic and Altaic Studies at Indiana University.

According to the 1959 Census, of the 208 million total inhabitants of the Soviet Union, 15% or 25 million were Muslims. This means that the Soviet Union contained one of the largest Muslim communities in the world, actually fourth largest following Indonesia, Pakistan, and India.

A great majority of the Soviet Muslims, 75% or almost 22 million, were of Turkish descent in 1959. This number had risen to about 30 million by 1970 and this meant that 8% of the total Russian population of 240 million was of Turkish origin. Between 1959 and 1970, the total population of the Soviet Union increased by 33 million, representing an annual growth rate of 1.4%. During the same period, the Turkish population increased by 7.5 million, a growth rate of 3.9% annually. If this tendency continues in the future, we can expect the Turkish population to play a larger role in Soviet society.

The table and map that follow are designed to inform the reader of the names, administrative status and geographical locations of the Turkish populations in the USSR.

**TURKISH-MUSLIM SPEAKING PEOPLES
OF THE SOVIET UNION
(1970 CENSUS)**

Union Republics	Population
Azerbaijan, USSR	4,143,000
Kazakistan, USSR	4,776,000
Kirgiz, USSR	1,320,000
Turkmen, USSR	1,147,000
Uzbek, USSR	8,941,000

Autonomous Republics and Autonomous Provinces		
Bashkir, ASSR		1,200,000
Tatar, ASSR		5,816,000
Karakalpak		230,000
Kumyk	(1959 census)	135,000
Uygur	(1959 census)	95,000
Balkar	(1959 census)	42,000
Nogay	(1959 census)	41,000
Mountain Altai		35,000

The figures include Turkish-Muslims living all over USSR, not only in the specific republics.

The interactions between the Muslim Turks and the Christian Russians go as far back as the 8th century A.D. in Asia, and follow two basic patterns throughout their history. Until the 15th century in Eastern Russia and until the 18th century in Western or European Russia, the Turks were on the attack and the Russians were in retreat. Ivan the Terrible, who captured Kazan in 1552 from the Mongol-Turkish Golden Horde Empire, reversed this trend in Asia. This led to the colonization of Central Asia by the Russians, a long and slow process which was completed at the end of the 19th century.

In the west however, because of the Ottoman domination and sovereignty in the Balkan countries, the northern Black Sea regions and southern Caucasia, the Turkish offensive posture continued. However, following a successful Russian campaign launched in 1771, these

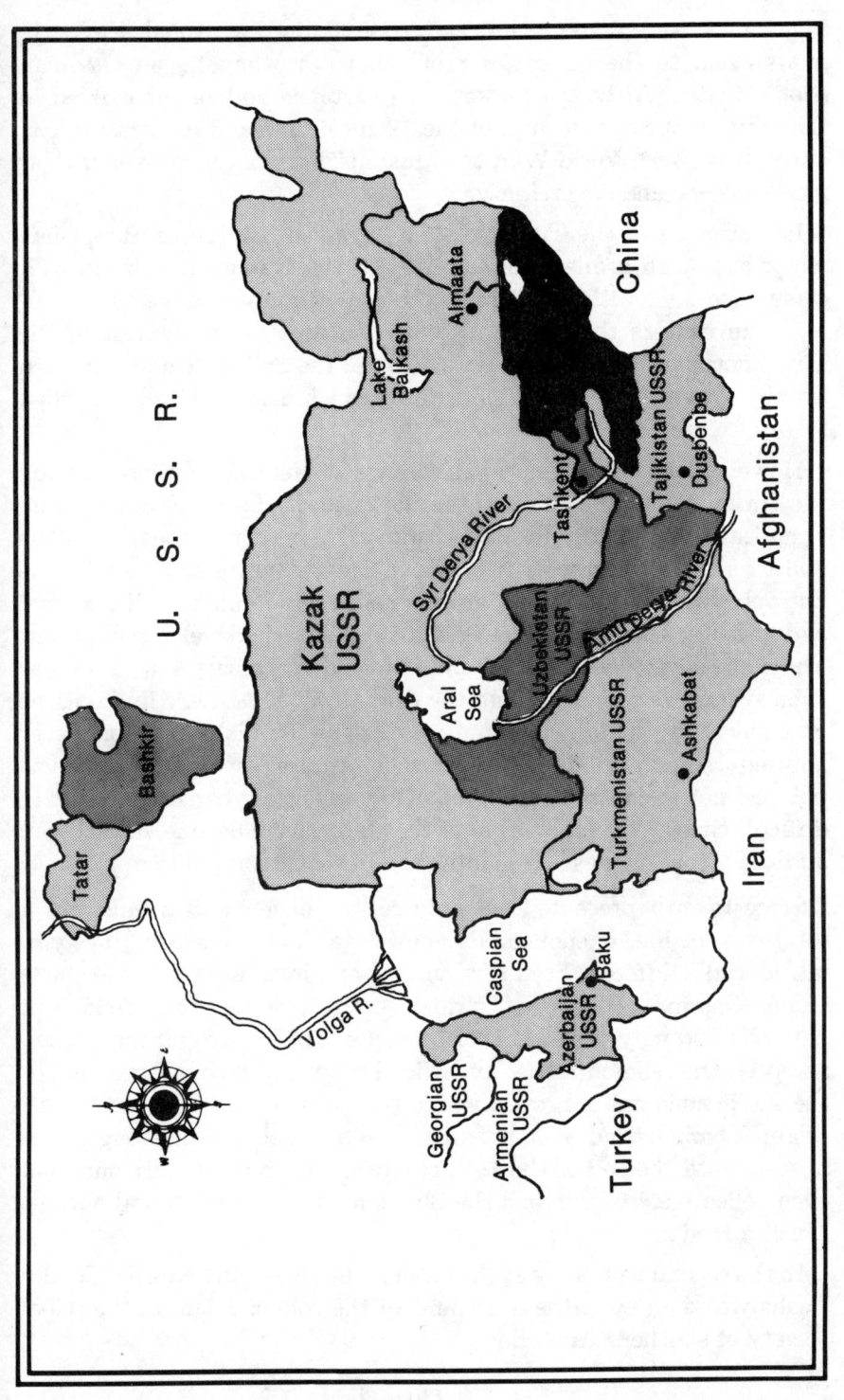

regions too were taken. The peace treaty signed at Küçük Kaynarja put an end to the sovereignty of the Tatar Khanate, an Ottoman protectorate. Although pockets of resistance and revolt existed in Caucasia in the second half of the 19th century and in Central Asia during the First World War, the Muslim Turks never recovered their independence and sovereignty.

Islamization of the Turks in Asia began in the 7th century when victorious Arab armies, having crushed the Iranian Empire in 642, came in contact with the Turks. The conversion was more successful in urban centers than in rural and tribal areas. Nevertheless, the Turks not only became Muslim but under the Seljukide and Ottoman Empires were the main religious force which defended and expanded Islam.

However, the new religion was rarely a strong unifying force among the Turks. It was the power of the state and the discipline of the social organizations which pulled the Turkish communities together. The state, as the strongest institution, not representing any social class but only the fighting forces, always kept religion under tight control and never let the *ulama* or religious intelligentsia develop real power. The state developed, codified and enforced customary law, a secular legal system (örf), while giving the Koranic law *(Shari'a)* a limited area of application, mainly in family life. The Turkish tradition never allowed religion to dominate worldly affairs — on the contrary, political power controlled religion. Only in large urban centers and in difficult times, when the power of the state was in decline, did religion and the *ulema* increase their influence in social and political life.

Since Islam represented not only certain beliefs and rituals, but a total way of life, it sponsored a new legal and educational system, introduced a different literature and art and inaugurated a whole new value system. However, Turkish nomadic society in Asia and Anatolia strongly resisted social change of this magnitude. They accepted the religion rather superficially but retained a large part of the indigenous culture, even where the culture was in conflict with Islam. Shamans and Shamanism, for example, survived among Turks in Asia until the end of the 19th century. In times of individual and even collective crisis, it was the Shaman who was called and not the Muslim Hodja.

In the second half of the 19th century, the Ottoman historian Cevdet Pasha wrote an eyewitness account of the role of Islam in the tribal society of southern Anatolia:

When was asked him why he was so sad, the chief of the Tecirli tribe told us that, on that very day, his wife had divorced him. To our surprise, we learned that in this tribe, a woman could divorce her husband. It sufficed for her to inform her husband that she did not love him any longer, and the marriage would thus end. There was not a single Hodja in this tribe to perform religious services such as marriage ceremonies and burial rituals. In addition, if a Hodja visited the tribe during the holy month of Ramazan, he would first be allowed to perform marriage ceremonies for those couples who already had children. He would then collect a large fee for his services, but as soon as he departed the people of the tribe would attack him and rob him of his money. He would be lucky if his life was spared.[1]

At the beginning of the 20th century, under the Tsars, the Turks in Asia were at varying stages of social and economic development. In the Crimea, among the sedentary Turks, a well-educated landed aristocracy and wealthy merchant class emerged. In Central Asia, on the other hand, on the high mountain plateaus, pastoral nomadism with pre-feudal tribal organization was the structure of the Kirgiz, Uzbek and Turkmen groups. However, these same peoples living in the rich valleys or in irrigated semi-desert regions were transformed into settled agriculturalists, and developed a highly urbanized civilization.

In order to change the role of Islam in Turkish societies, which were structurally and culturally diverse, an attempt at reform was made in the second half of the 19th century. The movement began among Tatar intellectuals in the Crimea and was called the Jadid (new reform movement). Jadid movement advocated a modernized religion with a new religious education which was to include the teaching of science and art in addition to the traditional theology. It also aimed at the transformation of the Tatar into a literary language which could be understood by all Turkish ethnic groups in Russia. In politics, the reform movement never had a cohesive, well-defined program which could be shared by all Turkish intellectuals. Instead, it zigzagged between nationalism and pan-Islamism, between liberalism and religious conservatism, and between pan-Ottomanism and pan-Turkism. The impact of the Jadid movement, a movement supported mainly by the Tatar merchants and intellectuals of aristocratic origin, was limited and varied from one Turkish group to another. Nevertheless, it was the first attempt at creating an intra-Turkish ethnic and religious consciousness, and it presented to the Russian Duma after 1905 a program representing all the Muslim Turks of Russia. The unified program demanded religious and political autonomy for the Turks. The Duma did not even meet the mildest demands of the Turkish Muslims, and this refusal was at least in part responsible for revolutionizing Turkish intellectuals.

Lenin, on the other hand, defined, as early as 1913, the position of his party with regard to the problem of nationality. This position could be termed as a recognition of the right of every nation in Russia to political self determination, even to the point of secession from Russia to create an independent government. Later, in 1917, this opinion was clarified by the Declaration of Rights of the Communist party. Signed by Lenin and Stalin, the declaration was worded as follows:

> Muslims of Russia, Tatars of Volga and the Crimea, Kirgiz and Sarts of Siberia and Turkestan, Turks and Tatars of Transcaucasia, Chechens and mountain peoples of the Caucasus and all you whose mosques and temples have been destroyed, whose beliefs and customs have been trampled upon by the Tsars and oppressors of Russia: your beliefs and usages, your national and cultural institutions are forever free and inviolate. Know that your rights are under the mighty protection of the Revolution and its organs, the Soviet of workers, soldiers and peasants.[2]

The promise was unprecedented and very attractive as the means for the Turks to achieve political and cultural independence. In the years following the Declaration, the October Revolution took place. The Muslim Turkish organizations neither joined in nor supported the revolution. They remained neutral and the revolution was fought only by the Russians.

Following the revolution, the Muslim Turks enjoyed a short period of good relations with the central Soviet powers. In 1918, a Central Commiseriat for Muslim Affairs was established in Moscow and was given full authority in the political, religious, educational and even military affairs of the Muslim community. Azerbaijanis and Crimean Turks enjoyed a period of independence. The local Soviet organizations of these minorities, which were dominated by non-proletarian individuals — nationalists and in some areas even conservative religious intellectuals — were tolerated by the new regime. They enjoyed independence in their cultural and political affairs.

However, the honeymoon soon ended, due to the hostile attitudes of the Russian settlers who now dominated the local communist party organizations of the areas populated by the Turks. Although the attitude of Moscow had been tolerant, the local party members of Russian origin neither trusted the Turks nor forgot their refusal to join the revolution. Thus they began, with some justification, to accuse the

Turkish organizations of being nationalistic and reactionary. This increased the already existing tension to the point where quarrels and open fighting ensued. The Russian Red Army then began to use force to crush every sign of Muslim and Turkish independence. This resulted in massacre and bloodshed, and the traditional hostility between the Christian Russians and the Muslim Turks re-emerged. A short era of good relations was thus shattered once again.

For this reason, when the Civil War broke out in Russia, Muslim Turks joined the counter-revolutionary forces of the White Army, which was controlled by social democrats and liberals in the initial phases of this internal struggle. The leadership of the White Army was not only tolerant of but extremely sympathetic to the aspirations of the Muslim Turks. Thanks to this alliance, the White Army quickly gained control of all the territories where the Turkish Muslim population lived, and the Red Army had to abandon these areas. However, soon Kolchak and Denikin, extreme rightists and loyalists, took control of the White Army. This caused the Turks to reconsider their alliance, since under the new regime, the White Army looked on minority independence even less favorably than had the Tsarist regime. This intolerance and oppression forced the Turks to shift their allegiance and they began to join the Red Army everywhere as the lesser of two evils. Zeki Velidi Togan, who was the leader of the joint Bashkurt-Kazak independence movement between 1918-1920 and played an active role in Muslim-Turkish and Soviet relations, explained in his memoirs the reasons for this shift:

> "Admiral Kolchak, appointed himself the absolute dictator of Russia on November 18th, thus our plans were destroyed. His first order was the abolition of joint government of Kazakistan-Bashkurdistan, and the elimination of Bashkurt-Kazak army. Some detachments from our forces defied the order and began to fight the White Army, the military force of Kolchak, . . . under these circumstances, we had only one alternative left, to begin immediately the negotiations with the Soviets."[3]

Following the victory of the Red Army and the end of the Civil War, and the subsequent consolidation of the Soviet regime, a mutual suspicion dominated Turkish Muslim and Soviet relations, although it never became a full-scale clash. Turkish intellectuals, who were mainly interested in ethnic and religious autonomy, cooperated with the new regime as long as their aspirations of independence were not denied.

At this time, the Turkish Muslim intellectuals developed their own theoretical understanding of Marxism which was called "nationalist Marxism." This concept made their ethnic consciousness ideologically tenable under the Soviet regime. Sultan Galief, a Tatar who was the leading theoretician of national communism, clarified his views in the following fashion:

> Since almost all classes of Muslim society have formerly been oppressed by the colonialists, all are entitled to be called proletarian. The Muslim peoples are proletarian peoples. From an economic standpoint, an enormous difference exists between the British and the French proletariat, for example, and the Afghan and the Moroccan. It is therefore legitimate to affirm that the national movement in the Muslim countries is in character a socialist revolution.[4]

Another theorist of the national communist movement, Ahmet Ozenbashly, wrote the following:

> A Soviet regime resting solely on the dictatorship of the working class is justified in Central Russia where industrial capital has already reached the peak of its development. But when this regime is applied to nomadic Muslim masses or to those who have only just entered the era of merchant capitalism, it fails to be viable. We ask then for assistance in passing through the stages of economic development naturally. . . . In Turkestan, in Kazakhstan, in Bashkiriya, in the Caucasus as in Tataristan and the Crimea, the principles of national government must be adopted, not the principles of class government.[5]

At a later date, Sultan Galief, because of his fear that even the Christian European working class would not change its position toward the poor Muslims of the world, no longer saw the world-wide struggle as between the proletarian and capitalist societies, but in current terms, between the developed Western world and the third world. He wrote:

> We feel that a plan which looks to replacing the world dictatorship of a class of European society by the world dictatorship of the proletariat, that is to say by another class of that same European society, will bring no appreciable change in the lot of the downtrodden colonial peoples. And even were there a change of any sort, it would not be for the better but for the worse.[6]

No matter how ideologically viable the theory was made, its primary function was to preserve the ethnic unity of the Muslim Turks under the new proletariat dictatorship and to insure the survival of numerous intellectuals who were not Marxists but nationalists of various colors. This fact did not escape the attention of the Communist rulers, but they tolerated it for a time. However, they soon began to accuse the nationalist Marxists of being reactionary, pan-Turkist and bourgeois nationalist — the right wing of the party.

After 1922 as the conflict heightened, measures were taken in the areas of education, administration and politics to exclude the ethnic independence movements from Soviet public life. The large Muslim Turkish population was administratively divided into small Soviet Republics, each having a different language, cultural identity and administrative structure. Next, a well organized attack was launched to put an end to the influence of the religion of Islam in social life. The *wakf* or pious foundations, the only source of income for religious schools, were liquidated. The schools themselves were then closed. In the 1930's the Koranic law or *Shari'a* was abolished and the Muslim clergy lost their posts and their power in religious and political affairs. A strong youth organization called the "Godless" on the one hand and an official policy of scientific atheism on the other were able to eliminate Islam from public life. The religious centers or spiritual directorates of Islam — in Ufa for Kazakhistan, in Tashkent for Central Asia, in Binayk for North Caucasia (for Sunni Muslims) and in Baku for the Shiites — were still preserved, but they were allowed to function only within the limits of governmental approval.

Where the private lives of individuals are concerned, a traveler to the Soviet Turkish Republics today will observe the survival of Muslim greeting formulas among friends, of the recitation of prayers when breaking the bread at the table or after the meal. However, these actions have lost their religious significance. It would be a mistake to consider them the continuation of Muslim practices. People view them as a part of traditional life, an ethnic heritage that may protect them from the onslaught of modern ways, brought to Central Asia by the Russian settlers.

This ethnic consciousness and the desire to preserve a national heritage are the most powerful social forces in the Turkish Republics today. They replaced religious identity, which was never a strong unifying force among the Turks to begin with, and which was eliminated from social life by sixty years of Soviet rule.

The development of national consciousness among the minorities in the Soviet Union was the result of complex interactions between the various nationalities and the Soviet central government. These interactions followed basic patterns of politics of the pre-Stalin and post-Stalin eras. Whatever the Soviet policy on nationality was, it resulted in the assimilation of small ethnic and linguistic groups. But larger minorities lost neither their languages nor their ethnic identities. Thus the same policies created what can be called "new" Turkish nations, such as the Azeri, Turkmen, Uzbek, Kazak and Kirgiz, within

Soviet society. Intensive interaction with Russian language and culture did not eliminate their national languages or cultures; instead these nations became bilingual. There are, in addition, other reasons to call these new nations. They each gained well-defined boundaries, developed their own literary languages and their own distinct national identities. The director of the Manuscript Institute in Tashkent, a native Uzbek and a distinguished scholar, explained the development of a nationhood under the Soviets in the following terms:

> Various small khanates, one each in Buhara and Hiyve and Tashkent, and several tribal units all lived in the land we call Uzbekistan today in the days before the Soviet revolution. Each Uzbek society used a different dialect of the ancient Chagatay language and did not know what was going on in the others. Tribal wars and disputes between small khanates divided the Uzbeks spatially, politically and culturally. But today, there is one Uzbek land, an Uzbek literary language and a distinct Uzbek culture shared by ten million people who call themselves members of the Uzbek nation. It was Soviet rule which was responsible for this development, since it destroyed tribal structures and unified small groups.[7]

Similar developments took place in Azerbaijan, Turkmenistan, Kirgizistan and Kazakhistan. Today, a visitor would be surprised to observe the degree of national pride and ethnic identity in the Turkish Republics, developed almost to the point of racial supremacy.

Each republic established local institutes, museums, and halls of fame to study and foster national culture, especially language, history, and literature, both oral and classical. Poets, artists, scholars and historians of the past are promoted to the status of national heroes. For example, Fuzuli, an Azeri classical poet of the 16th century, is memorialized by an institute in Baku; Mahdrumkulu, a 17th century Turkmen poet, has an institute named after him in Ashkabat. The 15th century statesman and poet Ali Shir Novai lent his name not only to a similar institution, but to other schools and institutes as well.

The days of the Stalin era, when every sign of national and traditional culture was condemned as "reactionary, racist and divisive," are gone forever. Since 1953, a new Turkish intelligentsia, less suppressed politically and more secure economically, have been engaged in the study and publication of their traditional culture. The *Manas* epic of the Kirgiz people and the *Dede Korkut* epic of the Azerbaijani and Turkmen peoples, which were once strongly condemned as "advocating the reactionary ideology of Islam, and disseminating the pan-Turkic racism" have had several printings since 1956. The Uzbek Institute for Language and Literature planned the publication of a folklore collection in fifty volumes, some of which have already been published. The important collections of folk literature which remained unpublished during the 1930's and 1940's are being systematically published. Native scholars in the local branches of the Russian Academy of Sciences are quite active in the study of their history, archaeology, language and literature.

In Baku, the capital of Azerbaijan, a scholarly journal called *Sovietskaya Turchologica* is being published. The journal is devoted exclusively to the study of Turkish linguistics and culture. A second journal, entitled *Edebiyat, Dil, ince Sanat* or "Literature, Language and Fine Art" appeared since 1978, and it publishes studies in Azerbaijani as well as Russian. In January of 1979, the Azerbaijani writer's union began publication of *Azerbaijan*, a monthly journal published in Azeri. The journal includes poetry and prose of Azerbaijani writers.

The best expressions of this national consciousness are found in the literary works of Turkish artists in the Soviet Union. Even a quick survey of the literature of these republics reveals that the main components of ethnic identity are love of the mother tongue, pride in national culture and history, and in particular an almost mystical devotion to the land. The Azery, Uzbek, Turkmen and Kirgiz poets speak in unison when they express their belief in the ultimate superiority of the motherland, which they call *vatan, yurt, il* or *anayurt* in their native languages.

A poem of the famous Azeri poet, Samet Vurgun (b. 1906-d. 1956) is carved into the stone of the ancient gate of the city of Baku:

> El bilir ki sen menimsen
> Yurdum yuvam meskenimsen
> Anam, dogma vatanimsan
> Ayrilar mi gönül senden
> Azerbaijan Azerbaijan

> Everyone knows that you belong to me
> You are my country, my home, my refuge
> You are my mother, you are my native land
> How could my heart leave you
> Azerbaijan Azerbaijan

Kemal Cemal, an Uzbek poet, expresses the same love for his motherland in a different manner:

> In the end, whatever fate is your choice
> Oh, homeland, you are the fountain head of happiness
> When you are well there is such joy and contentment in my heart
> When you are well the radiance of the world dances in my soul

> When the sun lowers its head toward your evening horizon
> With a tear of gladness in my eye
>   I place my head against your bosom.
> How happy the moment when I understood your pride,
> And in the world of my heart I enclosed your love.
> Your love became a melody unto my heart
> And without this melody, how sad, how forlorn is my soul.[9]

A young Kirgiz poet, Turar Kajamberdiev, also speaks of a homeland more primal than a mother's breast: "Remember, even before your mother's milk/ You drank the milk of the homeland."[10]

The novels and short stories of the Kirgiz writer Cengiz Aytmatof, an internationally recognized author whose major works have been translated into Western languages, show this love of homeland assuming an epic dimension. Landscape has always been a strong element in the Central Asian epic. In the life of pastoral nomads, the land was not only a source of sustenance for people and animals, but it was also a mystical source. The mountains, the lakes, the forests and the rivers of the motherland were deified and worshipped. Thus the material as well as the religious lives of the Turkish nomads were strongly connected to the land.

Thus, the epic devotion to the landscape and the mystical devotion to the land are followed by this new devotion to the motherland. There is a distinct continuity in the role of this important component of traditional culture among the Turks. Devotion to the homeland has become such an all-encompassing force among the Turkish Republics in the Soviet Union that every culture and civilization that resided on that land, no matter who the creators were, is considered a national heritage. Azerbaijani intellectuals will show you rock drawings dating from the 2nd century A.D. when the name of the Azeri Turks was unheard of, and proudly claim that these were the creation of Azerbaijan peoples. Al Biruni, (973-1051) a Persian scientist, is considered the pride of the Uzbek nation because he was born in Uzbekistan. Nizami, (1141-1209) the Persian author who wrote all his romances in Persian, is a national hero in Azerbaijan, because Gence where he was born is an Azerbaijan city today.

This feeling of nationality is being tolerated, even encouraged, today by the Soviet regime as long as it is fragmented and is not in conflict with the principles of economic socialism. The Azeri nationalism, the Uzbek nationalism and the Turkmen nationalism, while they foster pride in and encourage preservation of ethnic cultures also prevent the homogeneity of Turkish groups and block the ethnic and linguistic unity of various Turkish peoples. This way they will not pose a danger to the security of the Soviet Union.

The Sino-Soviet conflict in Central Asia will presumably play an important role in the future of the Soviet-nationality relationships. China has a Turkish-Muslim population of between four and ten million in Northwestern China, in the province of Sinkiang. They are of the same ethnic origin as the Russian Turkish groups. They are Uzbeks, Uygur, Turkmen, Kirgiz, and Kazak. As far as cultural and linguistic autonomy is concerned the Muslim-Turks in China are in worse condition than those in the USSR. The massive resettlement policy of China placed the Turkish minority in a great danger of complete assimilation or loss of national identity. But China's attitude toward tribal insurgence in Afghanistan made it very clear that the Chinese leadership would grab every opportunity to present itself as the defender of Turkish-Muslim peoples of Central Asia against the Soviet Union. The Afghani tribesmen who received political support and military equipments from China were the Uzbek, Turkmen, and Tajik peoples. By helping them China hoped to impress and gain the sympathy of the peoples of the same origin living on the Soviet side of the border. It is doubtful that this gesture of friendship could reverse the traditional hostility of Muslim Turks, who consider China the most dangerous enemy of Islam. But it will definitely have an impact on Soviet attitudes. Since it is China which could claim the leadership of the minorities in Central Asia — no other global power is in a position to play such a role — and since the political importance of Central Asia as a new sensitive area between India-Pakistan-USA-China-Iran and Soviet Union is increasing it is expected that the Soviet Union will pay more respect to the cultural and ethnic rights of Turkish-Muslim populations in that region.

Footnotes

[1]Cevdet Pasha, *Tezakir*, No. 21-29, T.T.K. publication, No. 17b. Ankara, 1963. p. 163.

[2]Alexandre Bennigsen and Chantal Lemercier-Quelquejay, *Islam in the Soviet Union*. Published in Association with the Central Asian Research Centre. London: Frederick A. Praeger, 1967. p. 82.

[3] Zeki Velidi Togan, *Hatiralar*. Istanbul, 1969. p. 236-241.
[4] Bennigsen-Quelquejay, p. 112.
[5] *Ibid.*
[6] Bennigsen-Quekquejay, p. 114.
[7] Interview which took place in 1978 with H. Suleyman, the director of the Manuscript Institute in Tashkent.
[8] *Azerbaijan*, (monthly literary journal of Azerbaijan writer's union), No. 4 (Jan. 1979), p. 1.
[9] Edward Allworth, ed., *The Nationality Question of Soviet Central Asia*. New York: Praeger, 1973. p. 31.
[10] Allworth, p. 16.

XV

ISLAM AND THE STRUGGLE FOR AFGHAN NATIONAL LIBERATION

Richard S. Newell

Soviet invasion of Afghanistan and the continuing resistance by nationalist tribesmen raised questions, among others, about the role of Islam in the struggle for national liberation. Professor Newell describes here the historic role of Islamic leaders and institutions in Afghan life and shows how these instruments of influence in the past are in a state of disarray now as a result of many decades of contention with the secularly oriented national government. While Islam still remains as the chief rallying point for the many tribes and factions that fight their own wars against the common enemy the formation of a common front will depend on the rise of charismatic leaders from either the religious or secular elite, Newell contends.

Richard S. Newell who has had many years of experience in Afghanistan is the author of **The Politics of Afghanistan** *and currently professor of history at University of Northern Iowa.*

Preservation not revival has become the central issue for Islam in Afghanistan. A conservative but fragmented Muslim nation is confronted by an attempted Marxist revolution protected by the military force of a neighboring superpower. This crisis arose at the end of a sequence of political developments which had kept Afghanistan's Islamic leadership on the defensive at every significant stage. This recent history and the political/cultural compartmentalization of Afghan society seriously limit the prospect that an Islamic revival could become a major factor in determining the outcome of Afghanistan's current tragedy.

These observations are offered in the face of the obvious fact that the resistance of the Afghan *mujahidin* is essentially by definition motivated by a commitment to defend Islam. This identification of religion with an ethnically composite way of life has already produced a remarkably tenacious defense by a population almost totally lacking the resources to wage modern warfare. Yet it is a defense; whether it can be transformed into a crusade which can eject the Russians by some combination of military and diplomatic means remains highly problematical. Should such a development take place, it seems highly doubtful that Islam in Afghanistan can generate the kind of assertive response that would dominate the struggle for national deliverance. The fervor is not lacking; the institutional foundations and ideological framework appear to be.

The basis for this conclusion is that Islam has been a particularist, not an integrative force in the process that has brought a degree of national unity to Afghanistan since the late 19th century. Success by the monarchy in bringing the fractious population and difficult terrain under increasing central control was achieved despite the opposition of the most prominent of Afghan religious leaders. They opposed Abdur Rahman's claim to religious authority. He responded by co-opting the leading *ullama;* incorporating them and religious properties into his royal system. Their greatest success against royal encroachment of their authority was the frustration of Amanullah's attempt at legal, educational and social reforms in the 1920's. This proved to be short lived. After having rebuilt the power of the central government the Musahibans, eventually under Muhammad Daoud, were able to crush conservative Islamic resistance to a far more sweeping introduction of modernism in the 1950's.

This history of retreat by religious purists had a minimal effect upon Afghanistan's overwhelmingly rural or pastoral population until the late 1960's. Before then few of the changes in government organization, constitutional arrangements, education, social practice, economic infrastructure or commerce introduced in Kabul and several of the major provincial cities had materially affected the rural majority. The isolation of Afghanistan's ethnic/regional communities from the center and from each other muffled the impact of modernist innovations and also the loss of political influence upon the government by religious conservatives. Hence when innovations were adroitly introduced — a requirement which Amanullah failed to meet — there was limited reaction among the population as a whole which might have fueled a strong fundamentalist or conservative opposition.

Most of Afghanistan's religious leaders continued to operate within a conventional rural milieu. Narrow in their experience and vision, most Afghan *ullama* could ignore the growing apparatus of a modern state while it accumulated the strength to impinge upon them. Their lack of preparation for a modernist challenge was demonstrated by the successful introduction of profound educational changes in the countryside in the late 1960's. A national system of secularly operated schools (religion was included in the curriculum) was rapidly spread throughout Afghanistan. This reflected a dramatic change in attitude towards government run schools: from resistance to what was seen as an intrusion to a demand for educational opportunities for rural children. For the most part this changed attitude applied to education for boys, but by the early 1970's public education for girls was gaining acceptance beyond the provincial cities, although it continued to be resisted in the more conservative Pushtun communities.

This revolution in education greatly affected the educational role of the typical rural *mullah*. Previously he had a virtual monopoly over what passed for formal instruction in his village. He now was enlisted within the centrally controlled system as a primary school teacher, an arrangement which was common in the smaller or more remote villages, or he was bypassed by the appointment of teachers trained in the new system of teacher academies. Either way, his educational and hence his social role in his community was substantially weakened or circumscribed.

At the same time similar inroads were made into the enforcement of justice, another bastion of traditional influence for rural specialists in Islam. With the establishment of the primacy of secular legislation in the liberal constitution of 1964 *qazis* and *muftis* were confronted by significant changes in the content, organization and spirit of the Afghan legal system. Secular law legislated by parliament and enforced and regulated by the Ministry of Justice now dominated the system. The ministry embarked upon programs of retraining incumbent judicial officials and recruitment from the modernist Faculty of Law and Political Science of Kabul University to insure effective implementation of the new constitution. These changes portended severe limitations upon the accustomed freedom of *qazis* to apply the *Shari'a* with a mixture of local usage and personal idiosyncracy.

Since the founding of the Afghan state in the eighteenth century the leaders of its dominant Sunni community had never played a prominent, direct role in politics. By 1970 they were rapidly losing their influence in education and law. Access to political influence was coming to require acceptance of a modernist, increasingly pervasive, role of government and a willingness to adapt social innovations from Western sources. Prominent religious leaders who advocated such changes could reach senior positions in government. The most notable case was that of Mussa Safiq, a graduate in Islamic Law from Kabul University who had studied at Al Azhar. After playing a major role in the drafting of the 1964 constitution and in the subsequent cabinets he was appointed Prime Minister prior to the coup that returned Daoud to power in 1973. During his short tenure he attempted to check some of the more obvious trends towards the relaxation of orthodox Muslim standards of behavior among Kabul's urban sophisticates, but his political prominence followed his willingness to accept a broad range of innovations.

Daoud's return to power with the help of the Parcham wing of the Afghan Marxists — the Peoples Democratic Party — placed the religious leadership even more on the defensive. The general tolerance even of reactionary Islamic critics by the liberal government came to an end. Public political comment was squelched in general, with particular attention paid to the arrest and expulsion of recalcitrant *ullama* who expressed their opposition to a regime in which Marxists were prominent. Muhammad Niazi, leader of the Afghan Ikwani Musalamin, was jailed and his organization driven underground. To some degree his fundamentalist followers resurfaced in Pakistan, some under Burhanuddin Rabani who organized the Jamiat Islami with help from the Pakistan Jamiat in Peshawar, and others under Gulbudin Hekmatyar, leader of the Hizb-i-Islami, also based at Peshawar. Thus, expatriate opposition movements led by conservative theologians began prior to the outright seizure of power by the Khalq wing of the PDP in 1978.

For the Afghan *ullama,* therefore, the process of political change over the past century has brought a progressive erosion of political independence and influence. With the sudden emergence of the Khalq regime their position became precarious. After several clumsy attempts to co-opt Muslim leaders and institutions in order to win popular acceptance, the Taraki/Amin government launched assaults against religious leaders who persisted in open criticism. The most notorious instance was a violent attack on the residence of the Hazrat Sahib of the Shor Bazaar. The arrest of more than 100 of his followers and his rumored execution clearly signaled an end to the regime's attempt to court Islamic support. Arrests and executions of prominent urban *ullama* virtually decimated the ranks of leading religious figures in the cities who refused to collaborate with the regime.

This resort to repression had little effect upon the rural religious leadership which continued to retain niches of influence upon local opinion and mores. When revulsion towards the Khalq regime spread across all of Afghanistan's rural sectors in early 1979, it was provoked by official disruptions of local socio/cultural traditions and conditions. Accordingly, the resulting resistance was led by combinations of local secular and religious leaders. These spontaneous and sporadic reactions against government intrusions demonstrate the shallowness of the impact of previous government attempts to control and transform the countryside. The Khalq regime had the ambition and the recklessness to attempt draconian changes without establishing the coercive means to achieve them. Programs intended to bring about the radical redistribution of land, to emancipate women from family control over marriage and to enroll both sexes in government schools with a Marxist curriculum assured a violent and nearly universal response.

Inevitably, this reaction included both religious and secular elements. Religious leaders have played prominent roles in organizing and carrying out insurgent resistance and in representing it to the outside world. Yet there are constraints on their roles in Afghan society which may severely limit the degree of political influence they can wield even in the apparently unlikely event that the Marxists and the Russians are driven from Afghan soil. These constraints are closely related to the anarchic character of Afghan society and culture as a whole.

Afghan Islam is divided between the two major sects with Sunnis accounting for approximately 80 percent of the population. Shi'ism is spread among some of the ethnic minorities with both Ashariyas and Ismailis represented. As a result of regional, ethnic and sectarian diversity, there is no single dominant religious institution even among Sunni Muslims. Despite the near totality of popular resistance to the Marxists and the Russians, no commanding figure analogous to the Ayatollah Khomeini has emerged in Afghanistan. This may be partially accounted for by the generally more passive Sunni theological position towards the authority of the state when compared with the elaborate Shia rationale for opposition. Religious influences in politics are more materially weakened by the absence of Islamic institutions which are truly national in scope.

Afghanistan's religious institutions faithfully mirror the diversity and fragmentation manifest in all aspects of society. This is most obvious within rural communities. The rural Afghan *mullah* has been constricted by limits of education and experience to a particularist, often distorted, understanding of Islamic doctrine which is diluted by autonomous tribal norms and survivals of pre-Islamic belief. Thus, while most *mullahs* would consider themselves to be strict enforcers of the *Shari'a*, there is much variety of detail and substance in their conservatism. Until very recently their services to their local constituents as teachers, mediators, mentors and models of piety were shaped by the specific conditions operative in their villages or nomadic groups. Such local religious leaders have had little reason or opportunity to respond to currents of Islamic thought outside of their limited social spheres.

This isolation reflects the failure of more sophisticated religious institutions to have an impact upon Afghan rural life. Extra-local institutions do exist, especially the numerous shrines to *pirs* — usually Sufis — which attract great attention as pilgrim centers. Yet few Afghans appear to be identified with the brotherhoods or religious orders which dominate much of the social order in other Islamic societies. When it does occur, affiliation is usually with a prominent regional institution or with an urban center of teaching and charity. Perhaps the most influential of the regional religious influences have been families accepted as *pirs* who in effect serve as chaplains to major tribes or regional groups. Outstanding in its impact has been the Gailani family which has great influence among the Mohmand, Afridi, and Suleiman Khel Pushtuns of the Janubi and Mashriqi areas of eastern Afghanistan. Within the cities the senior *ullama* of the *juma* mosques can generate influence beyond their urban congregations. However, the most notable urban based religious institution is the network of educational cum social service centers established and operated by the Mujadidi family of scholars led by the Hazrat Sahib of Kabul. Yet, taken together these atypically prominent institutions offer little means of bringing about cohesion in Afghan Islam. Modest in resources, limited in the number of followers who *actively* identify with them, the major mosques, shrines, regional chaplains and urban centers have not effectively drawn Afghan Islam into a coherent institutional system.

Underlying this fragmented situation is the glaring demographic contrast between Afghanistan and most of the Muslim Middle East. Despite rapid growth which began in the 1950's, Kabul and other relatively large Afghan cities account for probably less than seven percent of the population. This compares with a 50 percent urban proportion in the nearby Muslim countries of Iran, Jordan, Kuwait, Lebanon, the Trucial states and Egypt. Only Saudi Arabia, the Sudan and Yemen have similarly small urban populations. Consequently, the capacity of urban institutions in Afghanistan to reach and affect the overwhelming rural majority is relatively limited. Not only does much of the population have little access to urban, centralizing religious institutions but also Afghanistan's limited urban development restricts where the availability of persons educated beyond minimal literacy is variously estimated to be between five and ten percent of the adult population. This absence of a pool of educated persons means that few Afghans have the intellectual resources and interests to participate in religious movements dedicated to reviving, restating or reforming Islam. There is no Afghan counterpart to the partially educated, uprooted ex-rural conservative proletariat which has served as the social base for Khomeini's revolution in Iran. Not only is intellectual ferment restricted to a small educated elite in Afghanistan, the linkage between this elite — whether Marxist or Islamic in orientation — and the mass of the population is strictly limited. So far, the articulateness of the urban elite of all persuasions belies its impact upon Afghan society as a whole. This chasm grew rapidly during the period of foreign supported urban modernization. It persists in a new form during the course of a violent rebellion against rule by a Marxist splinter of the urban educated elite.

The diversity and disconnectedness which have consistently been features of Afghan politics mark the present resistance to the Russian military presence and the pretensions to authority by the Parcham government. The insurgency has almost always been generated by local issues between the population and the government and has been led by local notables both secular and religious. The internal struggle has been accompanied by the emergence of emigre groups, mostly quartered in Pakistan, who claim to have mobilized and to lead the *mujahidin* actually engaged in hostilities. The emigre organizations have achieved a degree of visibility in the international press which has drawn attention to the plight of the Afghan resistance, particularly in Muslim countries. This accomplishment has been accompanied by little positive evidence of their ability to coordinate, direct or materially support insurgent groups actively carrying out resistance inside Afghanistan. The position of these emigre organizations is thus analogous to that of Afghanistan's educated elite as a whole.

This gap between emigre organizers and the *mujahidin* remains open despite factors convenient to the formation of close connections between them: the general permeability of the Afghanistan-Pakistan border which permits constant movement and the consequent presence of a large refugee population — some one million in Pakistan — from which the emigre groups are in a position to recruit manpower. These circumstances and not the popular appeal of the Pakistan based spokesmen for the resistance account for much of the influence they have exercised upon events inside Afghanistan.

This weakness of linkage is partially attributable to the intergroup rivalries which have tended to discredit them from the point of view of *mujahidin* fighting inside Afghanistan. Emigre influence is further weakened by their inability to generate material support for the guerillas. The *jirgah* held in May, 1980 in Peshawar in which representatives of the insurgents fighting in Afghanistan ignored the emigre organizations is the latest indication of this lack of cohesion.

Differences of doctrine and leadership style have been largely responsible for the failure of these groups to find a formula for effective unity and cooperation between themselves. All claim to be conducting a *jihad* on behalf of Islam and Afghan independence, but all have leaders claiming to have unique religious credentials and specific programs for applying Islam to a restored Afghanistan. To these differences of ideology are added differences of social or regional bases of support within Afghanistan and different avenues of access to foreign assistance.

Thus, even when confronted with a foreign invasion which would impose a Marxist society upon Afghanistan, the leadership of contemporary Afghan Islamic institutions has not been able to transcend the divisions that have compartmentalized Afghan life. Islam has inspired and shaped much of the resistance to the Russians, but it has not provided the social means for focusing and coordinating an all embracing national struggle for liberation.

Should the resistance struggle persist indefinitely, it may produce a social/ideological dialectic that could create new leadership and institutions which may survive and prove themselves in battle. National deliverance from Russian control would require a remarkable combination of military, diplomatic and political achievements. As an elemental motivator and a primary component of what Afghan culture holds in common, Islam would likely be a primary factor in gaining such a deliverance. The emergence of a charismatic religious leader from the struggle itself remains a possibility. Otherwise, if national liberation is won, it will be through the political and military exploits of devout but secular leaders. That result would once again place Afghanistan's Islamic institutions in the uneasy position of accepting a political order which they did not create and cannot control. A secular leadership would continue to determine the mechanism and distribution of power. Islam would be restored to a venerated and secure status; to that extent an Islam revival would be assured. For this revival to extend to a reaffirmation of Islam as the guide and aspiration to an integrated Afghan national culture would require a broader view and a political genius that no religious figure has so far demonstrated.

But at this point projections on the aftermath of a successful struggle for Afghanistan's liberation seem an indulgence in fantasy. Indefinite struggle and tragedy are the immediate prospect. Eventually, to cut their own losses the Russians may agree to abandon Parcham and support a coalition government dominated by the leadership of the resistance. The nationalist *bona fides* of such a compromise government would be greatly enhanced if it were to be led by a religious figure credible to Afghan nationalists and acceptable to the Russians. Again, no such figure has emerged, but one might in the course of the struggle. And even if it came to pass, such an elevation of a religious leader to political power would not manifest a transformation of Afghan religious institutions. The mechanism that would have made it possible would be essentially political.

Secular considerations are likely to dominate the agenda of any government which restores Afghan independence. The most compelling priorities would have to be given to relations with the Soviet Union, the role of the regional and sectarian minorities, and the direction and means for resuming national development. Religious figures might lead such a government, but they could not ignore the primacy of these secular concerns.

Given its history, present circumstances and culture it is safe to predict that Afghanistan's restoration as an independent national state would be inspired by Islamic social goals and motivated by the desire to preserve an Islamic way of life, but such a restoration must be achieved through secular means. This reality, which has persisted through revolution and invasion, does not preclude deep religious influence upon politics, but it is likely to mean that intellectual and social initiatives in Afghanistan will arise from secular sources whatever the outcome of the present crisis.

Bibliography

Canfield, Robert L., *Faction and Conversion in a Plural Society: Religious Alignments in the Hindu Kush.* Ann Arbor: Museum of Anthropology, University of Michigan, Number 50, 1973.

Dupree, Louis, *Afghanistan.* Princeton: Princeton University Press, 1973. Especially chapters 6, 8, 12, 24, 25.

_____, *American University Field Staff Reports, South Asia Series,* Volume XX, No. 1 "Saint Cults in Afghanistan" and Volume XX, No. 7 "The Afghans Honor a Muslim Saint: Reprise".

_____, "Islam in Politics: Afghanistan", *The Muslim World,* LVI-4:269-276. 1966.

_____, "The Political Uses of Religion: Afghanistan", *Churches and States,* K. H. Silver (ed.). New York, 1967.

Fletcher, Arnold, *Afghanistan: Highway of Conquest.* Ithaca: Cornell University Press, 1965. Especially chapter 2.

Gregorian, Vartan, *The Emergence of Modern Afghanistan.* Stanford: Stanford University Press, 1969. Especially chapter 2.

Newell, Richard S., *The Politics of Afghanistan.* Ithaca: Cornell University Press, 1972.

Weinbaum, Marvin G., "Legal Elites in Afghan Society", Department of Political Science, University of Illinois at Urbana, unpublished thesis (N.D.).

XVI

ISLAMIC REVIVAL IN PAKISTAN

Mumtaz Ahmad

Pakistan was born in 1947 as an Islamic state. But after thirty-three years and over half a dozen constitutions and/or constitutional changes argument still rages on about the Islamicity of the state. While even the revivalist reforms of General Zia do not satisfy fully many orthodox/fundamentalist Muslim groups, on the other side stand the Western oriented modernists — who claim they are just as good Muslims — with their contention that traditional Islamic precepts about the state and society should be reinterpreted to suit the needs of our time. Indeed, what is shaping up in Pakistan is a classic contest between two concepts of state, traditional Islamic and modern Western, the end result of which may have far-reaching consequences in the Islamic world. Mr. Ahmad describes here the background, history and the characters of this drama.

Mumtaz Ahmad, a graduate of the University of Karachi and American University in Beirut is at present a Ph.D. candidate in the Department of Political Science at the University of Chicago. From 1968 to 1975 he taught at the National Institute of Public Administration, Karachi. He is the author of **Bureaucracy and Political Development in Pakistan, The Kashmir Dispute: A Study in Diplomacy, The Unfinished Revolution: Studies in Local Government and Rural Development in Pakistan,** *and numerous journal articles on Islam, development and Pakistan.*

Unlike Iran and some other Muslim countries whose Islamic enthusiasm is relatively recent, the Pakistani experience of Islamic revivalism is integrally related with the very idea of a separate homeland for Indian Muslims which took shape in the late 1930's. As long as the Muslim League — the political organization of the Muslims which was dominated by the landlords and urban elite of Northern India in its earlier phase — was engaged in constitutional struggle in order to seek separate electorate and nominated political and administrative positions in the British Indian political system, it had little or no appeal among the Muslim masses. After many years of persistent attempts to reach some reasonably acceptable settlement with the Indian National Congress, the Muslim League leadership eventually realized that the religious, cultural, and political interests of the Indian Muslim community could not be safeguarded in a post-independence united India dominated by the Hindu majority. The Muslim League, therefore, set for itself the goal of creating a separate state with a Muslim majority, to be known as Pakistan. The popular acceptance of the idea of Pakistan was, however, only made possible through the Muslim League's successful attempt to politicize the religious beliefs and sentiments of the Indian Muslim community. By the time the movement for the establishment of Pakistan came near the realization of its goal, the revivalist character of the movement had already been firmly established. But the revivalist dimension of the Pakistan movement was not entirely related to the exigencies of the Muslim League's political tactics; it had its firm historical roots in such pre-modern fundamentalist movements as that of Shah Wali Allah of Delhi and Sayyid Ahmad of Breli. This revivalist impulse, nevertheless, came to be intricately intertwined with the late nineteenth and early twentieth century Muslim modernist-nationalist tradition of the Aligarh School, Seyyed Amir Ali and Mohammad Iqbal with their concern for the restoration of Islam's political power and cultural glory.

When Pakistan came into existence in August 1947, there was a broad consensus that the constitution and the new government should be Islamic and relate to the teachings of the Holy Quran and the *Sunna* of the Prophet. The problem, however, was that interpretations of these teachings offered by the conservative *ulama* and the fundamentalist *Jamaat-e-Islami* (literally, the party of Islam, founded by Maulana Abul Ala Maududi in 1941) on the one hand and the modernists on the other, differed considerably. It was because of these differences that the final approval of the constitution by the parliament had to be delayed for about nine years in order to seek a middle point on which both conservatives-fundamentalists and modernists could agree.

Prior to the adoption of the 1956 constitution, the parliament had passed the "Objective Resolution" in 1949 which was incorporated as a preamble into all the subsequent constitutions of Pakistan. The resolution embodied the main principles on which the future constitution of Pakistan was sought to be based. It declared that "sovereignty over the entire universe belongs to God Almighty" and that the authority which He has delegated to the state of Pakistan through its people will be exercised "within the limits prescribed by Him". The resolution referred to the Islamic principles of democracy, freedom, equality, tolerance, and social justice as guidelines for state policy and undertook to create conditions wherein Muslims could order their individual and collective lives in accord with the teachings and requirements of Islam.

The "objective resolution" thus defined the framework within which future legislation was to be enacted. But this still did not resolve the conflict between the *ulama* and the modernist political elite of the new nation. The conflict eventually came on the forefront when the generalized principles of the "objective resolution" were sought to be translated into operational programs of action and concrete policy measures. While the religious leaders defined and formulated the goals of the newly born state in terms of Islamic revivalism, enforcement of Islamic penal code, and introduction of strict socio-moral norms of behavior, very few politicians and administrators saw these goals as anything else than secular development in economic and social fields. The only thing they could promise to the religious groups was that they would try to create conditions favorable for the realization of Islamic ideals. They would not, however, commit themselves to the actual legislation of these ideals. To the Western-educated politico-administrative elite the first and foremost task was the establishment of a viable civil order and the maximization of national production. They perceived the public policy issues in strictly pragmatic and technical terms and opposed the *ulama's* attempts to relate specific injunctions of Islamic *shari'a* to programs of socio-economic development. It is thus interesting to note that while the modernist political elite acceded to the *ulama's* demands to incorporate certain general Islamic provisions in the 1956 and 1962 constitutions, they did not, at the same time, accept their views on such issues as abolition of bank interest, banning of alcoholic drinks, disallowing birth control, instituting separate educational institutions for women, or keeping the Muslim marriage and inheritance laws as exclusive domains for the *ulama*. As for the Islamic provisions of the 1956 and 1962 constitutions which promised that "no law shall be enacted which is repugnant to the Quran and *Sunna*" and that the Muslims of Pakistan "shall be enabled individually and collectively to order their lives in accordance with the principles of Islam", these appeared to have been inserted in the constitutions, as Fazlur Rahman has observed," ... piecemealy, desultorily and rather mechanically ...

as several pieces of decoration and window-dressing". Also, these provisions were not made part of the operative sections of the constitutions and were referred to only as "principles of state policy", not enforceable through court action. Thus, notwithstanding the constitutional commitments and political rhetoric, the relationship between Islam and the national political system remained ambivalent and indeterminate throughout the first three decades of Pakistan's independent existence. It is only after the break-up of Pakistan in 1971 that we witness the resurgence of Islamic politics as an ideological response to Prime Minister Zulfikar Ali Bhutto's Islamic socialism. Although Bhutto's constitution of 1973 did include the Islamic provisions of the earlier constitutions and added some of its own, the *ulama* remained unconvinced of the regime's sincerity of purpose. The most important concession offered to the *ulama* in the 1973 constitution was the provision that the head of state and certain other important political officials would take the oath that they were not *Ahmadis* (a sect founded by Mirza Ghulam Ahmad who claimed that he was a prophet and received revelation from God) and that they believed in the finality of Mohammad's prophethood. As a logical consequence of this provision, the *ulama* and the *Jamaat-e-Islami* launched a movement in 1974 demanding that the *Ahmadis* be declared a non-Muslim minority. Bhutto gave in to the pressure of religious groups and declared officially, through an act of parliament, that the *Ahmadis* were outside the pale of Islam. But even this concession did not work and the relationship between Bhutto's regime and the religious groups remained estranged and tense. The *ulama* and the *Jamaat-e-Islami* were convinced that Bhutto's socialist rhetoric and secular policies were eroding the Islamic basis of Pakistani society. They also felt threatened because of the increasing intervention of state in the so-far autonomous religious institutions. The common fear of Bhutto's socialist-cum-authoritarian policies led the *ulama*, the fundamentalist *Jamaat-e-Islami* and other conservative political groups* to form an alliance, the Pakistan National Alliance (PNA) under the banners of (a) the restoration of democratic rights and (b) the introduction of a true Islamic system, described as *Nizam-e-Mustafa* (literally, the system of Prophet Mohammad). Bhutto tried to establish his Islamic credentials by hosting an Islamic summit conference, allowing more people to go for annual pilgrimage to Mecca, declaring *Ahmadis* as non-Muslims,

---

*For a schematic introduction of the Islamic parties, see Appendix A.

and introducing legislation for the error-free publication of the Holy Quran. During his last days in power he issued another package of "Islamic reforms" under the intense pressure built by the *Nizam-e-Mustafa* movement of January-July 1977, and banned alcoholic drinks, gambling, horse-racing, and dance clubs.

By the time Prime Minister Bhutto announced in December 1976 that he would hold general elections in the following March, the various opposition parties and Islamic groups had already launched a vigorous election campaign, starting from urban centers and then concentrating on small towns in Punjab, Sind and the Frontier province. The PNA movement gained considerable momentum in a very short time and its slogan of *Nizam-e-Mustafa* became a hallmark of an almost spontaneous mass movement against the Bhutto regime. It was at this time that Bhutto panicked and rigged the elections to such an extent that the entire process became a farce. Deeply resentful of the mass rigging of the elections, the PNA issued a general appeal to the people to protest against what it termed the "suppression of their democratic and Islamic aspirations". As is well known, the violent processions and demonstrations, barricade fighting between PNA supporters and the police and Federal Security Force, and the increasingly uncontrollable situation of lawlessness that followed the PNA appeal, subsequently led to the overthrow of the Bhutto regime and the imposition of martial law by the Army Chief of Staff, General Mohammad Zia ul Haq.

At the time of his coup in July 1977, General Zia said that his mission was to restore law and order and to hold fair and impartial general elections within ninety days. However, he later postponed the elections in order to "weed out" the corrupt political elements from the society and to "lay down the foundations of the Islamic system", the two tasks which, according to him, enjoyed the consensus of the entire nation. In 1978 he invited the *Jamaat-e-Islami* and certain other Islamic and conservative parties to join his civilian cabinet in order to help the martial law authorities "in the prompt and effective introduction of *Nizam-e-Mustafa*".

Even before their formal association with the martial law regime, the religious parties in the PNA had assumed an important role as unofficial advisors to General Zia on religious matters and were actively persuading him to introduce Islamic measures. An orthodox Muslim himself, Zia was fully convinced that it was the demand for *Nizam-e-Mustafa* that had moved the people to overthrow the Bhutto regime. Assuming that there was a general consensus on the demand for the Islamization of society, and believing that the success of the PNA movement in 1977 provided him with a sufficient mandate, Zia set for himself the goal of introducing "concrete steps and solid measures" designed to transform the country's socio-economic and political structures in accordance with the principles of Islam.

Zia's first step toward Islamization was to reorganize the Council of Islamic Ideology. The newly constituted Council, consisting mainly of conservative and fundamentalist *ulama*, was given the task of formulating guiding principles for the enforcement of the Islamic system and of suggesting ways and means to bring the existing laws in conformity with the Quran and the *Sunna*. The Council was specifically charged with recommending practical measures to introduce *Zakat*, *Usher*, an interest-free economic system, and the Islamic penal code. The general mood of self-confidence and optimism with regard to the success of Islamization program is reflected in a statement by Maulana Shah Ahmad Noorani, President of the *Jamiyat-e-Ulama-e-Pakistan* who said that the PNA had plans "to introduce interest-free banking in the country within one year." He declared that punishments in accordance with the *Shari'a* would be introduced within one month, the entire Pakistan penal code would be revised within six months, *Zakat* and *Usher* would be enforced within one year and the solution "of the country's economic problems . . . could also be (achieved) within a year".

The other major move toward Islamization was the *Shari'a* Bench Order which was introduced in December 1978. The order amended the constitution so as to confer on the High Courts the power to decide whether a law is repugnant to the injunctions of Islam and to provide that any law so declared would cease to have effect on the day the decision of the High Court became effective. This order was subsequently amended, abolishing *Shari'a* Benches at the level of High Courts and leaving only one *Shari'a* Bench in the Supreme Court of Pakistan. The Bench consists of five judges who are to be advised by competent *ulama* in matters of classical Islamic law. The *Shari'a* Bench Order was accompanied by other "Islamic" measures such as the observance of strict Islamic moral standards in the production and screening of T.V. programs; revision of all textbooks toward an Islamic bias; a promise to establish two separate universities for women; formation of a permanent law commission to simplify the process of justice and to bring the existing laws in conformity with Islam; the setting up of a *Shari'a* faculty at the Islamabad University, which began functioning in September 1979; declaring Friday as the weekly holiday instead of Sunday; and the obligatory prayer breaks during working hours in government and private offices, factories and other organizations.

The major thrust toward Islamization of society, however, came on 10 February 1979 (the birthday of the Prophet) when General Zia announced the amendment of the criminal jurisprudence based on Anglo-Saxon law and the introduction of the Islamic penal code. Ordinances were issued simultaneously which provided Islamic punishments for alcoholic drinks, theft, adultery and *Qazaf* (false accusations concerning sexual offenses) as well as "appropriate procedures" to make whipping the form of punishment for these crimes. Another ordinance sought to introduce the *Zakat* and *Usher* fund and the procedures for their collection, management, and distribution. While the laws *(Hudood)* regarding drinking, adultery, theft and *Qazaf* were meant to be enforced immediately, the implementation of *Zakat* and *Usher* was scheduled for July and October 1979, respectively. As for the issue of interest, General Zia said that his government was working to establish an interest-free economy but that could be done only gradually. As a first step it was decided that the House Building Finance Corporation, National Investment Trust and Investment Corporation of Pakistan would begin interest-free lending and deposits and would function on the basis of equity participation.

Immediately after these announcements, a Central *Zakat* fund was established with an initial amount of Rs. 225 crores to help widows, orphans and other needy persons. The major contribution to this fund came from Saudi Arabia and the United Arab Emirates. General Zia declared confidently that as a result of the welfare measures such as *Zakat* and *Usher*, Pakistan would be transformed into an egalitarian society in which "hunger and beggary would be eliminated" and "no citizen would go to bed hungry". It was General Zia's hope that with the introduction of the package of fiscal and penal laws of the *Shari'a*, Pakistan would soon become a true Islamic state — a dream come true after thirty-two years of betrayal of the Islamic basis of Pakistan.

General Zia's announcement of these measures was greatly hailed by the religious parties and their supporters. Here was a ruler who, for the first time in the thirty-two year history of Pakistan — nay, for the first time since the death of the Moghul emperor Aurangzeb in 1740 — had incorporated the Islamic punishments in state laws and had recognized the supremacy of the Islamic *Shari'a* in public policies. The invocation of Islam by the regime was seen by the *ulama* not only as a genuine revival of the Islamic *Shari'a*, but also as a recognition of their special sphere of influence in matters of public policy. The *Jamaat-e-Islami* initially supported these measures but later on went back to its original position formulated by Maulana Maududi that the introduction of the Islamic penal code prior to its socio-economic prerequisites (i.e., elimination of poverty, provision of the basic necessities of life to all citizens, and establishment of Islamic socio-moral order) was neither a sound policy nor was it warranted by Islam.

With the advent of the Islamic measures, however, the old questions of juristic, doctrinal and theological differences among the Islamic groups came to be revived to such an extent that the implementation of the *Zakat* and *Usher* ordinance had to be postponed pending an agreement between the government and the *Shia* minority. The *Shia* members of the Council of Islamic Ideology resigned from their positions to protest "these *Sunni*-oriented measures which disregarded the views and opinions of the *Shia* community". As a matter of fact, the *Shias* were never enthusiastic about the Islamization drive in the first place. They had generally supported the secularly-oriented Bhutto's People's Party in the 1977 elections, fearing that the rising tide of militant orthodoxy might turn against them, as it had against the *Ahamadis* in 1974. The *Shia ulama* launched a movement to resist the compulsory collection of *Zakat* from the *Shias* and raised quite a furore, creating serious law and order problem for the authorities. About thirty thousand *Shias*, most of them armed, marched toward the central secretariat buildings in Islamabad on 6 July, 1980 and threatened "violent action" if their demands were not met. Fully convinced that the success of the Islamization programs is contingent upon their concurrence, and emboldened by the moral and political support from the neighboring *Shia* Iran, the *Shias* were certain that General Zia could not but agree to their demands. The government immediately started a process of consultation with a group of *Shia Ulama* and promised that their viewpoint would be incorporated in an amended ordinance on *Zakat* and *Usher*. The new ordinance which was promulgated in September 1980, provided that the persons feeling that the compulsory deduction of *Zakat* at source was against their belief and sect, could seek an exemption from it by filing a declaration to this effect. The *Shias* will have their own *Zakat* committees to be administered voluntarily by their own leaders.

During the month of *Ramadhan*, 1400 A.H. (July-August, 1980), General Zia personally inaugurated the distribution of *Zakat* with great fanfare and extravagant publicity on the national radio and television. But the amount distributed was so meager ($4.00 per individual and $8.00 per family) that the entire process looked rather farcical, especially if one remembered General Zia's confident remarks that with the introduction of *Zakat* Pakistan would be able to solve the problem of poverty. Although the rate of two and a half per cent was the minimum allowed and there were large numbers of deserving cases, the suggestion of realizing *Zakat* at different rates from people in different income groups was outrightly rejected by the *Ulama* and the regime. The daily *Hurriyat*, a national newspaper published from Karachi, expressing the modernist viewpoint remarked that the existing rate of collection and system of distribution of *Zakat* would perpetuate the state of poverty in the country and that "this kind of '*Shariat*' has no connection whatsoever with Islam".

The progress toward introducing an interest-free economy was also not very encouraging. After about three years of deliberations, the Council of Islamic Ideology came out with an 118-page report which, except for a change of terminology, could not think of any solution to the thorny problem of giving an Islamic bias to the country's economy. The Council recommended that "in view of certain difficulties in the practical application of the profit/loss system" certain other methods like leasing, hire-purchase, speculative transactions, investment auctioning and financing on the normal rate of return would be allowed in "interest-free" banking operations. As if cognizant of its inability to find a feasible alternative to interest-based economy, the Council recommended the formation of more study groups and committees in order to prepare detailed blueprints for the switch-over to interest-free economy and concluded its report by emphasizing "the need for reformatory measures at moral building and eradication of false values of life".

Recently, because of the interplay of diverse political, social, economic, and religious factors, the general enthusiasm for Islamization seems to be on the decline. Only General Zia appears to have kept his faith alive. However, while the rhetoric about Islamic system still constitutes a major theme in his public speeches, practical initiatives and programs toward Islamization have been shelved or are at a standstill. Symbolic gestures, perhaps as substitutes for practical measures, have recently become much more common. This includes the holding of international conferences on Islamic law and Islamic education; centenary celebrations of Islamic calendar; hosting national conventions of *ulama* and *mashaikh* (spiritual leaders); and General Zia himself presiding over lower level bureaucratic meetings to decide the appropriate architectural design for the new shrine of Data Ganj Bakhsh, the patron saint of Lahore. Since the *Jamaat-e-Islami* has withdrawn its support for General Zia and is increasingly becoming critical of the way he is handling the Islamization programs, he is now looking for a support base among the non-political *ulama* and *mashaikh*. The *ulama* and *mashaikh* conventions held in Islamabad in August and September 1980 almost unanimously supported General Zia's efforts toward Islamization and noted that his government was "sincerely working for the glory of Islam".

By way of concluding this paper, certain important aspects of the Islamization movement in Pakistan need to be emphasized. The entire thrust of Islamization in Pakistan is based on certain legal changes with the assumption that the introduction of the Islamic penal code and the *Zakat* and *Usher* laws will help bring about desired Islamic changes in society. This is precisely the same methodology of change which the *ulama* and other religious parties have been following since the very inception of Pakistan. They have continuously demanded an Islamic constitutional law for Pakistan with the hope that the constitutional document itself will somehow bring about an Islamic state or Islamic society. The efficacy of law as an instrument of Islamic social reform was also an important methodological assumption of the Islamic modernists, who sought to change the established modes of social behavior and traditional functions of religious institutions through legal enactments. Much of the "Islamic engineering" by the Islamic modernists as well as by the Islamic fundamentalists has taken the implementing agencies and the affected groups in society essentially as passive recipients with no interests or ideological orientations of their own.

Even given the limited legal reforms and economic measures, it is doubtful that they can be successfully implemented in view of certain important structural constraints. The existing social and governmental institutions represent an admixture of varying degrees of the legacies of both the British colonial rule and the regional cultural traditions of Indian Islam. Family and tribal institutions in most cases are based on caste and kinship identifications. Educational institutions are essentially a continuation of the educational philosophy propounded by Lord McCaulay in 1835. The structure of recruitment, training, organization and orientation of the civilian and military bureaucracies is, to a very large extent, a continuation of the British Imperial tradition of authoritative rule, maintenance of law and order and collection of taxes. Political parties and other organizational interest groups represent a dual structure of traditionally sanctified social hierarchies, tribal loyalties and regional identifications on the one hand, and the constitutional legacy of the later day British rule on the other. Property relations in both the traditional rural sector as well as in the modern urban sector are highly exploitative and oppressive. It is obvious, therefore, that in a social structure that embodies systematic inequalities in distribution of power, status and resources, the *Fiqh*-oriented, legalistic definition of Islam which is propounded by the *Ulama* and General Zia and which is devoid of Islam's concern for social justice is likely to become an ideological tool of political control and a rationalization of the existing social formations. That an inherent contradiction exists between Islam and the present sociopolitical formations has not occurred to the Islamic parties in Pakistan. Whenever they talk about the Islamization of society they either seem to assume that this process will take place in a power vacuum, or that the existing social and state institutions will be passive recipients of the Islamic measures. Hence we find that they emphasize change in political personnel as the basic prerequisite for Islamization. The general assumption has been that the politico-administrative structures of decision-making are value-neutral, represent no special interests except those of the present incumbents, and do not in themselves constitute an obstacle to the programs which aim at the transformation of society.

Appendix A

MAJOR ISLAMIC POLITICAL PARTIES OF PAKISTAN

NAME OF THE PARTY	LEADER	RELIGIOUS IDEOLOGY	MAIN SUPPORT BASE
1. *Jamaat-e-Islami*	Founder: Maulana Abul Ala Maududi Current President: M. Tufail Mohammad	Fundamentalist; takes a comprehensive view of Islam as a way of life; non-sectarian; close relations with the Muslim Brotherhood.	Students; urban and small town lower middle classes in Sind and Punjab and some parts of rural N.W.F.P.
2. *Jamiyat Ulama-e-Islam*	President: Maulana Mufti Mahmud	Conservative; *deobandi*; *Fiqh*-oriented; literalist; puritanical; sectarian	*Madrasa* students and *ulama*; rural N.W.F.P., and Pushtun areas of Baluchistan
3. *Jamiyat Ulama-e-Pakistan*	President: Maulana Shah Ahmad Noorani	Conservative; *brelvi*; less oriented to *Fiqh* and more to folk and popular Islam of saint-worship and sufiism; highly sectarian	Refugee areas of urban Sind; small town merchants of Punjab; traditional *pir* families of Punjab

Suggested Readings

Abbott, Freeland K., *Islam and Pakistan*. New York, 1968.

Ahmad, Aziz, *Islamic Modernism in India and Pakistan, 1857-1964*. London, 1967.

Binder, Leonard, *Religion and Politics in Pakistan*, Berkeley, 1961.

Khan, Mohammad Ayub, *Friends Not Masters*. London, 1967.

Maududi, Abul Ala, *Islamic Law and Constitution*. Lohore, 1968.

Mujeeb, M., *The Indian Muslims*. London, 1967.

Qureshi, Ishtiaq Husain, *Ulema in Politics*. Karachi, 1974.

Rahman, Fazalur, *Islam*. Chicago, 1979.

Rosenthal, E. I. J., *Islam in the Modern National State*. Cambridge, 1965.

Sayeed, Khalid bin, *The Political System of Pakistan*. Boston, 1967.

Smith, W. C., *Islam in Modern History*. New Jersey, 1977.

XVII

ISLAM IN AFRICAN HISTORY

Ralph A. Austen

Islam was introduced in subsaharan Africa and it grew there over a period of several centuries as a major religion in a very different manner than in any other major Muslim territory. As a result of this and its two-pronged interaction with native African and European societies in the colonial period, subsaharan Islam developed certain unique characteristics of its own. But, the post-colonial thrust of new African countries into the outer world and the current sweep of Islamic revivalism are making a transformation which may bring African Islam closer to its Arabian counterpart and make it an instrument of change in African society. Professor Austen describes Islam's various phases of development in Africa and its current posture.

Ralph A. Austen is Associate Professor of African History, Director of the Master of Arts Program in Social Sciences, and member of the Center for Middle Eastern Studies at the University of Chicago. His research, publication and teaching have covered wide areas of Africa, most notably the pre-colonial and colonial histories of Cameroon, Nigeria and Tanzania as well as a quantitative study of the Islamic slave trade.

In strictly geometrical terms — as the crow flies — subsaharan Africa is very close to the core of the Islamic world: indeed, black Africans were present and active at the creation of Islam in Arabia. However, in more historical terms — measured by how a religion spreads — there are major barriers between the lands which are the classic *Dar-al-Islam* and *Bilad as-Sudan* — the Land of the Blacks.

First there are physical barriers: the expansion of Arabic-speaking peoples bearing Islam was inhibited by the Sahara desert and other impediments prevented them from reaching beyond North Africa, the lower Nile Valley, and the East African coast — these areas were relatively easily incorporated into the Islamic core and will not be discussed here. Islam did, however, have a considerable impact on more remote African areas which were never effectively conquered in the Middle Ages and it is on these which I wish to focus.

Another, no less significant barrier, is cultural. First of all the major portions of the African continent shared no unifying civilization or civilizations which could be "converted" to Islam through any form of external domination. Instead the lives of people were governed and expressed through a series of local beliefs, rituals, and images of the spiritual world which are remote from and inimical to the entire monotheistic, iconoclastic thrust of Islam.

Finally there is also the barrier of what we may call race. The central Islamic world knew black Africans essentially as slaves and the African world frequently knew Muslims — more often, of course, black ones than white ones — as slavers. Such a relationship hardly encouraged either efforts at, or receptivity to, conversion.

The spread of Islam in Africa has not been rapid or smooth. Nonetheless it has taken place wherever there were historical contacts between the external Muslim world and the interior of the continent and it has continued even under the apparently hostile aegis of European colonialism and Europeanized postcolonial regimes. In the space allotted for this presentation I cannot cover all aspects of the spread and development of Islam in Africa but will rather concentrate on one region, West Africa. This area displays a sufficiently wide range of experience with Islam to give an indication of its continent-wide significance.

The development of Islam in West Africa went through three forms which are often seen as more or less evolutionary phases, although it should be kept in mind that all three can be present at the same time. First there was what has been called "the dispersion of Muslims" in which the majority of the population in the areas affected gave little or no attention to Islam. Second there is syncretism, in which Islamic beliefs and practices are mingled with those of traditional African religion. Finally there is reformism in which broad African societies take on orthodox Islam as their major faith and even lifestyle.

The dispersion of Muslims in West Africa was essentially a peaceful process, involving first merchants in the transsaharan trade (beginning about the 8th century AD) and then scholars linked in various ways to these commercial communities. The earliest such Muslims were Arabs and Arabic-speaking Berbers from North Africa who only traveled as far as the southern edge of the Sahara desert where they settled temporarily in such cities as Kumbi (capital of ancient Ghana) or Timbuktu to exchange their Mediterranean wares for African goods such as gold and slaves. In time elements of these settlements became permanent but they always maintained a considerable degree of separation from the indigenous communities.

The activities of foreign Muslim merchants eventually gave rise — through a process whose beginnings we cannot trace — to local groups specialized in long-distance trade, both for supplying the transsaharan caravans and moving goods within the various ecological zones of West Africa. These indigenous merchants identified themselves in ethnic terms — they were called Juula in the regions to the west of the Niger bend and Hausa farther to the east; they also organized their enterprises along extended kinship lines. But the one common trait which linked them all is that they were Muslims. As such they did not spread Islam to other peoples because they settled in communities all over West Africa which replicated the kind of separatism that characterized the Arab-Berber merchants at the desert edge.

Within both the foreign Muslim communities and the scattered Juula-Hausa settlements, merchants were eventually joined by scholars. These were men usually from the same social groups as the merchants who had traveled to outside the region (or eventually to centers of learning within the region) in order to train themselves for careers as teachers and jurists within the Islamic community which needed such services to settle both personal and business affairs. Also — for reasons explained below — the powers of Muslim scholars were utilized in various ways by non-Muslims. Finally, Muslim scholars in West Africa often employed their pupils and slaves (the latter being a major form of payment for religious services) to establish centers of intensive commercial agriculture. In this they clearly resemble the monastaries of medieval Europe.

Neither these early generations of scholars nor the majority of their successors up to contemporary times have made serious attempts to convert the surrounding communities. This may appear a strange way for orthodox Muslims to behave since the Quran expressedly forbids tolerance of any religion not identified with "people of the Book", a category into which traditionalist Africans certainly did not fit. The practice of such quietist or separatist Islam may be explained in several ways. One probably quite important factor is that the North African communities which pioneered the transsaharan trade were *not* orthodox Sunnis, or even Shi'ites but rather members of the Kharajite

Ibadi sect. Kharajites are supposed to be highly dissident and anarchistic Muslims, although among this group the Ibadis come the closest to following orthodox belief and practice. Nonetheless Ibadis were persecuted within the core Islamic areas and in order to live peacefully in a situation where *they* required tolerance from the orthodox majority, they had developed a doctrine of *kitman* or quietism. It appears that this doctrine was carried with Ibadi merchants and scholars to subsaharan West Africa and became a major feature of the most pious Islamic communities there.

It is also easy to understand why such a doctrine would have survived in West Africa even after losing all obvious traces of its connection to the deviant Ibadi sect. After all, Muslims in this area had little hope of converting the large populations among whom they lived as vulnerable strangers. Moreover the major purposes of the Muslims themselves was to carry on trade, not expand their faith, and this would become difficult if not impossible were it accompanied by challenges to the religion of host societies.

Syncretism — the blending of Islam with other religious systems — must be sought in West Africa not from the side of the originally separate Muslim communities but rather in the local societies who came to see these Muslims as part of their own world. Another way to state this idea might be that the world of West Africans became broader as commercial relations brought it into contact with the Middle East and Islam became associated with one dimension — but not the totality — of this expanded world. Throughout the history of Islam in West Africa Muslim merchants and scholars have remained reasonably orthodox but local rulers as well as more common people have come to view them in terms which are neither normal to Islam nor entirely in keeping with traditional beliefs.

States and kingship existed in West Africa before the coming of Islam and Muslim merchants often lived under the protection of rulers who made no pretension to Islamic adherence. However the very fact of protecting such merchants put rulers in close contact with Muslims and obviously added to their wealth since local authorities could demand some share in the profits of long-distance trade. As some of these rulers also sought to increase their claims to political authority, an involvement with Islamic ritual also became desirable since Islam was associated in general with a wider universe and more specifically (although not *too* specifically) with a universal system of government. Conversion was thus attractive as a means both of improving relationships with Muslims from outside the region and adding to the status of rulers within the region.

On the other hand, such adherence by African rulers to Islam usually operated within major limitations. In the first place the notion that Islam was of some practical utility in organizing a West African state before the nineteenth century (to which we will return) must be dispelled. Even within the Islamic heartlands, there were constant conflicts between the practices of large states — in taxation, warfare, relations with non-believers, etc. — and Islamic orthodoxy; West African states certainly were in no better position than those of the Middle East to conform to the Islamic political ideal. Secondly, the literacy which came with Islam had virtually no secular utility before the nineteenth century; learning was entirely in Arabic and neither indigenous merchants nor states kept their records in writing; serious Islamic education was only pursued by those with some kind of scholarly-clerical career in mind.

Rulers therefore had no motives for pursuing Islamic piety beyond the sphere of public gestures — which might even include pilgrimage to the holy places of Arabia — and a number of reasons for not doing so. These latter had to do with the need to maintain ties with the population in their own societies which clung to traditional religion and expected the ruler to participate in it. Such beliefs and practices were intimately linked with the lives of farmers — the majority of people in West Africa — who saw their livelihood as dependent upon relationships with spiritual forces indigenous to — and graphically identified with — their immediate environment. Even artisan groups, partially grouped in towns and close to both rulers and merchants, perceived the maintenance of their specialized skills in terms of similar "pagan" beliefs.

West African rulers thus tended to present themselves alternatively as Muslims and traditionalists. We can find very striking examples of this in one of the classic documents of West African kingship, the Sunjata Epic, which is recited to this day by bards — griots — whose very status is defined in very complex indigenous cosmological terms. Sunjata is presented by these bards as a descendant of immigrants from Arabia, a man who must make his own *Hijra* (exile) from his agricultural homeland to the more Islamicized desert edge in order to prepare for his role as a regional emperor, and who sallies forth on his return to his inheritance "dressed like a Muslim." Once back in his native region however, Sunjata draws strength from his mother's totemic association with the buffalo, uses indigenous magic rather than Islamic science to defeat his enemies, and appears on all major occasions in the garb of a hunter — a figure who can deal directly with the forces of local nature. The Sunjata Epic represents an example of syncretism heavily weighted towards the traditionalist side; other documents give more importance to Islam. But the critical point is always the same: Islam is necessary to qualify the ruler for confronting and organizing the larger outside world; more traditional forces are needed to deal with the internal universe.

The syncretism of ordinary peoples in West Africa always tends to give a relatively limited role to Islam. Most of their lives were not very deeply affected by the activities of the larger economic and political systems in which Muslims and kings operated. Nonetheless they too recognized the efficacy of Islam as the agency of forces beyond those of their own environment. Thus they have always been ready to patronize Muslim scholars (or their less scholarly pupils) for purposes of divination, ritual healing, and the purchase of amulets. The link of scholars to these services does not necessarily make them less orthodox — often a greater reputation for orthodoxy adds to the alleged efficacy of the services. However for many West African peoples these functions are their only link to an Islam which has been constructed by them as a more universal equivalent of similar magic within their inherited religious systems.

Examples of this kind of folk syncretism may be seen in some of the masquerade festivals of indigenous societies in West African areas where Muslims have been present for a long time. The masks, usually in some kind of animal form, are meant to address the spiritual world in a way which is absolute anathema to Islam. Yet among these carved effigies are some figures in human shape which turn out to be representations of Muslim scholars!

At most times in most places in West Africa Muslims have tolerated both unbelief in the surrounding communities and the kinds of assimilation of Islamic belief to local religion just described. But there have been occasions, particularly since the eighteenth century, when the banners of *jihad* — holy war — have been raised in order to expand and purify the role of Islam in West Africa. Historians have, in general, tended to exaggerate the role of *jihad* and reform in African Islamic development both because it provides a dramatic focus for discussing a very complicated topic and because non-African scholars tend to put great value upon conformity to imported, universal values, whether they are religious or secular, Muslim or Christian. In concluding this discussion of precolonial Islam with a treatment of *jihads* I do not wish to suggest that they represent the goal towards which all Islamic development in the region has been or should be striving. That it has not been is obvious from the historical record; whether it should be is a matter on which I prefer to avoid judgment.

Even when we examine *jihads* in West Africa, we find that they fall into two categories with varying effects on the spread of Islam. In one kind the Islamic ideal order is evoked in opposition to the existing order for the purpose of promoting the interests of groups within society which are discontented with the status quo but not very positively committed to the Islamic alternative. In eighteenth and nineteenth century West Africa such discontented groups tended generally to be Fulani pastoralists under the control of various sedentary, i.e., agriculturalist states. The Fulani regimes which emerged from these *jihads* turned out not to be radically different from their predecessors because the Fulani way of life was not closely associated with Islam; it was only that as cattle keepers the Fulani found less obstacles in their traditional beliefs and practices to declaring themselves Muslims than was the case with farmers.

The other form of *jihad* is one which effectively transforms a West African society into something approaching the Middle Eastern model, if not the ideal theocracy of Mecca and Medina in the Prophet Muhammad's time. These transformations cannot be achieved by Islamic faith alone; they only occur when a society is already sufficiently shifted out of pre-existing economic and social patterns so that a new formulation for ordering the world becomes attractive and perhaps even necessary. Such was the case with two situations in nineteenth century West Africa where *jihads* did have a lasting social effect: those of the Hausa and Fulani in Northern Nigeria and the peasant populations among Wolof, Mandinka and other peoples of Senegambia. Both these sets of societies had become heavily involved in commerce, so that their lives were closely touched by forces of the broader market universe as well as central political authorities — which, in both regions, had come to appear intolerably oppressive.

The *jihads* in these regions were closely associated with organizations representing *tariqas,* Sufi brotherhoods, particularly the Quadariyya and the Tijaniyya. Scholars have often sought in the mystical practices of these orders some element of African syncretism. However, whatever mystical practices are associated with *tariqas* in West Africa they appear to have been imported from outside the region rather than developed as an adaptation of local religion. The *tariqas* here were and are essentially channels for the propagation of orthodox Islam and the *jihads* were one of their methods for doing so. The results of the transformative *jihads* in West Africa were to create new political structures, modes of expression and ritual patterns permeating entire lifestyles. The new rulers were orthodox Muslims who owed their legitimacy to this claim rather than to any indigenous status; they were the first to make serious use of Islamic law and presented a new model of behavior to their subjects which at least echoed that of the Prophet. It was in these *jihads* that Islamic literacy first became vernacularized and could thus reach a larger constituency and also become adapted to such secular ends as commerce and government. The communities transformed through these *jihads* came to celebrate the major points in the life cycle — birth, marriage, coming of age, death — through Islamic rituals and organized ties of personal status along lines prescribed by Islam.

Lest the above seem like an idealistic portrait, two sets of qualifications should be noted. First, none of the post-*jihad* societies ever fully conformed to all of the characteristics just cited. Rather they sought to, and succeeded in doing so to a far greater degree than other societies in West Africa. Second, a *jihad* was not the only, or perhaps the most critical factor in such a transformation. The Kanuri people of Borno, also in Northern Nigeria, successfully staved off the Hausa-Fulani *jihad* in this same region. However Kanuri society, by the late nineteenth century at least, was about as thoroughly Islamized as the world of the Hausa-Fulani. The main factor here appears to have been a mobilization out of subsistence-oriented agriculture into a more commercialized, urbanized way of life for which Islam offers an appropriate and easily accessible cultural model.

The spread of Islam in West Africa and elsewhere on the continent was ultimately limited in certain respects by the imposition of European colonial rule. Even before the colonial period European contacts with Africa provided an avenue to the broader universe which served as an alternative to Islam. Europeans, moreover, directly came into conflict with Muslim merchants in many areas (not always successfully as with the Portuguese in East Africa) and by the nineteenth century were sending out large numbers of missionaries to compete with the Muslim faith.

This process of competition appeared to reach its climax with the colonial conquests of the late nineteenth century when Europeans abolished the Muslim slave trade, undermined transsaharan trade by building railroads in from the West African coast, and suppressed

Muslim political and religious authorities who offered actual or potential resistance to Western imperialism.

As it turned out, however, the European presence actually accelerated the spread of Islam in Africa. Even before the formal colonial period of the late 1800's European activities expanded African markets in ways that benefited more than the limited Islamic commercial expansion. Once safely installed in Africa European colonial regimes usually found (and this applies to the supposedly assimilationist French as much as to the "pragmatic" English) that Muslim elites functioned very effectively as intermediaries. They were thus given additional political resources, mosques were built for them, schools supported, etc. Even the transport networks which damaged Muslim trade (although not always) facilitated participation in the *Hajj* — the pilgrimage to Mecca — in which millions of black African Muslims could now participate. Finally colonialism encouraged migration to towns and participation in trade and commercial agriculture, processes which continued to encourage conversion to Islam, even when the alternative of Christianity was made readily and aggressively available.

Despite this expansion of its adherents, African Islam has been faced by colonial and postcolonial situations with the same dilemmas of modernization as Islam everywhere. The African situation is somewhat more acute insofar as individuals and groups who chose Christian conversion ended up with advantaged access to European dominated sectors of employment (although not necessarily commerce or political office). On the other hand, developments of very recent years have shifted balance somewhat in favor of Islam, which has come to be associated with both the struggles of an oppressed Third World and the power of OPEC, to which a number of African states belong. The shift in orientation, possibly at a very superficial level, is illustrated by the case of President Omar Bongo of Gabon, a highly assimilated French-speaking ruler of an oil-producing state who recently converted to Islam. At a deeper but less specific level we may see Islam as the cultural equivilent of an intermediate technology which may link Africa more gradually and effectively to a larger universe than can Christianity or the secular faith of modernization. Certainly in the past Islam has served as an important vehicle or medium for change in Africa and it may well serve in that role again, although that is not quite certain.

Bibliography

Austen, Ralph A., "The Trans-Saharan Slave Trade: a Tentative Census" in Henry A. Gemery and Jan S. Hogendorn, eds., *The Uncommon Market.* New York, 1979.

Bravmann, Rene A., *Islam and Tribal Art in West Africa.* London, 1974.

Cohen, Ronald, *The Kanuri of Bornu.* New York, 1967.

Cruise O'Brien, Donal, *The Mourides of Senegal. The Political and Economic Organization of an Islamic Brotherhood.* Oxford, 1971.

Hiskett, Mervyn, *The Sword of Truth: the Life and Times of Shehu Usuman dan Fodio.* New York, 1973.

Kaba, Lansine, *The Wahabiyya: Islamic Reform and Politics in French West Africa.* Evanston, Illinois, 1974.

Levtzion, Nehemia, *Ancient Ghana and Mali.* London, 1973.

Lewicki, Tadeusz, "al-Ibadiyya," *Encyclopedia of Islam.* New Edition, Vol. IV, Leiden, 1971.

Martin, B. G., *Muslim Brotherhoods in Nineteenth Century Africa.* Cambridge, U.K., 1976.

Morrison, Donald, Robert Mitchell, John Paden, *Black Africa: a Comparative Handbook* (second edition). New York, 1980 (contains excellent data on the contemporary spread of Islam).

Niane, Djibril Tamsir, *Sundiata: an Epic of Old Mali.* London, 1971.

Sanneh, Lamin O., *The Jakhanke: the History of an Islamic Clerical People of the Senegambia.* London, 1979.

Stewart, Charles C. and Elizabeth K., *Islam and Social Order in Mauretania.* Oxford, 1971.

Trimingham, John Spencer, *The Influence of Islam upon Africa.* London, 1968.

XVIII

AFRICAN-AMERICAN MUSLIMS AND THE ISLAMIC REVIVAL

Umar A. Hassan

The Islamic heritage of African-Americans had not been allowed to surface, let alone flourish, in their years of slavery or near slavery in the Americas. Yet through memories, oral traditions and myths transmitted from generation to generation they kept alive a flicker of Islam which started to shine brightly once the Blacks moved in large numbers to the industrial urban centers which offered a bit more favorable atmosphere and their slavish conditions gradually changed. But by then the Islam they brought from Africa, syncretized as it had been, was further distorted by accomodations with American customs and values which they had to make over the years. In recent decades, however, contacts with the Islamic world caused African-American Muslims to refine their religious perceptions, but as Mr. Hassan points out below this process is not likely to result in the adoptation of an Arabian model; rather, Islam's expression in America, unique as it is, will probably develop structures that are suitable to its own environment.

Umar A. Hassan, who has done graduate work in the department of Near Eastern Studies of the University of Michigan and the department of religion at Temple University, now resides in Los Angeles.

For more than half a century many Americans have joined "back to Islam" movements which were, perhaps, only nominally Islamic. Yet these movements have succeeded in creating a Muslim community identity — a success which can be explained only in terms of the Islamic roots of many black Americans and the sociological use they found in Islam for self assertion. The purpose of this paper is to examine the historic roots of Islam in this country, sketch the developments in recent decades and to analyze American Muslims' reactions to the current Islamic revival.

There are a number of ways to examine the phenomenon of Islam in America. A sociological approach could focus on the composition of Muslim groups, their internal and external relationships, demographic data and community profiles. Islam in America may also be examined from the points of view of disciplines such as religion, anthropology, political science and economics. While many disciplines can provide a helpful focus for our efforts to understand Islam in the American context, the methodology I adopt here — one that is perhaps a prerequisite to others — is to examine Islam in America from a sociohistorical point of view. From this approach we gain an overview of how Islam came to North America and how and in what form it was preserved.

The fact that Islam came to the Americas in the hearts and minds of captive Africans must be put in perspective. The central concern of this presentation is to propose how Islam came to and survived in the American environment. The fact that Islam came to America via Africans is really secondary. What is critical is that the history of Islam in this hemisphere be interpreted in the context of a vital belief system withstanding the vagaries of time. What I propose here, therefore, is a thesis that Muslims brought to America formed an abstract social class and some eventually organized themselves into voluntary associations in order to preserve their religion and culture. Furthermore, severe collision of Islam with heretical, syncretized expressions of itself and non-Islamic belief systems (African, European, and native American) made the role of these voluntary associations vitally important to this social class.

By 1850 a full one third of the people of African descent lived outside of Africa. For various reasons, we shall never know the precise number of Africans brought to the Americas. The estimates of historians vary significantly. Some records that exist show a catastrophic population shift from Africa to America. South Carolina census of 1860, for example, counted 291,000 whites to 412,320 blacks.[1] As early as 1742 in Maryland there were 100,000 whites to 140,000 blacks.[2] Furthermore, in the nineteenth century 80,000 Africans were imported to the United States annually.[3] It is clear that the Middle Passage was the most massive involuntary migration in recorded history which, while retarding the development of Africa, accelerated the economic expansion of Europe and America.

The majority of the captives were from West Africa, although not much is known about their specific source areas. But it is clear that the trade shifted from region to region depending upon political conditions in Africa.

The source areas of the captives included regions which were Islamicized long before the trade began. Of course, Muslims entered Africa before they settled in Madinah. It is, however, less certain as to when they entered West Africa. But we do know that in 1054 Ibn Yasin marched into Sub-Saharan Africa from the Maghrib. Twenty two years later, Abu Bakr conquered Ghana. Three hundred years after that Ibn Khaldun wrote about the Muslim destruction of Ghana. In 1213 Allakoi Keita founded the Mandinka Empire of Mali. Sundiata came to power in 1238 and by 1307 Mansa Kankan Musa began the expansion of the dominion of Mali.[4]

For the vast majority of West Africans, therefore, Islam had become a way of life generations before the slave trade. Highly advanced Muslim societies also blossomed there. For example, Leo Africanus recorded that "in Timbuktu there are numerous judges, doctors, and clerics, all receiving good salaries from the king. He (Muhammad Askia of Songhay) pays great respect to men of learning. There is a big demand for books in manuscript, imported from Barbary. More profit is made from the book trade than from any other line of Business."[5]

Ibn Battuta wrote about Mali in these words, "These people are Muslims, punctilious in observing the hour or prayer, studying books of law, and memorizing the Koran." But that is not all Ibn Battuta saw. He bears witness also to some native customs which Muslims of Mali followed: "One day at Walata I went to the Qadi's house, after asking his permission to enter, and found him with a young woman of remarkable beauty. When I saw her I was shocked and turned to go out, but she laughed at me, instead of being overcome with shame and the Qadi said to me, 'Why are you going out? She is my companion.' "[6] It was customary that both men and women took companions.

Just as Mali followed Ghana, Songhay flourished after Mali. It has a history of literacy in Arabic which extends over a period of nine hundred years. Although as a dominant kingdom in West Africa, Songhay followed Mali, it had begun to be Islamicized as early as 1009 when King Kossoi accepted Islam. By 1464 Sonni Ali had made Songhay the most powerful state in Africa, excepting, perhaps, Bornu. Ascending the throne in 1493 Muhammad Toure Askia the Great expanded the realm of Islam during a successful thirty five year reign. During his reign Islam was extended "as far as Segu in the west and the sub-suharan region of Air in the northwest realizing once again something of the unified control of far north and far south that Mansa Kankan Musa had achieved."⁷ These were the greatest kingdoms known to have been established in Africa. There is no question, therefore, that large populations in this region which centuries later became the target for the slavers had not only accepted Islam but also had developed various syncretized expressions of this faith.

The definitive history of Islam in early America is yet to be written. The problem is lack of written materials. What is available are narrative accounts by various victims of the slave trade many of which indicate their deep commitment to Islam. One such slave, Ayube Suleiman for example, had memorized the Qur'an at fifteen years of age. Later while in captivity he produced two complete copies of the Qur'an without any assistance. Another, Salih Bilali, a Fulani captive in Georgia from 1816, was born in a society in which all children were taught to read and write the Qur'an. Still another, Abu Bakr al-Siddiqi, born as the son of a *mufassir* in Timbuktu around 1790, had studied at a prestigious center which was "far south, on the frontiers of the Ashanti Empire, is otherwise known only from Bath's short reference to it, as a place of great celebrity for its learning and its schools, in the countries of Muhammadan Mandingoes to the south, although it is mentioned in extant works in Arabic."⁸ Abu Bakr exchanged letters with Muhammad Caba, another Muslim in captivity who was forced, as was himself, to use a Christian name imposed by his master. There are still many others who left records of their Islamic background such as Omar ibn Said who lived in South Carolina around 1830; the Moorish Prince Abd al-Rahman; a Mandinka Muhammad Sisei; Wargee of Astarkhan; and Ali Eisami, also known as William Harding. From their narratives, descriptive of their respective societies, it is clear that they had been Muslim for generations. They came from societies in which Qur'anic and other Islamic scholastic traditions were highly valued.

Although the personal histories of these few men do not account for the millions of Africans brought to the Americas, they do provide a dramatic and coherent picture of many of the Muslim societies victimized by the slave trade. They also provide an insight into a segment of 18th and 19th century African-American community which must be described as Muslim.

Just as the historical materials concerning the Islamic background of the African slaves are sparse, the materials concerning the new African-Americans' social and spiritual responses to captivity are extremely limited and often willfully distorted. This is especially true of African Muslims in North America. Records of the experience of Muslims in South America are more available, however, and may be used to suggest certain behavior patterns which may have paralleled the experience of Africans in the United States. Such South American records include accounts of many rebellions as the following selection from Freyre indicates.

> The Abbe Etienne reveals to us some aspects of the Male uprising in Bahia in 1895 that identify this supposed slave revolt as an outbreak or eruption of a more advanced culture downtrodden by another, less noble one. Let us not romanticize. This was purely a Male or Mohammedan movement, or a combination of various groups under Mussulman leaders. One thing is certain, it is to be distinguished from slave revolts in colonial times. It deserves a place, indeed, among the libertarian revolutions of a religious, social, or cultural nature.[9]

Freyre continued his account of this revolution, which he reconstructed from original documents, noting that the revolutionaries communicated with each other in Arabic and that the masters could not accept the possibility that those scrawlings actually represented an advanced language.

Having expressed no interest in the captives, other than the strength of their backs, it is not surprising that the masters committed many errors in identifying their tribal backgrounds. Freyre pointed out a major yet common error made by the slavers. At one time in Brazil it was assumed that most of the captives were Bantu (also a common supposition in the United States). However, it is now clear that the predominant group, at least in Brazil, was Sudanese.

It is also clear that their reaction to captivity was covert as well as overt resistance. But this resistance should not be romanticized nor attributed exclusively to Muslims, although most often Muslims were the leaders of revolts, at least in Brazil. Although many rebellions were spontaneous, others were planned and led by Muslim Imams or holy men. It must also be noted that Africans from Mali and Hausa states, mostly Muslims, were the most active resistors to captivity. In North America where, some have argued, existed a more controlled environment than in South America, the situation was less dramatic. However, Aptheker has documented at least one hundred and eleven (111) revolts from 1663 to 1864, with the majority occurring in the last one hundred years of this period. Although many were spontaneous, others were planned and led by religious figures.

Despite this rebellious attitude, it is clear that African Muslims gradually made accomodations with native cultures, as Freyre documents:

> Mello Moraes Filho describes a feast of the dead in Penado (Alagoas), which, as Nina Rodrigues sees it, is without doubt Mussulman in character. Long prayers and fastings. Abstinence from alcoholic beverages. The relating of the feast to the phases of the moon. Sacrifice of sheep. Vestments consisting of long white tunics.[10]

Bastide offers more examples of this phenomenon:

> They worshipped Allah or Olorum-ulua (a syncretism current among the Yoruba Muslims, combining Allah with their own chief deity Olourum), the Mother of God. They had no mosques but met in the houses of their priests, or alufas, to celebrate their cult, under the direction of the lessano (corruption of imam), assisted by ladano or sacristan. Cult practices consisted of two prayers, one in the morning and the other in the evening, saying which the inhabitants of Bahia referred to as fazer sala ... and a more important ceremony known as the 'Mass of the Malis,' or sara. ... In Brazil they continued the practice of circumsizing young children (kola), and observed the annual fast (assumy), which terminated in a great feast and gifts (saka) exchanged.[11]

The syncretism which Ibn Battuta noted in his travels in Muslim Africa and which Freyre and Bastide described concerning African Muslims in the Americas seems to have been a pattern established in Africa, long before the slave ships started to cross the Atlantic. In spite of the accomodation with the cultures of their new homeland which African Muslims, and by extension all Blacks, made — as manifested in the syncretism we noted — they did not hesitate to take adequate steps to preserve their African identity. Creation of the so-called "nations", which sprang up in all captive holding countries, was such a step. "... urban slaves and free blacks were formed into 'nations' with their own kings and governors.... These nations were organized with most admirable efficiency, and numerous examples of them are on record, ranging from the United States (where in the north at least, the Negroes elected their own governors) down as far as Argentina."[12] Although these nations were often an oppressive tool, participation in them by the African Americans emphasized their apartness and provided organizational experience which may have encouraged the continuation of the process of 'national identity' in the early black nationalism of Marcus Garvey, Noble Drew Ali, and Elijah Muhammad.

Within the framework of these major themes — rebellion, syncretism, and a racially defined nationalism — the social expression of Islam in America can be understood. The Georgia Writers Project of the 1930's, perhaps the most comprehensive attempt ever undertaken to record the oral history of slavery in the United States, refers to many concrete manifestations of these themes. Parallel arguments based on other nations in the Western Hemisphere can be suggestive, but recorded references to Muslims in this Georgia Project provide the kind of data required to theoretically establish links between a syncretized expression of Islam extant during slavery and the first recorded appearance of Muslim oriented voluntary associations in the United States. One such reference deals with a Muslim named Bilali Muhammad and his Muslim descendants. It is reported that he and his family came to America on the same slave ship. For at least three generations this family practiced Islam. Another deals with a woman from Africa named Patience Spaulding who was a Muslim as shown by her punctilious performance of *salah*. Still another recounts the story of a Muslim in this manner:

> Ole Israel he pray a lot wid a book he hab wut he hide, an he take a lill mat an he say prayuhs on it. He pray wen duh sun go up an wen duh sun go down Dey ain non but ole man Israel wut pray on a mat. He hab he on mat. He aluz tie he head up in a wite clawt, an seem he keep a lot uh clawt on hand fuh I membuh yuh could see em handin roun duh stable drying.

These references to the transmission of Islam from generation to generation, Muslim style dresses, and the Qur'an not only suggest the strong presence of Islam in Georgia but also its unbroken continuity.

Thus far we have dwelt on three major theses: rebellion, syncretism, and a racially defined nationalism. We have also noted a surprisingly high incidence of Muslims in Georgian society with generational overlapping. Furthermore, it is noteworthy that the major figures in the history of the resurgence of Islam among the descendants of American slaves were born and raised in those states which have been demonstrated to have had Muslim residents. Noble Drew Ali, the first recorded instance of a Muslim-syncretist organizer of a voluntary association, was also the first among these figures.

Timothy Drew, later to be known as Noble Drew Ali, was born in 1886 in North Carolina. He was the central organizer of the Moorish Science Temples in America. He established temples in seventeen cities, most notably Newark, Pittsburgh, Chicago, and Detroit. What is suggested here is that some of his followers belonged to an abstract social class which he effectively organized into a Muslim oriented voluntary association. However, this is not to suggest that all or most members were already Muslims. That he expressed the themes of rebellion and separation is known. For example, he termed his relationship with Marcus Garvey, the father of Pan Africanism, as that of John the Baptist to Jesus. This spiritual connection validates Noble Drew Ali's racially defined nationalism and his unique world view. His followers were taught:

> Before you can have a God, you must have a nationality. Allah is God and He ordained His prophet, Noble Drew Ali, to divulge His secrets to the dark fold of America.
>
> Moslems belong to certain areas of the world including the American continent.
>
> There is not black, colored, or Ethopian — only Asiatic or Moorish-American.
>
> Christianity is for whites.
>
> Noble Drew Ali is a kindred personage and spirit to Confucius, Jesus, Buddha, and Zoroaster.
>
> Two words of greeting: Peace! and Islam!
>
> The red fez should be worn by all men at all times.
>
> Meatless diet.
>
> European games, attendance at movies, secular dancing — all forbidden.
>
> Prayer is performed by facing the east and outstretching the hands with the palms up and the head slightly bent.
>
> Shaving, cosmetics, straightening the hair, intoxicants, and smoking are forbidden.

This list, is not exhaustive. Some of these prescriptions are not in accordance with traditional Islamic practices. They do, however, make it clear that Noble Drew Ali was a Muslim-syncretist who expressed the themes important to the development of Islam in America. He, as has been noted, taught that before a people can have a God they must first have a nationality. Ali's thought (obviously not Islamic) is in harmony with, of all people, Nietzche who wrote, "A people which still believes in itself still also has its own God. In him it venerates the conditions through which it has prospered, its virtues — it projects its joy in itself, its feeling of power to a being whom one can thank for them ... a proud people needs a God in order to sacrifice. Either they are the will to power — and so long as they are that they will be national gods — or else the importance for — and then they necessarily become good."[13]

Nietzsche's philosophy certainly is not the stuff with which Muslims can construct their cosmology. But this example from Noble Drew Ali is illustrative of a tendency among Blacks to construct their world view in a racist context, one in which philosophical implications are rarely considered. It is quite doubtful that Ali had read or heard of Nietzsche. What is likely, however, is that he understood the necessity of realizing an identity within a cosmological framework which would enable people to act in ways in which their power to effect change was a demonstrable reality.

Behavioral proscriptions are far from alien to Islam. The renunciation of intoxicants, gambling, and secular dancing are relevant to Islam. The question of the origin of Ali's knowledge about these prohibitions must be addressed, however. What is suggested here is a confluence of factors ranging from personal research to residues of African practices maintained by members of what has been termed here a Muslim abstract social class.

The connection between Noble Drew Ali's movement, Fard Muhammad, and Elijah Muhammad has been well established by Essiem-Udom in his work *Black Nationalism*. In addition, Dr. Zafar Ishaq Ansari's researches have demonstrated the connection between these two movements. At any rate, those who have come in contact with the 'Nation of Islam' now called 'The American Muslim Mission', have little difficulty noticing the conceptual affinity between these movements.

The connection between the movements may be explained by the involvement of Fard Muhammad and Elijah Muhammad in the Moorish Scientists movement. The former claimed to be the reincarnation of Noble Drew Ali in order to gain influence within Moorish Science temples while the latter was a member of the Moorish Scientists during Ali's time.

Apart from these two broadbased movements of 'Moorish Scientists' and 'Nation of Islam' there were also several Muslim oriented small movements among the Blacks as oral history and scattered newspaper accounts from the early part of this century indicate. Two such movements were based in Cleveland — the 'Web of Destiny' and the 'Clock of Destiny' — where the activities of Ahmad Evans also held the attention of America for a short period. That he also identified his militancy with Islam is clear. In Detroit, Michigan there were the 'Bey Tribe,' the 'Tribe of Muhammad,' and the 'Malcolmites' which later emerged as the 'Republic of New Africa.'

It must be clear from what is said above that Islam in the Americas has been the religion of Black people; it has been the vehicle of armed struggle against slavery in South America and probably the Southeastern United States as well. "Militant Islam," therefore, among the African-Americans, is an important dimension of their history in America. Islam, for this reason, has been given a racial definition, one which is coined in the terms of cultural rejection, social resistance, rebellion, Black nationalism, and a simmering anger which, in turn, frightens those who have invested their identities in a white America.

Islam has provided psychological comfort to the dispossessed by offering a cosmology woven out of shared experiences in America and the mythologies fabricated by these people to salvage their own humanity. Since Muslims in America have always been militant, the apparent revivalism and militancy of the Muslim world is reassuring to many African-American Muslims.

Whether the revivalism and militancy of the Muslim world is a media sham is not crucial to its influence in America, because many American Muslims want to believe in the revival of Islam and its rediscovered militancy as they reinforce their understanding of their own experiences.

The Muslims in America have been following for quite some time the struggle of Islamic movements in the Muslim world with great interest. Those who support the establishment of Islamic governments have been encouraged by the work of the Muslim Brotherhood in Egypt, the Sudan and Syria. They have been cheered by the progress of the Islamic Party of Pakistan also. These movement oriented Muslims have read eagerly the works of the men who are credited with laying the groundwork for today's movements, especially Hasan al-Banna, Seyyed Qutb, and Maudoudi. Many of their works have been translated into English and have been used as introductory materials to Islam. Therefore, many young men and women accept their premises for work as Islam's premises, which turns them into movement oriented persons. This has been especially true in the prisons. A consequence of being in prison is having time to think. This has been exploited by Muslims in the sense that they have given these men an opportunity to think through the implications of their incarceration within the context of Muslim revolutionary thinkers.

It is, finally, not at all surprising that African-Americans, alienated for so long from the sources of power in their country, have resorted to resistance and sought a separate identity within Islam.

But the resurgence of the Islamic identity and a commitment to the Muslim world view must be viewed in the American context as a dynamic which has catalyzed Islamic movements. Although these developments coincided with the Islamic revival outside, the future of Islam in America does not hinge on the success or the continuation of this outside revival. Rather, the Muslims in America, although part of the world Muslim community, will forge institutions and structures in their own environment. The encouragement the Muslims in America have received from abroad might lead to such a result.

Moreover, the ethnic and cultural diversity of the Muslims in America might be used constructively as the socio-political visions of the movement oriented Muslims become one. The range of resources, human and fiscal, that they share is impressive and once the walls of cultural nationalism are removed, a strong organization, might emerge. What the ultimate direction of such an organization will be can only be surmised by what has already happened. Organizations that have emerged in the past generally projected a positive — that is to say acceptable to mainstream Americans — point of view. The radicalism that is characteristic of the Middle East and Africa may not be openly adopted here because of the fear America has for it, but it will remain as an undercurrent for quite some time. In the meantime, reports of Muslim militancy from the larger Islamic world will be a source of inspiration.

Footnotes

1. W. E. B. Dubois, *Black Reconstruction in America: 1860-1880*. New York: Atheneum, 1975.
2. *Ibid.*
3. *Ibid.*
4. Melvin Drimmer, ed., *Black History*. Garden City, New York: Doubleday, 1969.
5. Basil Davidson, *Lost Cities of Africa*. Boston: Little Brown, 1959. pp. 81-103.
6. *Ibid.*
7. Philip D. Curtin, ed., *Africa Remembered*. Madison: University of Wisconsin Press, 1967. p. 53.
8. *Ibid.*, p. 146.

9. Gilberto Freyre, *The Masters and the Slaves*. New York: Knopf, 1946. pp. 264-5.
10. *Ibid.*
11. Roger Bastide, *African Civilization in the New World.* New York: Harper & Row, 1971. p. 6.
12. Elliot P. Skinner, intro., *Drums and Shadows*. Garden City, New York: Doubleday, 1972. p. 152.
13. Frederick Nietszche, *The Anti-Christ.* New York: Arno Press, 1972.

Bibliography

Bastide, Roger, *African Civilization in the New World.* New York: Doubleday, 1972.

Curtin, Philip D. ed., *Africa Remembered.* Madison: University of Wisconsin Press, 1967.

Davidson, Basil, *Lost Cities of Africa.* Boston: Little Brown, 1959.

Drimmer, Melvin, ed., *Black History.* Garden City, New York: Doubleday, 1969.

Dubois, W. E. B., *Black Reconstruction in America: 1860-1880.* New York: Atheneum, 1975.

Essien, Udom, E. U., *Black Nationalism: The Search for an Identity in America.* Chicago: The University of Chicago Press, 1962.

Freyre, Gilberto, *The Masters and the Slaves.* New York: Knopf, 1946.

Jansen, G. H., *Militant Islam.* New York: Harper & Rowe, 1979.

Skinner, Elliot, P., *Drums and Shadows.* Garden City, New York: Doubleday, 1972.

XIX

ISLAMIC LAW AND ISLAMIC REVIVAL IN LIBYA

Ann Elizabeth Mayer

From its earliest beginnings, Islam considered the Quranic prescriptions and the practices of the Prophet, collectively known as the Sunna, *to be normative of positive laws governing all aspects of Muslim life — religious and secular, private and public. However, when Islam spread into various parts of the world and large empires were erected under its banner, the complexities that arose as a result of all these on the one hand and the difficulty in determining who should be the innovators, interpreters and implementors of the law on the other caused serious problems between the religious scholars and the secular rulers. As a result, legal formulations that occurred in the Islamic world did not follow a uniform pattern but were dependent on which of these two factions were dominant in given times and places. But the issue of who should be the guardians of Islamic law became a moot point by the late nineteenth century when practically all but a few pockets of the Islamic world came under European domination and/or influence, including European legal systems. In the post-colonial era, however, attempts have been made, mostly* ulama *inspired, to reestablish the dominance of Islamic legal system in many countries, starting with Pakistan — all of which failed due to the resistance of the Western educated ruling elite in these newly independent countries and due to the general unsuitability of old Islamic laws to conditions of modern life. In the current Islamic revival, the issue is revived again, this time with the support of a new generation of national leaders whose commitment to Islamic law is intense, open and vocal but whose understanding of it is often open to question. Libya under the leadership of Colonel Qadhdhafi is a case in point, which Professor Mayer discusses below.*

Ann Elizabeth Mayer who holds degrees in law and Islamic

studies and has wide ranging experience in the Middle East is currently a professor in the Department of Legal Studies, The Wharton School, University of Pennsylvania.

The current Islamic revival in the Middle East has many dimensions, some of which involve the individual believer — such as renewed strictness of observance of Islamic precepts governing the private lives of Muslims and enhanced piety, while others relate to the public sphere — such as the relationship between Islam and the State. The relationship between Islam and the governments of the contemporary Middle East has in turn many dimensions — such as the relationships between governments and the *ulamā*, religious educational institutions, and sectarian and minority religious groups. However, the dimension of the relationship between Islam and the State that has the most far reaching implications for the Islamic revival lies in the legal sphere and involves the issue of whether and in what manner Islamic law is to be revived as the law of the land. Everywhere where the phenomenon of Islamic revival has arisen there have either been popular movements demanding the reinstatement of Islamic law or governmental measures aiming at the reinstatement of Islamic law, or sometimes both. It was in Libya, in the wake of the 1969 coup that brought Colonel Mu'ammar al-Qadhdhafi to power, that the first experiment was made with reinstating Islamic law. This experiment is examined in what follows, with a view to assessing its significance in terms of the relationship between Islam and the State in Libya and with regard to the reinstatement of Islamic law as a feature of contemporary Islamic revival.

First, it should be pointed out that Islamic law, or the *shari'a*, in its traditional formulation in the *fiqh*, or Islamic jurisprudence, was not a law made or enacted by the State. Rather, it was above the State as the creation of Allah, the Divine Legislator. The *shari'a* was derived from Allah's Revelation to mankind in the Quran and the custom, or *sunna*, of His divinely inspired messenger, the Prophet Muhammad. No other authoritative sources of law could exist according to traditional Islamic views, views which prevailed until the last century, when governments of Muslim countries for the first time openly assumed the legislative prerogative. However, when these governments began to legislate, it was simultaneously the beginning of the process of abandoning the Divine Law as the law of the land and replacing it by man made laws in the form of codes borrowed from the legal systems of Western Europe, particularly that of France. Adherence to the *shari'a* began to be perceived by the elite as an obstacle to the modernizing of Middle Eastern societies, and by the middle of the twentieth century, outside of Saudi Arabia, all Middle Eastern governments had imported Western codes to cover all spheres of law save those of personal status. The progress towards Westernization of Middle Eastern law was so steady over many decades that until the recent Islamic revival its continuation seemed inevitable. When Qadhdhafi signalled, soon after coming to power in 1969, that he favored the reinstatement of the *shari'a*, this came as a startling break with the overall pattern of legal development in the area. However, Qadhdhafi did not advocate the reinstatement of the *shari'a* in its traditional form, which would have meant imposing the classical medieval treatises of *fiqh* as the law of the land and leaving the interpretation of the rules of the *shari'a* to scholars of *shari'a* law known as the *fuqaha*. Instead, as it emerged, the government was to enact *shari'a* rules into statutes which would then be interpreted and applied by Libya's secular courts just like any other part of Libyan law, which was largely French and Italian in its derivation.

When Qadhdhafi came to power in 1969 he was an unknown army officer of the middle rank with no political or religious following. Although King Idris, whom he had overthrown, was the hereditary leader of the Sanusi religious order, by far the most powerful religious organization in Libya, and a devout Muslim, Qadhdhafi by his widely advertised commitment to reinstating the *shari'a* was able to establish a reputation as a great champion of Islam. This reputation can only have been helpful to him in a society like Libya's, where religious feeling has remained intense and Islamic fundamentalism has many adherents.

Qadhdhafi's first enactments, which betokened his public commitment to stamping out practices that violated Muslim mores and offended Libyan customs, were not enacted as Islamic laws but as standard legal measures. Soon after his takeover on September 1, 1969, Qadhdhafi imposed a ban on alcohol throughout the country. In 1970 he banned all "indecent" performances in public entertainment spots.

The Islamic laws that were enacted under Qadhdhafi were not his own creations. Lacking the kind of specialized education that would be necessary to draft codified provisions based on Islamic law, Qadhdhafi entrusted the job of drawing up proposals for new laws to a taskforce of experts from both the civil and Islamic law fields. Beginning in 1971 these experts worked as members of a special commission charged with reviewing existing Libyan law for the purpose of eliminating laws that violated the *shari'a* and preparing new ones that would embody the basic principles of the *shari'a*. The period in which the commission was active was very brief, lasting only a few years, and only a small number of new Islamic laws were produced. Nonetheless, these were enacted with enough publicity that a widespread impression was created that Libya was reverting to the *shari'a*.

In part, the illusion that Libya had reverted to *shari'a* law was due to the fact that the laws that were enacted included some of the Quranic criminal provisions that are regarded as being the most problematical aspect of *shari'a* law since they deviate most radically from widely accepted contemporary legal norms. It was easy to assume that a government that would adopt such extreme measures would not hesitate to enact the less controversial portions of the *shari'a* into law, but, in fact, the Islamicizing process did not go much beyond the reinstatement of the Quranic criminal penalties — and these were only reinstated in modified form.

The first of the criminal laws inspired by the Quran was a law on theft and brigandage, which was enacted in 1972. The traditional penalty of cutting off the hand of the thief and the hand and foot of a brigand were reinstated, but the law included many modifications of the *shari'a* rules which were designed to mitigate some of the harsher features of the classical *fiqh*. A second Quranic criminal law was enacted in 1972, when the penalties of flagellation and stoning to death were revived for fornication by single people and people who were or previously had been married, respectively. Far from embodying slavish adherence to the traditional *shari'a* rules, this law contained features that were shaped by secular influences, such as the abandonment of the Quranic requirement that four male Muslim eyewitnesses were needed to prove the offense. Of all the criminal laws, the one that most closely approximated the traditional law was the law of 1974 reinstating flagellation as the penalty for slanderous accusations of unchastity. The law reinstating flagellation as the penalty for consuming alcohol, also enacted in 1974, modified the traditional rules, but in the sense of making them generally harsher and the range of conduct affected broader.

The only other important Islamicizing laws to emerge under Qadhdhafi were three laws enacted in 1972. In one the Islamic almstax was placed under governmental regulation instead of being left solely to the discretion of the individual, as was customary in the traditional law. Another reinstated the Islamic prohibition of interest, but limited the prohibition to transactions between natural persons.

This important limitation meant that the prohibition had much less scope than it did in the classical *fiqh*, where dealings involving interest were absolutely prohibited, and also less scope than it has in many of the theories of Islamic economics that have recently been developed by Muslim thinkers. The third law outlawed a number of transactions on the grounds that they contravened the Islamic prohibition of gambling, making such activities as lotteries and betting on races illegal.

At the same time that these much vaunted Islamicizing enactments were going forward, however, there were also two important changes that reduced the role of the *shari'a* in the legal system. In line with earlier developments in other Middle Eastern countries, Libya in 1973 abolished the Islamic family trust, a venerable institution of Islamic law, and unified the court system, eliminating the separate jurisdiction of the *shari'a* courts.

Unlike the Islamic principles that Qadhdhafi did reinstate, the *shari'a* rules regarding the jurisdiction of the *shari'a* courts and Islamic trusts are not based on Quranic verses. Given the balance sheet of Qadhdhafi's achievements in Islamicizing Libyan law, it is clear that he did not reinstate Islamic law in Libya but only revived rules, and then only selectively, that were contained in verses of the Quran. This is significant, because only a very small part of Islamic law consists of rules taken from the Quran. By far the greater part of the Quran is concerned with matters other than law, and of the six hundred verses that do touch on legal issues, the overwhelming percentage concerns family law and inheritance, areas where Islamic law was still in force in Libya. A policy of reviving only those laws that were in the text of the Quran could therefore never lead to a widescale reintroduction of Islamic law. In the aftermath of Qadhdhafi's Islamicizing enactments, it was therefore appropriate to ask whether when he talked of reinstating "the *shari'a*" he in fact meant the *shari'a* as it has traditionally been known, or whether he was redefining the *shari'a* so as to exclude all but the small number of legal provisions set forth in the Quran. If the traditional definition of the *shari'a* were taken, Qadhdhafi's campaign to Islamicize the law had fallen far short of the mark; if the *shari'a* was given the latter redefinition, he could contend that the Islamicizing campaign had achieved its goals — although the question would then become one of whether his fellow Muslims accepted his new, restrictive definition of the scope of *shari'a* law.

In his first years in power Qadhdhafi gave no indication that he did not share the traditional view that the *shari'a* was based on the Quran and the traditions of the Prophet and that its authoritative formulations were to be found in works of classical jurisprudence. In the official memoranda accompanying the Islamicizing laws there are ample references to the traditions of the Prophet and to works of *fiqh.* By 1977, however, there were indications that Qadhdhafi was promoting just such a restrictive redefinition of the *shari'a.* In the new Libyan Constitution of that year, which was shaped by the fresh ideology that Qadhdhafi began expounding with the publication of the first volume of his *Green Book* in 1976, the Quran was stated in Article II to be "the *shari'a* of society." Developments in 1978 proved that Qadhdhafi was mounting a campaign to have the Quran accepted as the sole source of *shari'a* law.

In public presentations that he made in February and July of 1978 Qadhdhafi unequivocally stated his view that the only Islamic laws were those contained in the Quran. He dismissed the *fiqh* as being without legal force, contending that it should be treated as a part of the Islamic cultural legacy to which Muslims could turn to for guidance on matters of private ethics. He also rejected the authority of the *sunna* of the Prophet Muhammad as a source of law, claiming that many of the traditions of the Prophet were forgeries, and that it was impossible to distinguish between those that were authentic and those that were not. He further chastised his fellow Muslims for following the Prophet's example, contending that in so doing they were elevating him to a god-like status and were thus guilty of the heinous offense of *shirk,* or associating someone else with God. The only rules binding on Muslims were those set forth in Quran, he contended, and these he had already had enacted into law. Thus, although Libyan law had not as a whole become significantly more Islamic since he assumed power in 1969, he was able to maintain that he had kept his promise to reinstate Islamic law.

However, this was not a reinstatement in keeping with the objectives of Islamic revival, according to which Islamic law, whether in its traditional guise or in updated interpretations, should be the ultimate criterion for ordering all activities in human society. In Libya under Qadhdhafi the relationship between Islam and the State is the reverse; Islamic law is subordinated to the will of the secular legislator, and only those *shari'a* rules which he chooses to enact as statutes have the force of law. Given the fact that Qadhdhafi has chosen to discard all but a small fraction of the rules that most Muslims believe constitute the *shari'a,* the outcome of the State's monopoly of the law making function has meant in the final analysis a forestalling of any real attempt to Islamicize Libyan law.

Not only did Qadhdhafi maintain that the *shari'a* was limited to those rules set forth in the Quran, but by 1976 he had become bold enough to propound his own interpretations of Quranic verses. These new interpretations of the Quran were in accord with Qadhdafi's political and economic philosophies, which seem to have verged sharply to the left in the mid-Seventies. Qadhdhafi's credo has been officially set forth in the three parts of his *Green Book,* which came out in the late Seventies and were subsequently imposed on Libyan society as the law of the land. *The Green Book* purports to supply the solutions to the political, economic, and social problems of today's societies. The book's green color and the word green in the title evoke Islamic associations, green being the color associated with the Prophet and with Islam, but the solutions that it proposes would not strike the average readers as Islamic in inspiration.

According to Qadhdhafi the system of government by popular committees which he advocates in the first part of *The Green Book* resulted from his *tafsir,* or commentary on the word *shura,* or consultation, in a verse of the Quran. Thus, when he imposed this new system in 1977, turning Libya into the first "Jamahiriyya," or state governed by the masses, he was able to claim that he was implementing the true Islamic form of government. In connection with the many deviations from *shari'a* rules in the area of family law that are mandated by positions that he has taken in the third part of *The Green Book,* Qadhdhafi has also offered new interpretations of the Quran. Thus, for example, he has offered his reading of Sura 4: 3, which Muslims have traditionally understood to permit a man to take up to four wives. Qadhdhafi argues that the verse permits polygamous marriages only for those men entrusted with the care of orphaned females, a very exceptional situation. Few Muslims would be likely to accept either of these interpretations as being grounded in Quranic scholarship.

As idiosyncratic as Qadhdhafi's purported interpretations of the Quran are with regard to the first and third parts of *The Green Book,* it is with regard to the second part of that work that his interpretations have provoked the greatest controversy. The second part, which deals with economic matters, is particularly difficult to reconcile with Islamic law. Among the measures taken, pursuant to the second part, were the total elimination of the private sector of the economy and a nationalization of all economic activity, draconian confiscations of private property and wealth, and the limitation of individual ownership to a few basic needs such as housing, clothing, food, and transportation.

The Green Book philosophy is at odds with mainstream interpretations of the requirements of Islamic law, according to which private property is given strong protection, commerce and profit are licit, and disparities in income and wealth are seen as part of God's design for human society. Not surprisingly, Qadhdhafi's *Green Book* was roundly denounced by Islamic scholars in Libya as being contrary to Islam, and many were jailed as a result of their public protests. In a confrontation with Islamic scholars in July of 1978 Qadhdhafi sought to meet the objections that were raised to his *Green Book* on Islamic grounds, and, in so doing, made explicit many of his positions regarding the role of Islamic law in contemporary society. He denied that any special expertise or learning was needed to interpret the Quran — a necessary prelude to his discounting the *ulamā's* opposition to his views. He insisted that the Quran provided guidance only on matters of personal ethics and did not cover the problems that were dealt with in *The Green Book,* so that there was no possibility of conflict between the two. In so doing, he was in effect arguing that Islam was like Christianity in being concerned with morality and the afterlife, not a religion which offered guidance in mundane matters. When the *ulamā* brought up verses which contradicted *The Green Book's* philosophy, Qadhdhafi insisted that they had been directed at conditions prevailing in Seventh Century Arabia at the time of the Revelation and were therefore historically linked with that milieu and irrelevant for today's Muslims. With little concern for the consistency of his arguments he also offered interpretations of Quranic verses that supported his theories, such as claiming that Sura 9: 34 condemning those who hoard up gold and silver was an Islamic justification for his confiscations of private wealth and property. However, he did not claim that it was because there was specific Islamic authority for the teachings of *The Green Book* that the *ulamā* should abandon their opposition to his economic program. Instead, he threatened them that if they were unwilling to accept his work, which was a work by a Muslim coming from a Muslim environment, the alternative would prove to be a red book — with the implication that there would then be no pretense of according Islam even a modest role in Libyan life.

The positions that Qadhdhafi took in the July 1978 debate with the *ulamā* indicate the great gap that now separates him from contemporary advocates of Islamic revival. Rather than turning to the *shari'a* — as interpreted by knowledgeable persons — for guidance in political, economic, and social matters, Qadhdhafi has subordinated the *shari'a* to his own ideology and has interpreted it with a view to rationalizing policies that owe nothing to Islam. Instead of expanding the authority of the *shari'a* in Libyan life, he has precluded revival of the *shari'a* as law by denying that it has potential viability as a legal order for today's Muslim societies and relegating it to the role of a scheme of ethics. In order for there to be Islamic revival in any meaningful sense of the term, there must at a minimum be an Islamic impetus shaping political life. In Libya, on the contrary, recent developments indicate that Islam has become more than before a captive entity at the mercy of the State, and its integrity has been undermined by the State in the person of Qadhdhafi intervening in the formulation of *shari'a* doctrine and propounding new "Islamic" rules. Although the recent trend towards reinstating the *shari'a* was inaugurated in Libya, *The Green Book* has since supplanted the *shari'a* as the actual inspiration for legal change. As a result, if a campaign on behalf of Islamic revival is launched in Libya, it will be in opposition to the policies of the Qadhdhafi government rather than one that emerges under its auspices.

Bibliography

Atallah, Borham, "L'Acculturation juridique dans le nord de l'Afrique." In *Independences et interdependences au Maghreb.* Paris: Centre National de la Recherche Scientifique, 1964. 159-200, and "Le droit penal musulman ressucite," *Annuaire de l'Afrique du Nord — 1974.* Paris: Centre National de la Recherche Scientifique, 1975, pp. 227-252.

Bianco, Mirella, *Gadafi: The Voice from the Desert.* London: Longman, Green & Co., 1975.

Evans-Pritchard, Edward Evan, *The Sanusi of Cyrenaica.* Oxford: Clarendon Press, 1949.

El-Fathaly, Omar; Palmer, Monte; and Chackerian, Richard, *Political Development and Bureaucracy in Libya.* Lexington, Mass.: Lexington Books, 1977.

First, Ruth, *Libya: The Elusive Revolution.* New York: Africana Publishing Co., 1975.

Hudson, Michael, *Arab Politics: The Search for Legitimacy.* New Haven: Yale University Press, 1977.

La Libye nouvelle: rupture et continuite. Paris: Centre National de la Recherche Scientifique, 1975.

Mayer, Ann, "Libyan Legislation in Defense of Arabo-Islamic Sexual Mores," *The American Journal of Comparative Law,* 28 (1980). pp. 287-313, and "The Regulation of Interest Charges and Risk Contracts — Some Problems of Recent Libyan Legislation," *The International and Comparative Law Quarterly,* 28 (1979). pp. 541-559.

Qadhdhafi, Mu'ammar, *The Green Book.* London: Martin, Brian & O'Keefe, 1976-1978.

XX

ISLAM IN IRAQ'S PUBLIC LIFE

Daniel Pipes

The Iran-Iraq war, coming as it did on the heels of the Iranian revolution, caused many people to wonder whether the Shiite religious revival inspired by Ayatollah Khomeini had anything to do with the conflict. It is fairly clear now from reports on the war that its causes lie in a dispute over the very valuable Shatt al-Arab waterway, not in any religious difference. But not to be discounted are the historic Shiite-Sunni and Arab-Kurd rivalries that will figure prominently in the political future of Iraq, if not in the current war. Dr. Pipes describes the nature of these rivalries, their impact on Iraq's history and their possible influence on the future of this nation.

Daniel Pipes, the author of **Slave Soldiers and Islam** *and frequent contributor to the national press on current developments in the Middle East and the Islamic world, is currently associated with the Department of History, the University of Chicago.*

Iraq is perhaps the most fragile nation in the Middle East; its peoples show few of the characteristics requisite for developing a single nationality. Instead, they are divided into a multitude of distinct communities, all but a few of which are defined along religious lines. In the six decades since Iraq emerged as a political entity in 1920, these divisions have prevented the country from attaining a unified or integrated public life. Like many new states, Iraq faces the acute problem of forging disparate groups into a nation; unlike most other countries with this problem, however (such as many in Africa), Iraq's divisions are primarily religious rather than ethnic, tribal, linguistic or regional — although these too play a role. Thus, this essay stresses the place of Islam in Iraqi national development during the 20th century.

Islam in Iraqi public life today reflects age old patterns of Middle East religion. Monotheism, the unique quality of Middle East spiritual life, centers on the concept of a single jealous God. He demands exclusive adherence and worship in a specified way. The major religions of Western Eurasia — Judaism, Christianity, Islam — and innumerable minor ones share this basis. Over the millennia, more and more religions, sects and subsects appeared, each with its own rituals and customs, each one prepared to fight others who differed. Most wars had a religious justification and few aspects of life did not have reference to God's commands. Faith gained a major significance in defining political communities among monotheistic peoples.

No where is this clearer than in the homeland of monotheism, the Middle East. Still today, in the age of nationalism (with its territorial, not spiritual concerns), this region divides profoundly by religion. Lebanon represents the quintessence of this tendency: it contains some eighteen communities and virtually all politics in the country is conducted along communal lines. In other parts of the Fertile Crescent, in Israel, Syria and Iraq, religion has a nearly comparable importance.

Iraq's population in 1980 has been estimated at about twelve million persons. Arabic speakers constitute some 80% of the population and Kurds the rest, except for about 100,000 Turkmans speaking a Turkic dialect. Although Iraq is always portrayed as an Arab state, it contains a compact and powerful minority speaking a different language. (Kurdish, an Indo-European tongue closely related to Persian, is utterly different from Arabic.)

The religious map of Iraq is yet more fragmented. Muslims make up all but 5% of the population. Non-Muslims, about whom little will be said here (because they play so small a role in the public life of Iraq) number about 600,000, most of them Christians. Virtually all Christians belong to Eastern rites or uniate churches, including 250,000 Chaldeans, 100,000 Syrian Catholics and smaller numbers of Syrian Jacobites, Nestorians, and Armenians. Yazidis, a quasi-Muslim people probably of Kurdish extraction (often known as "devil-worshippers") living at the far north of the country, number about 40,000. Sabaens, another religious group with mixed religious practice, in this case predominantly Christian, live in southern Iraq and number as many as 30,000. Jews are restricted to Baghdad; heirs to 2,500 years of tradition in Iraq, they are old and emaciated, numbering only a few hundred, soon to become extinct.

Iraqi Muslims, 95% of the population, divide into three large groups: Shi'i Arab, Sunni Arab and Sunni Kurd. Roughly speaking, each predominates in a third of the country. Taking Baghdad as the central point, Shi'i Arabs live to the south, Sunni Arabs to the northwest, and

Kurds to the northeast.

Shi'is constitute slightly more than half of Iraq's population. They inhabit the alluvial plains and marshes of the Tigris and Euphrates rivers. Sunni Arabs live in the upper reaches of these rivers and in the deserts; they make up about one-fifth of the Iraqi population. Kurds, also about one-fifth of the population live in the mountainous regions where most of Iraq's oil lies. Other Kurds, perhaps numbering eight million persons, live in Iran, Turkey, Syria and the Soviet Union. Numerous attempts at Kurdish independence have failed in all these countries, partly because few Kurds have modern skills, living in remote and isolated regions as most of them do, and partly because they took up nationalism too late, after the Middle East had already been divided into modern countries.

Islam's two sectarian branches, Shi'ism and Kharijism, both developed in Iraq in the later 7th century A.D., just decades after the inception of Islam itself. The sects emerged from conflicts over the leadership of the Muslim community: those who later came to be known as Sunnis supported as caliph Mu'awiya b. Abi Sufyan, a distant relative of the Prophet Muhammad; Shi'is advocated 'Ali b. Abi Talib, cousin and son-in-law of Muhammad; and Kharijis, who began as extreme supporters of 'Ali, became disillusioned with him and turned into radical egalitarians.

Three political principles lay behind these movements: while Shi'is insisted on purity of lineage and Kharijis on purity of faith, Sunnis compromised and included elements of both in their selection of a leader. Over the centuries, Sunnism proved more flexible and resilient than the alternatives. Kharijism nearly died out (the Ibadi branch alone remains extant and it is found almost only in Oman) and Shi'ism was reduced to minority status in all but a handful of Muslim regions. Most Shi'is today live either in Iran or Iraq; and though Iran's are far more numerous, Iraq remains central to Shi'i religious and cultural life due to the holy shrines 'there (most especially those in Karbala and Najaf) and the schools nearby.

Shi'i Islam subsequently split into a great many subsects; by far the most populous of them is the Twelver (Arabic: Ithna'ashari) branch, Shi'is who believe that twelve imams followed Muhammad until the last of them disappeared in 965 A.D. For centuries thereafter, Twelver Shi'is were among the most quiescent and inward-looking Muslims, those who generally most avoided contact with the state. This attitude changed in 1500 when the Safavids, espousing Twelver Shi'ism, conquered Iran and imposed Twelver doctrines on the country. Safavid power raised many questions for Twelvers concerning their relations to the state: can lay rule by a Twelver be legitimate, what authority should the religious men have in politics, how does one deal with an unjust king? These questions have not been answered — as the Khomeini revolution and its aftermath in Iran demonstrate.

Twelvers in Iraq watched the Safavids with interest and concern but they hardly ever acted with similar purpose. Instead, just fourteen years after the Safavids came to power, they fell under control of the Ottoman empire. For four centuries, until World War I, Iraq remained under Ottoman dominion; at times this meant real subjection to Istanbul, at others considerable real local autonomy.

Early in the Ottoman period, Sunni Arabs, neither as numerous as the Shi'is nor as martial as the Kurds, emerged as the leading actors in the public life of Iraq. Iraq was a further outpost of the Ottoman Empire; to control it and to help fight off the Safavids, the Sunni Turks relied on the Iraqi people closest to them geographically, those least influenced by Iran, and those sharing their sect, the Sunni Arabs. Persistent efforts by the Iranians to tear Iraq from Ottoman control made this local source of support crucially important. Relative to the other Muslim groups of Iraq, Sunni Arabs flourished under Ottoman rule, acquiring a solid grip on the government and the army. Once organized, they had both the means and the ambition to run the region; and this they have been doing, virtually without interruption, ever since.

Besides Ottoman favor, two other factors contributed to Sunni predominance. First, they are urbanites; except for Basra in the far south, Sunni Arabs predominate in every major Iraqi city. As city-dwellers, they were well placed to gain skills and contacts useful for politics. They knew foreign languages and became literate, amassed wealth, and gained prestigious positions. Shi'is, though far more numerous, could not compete with Sunnis in skills or in gaining favor with the Ottomans. The same thing held true later, under British control; Sunni Arabs went off to European schools and acquired modern skills much more commonly than did the Shi'is or Kurds. Second, the bonds that Sunni Arabs share with Shi'is and Kurds may contribute to their mediating status: like Shi'is, they speak Arabic; like Kurds, they are Sunnis. By linking the other two Muslim groups, Sunni Arabs gain ties to both which have translated into political power.

Sunni Arab control of Iraq persisted beyond the Ottoman period until the present time. After the collapse of Ottoman power in World

War I, the British imposed a mandate on Iraq. When they met violent Iraqi resistance, the British authorities installed a king, Faisal I, in 1921. Full independence followed in 1932. The monarchy was never very secure but it lasted until Faisal II was bloodily overthrown in 1958. For ten years, unstable republican governments frequently replaced each other; then, in 1968 the more steady rule of Ahmad Hasan al-Bakr and Saddam Husain began.

Despite these changes in the political structure — mandate, kingdom, republics — Sunni Arabs remain in charge. Coming as it does in a country deeply split by religious and ethnic loyalties, this dominance has profound implications for all aspects of public life in Iraq. It has always been a fertile source of instability and envy; this remains true today.

Sunni Arab dominance implies the exclusion of Shi'is and Kurds from power. With limited roles in the central government and the army, absent from most of the cities, and economically disadvantaged, they have less power than either their numbers or official ideology would suggest. Recently, however, both Shi'is and Kurds have indicated that they will no longer accept Sunni Arab control. The Kurds have frequently revolted against the central government during the last generation; more recently, the Shi'is too have shown signs of restlessness, especially since 1978, when Ayatollah Ruhollah Khomeini emerged from political obscurity to spearhead the Iranian people against the shah's government.

The Iranian revolution had an electrifying effect on Iraqi Shi'is. Although Khomeini repeatedly stressed the universal import of his ideology for all Muslims and in the process de-emphasized his own Shi'i adherence, his message resonated most strongly among Shi'is. This was especially so in Iraq, where the sectarian split so permeates public life. Ayatollah Khomeini's fifteen year sojourn in southern Iraq at Najaf, the Shi'i sanctuary town, also amplified his impact in that area. He knows Iraqi Shi'is and their predicament first hand and has no trouble finding the right words to encourage or to incite them against the Ba'th regime. Also, Khomeini addresses himself largely to the poor and the politically oppressed, two qualities which accurately describe Iraq's Shi'is.

Despite Khomeini's massive appeal among them, Shi'is in Iraq are unlikely to replicate the Iranian revolution in any form. The Iranian situation had many unique qualities — not the least of which being the personal characters of its two central protagonists; but most important was the independence of the religious establishment there.

To an extent unparalleled in other Muslim countries, Iranian *mullahs* could resist the government because they had financial freedom. Religious leaders and mosques elsewhere are paid for out of taxes, money collected and controlled by the government; as a result, politicians exert great authority over the policies of religious leaders. For example, Anwar as-Sadat had no trouble winning religious sanction for his war against Israel in 1973 and four years later he easily got approval from the religious establishment for his moves toward peace (though non-official religious groups protested vehemently).

In contrast, Iranian *mullahs* have long enjoyed virtual autonomy from the government; they receive funds directly from individual believers. As the shah cracked down on dissent and opposition activity, only *mullahs* were left to organize resistance. As other associations faded, the mosque network emerged as the one structured form of opposition to the government. This was one important reason for the highly religious tone of the Iranian revolution.

There appears to be little basis for comparable Shi'i opposition in Iraq, where the religious establishment resembles Egypt's much more than Iran's. Shi'is lack organization and independence and pose no real threat to the Iraqi government. They can grumble and riot, perhaps even cause a government to fall, but they cannot mount a sustained opposition to challenge the state. This would change if the Shi'is ever organized effectively to resist the central government; but for the foreseeable future, they have no answer to the Ba'thist ideology propounded by the government.

Ba'thism, the official ideology of the state since 1968, is particularly well suited to the needs of Sunni Arabs in Iraq. Its stress on secular pan-Arabism has two virtues for them. First, secularism serves the needs of any rulers of Iraq by de-emphasizing sectarian differences within the country. Only when Iraqis devote less attention to religious bonds will they find room for strong allegiance to their state. Secularism also defuses the importance of Sunni Arab preponderance in the government of Iraq; if religion is irrelevant to politics, who cares that Iraqis of the Sunni persuasion are in charge?

Second, pan-Arabism serves Sunni interests in its claim that Iraq is part of great Arab nation stretching as far as Morocco. Pan-Arabist ideology disdains boundaries currently in effect between Arab states, calling them arbitrary and meaningless; it aims to unite the entire Arab world into a single nation far more powerful than its small parts. As nearly all Arabs outside Iraq are Sunnis, Arab nationalism implies annexing Iraq to a much larger entity within which Sunnis vastly outnumber Shi'is. This clearly holds appeal to Iraq's Sunni Arab leaders, if not to the Shi'is and Kurds.

For these two reasons, Shi'i Arabs resist Ba'thist ideology. They wish to maintain the religious basis of their communal ties; they dislike the prospect of submergence into a vast sea of Sunni Arabs. Ba'thism implies the continued exclusion of Shi'is from political power in Iraq. (Ironically, in Syria it has the opposite purpose serving as the basis of 'Alawi Shi'i power over Sunni Arabs.) A more integrated government cannot be established until the principles of pan-Arabism have been muted or eliminated from the Iraqi state.

The Islamic revival, so celebrated in other Muslim countries during the late 1970's, hardly affected Iraq. The term "Islamic revival" refers most usefully to the increased tendency of Muslims to undertake political action in the name of Islam rather than some other ideology, say nationalism or socialism. Its manifestations in Iraq have been few and usually limited to expressions of Sunni-Shi'i differences. Shi'is caused civil disturbances several times during the 1970's but nothing major occurred until Ayatollah Khomeini came to power. Since then, they have rioted more frequently and with greater ferocity. The Ba'th regime, frightened by Khomeini's charismatic popularity, cracked down severely on the rioters, executed a leading Shi'i imam, and expelled many Iranian Shi'is back to their home country. In a mood of conciliation, Saddam Husain has also allowed pictures of himself praying in mosques to be distributed to the national press.

What role did Islam play in the outbreak of war between Iraq and Iran in September 1980? Many analysts interpreted this as part of an age-old conflict between Sunni and Shi'i, Arab and Persian, Semite and Aryan. Sectarian differences may have added to the general animosity between the two governments, but far more important was the fact that the Ba'thists espoused a diluted version of Islam while the Iranian revolutionaries were inspired by Islamic fervor.

The notion that Iraq went to war out of fear of Khomeini's influence over Iraqi Shi'is is not convincing. If Saddam Husain, President of Iraq, genuinely feared a Shi'i uprising, he would avoid engaging Iran in war and killing its Shi'i soldiers. Further, the war was launched from the south, the most thoroughly Shi'i region of Iraq. Nor would the Iraqi air force have bombed Iranian civilians if this were the key consideration. Even if the Iraqi invasion were intended to eliminate Khomeini's regime, the government that undertook it could not have been too very afraid of its Shi'i populace.

(Arab-Persian differences may also have played a role, but not one great enough to provoke a war. As for the Semite-Aryan explanation, the less said the better; these are specious terms not useful in any political analysis.) More important than either religion or language was a mundane conflict over border details along the Shatt al-'Arab waterway, confluence of the Tigris and Euphrates rivers. This dispute dates back only to the 1920's; it erupted in 1980 because the Iraqis perceived a unique opportunity at that time to regain river rights they had signed away, under duress, in 1975. In short, Islam played only a minor role in the outbreak of hostilities.

When non-Muslims threaten, Islam consolidates Muslim peoples by bringing Islamic bonds to the fore. The Afghan rebellion against a Soviet sponsored government demonstrates this, as do Muslim rebellions in the Philippines and Thailand against non-Muslim central governments. In Iran this sentiment had a leading role in galvanizing popular sentiment against the shah. Although a Muslim, the shah was characterized by Khomeini as an American puppet and this made him fair game.

But Islam plays a different role in Iraq. Here, as in few other countries (North Yemen; also Bahrain and Lebanon) where Sunnis and Shi'i are both numerous, Islam divides Muslims rather than binds them together. Other aspects of Islam have had limited importance in Iraq. The country has not spawned leading Islamic modernist thinkers nor has it witnessed major movements reasserting traditional Islamic ways of life; and its resistance to British rule between 1920 and 1932 did not depend on Islamic leaders or organizations. Islam has influenced national life in Iraq primarily through its role segmenting the country.

Each of Iraq's major Muslim groups looks outside the country for moral and material support. Shi'is, especially since the Khomeini revolution, look to Iran; Kurds dream of combining with their scattered brethren into a nation; and Sunni Arabs hope to blend Iraq into a pan-Arab nation. None of the three groups, not even the Sunni Arabs in control, accept Iraq's boundaries as presently drawn. In times of crisis, these differences are accentuated, as each community looks to its outside constituency.

Iraqi leaders will not succeed in establishing internal equilibrium until religious and ethnic divisions are reduced. Substituting Shi'i rule for that of Sunni Arabs will not help; that only will make the Sunni Arab population bitter. Either an impartial ideology must be developed allowing participation in public life in proportion to communal numbers (as in Lebanon) or else without regard to religious and ethnic background (as in the industrial democracies). Until that day, Islam adds to the divisions in Iraqi public life. Those divisions make it impossible for the government to rule by consensus — instead, they must rely on force. This means that the military must play a major role in politics; and since the army has long been a Sunni preserve, rule by force implies rule by Sunni Arabs. Iraq is a new country, young in years, even if ancient in history; its political discourse, institutions and social bonds are yet undeveloped. For Iraq to become stable religious ties must either be withdrawn from public life or allowed to balance each other; then political integration and participation will follow.

Selected Readings

Atiyyah, Ghassan R., *Iraq 1908-1921, A Socio-Political History*. New York: International School Book Service, 1975.

Fichter, George, *Iraq*. New York: Watts, 1978.

Foster, Henry D., *The Making of Modern Iraq: A Product of World Forces*. New York: Russell, 1970.

Gobbay, Rony, *Communism and Agrarian Reform in Iraq*. New York: Biblio. Dist., 1978.

Ireland, Philip W., *Iraq: A Study in Political Development*. New York: Russell, 1970.

Jalal, F., *Role of Government in Industrialization of Iraq*. New York: Biblio. Dist., 1972.

Khaduri, Majid, *Socialist Iraq: A Study in Iraqi Politics Since 1968*. Washington, D.C.: Middle East Institute, 1978.

Kimball, Lorenzo K., *The Changing Patterns of Political Power in Iraq 1958-1971*. New York: Speller, 1975.

McLaurin, R. D., *Foreign Policy Making in the Middle East: Domestic Influences on Policy in Egypt, Iraq, Israel and Syria*. New York: Praeger, 1977.

O'Ballance, Edgar, *The Kurdish Revolt 1961-1970*. Boston: Shoe String, 1973.

Penrose, Edith and Penrose, E. F., *Iraq: Economics, Oil and Politics*. Boulder, Colorado: Westview Press, 1978.

Penrose, Edith Tilton, *Iraq: International Relations, National Development*. Boulder, Colorado: Westview Press, 1978.

Samarraie, Husain, *Agriculture in Iraq*. New York: International Book Center, 1972.

XXI

ATATÜRK'S SECULARIZING LEGACY AND THE CONTINUING VITALITY OF ISLAM IN REPUBLICAN TURKEY

Howard A. Reed

The historic legacy of Turkey in the Islamic world is paradoxical. On the one hand, the Turks and their national leaders played the role of principal defenders and spreaders of the Islamic faith since the late Middle Ages. On the other, they held Islam in check within the framework of their political interests by controlling traditional Islamic institutions. This dual approach of protection and control gradually gave way to an increasingly secularist approach in the last two hundred years, and dramatically in the last fifty, since the rise of Mustafa Kemal Atatürk to power. Yet a strong commitment to Islam as the basis of Turkish culture has never been abandoned. However, in the aftermath of the September, 1980, change of government questions have been raised whether Turkey's secularist tradition is weakening in the wake of the current Islamic revival. Evidence is to the contrary, as Professor Reed points out. He also describes the balance that Turkey maintained between religion and state in various periods of its long history.

Howard A. Reed, Professor of History, University of Connecticut, was born in Turkey. He has lived, worked, lectured and studied extensively in the Middle East as a Ford Foundation program officer and in other capacities. Author of many books and articles on Turkey, Reed is also a member of the editorial boards of **The Muslim World** *and the* **Middle East Journal,** *an elected member of the boards of both the Middle East and Turkish Studies Associations and Director of the state-wide Undergraduate International Studies Program in Connecticut.*

Turkic speaking peoples and the Turks of Anatolia have had distinguished, dynamic and paradoxical roles in Islamic history for over a millenium. Islamic faith in Republican Turkey continues to be vital, yet its role is ambiguous as it was in the career of Mustafa Kemal Atatürk whose reforms dramatically accelerated earlier secular trends. Islam is an explicitly stated concern of the National Security Council armed forces commanders who seized power on September 12, 1980, in order to protect and restore Atatürk's reforms. This essay will explore some of the implications of these propositions and the role of Islam in contemporary Turkey.

Many Turkish speaking peoples of Central Asia were gradually converted to Islam after the eighth century A.D. The majority came to adopt the dominant sunni form of Islam as this evolved into widely held orthodoxy by the mid-tenth century. However, many Turks were attracted to Islam by heterodox, mystical Muslim leaders known as *babas* (literally, "fathers") or sheykhs. Although attempts were made, over the centuries, to bring them also into Muslim orthodoxy, substantial numbers of Turks who settled in Anatolia after the battle of Manzikert (Malasgırt) in 1071 still were or became *Alevis* or followers of Ali (d. 661 A.D.), cousin and son-in-law of the prophet Muhammad, on whom be peace.

In 1980, some 99% of Turkey's roughly 45 million citizens were Muslims. The official *Statistical Yearbook of Turkey* currently gives no data on religious affiliation of the population. The Republican government has consistently declined to publish figures on the number of Muslims who are shii, or *Alevi*, claiming, as General Evren did in his press conference on September 12, 1980, that Turkey's citizens are Muslims and "united in a single body in complete brotherhood which has forgotten sectarian differences." However, well-informed observers estimate that from five to eight million, or some ten to fifteen percent of Turkey's population, may be *Alevi*.

Sunni Turkish generals became very influential as commanders of the Caliph's bodyguard and of the army of the Abbasid Caliphs in the ninth and tenth centuries. For about a century after 1055 the sunni Turkish Seljuk Sultans effectively controlled the Abbasid Caliphate. In the twelfth and thirteenth centuries their cousins, the Seljuks of Rum, ruled most of central and eastern Anatolia (Asia Minor). As their power declined following loses to the Mongols in 1243 and later, the principality of Osman (Ottoman) arose in northwestern Anatolia near the Sakarya river marches athwart the main routes to Constantinople, capital of the Byzantine Empire.

From the late thirteenth century to the early twentieth, the Ottoman Turks were strongly motivated by the *ghazi* ideal of striving to extend the domain of Islam against Christian or pagan lands, as brilliantly argued by the late Professor Paul Wittek. Ottoman rulers always identified themselves with Islam and with Muslim religious leaders, both scholarly specialists known as *ulema* and more popular, mystically inclined leaders. The Ottoman state developed special links with leaders of two influential dervish brotherhoods or orders, the eclectic, heterodoxically inclined Bektaşi's, and the more orthodox Mevlevi's, or so-called whirling dervishes. Hacı Bektaş became the patron sheykh of the dreaded infantry standing army of converted slaves known as the Janissaries. These troops became the elite core of the Ottoman army in the fourteenth century and were not finally disbanded until 1826. The *dede* (literally, "grandfather") of the Mevlevi order (centered in Konya [anc. Iconium], home of its eponymous inspirer, Jalal ed-din Rumi, the great mystic poet who died in 1273), for centuries had the honor of girding the alleged sword of Osman on each new Ottoman sultan in confirmation of his accession. This ceremony was traditionally performed at the shrine of Abu Eyub al-Ansari, revered martyr of one of the early Muslim attacks on Constantinople in 670. This shrine is located just outside the triple Theodosian walls that still guard some of the land and sea approaches to the city.

The late great Turkish historian, Ömer Lütfi Barkan, has demonstrated the ambiguous role of Islam in the Ottoman state and polity. On the one hand, the Ottoman state was more successful than any earlier Caliphate in extending the application of Islamic law, the *shari'a*, and in organizing the scholar-legists of the learned *ulema* into a systematic hierarchy culminating in four great officers of the empire, the *kadı-askers*, or judge advocates general of Anatolia and of Rumeli (the Ottoman domains in the Balkans and southeast Europe); the *Mufti*, or jurisconsult whose legal interpretations known as *fetvas* could even deter the Sultan from acting in what was considered an un-Islamic way; and at the apex of the so-called "Muslim Institution," the *Sheykh ül-Islam*. As leader of the free-born Muslim *ulema* corps, he met regularly with the Imperial Council or *Divan*, under the leadership of the Sultan or his all-powerful representative, the Grand Vizir. The corps of *ulema* was educated systematically in an ascending range of scholastically organized *medreses* or theological colleges. Those completing various levels of study were certified, then served appointments appropriate to their attained levels of education and experience in relevant posts in various parts of the Ottoman Empire. In theory, the most learned and pious eventually gained appointment to the most senior positions. In the sixteenth century, during the apogee of Ottoman power, the entire administration was run primarily as a meritocracy of free-born Muslims and converted slaves serving the Sultan. He acted as God's vice-regent on earth, limited only by the sanctions of Islamic law, the sultanic administrative regulations, known as *kanunnames*, and *adat*, or customary law.

Over time, the *ulema* group came to control great wealth, largely as trustees or administrators of Muslim charitable trusts, known as *vakıfs* (Arabic, *waqf*, plural *awqaf* or, in Turkish, *evkaf*). It was in part to curb the relative independence and wealth of the *ulema* that Sultan Mehmed Fatih, the Conqueror of Constantinople (r. 1451-1481), seized control over the income of some of these philanthropic trusts, counter to Islamic law, alleging that he did so for the greater welfare of the Islamic community and the Ottoman state. His more cautious, pious son Bayezid II (r. 1481-1512) reversed this policy.

The very large number of shii and *Alevi* Turks in Anatolia early in the sixteenth century represented a threatening potential fifth column, sympathetic to the propaganda of the charismatic shii Shah Ismail of Safavid Iran. Consequently, the Ottoman Sultan Selim I (r. 1512-1520) took the unprecedented precaution of ordering the massacre of some forty thousand of these suspect subjects before his victorious campaign against Shah Ismail in 1514.

During the long decline of Ottoman power in the seventeenth and eighteenth centuries the *ulema*, often acting in concert with reactionary Janissary officers, or quasi-independent provincial notables known as *ayans*, gained increasing control over trust properties or subverted other income yielding positions to their benefit. At the same time, unscrupulous *ulema* managed illegally to corrupt the earlier process of promotion based on merit in order to obtain influential and lucrative posts within the *ulema* hierarchy for their sons or relatives, sometimes at a ridiculously early age.

Sultan Mahmud II (r. 1808-1839) finally managed to reassert central authority in most of his domains (despite the loss of much of Greece and virtual independence of his vassal governor Mehmet Ali in Egypt), by abolishing the ineffective and rebellious Janissary Corps in 1826. He also proscribed their coherts, the Bektaşi order of dervishes, who went into hiding for some time. In addition he weakened the *ulema* further by placing the administration of Islamic trusts under a central government supervisor.

The major nineteenth century reform era known as the *Tanzimat*, or reorganization, starting after 1826 and most clearly enunciated in the 1839 Edict of Gülhane, or The Rose Garden, culminated in the Constitution of 1876 and subsequent reforms under Sultan Abdül Hamid II (r. 1876-1909). Somewhat paradoxically, these centralizing, modernizing reforms introduced new concepts such as that of public as distinct from divine law, after 1838. The reforms also restricted the application of Islamic law. As a consequence the *shari'a* was partly codified between 1869 and 1876 in the remarkable *Mecelle* books of law prepared by a committee chaired by a leading, liberal, former member of the *ulema*, Ahmed Cevdet Pasha. Other liberal *ulema* favored certain modernizing trends, as Berkes and Heyd have shown.

The nineteenth century reforms resulted in frustrating dichotomous tendencies. The first tended to eschew reforms and hold fast to traditional institutions identified with changeless Islamic norms. The second sought to remove religious values from the stresses of rapid material and intellectual changes by narrowing the application of traditional belief, eventually focusing on the core elements of the *shari'a*, family law and inheritance. Efforts to balance state and Islamic faith in a new relationship failed. The result was "not a secular state with a religious organization outside it, but rather a series of divisions in the political, legal, and educational institutions, each of which manifested a religious-secular duality" according to Berkes in his masterful book on *The Development of Secularism in Turkey*.

The abortive reactionary 31 March incident (9 April 1909) represented resistance of traditionalists to the growing secular trends exemplified in the restored constitution adopted and amended after the Young Turk revolution of 1908. Traditionalists also questioned new tendencies in literature favoring Western liberal or social ideas; the emergent autonomous or nationalist aspirations of subject peoples such as Arabs, Armenians or Kurds; romantic visions of an idealized Turkic culture; a revitalized Ottoman multi-nationalism or a Turkish nationalist elite dominant in the Ottoman polity. Ziya Gökalp (d. 1924) linked some of these disparate trends in what became the widely accepted aims of Islamization, Turkization and Westernization.

During World War I the Young Turk triumvirate of Cemal, Enver and Talat Pashas brought the Ottoman Empire into the war as an ally of the Central Powers. The image of the Ottoman Sultan-Caliph became an effective rallying point for Turkish Muslim and international Muslim loyalty. The Sultan's call for Muslims to support a *jihad* or sacred war was used with some effect to appeal to Muslim groups in India, North Africa and Russia to turn against their rulers who were fighting Turkey. However, the Arab nationalists under the treacherous Sharif Hussein of Mecca put nationalism ahead of their allegiance to the Sultan-Caliph when they took part in the temporarily successful Arab Revolt after 1916.

The Ottoman general who emerged from defeat in 1918 with the best reputation for outstanding bravery and success against the enemy was Mustafa Kemal. He had distinguished himself by his attacks against the Western Allied forces at Gallipoli in 1915, then on the Russian front in Eastern Anatolia, and finally by his skillful retreat from Palestine in 1918.

The discredited Ottoman government accepted the armistice of Mondros (or Moudros) in October 1918 and subsequent Allied occupation of the Straits. Italy was assigned the Antalya region and France took over the Adana and Cilicia region in accord with secret Allied wartime agreements.

Early Turkish resistance to occupation was scattered, localized and rather ineffective at first. It became much more general after the Greek forces were allowed to land in Izmir on May 15, 1919 and begin the take-over of the fertile Aegean region. This event, and the landing of general Mustafa Kemal in Samsun on May 19, 1919, ostensibly to supervise the disarming of Ottoman forces in the area but in reality to rally and organize nationalist resistance against occupation, mark the real beginning of Turkey's War of Independence. This nationalist struggle eventually led to the expulsion of the Greeks from Anatolia in August and September, 1922. International recognition of nationalist Turkey's new frontiers and status in the treaty of Lausanne of July 1923 confirmed the demise of the Ottoman Empire and paved the way for the establishment of the Turkish Republic on October 29, 1923.

The nationalist struggle for independence was at first justified as an effort by loyal Muslim subjects to liberate the allegedly captive Sultan-Caliph and his pusillanimous cabinet in Istanbul (which was formally occupied by the Allies on March 16, 1920) from infidel enemy occupation. Many deputies elected to the Ottoman parliament of 1920 were nationalists and supported the National Pact *(Milli Misak)* insisting on an undivided, free Turkish state, which was adopted on January 28, 1920. The fiction of cooperation between the nationalist resistance forces (which were gradually consolidated under the leadership of Mustafa Kemal and his colleagues such as generals Kazim Karabekir, Ali Fuat Cebesoy, or the naval hero Rauf Orbay) and the Sultan's ineffectual administration in Istanbul was unmasked by the *fetva* of Sheykh ül-Islam Durrizade, which in 1920 attacked Mustafa Kemal and the nationalist forces as "a band of common rebels whom it was the duty of any loyal Muslim to kill." Mustafa Kemal had prudently taken the precaution of resigning his military commission in July, 1919, and got the *Mufti* of Ankara to issue a counter *fetva* declaring that the alleged rebels were loyal Muslims deserving of full support.

The establishment of the Grand National Assembly at Ankara in April, 1920, and adoption of the Constitutional Law on January 20, 1921, mark the first attempt to set up a republican form of government in the Islamic world. The first article of this new Constitutional Law states that "Sovereignty belongs unconditionally to the nation. The government is based on the people's direct rule over their own destiny." This superseded the 1876 abortive experiment in constitutional monarchy and signalled the end of theocratic rule. The subsequent termination of the sultanate, the flight of Sultan Mehmed VI on a British warship in November, 1922, and the abolition of the Caliphate in March, 1924, were logical outcomes of the new regime set up by the Turkish nationalists at Ankara.

The Turkish Republic was declared by the Assembly on October 29, 1923, and Mustafa Kemal was elected President. He remained President until his death on November 10, 1938. Mustafa Kemal, who was given the surname Atatürk (Father of the Turks) by the Assembly in 1934, and his associates introduced a major series of secularizing reforms. It has often been thought that this secularism signified the separation of state and religion somewhat along the lines of French laicism and that it involved an anti-religious policy seeking to eliminate Islamic faith. These assumptions are not correct. In fact, the new Turkish Republican regime tried to implement its constitutional mandate of freedom of conscience by setting up government agencies charged with helping citizens to approach Islam through reason rather than tradition. In 1924 the Presidency of Pious Affairs was set up to manage the administrative affairs of religion and the Presidency of *Evkaf* was authorized to administer the finances of the religious trusts. Both were to report directly to the Prime Minister's office. A Faculty of Divinity was constituted in Istanbul University to engage in research and foster the new religious outlook. Schools were opened to train *imams* (prayer leaders) and *hatips* (preachers) to care for religious functions along the desired more enlightened lines. These schools, like all educational institutions, public or private, domestic or foreign, were placed under the supervision and control of the Ministry of Education in accord with the basic law on the Unification of Education of March 3, 1924.

The Presidency of Pious Affairs was responsible for translating, editing, and publishing authentic religious works for the public, and for supplying qualified *muftis* and other religious staff to perform necessary administrative functions such as announcing the start of Islamic festivals which fluctuate according to the lunar calendar.

This somewhat paradoxical situation represented the dualistic Kemalist approach to secularism and was made even more official by the Constitution, adopted in 1961, and suspended after the military takeover of September 12, 1980. Article 19 of this constitution guaranteed absolute freedom of religion and belief to every citizen. Article 154 affirms the Turkish State to control and direct religious affairs. In 1972, the Presidency of Pious Affairs, which deals almost exclusively with Islamic matters, paid and supervised a substantial number of field staff on duty all over Turkey's 67 provinces. These included: 639 *Muftis* (in principle there should be one in every district or *kaza* of Turkey); 75 assistants to *Muftis;* 826 *Vaiz,* or weekday preachers; 1,130 Teachers of Qur'an (memorization) courses; 9,100 *Imams* and *Hatips* (congregational prayer leaders and Friday noon preachers); 14,446 substitute prayer leaders; and 5,761 *muezzins* or callers to prayer. These last appear somewhat redundant as for decades modern technology, in the form of loudspeakers connected to recording devices, have invaded the minaret balconies from which traditionally the *muezzin* has chanted the *ezan,* or call to prayer for the five daily prayers required of Muslims.

The Constitution adopted in 1924 stated in Article 2 that "The Religion of the Turkish State is Islam; the official language is Turkish; the seat of the government is Angora." This was amended on April 10, 1928, by deleting the first phrase, and again on February 5, 1937, to read: "The Turkish State is republican, nationalist, populist, etatist, laic, and revolutionist. The official language of the State is Turkish, its capital is the city of Ankara." Other references to Islam and the enjoining of office holders to swear by Allah were also removed. These amendments obviously underscore some of the secularizing tendencies of the period. However, there were also other significant reforms whose aim was not weakening but strengthening Islam by breaking the traditional sway of superstition and by improving outmoded Islamic practices.

The first phase of the Kemalist secularizing reforms between 1924 and 1928 included the abolition of the Caliphate, and of the Ministries of *Seriat* (the *shari'a*) and *Evkaf,* the closing of the *medreses* and of tombs of Muslim saints, the prohibition of the dervish orders and shutting of their cloisters, the outlawing of the fez and other types of hat without a visor, and a cabinet ruling that only certified Muslim functionaries could wear religious clothing. This was followed by the December, 1934, law prohibiting the wearing of ecclesiastical garb outside mosques or churches after June 15, 1935. The erection of statues of Mustafa Kemal, first in Istanbul's Sarayburnu (Palace Point) Park on October 3, 1926, then in Ankara on November 4, 1927, was an innovation disregarding Islamic prohibitions against the creation or use of images of humans or animals, even if worship is not involved.

A most important legal step was the adoption of a new Civil Code, patterned after the Swiss Civil Code of 1912, on February 17, 1926. This code signified the full secularization of civil life. Among other things, it abolished polygamy and equalized the rights of women and men in regard to divorce, inheritance, succession and guardianship of children. A new law of Obligations and Commercial and Penal Codes based on European models was also enacted, thus entirely superseding the *Mecelle* and any remnants of the *shari'a*. Two other important results of the Civil Code were the Law of Family Names of 1934, and full suffrage for women. Women were allowed to vote and stand for office in municipal elections in 1930, gained full political rights and duties in 1934, and seventeen were elected to the Grand National Assembly of 1935.

Adoption of the Latin script in 1928 was another great reform with wide-reaching educational, cultural and intellectual ramifications. Discussion on the introduction of the Latin alphabet went back at least to debates on the issue in 1912. The matter had been proposed again at the Economic Conference in Izmir in 1923, in parliament in 1924 and by Turkish delegates to the international Congress held in Baku in 1926. All of these suggestions had been rejected. Late in 1927, however, the Turkish linguist Cevat Emre began publishing a series of articles which represents the first serious application of the Latin letters to the Turkish alphabet. His experiments drew on earlier experience in Muslim Albania and among the Turkic peoples of the U.S.S.R.

In 1928, a committee was finally appointed to prepare a draft alphabet and a new grammar applicable to it. The recommendation of the committee was that ten years be allowed for the transition. Mustafa Kemal recognized the dilemmas involved in such a delay, which would have meant the simultaneous use of two writing systems for a decade. He met with the Committee and finally concluded that the experts would never agree on a viable alphabet. It is reported that he then worked all night to devise the new Turkish script, based on the Latin alphabet, which was announced at the start of a national campaign to promote it on August 9, 1928. On November 3 a law was enacted which prohibited the use of the Arabic script in all public affairs after December 1, 1928.

The results of this dramatic change were fundamental. The entire nation had to go back to school and take special courses to learn the new script. It turned out that primary school children learned to read and write in just a few months — a fraction of the three years it took them in the old system. There were, of course, many gains, but also many practical and psychological losses. At a stroke most younger Turks and all who had not learned the traditional Arabic script were cut off from the rich literary heritage of Ottoman Turkish. Yet the new script was far better suited to Turkish phonetics and it greatly facilitated access to education and literature. It also made printing much cheaper and simpler.

The culminating step in this first phase of secularizing reforms was the deletion of any reference to Islam as the religion of the State from the Constitution in 1928.

Mustafa Kemal's personal concern for religious enlightenment was expressed in several ways. He sought to Turkify Islam and make it accessible to all as a natural and rational religion. In 1923 he announced preparations for constituting a government sponsored board of Islamic studies. Its goals would be "to study Islamic philosophy in relation to Western philosophy, and to study the ritual, rational, economic, and demographic conditions of the Muslim peoples." On February 7, 1923, he spoke to the inhabitants of Balikesir from the *minber* (pulpit) of the Pasha mosque suggesting that preachers should speak in Turkish rather than in Arabic, which is incomprehensible to most Turks. He reminded them "that in early Islam national affairs and social problems had also been the subject of Friday sermons . . . and assured his audience that 'our religion which gave the human race the spirit of progress is the last and most perfect religion." Mustafa Kemal stressed the importance of Turkish as the language of worship for Turkish Muslims. Largely as a result of his encouragement, the call to prayer *(ezan)* and sermons *(hutbes)* came to be given almost universally in Turkish by 1931, entirely on a voluntary basis. It was only in 1941, three years after his death, that the Turkish *ezan* was made legally compulsory. He also did much to encourage the translation of the Qur'an into Turkish, so that it could be available to all Turks in their own language and obviate the need for any specially learned intermediaries versed in the Arabic language in which the Holy Book was originally written. Mustafa Kemal said, "The Turk believes in the Book, but he does not understand what it says to him. First of all, he himself must understand directly the Book that he so seeks" (Osman Ergin, *Turkiye Maarif Tarihi*, Istanbul, 1943, V, 1633-34, as cited in Berkes, *op. cit.*, 486).

Despite much controversy and conservative questioning several translations of the Qur'an into Turkish were made. The first, which appeared during the Constitutional period before 1914, was confiscated by order of the *Sheykh ül-Islam*. Another complete translation in 1923 was soon rejected by the Presidency of Pious Affairs as having too many errors, but its reissue some years later underscored the need for such a translation. Various other, more accurate and readable, translations appeared in 1924, 1926 and 1927. Mustafa Kemal and the Grand National Assembly took up the matter in 1926, when they allotted funds for a special translation to be made by the Islamist poet Mehmet Akıf, author of the National Anthem. Akıf eventually refused this commission, partly in protest against Kemalist reforms. The translation fund was kept in trust for him in the hope that he would undertake the work and Mustafa Kemal kept the offer open until 1936 without success.

Yet many other Turkish translations of the Qur'an started to appear. Of special interest is the one by the son-in-law of Mehmet Akıf (whose translation of selections of Qur'anic verses was finally published in 1944). Ömer Riza Doğrul's Qur'an translation appeared in 1934 and again in 1947. Another popular version was by Elmalılı Mehmet Hamdi, 1935-1938. The translation by Hasan Basri Çantay is reputed to be the best. It was reprinted four times between 1953 and 1964. Professor Abdülbaki Gölpinarlı's serialized translation which appeared in a newspaper in 1955 was a major innovation later repeated by Hacı Murad Sertoğlu in the daily *Tan*. In 1961 the Presidency of Pious Affairs began to issue an official translation of the Qur'an prepared by two younger scholars in the Faculty of Divinity of Ankara University under the supervision of an editorial committee. It is not for sale, as copies of the Holy Book must never be for sale. Instead, the price donated is termed a gift, or *hediye*. This translation is termed, "perhaps the most correct" of the more than one hundred existing translations aimed at making the Holy Qur'an more accessible to and better known among modern Turks.

The central problem of whether the Qur'an can, or should, be translated has not yet been entirely resolved. The late John Kingsley Birge, who lived in Turkey for some forty years, declared in 1951, "I do not remember having talked with a single Turk who likes the Qur'an read in Turkish." Many Turks and knowledgeable foreign scholars agree that the sound of the Arabic original affects Turkish listeners powerfully, even if they do not understand the meaning. The substantial and continuing popularity of courses in Qur'an memorization, and the fact that there are an estimated 200,000 Turks who know the Qur'an by heart, known as *Hafız,* suggests the profound appeal of the Arabic Qur'an to contemporary Turks.

In 1950, the newly elected Democrat government capitalized on this appeal by announcing, as one of its first acts, the reintroduction of the call to prayer in Arabic on June 16, 1950, so that it could be chanted in the favored traditional tongue the following day, which was the first of the fasting month of Ramazan. Nowadays, the Friday sermon is delivered in Turkish but is introduced by the recitation of Arabic verses.

The questions of religious reform and secularization are all closely related to religious education. In their desire to change and rationalize access to basic knowledge about the Islamic faith, the Kemalists sought to avoid the influence of religious conservatives, obscurantism and the exploitation of religion in any form. As a result, religious education in the Republic has gone through a number of phases, including one which might be called "benign neglect" from about 1933-1949. Since about 1950, however, there has been a fairly steady growth in the number of formal learning institutions and opportunities for Islamic religious education. Before discussing that growth, it may be helpful to review briefly some of the early phases of religious education for Muslims during the Republican era.

The law of Unification of Education of March 3, 1924 placed responsibility for all formal education in the national Ministry of Education which supervises even special training institutions set up by other ministries. This law led to the closing of the *medreses* and ended the age-long leadership in education exercised by the *ulema.* Some special religious training was continued in a number of *Imam-Hatip Mektepleri* (Prayer Leader and Preacher Schools) and in the new Faculty of Theology set up in the University of Istanbul. This faculty replaced an earlier one attached to the University between its constitution in 1900 and 1919. The faculty began issuing a quarterly journal in 1926. In 1928 a special committee of the Faculty, whose dean was the renowned turcologist Mehmet Fuat Köprülü, produced a controversial proposal for the reform of Islamic worship in Turkey which stated in part:

> . . . it is almost impossible with the modern views of society, to expect such a reform . . . from the working of mystic and irrational elements. Religious life like moral and economic life must be

> reformed on scientific lines. . . . First of all the form of worship . . .
> sanitary conditions. . . . The language of worship must be
> Turkish. . . . The character of worship — singers and imams
> equipped with a fair knowledge of music, instruments of music. . . .
> The intellectual side of worship . . . the important thing is a philo-
> sophical view showing the human and permanent nature of the
> Islamic religion. . . . The new Turkey will be the guide to freedom
> and progress of all the Muslim countries which are still enslaved
> and backward in civilization. . . . (quoted in full in Jäschke, *Der
> Islam in der neuen Turkei*, 1951, p. 66 ff., with further references in
> H. A. Reed, "The Faculty of Divinity at Ankara," *The Muslim
> World*, xlvi, 4, 1956, p. 300).

This report, which suggested the introduction of special prayer mats and pews along with the regular use of instrumental music in mosque worship, was not implemented in part because of protests from traditionalists. The Faculty of Theology itself had dwindling enrollments and did not survive the reorganization of Istanbul University in 1933. It was transformed into an Institute of Islamic Research in the Faculty of Letters, which was inoperative from 1942 to 1955, when it was reactivated as a research center directed by the late Professor Zeki Velidi Toğan.

Proposals to establish a new Faculty of Divinity were made in January, 1948, and part of the rationale was that the Minister of Education and some Deputies thought that the faculty had "to work against reactionary trends." This unique faculty was set up by law No. 5424 adopted on June 4, 1949, and was opened as part of Ankara University on October 31, 1949. Only two members of the teaching staff, O. H. Budda and Y. Z. Yörükan, had served in the previous Istanbul faculty. Professor Annemarie Schimmel, who taught in this faculty for five years has written as follows about it:

> The programme was well designed, containing not only purely
> Islamic subjects but also History of Religion, Psychology and
> Sociology of Religion, etc. But it was quite impossible to find
> qualified teachers for all these subjects. The deaths of four eminent
> professors during the first years added to the difficulties the new
> faculty had to face. Professors from Morocco, Yugoslavia and other
> Islamic countries were invited and some stayed as permanent
> members of the staff.

Among the problems faced by the faculty were:

> not enough reliable textbooks, and the students suffering from a
> very poor knowledge of Western languages in spite of foreign
> language classes; as to Arabic the students had to learn it during
> their four years' studies, not in a preparatory course. Nevertheless,
> they were very eager to gain knowledge about foreign religions, and
> lively discussions were held in my classes on problems of Christian
> dogmatics.

Next to no importance was given to "practical theology." A research institute with its own magazine . . . was added in 1959. Homiletics were not taught. The faculty issues a quarterly which was welcomed in Europe as 'scientific, critical and original' (Cf. Taeschner, *W. I.*, n.s. vol. II, pt. 2, 1953). Both textbooks and research work are being published. I am quite sure that some of the former assistants, trained in Europe and Canada, who have now joined the staff, will eventually provide this faculty with the dreamt-of combination of Western scientific methods and personal piety.

She adds the following observations:

Oddly enough, prayer was not offered regularly, and fasting not observed by all members of the staff, but, I think, by the overwhelming majority of the students.

In fact, a special room for prayers was set up and plans for a small mosque for the use of the staff and students of this faculty were made some years ago when it moved to larger quarters in a new building. Dr. Schimmel states:

I may add that there was no discrimination against women either in the staff or among the students. . . .

The number of students during the first years was always between seventy and ninety, among them on the average fifteen girls; in 1959 the figures had increased to 141 boys, thirteen girls; in 1964 to 348 boys, thirty girls; so that a new building was required. About sixty students are receiving scholarships from different organizations . . . sometimes also from the army where the young men will serve as religious and moral leaders attached to military units. Only a limited number of those who have completed the course have joined the 'imam-hatip' schools; others have become *muftis*, some girls are religious teachers in middle schools. . . . Since 1966, some of the graduates have been appointed 'religious attaches' at Turkish embassies abroad, e.g., in Germany and Austria, to look after the religious problems of the Turkish workers in these countries (Cf. Schimmel's study cited in bibliography).

In recent conversations with two former deans of the Faculty of Divinity, one of whom is a leading historian who did post-graduate study at the Institute for Islamic Studies at McGill University, and the other, who has also studied and lectured abroad and is also a widely published scholar, I gained the following impressions. Both professors are proud of the progress achieved by the Faculty of Divinity, yet they agree that it has not attained its full potential and still has to resolve some of the problems noted by Dr. Schimmel.

The Universities Law of 1946 and subsequent amendments, notably the 1973 law on universities, granted an autonomous status to Turkish universities. All other educational institutions in Turkey come under the supervision of the Ministry of Education. It is thus responsible for various programs and special schools concerned with Islamic religious instruction as it has been since 1924. In the early years of the Republic, religious classes were offered in the primary schools and taught by regular teachers. From 1927 on these classes were voluntary, with students participating if their parents so desired. Classes in religion were dropped fairly soon after the article stating that Islam was the religion of the state was deleted from the Constitution in 1928. Classes in religion in primary grades were dropped from urban schools in 1930, and from village schools in 1933. They were recommended on a voluntary basis until 1935. Religious classes in middle schools were abolished in September, 1931. In 1933 a law on the organization and functions of the Ministry of Education rescinded earlier provisions concerning religious teaching in schools and confirmed secular education. The teaching of Arabic and Persian was also removed from school curricula in 1928, when instruction in these languages was left to specialized departments at the university level. The number of *Imam-Hatip* Schools and their enrollments declined steadily from over twenty-nine in 1924 to two in 1932 and these institutions ceased operations in 1932-1933. They were to be revived as special courses between 1949 and 1951, when seven new *Imam-Hatip Okullari* were established to become the vanguard of 437 such schools by 1977-1978.

From 1934 to 1948, the only indigenous, legal Islamic religious training available to Turkish Muslims was either as a routine part of basic Armed Forces training for recruits, or in the very elementary courses for memorizers of the Qur'an and on the Qur'an *(Hafız ve Kuran Kursları).* These were operated under the supervision of the Presidency of Pious Affairs. The number of teachers and students grew steadily after 1934. By 1949 there were 130 teachers, 6,403 male, and 2,303 female students, all of whom were required to be primary school graduates.

In 1949, Muslim religious education for two hours weekly was made available in the fourth and fifth grades of all public elementary schools in Turkey, on a voluntary basis with two exceptions. The first was where, for any reason, such as shortage of qualified and acceptable teachers, the classes could not be offered, and second, in many villages inhabited by *Alevi* (heterodox, or shii) peasants, where the course options were simply neglected because no one wished their children to take what were considered faulty, sunni oriented courses.

After the end of World War II, during most of which Turkey remained neutral, war time authoritarian controls were relaxed. Citizens began to demand that the human rights recognized in the United Nations Charter, to which the Turkish government subscribed, be made more operative within Turkey. This led to the movement toward multi-party politics initiated late in 1945 and culminating in the Democrat party's victory in the May, 1950, election, upsetting the Republican People's Party's control of government since its establishment by Mustafa Kemal Atatürk in 1923. The freer atmosphere in the late 1940's also permitted more open expressions of Muslim piety than had been deemed fashionable or prudent, especially in urban centers and among the bureaucracy, during the secularizing reforms under Atatürk and before his successor, President Ismet Inönü, sanctioned a more pluralistic approach to politics. In the intense competition for votes, more attention was paid to the village peasant majority of the citizenry. The peasants had been less directly influenced by many of the secularizing reforms and most seemed to retain their devotion to traditional forms of Islamic worship and practice, often regardless of Republican law codes or regulations. According to Paul Stirling, in his *Turkish Village* (London, 1965), "to the villagers the Civil Code is irrelevant." There was, therefore, a kind of rediscovery of the continuing attachment of the peasant majority to traditional Islamic values and rituals. The peasants, who were unaccustomed to being given so much attention by politicians, made known their requests for better water, access roads to markets, and also for help with repairing or enlargening their mosques or in finding replacements for their aging prayer leaders.

One result of this rediscovery of traditional Islamic allegiance, especially among peasant villagers, coupled with the freer atmosphere, was the reappearance or resurgence of many customary Islamic practices in public. There was a notable increase in the building of new mosques and the repair of older ones, often adding a minaret or portico, usually in traditional Ottoman style. Vehbi Koç, one of Turkey's most successful businessmen, is alleged to have contributed toward the building or repair of some hundred village mosques in the late 1940's. The Democrat Party not only reinstituted the call to prayer in Arabic in June, 1950, but also made many appeals to Islamic religious sentiments, especially among the peasants and small town or urban lower and middle classes, during the decade of the 1950's. These appeals tended to disregard the legal restraints in article 163 of the 1926 Penal Code which prohibited propaganda against the principles of secularism, or article 241 which makes religious functionaries liable to prosecution for speaking derisively of the laws and public authorities in the course of their duties. Article 9 of the Law of Associations *(Cemiyetler Kanunu)* of 1938 prohibited parties from engaging in religious activities and making religious propaganda. It also prohibited the formation of societies based on religion, sect, and *tarika* (dervish order). However, it was permissible to form societies for the purpose of religious prayer and practice or to open schools for the purpose of religious instruction provided that these did not interfere with regular schooling, were authorized by the Ministry of Education, met public health requirements and had qualified instructors.

The current situation in regard to formal, legal religious education is this. In the universities, there are two Faculties of Divinity, one at Ankara and the second at Atatürk University. There is also the Islamic Research Institute at Istanbul University. Next there are Higher Islamic Institutes, the first established by law No. 7344 of June 10, 1959, in Istanbul and the second in Konya. Below these come the *Imam-Hatip* Schools, operating at both the *orta* (middle) school level (roughly sixth-ninth grade) and the *lise* (high school) level, the first with a four year and the second with a three year curriculum. The primary school religious classes in the fourth and fifth grades continue on the basis that students are required to take them unless their parents request in writing that they be excused. Finally, there are the voluntary courses on the Qur'an and for Qur'an memorizers operated under the aegis of the Presidency of Pious Affairs.

There has been a remarkable growth in the number of *Imam-Hatip* Schools since their inception in 1951, when the first seven were opened. By 1956 there were sixteen of these schools. In 1970-1971 there were 72 of these at the junior high school level with 917 teachers of whom 106 were female; 40,775 students of whom 764 were female; and 5,707 students earned diplomas that year, of whom 57 were female. The latest year for which comparable figures are available is 1976-1977, when there were 248 schools at this junior high level with 1510 teachers of whom 118 were female; 86,053 students, of whom 1,540 were female; and 9,830 students earned diplomas, of whom 73 were female. In 1977-1978, the number of these schools rose rapidly to 334, with 1,872 teachers of whom 192 were female; and 108,309 students, of whom 6,686 were female. Figures on diplomas awarded in 1978 are lacking.

The *lise*, or high school level *Imam-Hatip* School figures for the same years also show rapid growth. In 1970-1971 there were 40 schools with

631 teachers of whom 31 were female; with 6,648 students, of whom 19 were female; and 1,601 earned diplomas, one of whom was female. By 1976-1977, there were 72 schools, with 2,342 teachers, of whom 258 were female; with 25,688 students of whom 92 were female; with 6,015 diplomas earned, 118 by females. In 1977-1978, the number of schools had increased substantially to 103, with 3,050 teachers of whom 399 were female; and 26,177 students of whom only 45 were female. The number of diplomas awarded at this level in 1978 is also not available (*Statistical Yearbook of Turkey* 1979, p. 110). When one adds both levels of *Imam-Hatip* Schools, he gets the impressive total number of 437 schools with 4,922 teachers of whom 591 are female; and 134,486 students, of whom 6,731 are female. This is a substantial number of specialized Islamic educational schools for an avowedly secular yet Muslim Turkey. These figures need to be put into the context of the entire Turkish educational system for comparative purposes.

For example, in 1977-1978, there were 3,310 *orta* (middle) schools in Turkey with 32,430 teachers and 1,105,000 students. Thus, the *orta* or junior high level *Imam-Hatip* Schools made up roughly one tenth of the total. In the same year there were 979 *lises* with 31,310 teachers and 454,000 students. While at the *lise* level the number of *Imam-Hatip* Schools again was roughly ten percent, they enrolled only some five percent of the total number of students at this level nationally. Viewed in this context, this type of specialized religious education plays a significant, though relatively modest, role in Turkish secondary education.

The secularizing Kemalist reforms have been perceived in various ways by Turkish citizens during the first fifty-seven years of the Republic. There is no coercion of conscience or of Islamic faith in Turkey although traditionalists, modernists or *Alevis,* to say nothing of non-Muslim religious minorities, may feel that their points of view receive inadequate attention or that they suffer subtle if not more open discrimination. However, it is clear that ambiguities continue. Constitutional specialists differ in their assessment of this paradoxical situation. The liberal professor Tarık Z. Tunaya, dean of the Faculty of Economics at Istanbul University, argues for formal control of Islam. He claims that otherwise, "religion will invade the government institutions." His more conservative colleague, Professor Ali Fuat Basgıl disagrees. He calls for a total separation between the government's political preoccupations and the religious life of the people in a way somewhat analogous to the U.S. doctrine of the separation of powers between church and state. Of course, there is no formal equivalent of an ordained or apostolic clergy or church in Islam. However, scholarly specialists in Islamic tradition and law, the *ulema*, act somewhat as a lay clergy and jurisconsults in respect to religious law in the Islamic community.

The liberal Turkish Qur'an translator Hasan Basri Çantay wrote in 1958 that "All rules and commandments of the *shari'a* concerning beliefs, prayers, and morals, are in force and observed by the people" (Cf. Kenneth Morgan, ed., *Islam, The Straight Path*, New York, 1958, p. 280). The reality of the variety and continuing vitality of Islam in secular Turkey should not be overlooked. It is virtually impossible to conduct a general opinion poll on Turkish attitudes toward Islam and to ascertain exactly how many Turks pray regularly, fast during Ramazan, or go on the *hajj* (pilgrimage). However, the following figures, derived from surveys of a few hundred individuals primarily in urban Turkish centers some ten years ago are suggestive.

Among urban dwellers of all classes and both sexes, 20.6% said that they performed the five daily prayers and 41.5% said that they fasted regularly during the days of Ramazan. By contrast, residents of squatter communities which ring most cities (and compose some 70% of Ankara's three million population), who are often fairly recent migrants from religiously more traditional rural villages, reported that 54% perform the five daily ritual prayers and that 94% fast during the fasting month of Ramazan. In recent years inhabitants of these squatter communities around cities such as Ankara, Istanbul and Izmir have erected mosques of some size in their impoverished neighborhoods. In the summer of 1980 I was surprised to see two new mosques being erected on the very steep slopes of hills on the northern outskirts of Ankara which can only be approached on foot. Although prayers may be performed at home or elsewhere, many Turks prefer to do so in a mosque or *mescit* (Islamic chapel). Detailed restrictions on mosque upkeep and construction issued on December 25, 1932, resulted in the closing of many, despite the 1924 law charging the Presidency of *Evkaf* with the upkeep of many mosques. According to law No. 2845 of November 15, 1933, a mosque had to be at least 500 meters from the next, or it would be used for non-religious purposes. Consequently, some mosques were used as military barracks or warehouses. Recently, a Turkish Society has issued an illustrated booklet documenting the desecration of mosques, shrines and Muslim cemeteries on the Dodecanese islands of Cos and Rhodes ceded to Greece in 1948. Partly as a result of changing attitudes after World War II, the Turkish state assumed responsibility for maintaining

2,997 additional mosques. For example, in 1953 the Presidency of *Evkaf* spent some 22.5 million liras for the repair of mosques, many of which are built, and maintained privately.

In 1935 Aya Sofya (Haghia Sophia) mosque was converted into a museum. In recent years some ardent Muslims have agitated for the reconversion of it into a mosque. These requests have been denied. However, the Sultan's loge in Aya Sofya, which was begun by Sultan Mahmut II (r. 1808-1839) and enlarged by his son Sultan Abdülmecit, was opened as a *mescit* (small prayer chapel) for public prayers on the Night of Power in Ramazan, or August 7, 1980. It was announced that it would continue to be used as a *mescit* regularly henceforth. In another concession to Islamic sentiment, Tevfik Koraltan, Minister of Culture in the summer of 1980, announced that the Qur'an would be recited continuously every day in the Hirka-i Saadet room which contains relics of the Prophet Muhammad at Topkapı Palace, Istanbul.

Almsgiving, or *zakat* (in earlier times a tax of some 2.5% on certain types of property) has long been purely voluntary in Turkey. However, there are thousands of charitable trusts, or *vakıfs*, being established these days and many citizens contribute toward the building or upkeep of mosques, fountains, *Imam-Hatip* Schools, orphanages, student hostels, scholarships and similar worthy enterprises thus continuing the traditional obligation to be charitable.

The *hajj*, or pilgrimage to Mecca, is only incumbent once in a lifetime on those mature Muslims who can afford the journey without undue neglect of family or business responsibilities at home. Available figures reflect great variations in the number of Turks who made the pilgrimage in selected years since 1934, when 104 went. It was then prohibited until 1947. By 1952 there were 10,220 Turkish pilgrims granted official visas and foreign exchange permits. In 1964 there were 3,261; in 1970, 49,676 and some 35,000 in 1974. These data, although partial, suggest that H. B. Çantay's sweeping claim cited above has considerable validity. Professor Schimmel concurs with this assessment and states that even among middle class Turkish Muslim families, "Every act, even the conjugal act, is begun with the *basmala*" (i.e., the pious affirmation, "In the Name of God, the Merciful, the Compassionate").

She adds:

> In the development of Turkish Islam mystical currents have played a more important role than the official orthodox creed, and the amalgamation of mystical brotherhoods and their sometimes

heterodox ideas under the rule of orthodoxy was only achieved from the time of Selim I onwards. The influence of Sufism on Turkish cultural life cannot be estimated highly enough, and it is quite natural that even today Turkish religious feeling is more imbued with mystical feelings than is the case in other parts of the Islamic world (Schimmel, *op. cit.*, p. 87).

All mystical dervish orders were outlawed in 1925. Yet many continue alive and apparently are growing in clandestine membership in recent years. Since 1954 the government has allowed public performances of the worshipful whirling dance of the Mevlevi dervishes in Konya, Istanbul and abroad, allegedly for cultural and touristic rather than religious purposes. Such *zıkr* (Arabic *dhikr*), or worshipful recollection of God is an act of religious devotion. The Mevlevis performed their whirling devotions in Boston and New York in 1972. The Halveti-Jerrahi (or "Howling") dervishes performed their *zıkr* under the sponsorship of the Cathedral of St. John the Divine and the Cooper Union in New York City and of the Middle East Institute and the Smithsonian Institution in Washington, D.C. in the Spring of 1979. The annual performances of the Mevlevis at the shrine of their leader the great sufi poet Jalal ed-Din Rumi (d. 1273) in Konya on his December 17th birthday now attract senior government officials, members of the diplomatic corps and thousands of spectators. Public dervish chanting and *zıkr* in some Istanbul mosques and frequent private gatherings of mystics seem to be overlooked by the authorities who recently restored and reopened the once famed Galata Mevlevihane as a museum where classical Turkish musical and even on occasion Mevlevi whirling dances have been performed.

Traditional sunni-shii tensions and the presence of substantial numbers of *Alevi* Turks have been noted above. In recent years over 12,000 shii pilgrims have assembled each August to honor their saint, Hacı Bektaş, at his tomb near the small town of Kirşehir in Central Anatolia. This formally illegal gathering is winked at by the rural gendarmerie and other officials, including some members of parliament who have attended. The *Alevis* have rallied around a minority political party aptly named Birlik Partisi, or Unity Party. Turkish *Alevis* tend to cluster in their own villages and districts, to avoid intermarriage with sunnis, and to adapt more readily than other Turks to rapid change and so-called modernization. *Alevis* form a fairly autonomous, upward mobile and innovative minority among contemporary Turkish Muslims, and some are excellent entrepreneurs. Latent animosities between sunnis and shiis broke out into tragic confessional rioting in December, 1978, in Kahramanmaraş (formerly

Maraş) in southeastern Turkey. Over a hundred people perished, mainly shii Muslims attacked during a funeral by their sunni neighbors. After a year long trial, some of the instigators received heavy sentence in 1980.

Despite the tremendous progress in education, literacy and in many other fields, ignorance, superstition, and tradition continue to influence many. While some of the dervish orders have been relatively liberal and tolerant of, if not cooperative with, the Kemalist reforms, others tend to be more conservative or even reactionary. Orders such as the Nakşibendis, Nurcus or Süleymancıs have substantial followings. They continue to be active in more reactionary ways with repeated calls for a return to the *shari'a*. This would mean the reversal of secularizing trends extending back 250 years and constitutional guarantees of over half a century.

The recent charges leveled against Professor Necmettin Erbakan, leader of the National Salvation Party, of illegally exploiting religion for political ends, and against Colonel Alpaslan Türkeş, leader of the National Movement Party, of inciting to violence and terrorism by the National Security Council now ruling Turkey are very grave. They underscore the determination of General Evren and his colleagues to defend the Kemalist secular reforms. The very strong popular support for their coup d'état and for legal proceedings against these two former deputy prime ministers indicate that there is little support for reaction or for Islamic Fundamentalism in Turkey. The ambiguities and strains within the secular Republic established by Atatürk and his associates are serious. The National Security Council and the people of Turkey have recognized the issues and are struggling to resolve them creatively and harmoniously. The manner in which they do so, hopefully in the spirit of Atatürk's goal of "Peace at Home and Peace in the World," will give new meaning and substance to the Kemalist reforms and to the secular Republic which has evolved from them.

Suggested Readings on Islam in Turkey in English*

Abadan-Unat, Nermin, and Yücekök, Ahmet N., "Religious Pluralism in Turkey," *Milletlerarası Münasebetler Turk Yıllığı/The Turkish Yearbook of International Relations*, X, 1969-70, 24-49.

Adnan-Adıvar, Abdulhak, "Interaction of Islamic and Western Thought in Turkey," T. Cuyler Young, ed., *Near Eastern Culture and Society,* Princeton, N.J., 1951, 119-29.

Allen, Henry E., *The Turkish Transformation: A Study in Social and Religious Development.* Chicago, 1935.

Berkes, Niyazi, *The Development of Secularism in Turkey.* Montreal, 1964.

Birge, John Kingsley, *The Bektashi Order of Dervishes.* London and Hartford, 1937.

Çantay, Hasan Basri, "Islamic Culture in Turkish Areas," Kenneth W. Morgan, ed., *Islam — The Straight Path: Islam Interpreted by Muslims.* New York, 1958, 253-95.

Ergil, Doğu, "Secularization as Class Conflict: The Turkish Example," *Asian Affairs,* v. 62, February, 1975, 69-80.

Fallers, Lloyd A. & Margaret C., "Notes on an Advent Ramadan," *American Academy of Religion, Journal,* v. 42, March, 1974, 35-52.

Gallagher, Charles F., *Contemporary Islam; The Straits of Secularism; Power, Politics and Piety in Republican Turkey.* American Universities Field Staff, New York, 1966, 1-28.

Heyd, Uriel, "The Ottoman 'Ulema and Westernization in the Time of Selim III and Mahmud II," *Scripta Hierosolymitana,* IX, 1961, 63-96.

Jäschke, Gotthard, *Der Islam in der neuen Türkei. Die Welt des Islams,* N.S., Leiden, 1951. *(This basic study is cited even though it is not in English.)

Kinross, Lord, *Atatürk: The Rebirth of a Nation.* London, 1964.

Lewis, Bernard, *The Emergence of Modern Turkey.* London, 1961, 2nd edition, 1968.

Magnarella, Paul J., *Tradition and Change in a Turkish Town.* Cambridge, Mass., 1974.

Makal, Mahmut, *A Village in Anatolia.* London, 1954.

Mardin, Şerif, "Ideology and Religion in the Turkish Revolution," *International Journal of Middle East Studies,* v. 2, no. 3, July, 1971, 197-211.

Reed, Howard A., "The Religious Life of Modern Turkish Muslims," Richard N. Frye, ed., *Islam and the West.* The Hague, 1957, 108-48.

Robinson, Richard D., "Mosque and School in Turkey," *Muslim World*, v. 51, April and July, 1961, 107-10, 185-88.

Rustow, Dankwart A., "Politics and Islam in Turkey 1920-1955," Richard N. Frye, ed., *Islam and the West.* The Hague, 1957, 69-107.

Schimmel, Annemarie, "Islam in Turkey," Arthur J. Arberry, ed., *Religion in the Middle East: Three Religions in Concord and Conflict.* Volume 2, *Islam.* Cambridge, 1968, 68-95.

Scott, Richard B., "Qur'an Courses in Turkey," *The Muslim World*, v. 61, October, 1971, 239-55.

Smith, Wilfred Cantwell, "Modern Turkey: Islamic Reformation?," *Islamic Culture*, v. 25, January, 1951, 155-86, revised in his *Islam in Modern History*, Princeton, 1957.

Stirling, Paul, *Turkish Village.* London, 1965.

Webster, Donald E., *The Turkey of Atatürk: Social Process in the Turkish Reformation.* Philadelphia, 1939. (Note also his forthcoming, *Kemalism as a Civil Religion.*)

Wittek, Paul, *The Rise of the Ottoman Empire.* London, 1938.

XXII

ISLAM IN INDONESIA: CHALLENGES AND OPPORTUNITIES

Nurcholish Madjid

Islam arrived in Indonesia through the trade routes. Having penetrated the port cities and spice islands in the Middle Ages it gradually engulfed the entire archipelago very peacefully over a period of several centuries. In doing so, it blended with, not replaced, existing Indonesian cultures and religions, whether native (such as the animistic cults) or imported (such as Hinduism and Buddhism). This explains the uniqueness of Indonesian Islam.

In the nationalistic phase of Indonesian history, Islam, however diverse it was from island to island, served as a, nay the only, unifying force for all Indonesians. The post-independence phase has not been different. Both Sukarno in his, what is now called, "Old Order" and Suharto in his "New Order" used/uses Islam as a chief base for political power. Mr. Madjid describes here the role Islam played/plays in Indonesia's history and in its contemporary life.

Nurcholish Madjid who had a distinguished career in Indonesia as president of the Muslim Students Association of Indonesia (1966-1971), a lecturer at the State Institute of Islamic Studies and a researcher at the National Institute for Economic and Social Research is currently completing a doctorate in Islamic thought and philosophy at the University of Chicago.

There has been a growing consciousness among Indonesian Muslims since the last ten years or so that they are the largest Islamic nation in the world. Official figures based on the census of 1973 show that Muslims constituted 87 percent of the then about 120 million Indonesian citizens, Protestants 5 percent, Catholics 2.5 percent, Hindus 2 percent, Buddhists 1 percent, and adherents of *Aliran Kepercayaan* (Javanese mysticism) 2.5 percent. With a currently estimated population of 140 million, and assuming that the percentage of the Muslims has remained the same since the census, Indonesia now has a larger number of adherents of Islam than any other country, especially after the separation of Bangladesh from Pakistan. But the numerical aspect of Islam in Indonesia can be very misleading. In fact, the leaders of the nation have continuously and consistently rejected the idea of an Islamic State for Indonesia. Even more, most of them consider that such an idea is one of the two political ideologies most detrimental to the Republic, the other being Communism. The Republic is officially based on what is known as *Pancasila* or Five Principles: the principles of Monotheism, Humanism, National Unity, Democracy, and Social Justice.

The seemingly anomalous situation of Indonesian Islam can be partially explained by the nature and method of Islamization of the archipelago, and by the colonial history under the Dutch. The Islamization of the Indonesian people was, in fact, never fully consummated. The process of proselytization was what is known as *pénétration pacifique* which allowed a great extent of tolerance and compromise on the part of Islamic tenets in their encounter with the pre-existing cultural and social value-systems of the native people. As a result, and because of the fact that Indonesia is geographically the farthest Muslim region from the heartland of Islam, Muslim societies in the archipelago are also the least Arabized, even less than Pakistan to the west. Having, therefore, no unified cultural focus, three main streams of world-view or *alirans* emerged among Indonesians, particularly the Javanese. They are held by three distinct groups — the *Santri* (the more orthodox Muslims), the *Abangan* (the less orthodox and the more syncretic Muslims), and the *Priyayi* (the Indicized aristocratic Muslims).

An important development of the three *alirans* that occurred during the colonial era is that the Dutch invariably took the side of the *Priyayi* and the *Abangan* in the latters' struggle against the *Santri*. The *Priyayi* group were also the first Indonesians to be recruited in the colonial administration, and the first to be educated in modern Dutch schools.

Projected against this historical background, it should be no surprise that from its beginning, the nationalist movement in Indonesia was strongly Islamic, anti-colonial, and anti-*Priyayi* (because of their identification with the colonial government). The first organizational expression, in a modern sense of that Indonesian nationalist movement with nation-wide mass support was *Sarekat Islam* (Islamic

Association) which stemmed from *Sarekat Dagang Islam* (Muslim Traders' Association) established in 1911. The first decades of the twentieth century also witnessed the growth of Muslim religious movements proper, which constituted a veritable renaissance of Islam in Indonesia spearheaded and inspired by the Islamic modernist thoughts of Muhammad 'Abduh and Rashid Ridha of Egypt. The most important organizational expression of Indonesian Islamic modernism was *Muhammadiyah* which was established in 1912. *Muhammadiyah* subsequently inspired the Indonesian traditionalist *ulamā* to establish *Nahdlatul Ulama (Nahḍa al-'Ulamā'* — the Resurgence of the *Ulamā)* in 1926. Since this stage of development, a sub-variant of Islam in Indonesia had emerged, this time within the *Santri* group, that is the modernist variant as against the traditionalist majority. This schism would have major impact upon Indonesian Islam and the history of Indonesia in general as this Islamic modernism would later contribute tremendously to the emergence of modern Muslim nationalists in the revolutionary period.

However, after 1929 the *Santri* Muslims ceased to lead the nationalist movement of Indonesia, and the initiative was taken over almost entirely by secular Western-educated and politically-oriented intelligentsia, partly as the unintended consequence of the modern education that had been introduced by the colonial government itself. These Western-educated people were, therefore, recruited almost exclusively from among the *Priyayi* group who by and large stood aloof from Islam and its movements. They played a dominant role in Indonesian politics during the pre-war years, the last years of the Dutch rule, while Islam was as yet politically inarticulate.

The brief Japanese occupation of Indonesia during the War gave Islam its new political articulateness. The greatest contribution that Japanese made to the awakening of Indonesian political Islam was, perhaps, their patronizing efforts to unite all Indonesian Muslims under *Masyumi (Majlis Syura Muslimin Indonesia* — The Consultative Council of Indonesian Muslims), comprising the two most important Islamic religious organizations: the modernist *Muhammadiyah* and the traditionalist *Nahdlatul Ulama*. In addition, the Japanese also established an Office for Religious Affairs in the capital as well as in other major cities, which was to be responsible for the protection of Muslim interests. At the national level, the Office was presided by the leader of *Nahdlatul Ulama*. These two bodies, the *Masyumi* and the Office for Religious Affairs, survived the War and the defeat of Japan, and they continued to play important roles in independent Indonesia, after undergoing some modifications.

The Japanese Islamic policy in Indonesia originated from their interest in the War, and it was pursued because they very likely "may have felt a greater affinity with the apparently far more genuine anti-Western orientation of the Islamic leadership as a whole, than with that of the 'secular' but Western-educated Indonesian intelligentsia." (Harry J. Benda, 1972).

Toward the end of their occupation of Indonesia, however, and toward the time when apparently independence for Indonesia would be inevitable, the Japanese gradually gave more and more support to the secular nationalists rather than the Muslims, although they continued to give their protection to the latter. This development of Japanese policy explains why Muslims were extremely underrepresented in the Japanese-sponsored committee making efforts to prepare independence for Indonesia in 1944-1945. In the committee began the struggle between political Islam and secular nationalism concerning the philosophical basis of an independent Indonesia, with the Muslims advocating the creation of an Islamic State and the nationalists rejecting the idea. The conflicting ideas were finally resolved in a *modus vivendi* in the form of what was later called the Jakarta Charter, in which it was agreed that Indonesia would be based on *Pancasila* (see above), but which also provided that there would be an obligation upon the Indonesian Muslims to observe the Islamic *Shari'a* (Sacred Law).

The Jakarta Charter was signed by the representatives of the Indonesian people on July 22, 1945, and was intended as the text for the declaration of independence of Indonesia. However, for reasons that have yet to be more fully unfolded, when Sukarno and Hatta proclaimed the independence of the country on August 17, 1945, they did not use the Jakarta Charter as the text. Instead, they drafted a new text, which was relatively very short, apparently because it was written in a great hurry. The text, titled *Proklamasi* (Proclamation), did not mention Islam or any other religion. On August 18, 1945, one day following the proclamation of independence, a conference of Indonesian leaders was convened to discuss the constitution of the new country. There the Jakarta Charter was discussed again, and finally revised by omitting 'the seven words' that provided for the obligation of the observance of the *Shari'a*, "for the sake of national unity". The revised Jakarta Charter was then adopted as preamble of the Constitution of the Republic of Indonesia, and thus the country was firmly and solely based on the philosophy of *Pancasila*.

The decision to adopt *Pancasila* as state ideology could be viewed as a defeat for political Islam in Indonesia. But clearly the proponents of the idea of an Islamic State would not easily give up their aspirations. The aspirations were put aside temporarily because of the physical struggle against the Dutch who came back to the archipelago to restore their colonial domination and to destroy Indonesian independence. But in the Constituent Assembly that was formed on the basis of the result of the general elections in 1955, the Muslim representatives came back to their demand of a state based on Islamic principles. Although Muslim representatives got less than 50 percent of the votes, which meant that they had no real hope of obtaining two thirds of the votes needed to pass a constitutional resolution, the Muslims continued to fight for their idea of an Islamic State until the last meetings of the Assembly. Finally President Sukarno dissolved the Assembly and decreed the reenactment of the 1945 Constitution, declaring that the Jakarta Charter had a special historical connection to the Constitution and should be considered an integral part of it. The recognition extended to the Jakarta Charter could be interpreted as stressing the exceptional position of Islam within Indonesian society. But the Guided Democracy conception pursued by President Sukarno from 1959 onwards, which gave a tremendous role to the Indonesian Communists, amounted to a policy of "domestication and neutralization of Islam within a larger whole." (W. F. Wertheim, 1974).

One year later, Sukarno outlawed *Masyumi*, the then modernist Islamic political party and the most dynamic one in Indonesia, because of the involvement of some of its leaders in the 1958 regional rebellions. Political Islam was then represented mostly by *Nahdlatul Ulama*, the traditionalist religious organization turned into a political party in 1952 after its secession from the then almost all-embracing *Masyumi*.

Immediately following the abortive Communist-sponsored coup d'état in 1965, *Santri* Muslim groups in many parts of Indonesia, but particularly in Java, took a terrible revenge against the Communists and the ultra-nationalists who were suspected of having been involved with, or sympathetic to, the coup. With substantial help from army units, Muslim youths in rural areas, especially members of *Ansor (Anṣār,* Partisans, the youth organization of *Nahdlatul Ulama)* rounded up and executed members of PKI *(Partai Komunis Indonesia,* Indonesian Communist Party), and other ultra-nationalists, almost indiscriminately. The estimated number of people liquidated in the mass slaughter is from 500,000 to 1,000,000. (Oey Hong Lee, 1979).

But the Muslim leaders were to be disillusioned by their own miscalculation. Their expectation of gaining ascendency in Indonesian national politics after their communist and ultra-nationalist adversaries had been eliminated proved to be false. "Suharto's military Government proved to be as wary of Islamic domination as Sukarno's populist regime." (Wentheim, *op. cit.*) The dissolved *Masyumi* was not allowed to be rehabilitated, and the party that was allowed to be founded as a successor to *Masyumi*, the *Parmusi (Partai Muslimin Indonesia*, The Muslim Party of Indonesia) was to be put under strict control by the Government. Worse still, the former leaders of *Masyumi* were barred from participating in political activities, including from being nominated as candidates in general elections.

General Suharto's policy to keep political Islam in check reflected the Army's political outlook. And this outlook, in turn, reflected the "cultural roots of its officers, among whom orthodox *Santri* Muslims were underrepresented while, especially at the higher levels, Javanese of *Priyayi* outlook were heavily overrepresented." (Harold Crouch, 1978). The policy is also a consistent continuation of what was pursued by the military leadership since Sukarno's time. "Given its factionalism, some of which centered on different attitudes concerning Islam, the military leadership had generally favored a secular state during the Constitutional period. Almost without exception, military officers gave their support to Sukarno's *Pancasila* doctrine, the leading expression of secularism in that period. . . ." (Howard M. Federspiel, 1973).

President Suharto has also had to face some difficulties in persuading some Muslim leaders to accept his version of the meaning of *Pancasila* philosophy and to abandon their traditional goal of restructuring the state on Islamic principles and laws. In 1967 the Islamic political parties indicated that they were still upholding the aspirations of an Islamic State ideology through their efforts in the Provisional People's Consultative Council (MPR-S) to have a stronger constitutional position for the Jakarta Charter that provided mandatory observance of Islamic *Shari'a*. The efforts ended in failure, and what political Islam had experienced in the Council would foreshadow greater difficulties that it had still to face in further developments in Indonesian politics.

The relationship between political Islam and Suharto's Government went from bad to worse when there emerged on the Indonesian political stage the issue of Christianization. The issue came to the surface after hundreds of thousands of *Abangan* Muslims abandoned

Islam and were converted to other religions: Buddhism, Christianity, and Hinduism, but mostly Christianity, whether Protestantism or Catholicism. This happened as a reaction of the *Abangan* people against their political persecution by the *Santri* Muslims following the 1965 debacle. This caused "protests among Muslim leaders who are always incensed by the proselytizing activities of the Christians." (Oey, *op. cit.*) The Muslims even went so far as to have "the impression that the ultimate aim of the Christians is to *menaklukkan* (subjugate) Islam." *(ibid.)* And Muhammad Natsir, the leading figure of modernist Islam in Indonesia and the former chairman of the dissolved *Masyumi*, in an Inter-Religious Conference sponsored by the Government in 1967, accused the Christian leaders of "attempting to expel Islam from Indonesian territory and insisted that people who had already a religion should not become the target of proselytizing activities of other religions." *(ibid.)* And when the Government refused to accept the demands of the Muslim leaders to stop the Christian proselytizing activities, the Muslims began to see it as too lenient to the Christians if not outright supportive.

The inclination of many members of the regime towards *Aliran Kepercayaan* (Javanese mysticism) also became the target of strong resentment by the Muslim leaders. The proponents of the *Aliran Kepercayaan* had continuously lobbied at the highest level in Jakarta in an effort to win government support to have their belief systems elevated to and recognized as an independent religion. But unlike the case with the Christianization issue, this time President Suharto's decision was more sympathetic to Islam as he refused to recognize *Aliran Kepercayaan* as an independent religion. In February 1979 it was officially announced that the Government recognized *Aliran Kepercayaan* only as an aspect of Indonesian culture, and that its supervision was entrusted to the Ministry of Education and Culture rather than the Ministry of Religious Affairs.

The New Order of Suharto in Indonesia has been marked by more religious conflicts and incidents of a violent nature than the Old Order of Sukarno. During the first years of the New Order, dozens of Christian churches and schools were burned down by Muslims in South Sulawesi, North Sulawesi, North Sumatra, East Java, Central Java, and Jakarta. "The contradictions between the Muslims and the Christians have come out into the open with some Muslims strongly resenting the presence of Christian churches and the Christians being frightened by the idea of Islamic hegemony in the form of an Islamic state." *(ibid.)* It is the fear of an Islamic State which has always given impetus to the formation of a united front by the non-Islamic forces against political Islam, and which has instigated the limited resurgence of Hinduism, Buddhism, and Javanese mysticism. It has also offered better opportunity for the Christians to foster their political role at the national level. And all this has contributed to the growing isolation of Islam from the political scene in Indonesia.

The Chinese also constitute anti-Islamic elements in Indonesian society. Having been traditional adversaries of *Santri* Muslim traders and the targets of the earliest nationalist movements, many Chinese, being suspected of adhering to pro-Communist outlook, adopted Christianity rather than Islam to find refuge and political legality. *(ibid.)* The Indonesian Chinese Muslim Association still has little success in its efforts to spread Islam among the Chinese.

Nevertheless, after ten years of resistance the Government finally gave in to some of the Muslims' demands to ban or limit the activities of other religious groups. On December 7, 1976, the Jehovah's Witnesses were banned from the entire territory of Indonesia by the order of the Attorney General Ali Said, "to preserve tranquility, security, and harmony." *(ibid.)* About two years later on August 1, 1978, a governmental decision was issued on Guidance of Religious Propagation, known as Decision No. 70/1978, by the Minister of Religious Affairs, General Alamsyah. The Decision banned proselytizing activities among people already adhering to a religion. This Decision was to be followed by another, known as Decision No. 77/1978, dated August 15, 1978, on Foreign Aid to Religious Institutions in Indonesia. This placed foreign aid to religious institutions, mostly Christian churches but also some Islamic organizations, under strict control of the Government, and it demanded such aid be recorded with the Government and be formally approved. Foreign missionaries were also considered in the category of foreign aid and therefore needed formal approval from the Government to work in Indonesia. Christian institutions and other religious bodies concerned were instructed to replace foreigners within two years. *(ibid.)*

The Muslims, as expected, reacted positively to the decisions, despite the fact that they also suffer from the policy, although relatively little, especially in regard to foreign aid (some Islamic institutions receive contributions from some Arab countries). The Hindus and the Buddhists made a joint statement supporting the Government. The Christians, both Protestants and Catholics, quite naturally, protested the decisions, accusing the Government, in this case the Minister of Religious Affairs, of violating the principle of religious freedom guaranteed by the Constitution. *(ibid.)*

As to the reasons why President Suharto finally took the side of the Muslims in their dispute with the Christians, one speculation is that the answers could be found "within the context of the balancing act of the Government." *(ibid.)* Corruption has always been the primary target of criticism of Suharto's regime by many Indonesian political groups, including the Muslims. But secular intellectuals and university students were particularly articulate in their criticism. Some cases of anti-corruption activities, as *Malari* (January 15 affair of 1974), indicated the seriousness of the intellectuals' opposition to the regime. An assessment of the growth of the secular — that is, non-Islamic — forces critical of Suharto's Government in these recent years would give some justifications to the view that the President's rapprochement with Islam was within the context of balance of power politics.

> In 1978 the student demonstrations against the regime were nationwide compared to those of four years earlier during *Malari*, limited mostly to Jakarta. Also the target of attack was not anymore the generals around Suharto but the President himself. He was directly accused of corruption and asked not to put his name as candidate for the Presidency in the MPR-session of March. The anti-corruption and anti-foreign capital secular forces have increased tremendously since 1974 instead of decreasing and dwindling away. Is it a wonder that the Government, similarly as in the post-1974 period, is now looking for support from the Muslim country? *(ibid.)*

But all this does not mean that the situation in Indonesia has paved a smooth way for political Islam to come back to gain real political benefits. For one thing, the most dynamic segment of political Islam, the *Masyumi* and its leadership, has apparently been permanently blocked from any practical political initiative. For another, anti-Islamic forces are always there, which would quickly check any possibility of the development of an Islamic State ideology.

> It is not only Christians and Chinese groups who are worried about this possibility; Westernized intellectuals, to whom Islam in its stricter form represents a conservative and authoritarian traditionalism, were no less appalled by the prospect of an Islamic victory....
>
> There are also liberal foreign circles who tend to condone the harsh authoritarian traits of Suharto's military regime because the alternative would appear to be an Islamic state, harsher still than one based on *Pancasila* and allegedly opposed to "modern" development — whatever that may mean. (Wertheim, *op. cit.*)

Nevertheless, and in spite of all difficulties that the Muslims have confronted during all those years that elapsed, Islam in Indonesia has recently shown some signs of resurgence. The most visible phenomenon is the appearance of new Islamic buildings: mosques, *madrassas,* and *pesantrens* (traditional Islamic educational institutes), throughout the country. Thousands of new mosques have been and being built everywhere, mostly with the initiative and financial aid coming from the Government. Some of them are even built using the state budget. As a result, in Jakarta alone, for example, the number of mosques has risen from 460 in 1965 (the year when the New Order of Suharto began to take hold of the country) to 1,186 in 1978. Besides these there are now 4,413 *mushallas* (smaller places of prayer). Most of the new mosques are built using modern technology and architecture, and have modern equipment. These "modern" mosques have attracted hundreds of thousands of worshippers, with young people comprising up to 85 percent of attendance in some places. *(Far Eastern Economic Review,* 1979). Consequently, there are now flourishing associations of *Remaja Masjid* (Mosque Youths) throughout the country, especially in the big cities. A wide range of social and religious activities are covered by these associations, from sport and self-defense arts to music to academic discussions. Most of the members are recruited from among the university students, but many younger and older people also join them. They held their national convention in March 1980 in which the programs underscored the importance of the present century, the 15th century of the *Hijra,* as the Revival Century of Islam.

Indications of an Islamic resurgence in Indonesia are also evident on university campuses. During the fasting month of *Ramadan,* many campuses are marked with major religious activities, as if they were converted to Islamic centers. "*Ramadan* on Campus", as they call it, has become increasingly popular among university students and includes such socio-religious activities, unconventional for Muslims as poetry readings, dramas, and even musical shows, besides the traditional *tarawih (Ramadan* nightly prayers), *tadarrus* (Koranic studies), and religious lectures.

Many Indonesian university campuses now have their own mosques. The most conspicuous of them is the Salman Mosque on the campus of ITB *(Institut Teknologi Bandung* — The Bandung Institute of Technology), one of the most highly respected centers of learning in Indonesia. It is interesting to note that it was Sukarno who gave his blessing to the idea of having a mosque for ITB (he is an alumnus of the Institute), and it was he who gave the mosque its name Salman (after the name of one of the Prophet Muhammad's companions, Salman al-Farisi, considered to be the first "technician" of Islam).

In fact, President Sukarno indeed had many things to do with the current phenomena of Islamic resurgence in Indonesia. For one thing, he was responsible for the building of the *Baiturrahiem* Mosque within the compound of the Presidential Palace in Jakarta. Some view the Mosque of Sukarno as a symbol of "officialization" of Islam in Indonesia. Sukarno was also responsible for the decision to build the gigantic *Masjid Istiqlal* (Independence Mosque — the mosque erected to commemorate the independence of the nation), in Jakarta, the largest mosque in the world after the Grand Mosque of Mecca. It was the building of the *Istiqlal* mosque which inspired many governmental officials to build mosques in various parts of the country.

Another thing that Sukarno is to be credited with is the Palace tradition of celebrating Islamic anniversaries, as *Maulid Nabi* (The Birthday of the Prophet Muhammad), *Nuzulul Qur'an* (The Descent of the Koran), and *Isra'-Mi'raj* (The Nocturnal Journey of the Prophet and his ascent to Heaven), besides the two 'Id festivals. He was also responsible for the popularity of making the pilgrimage to Mecca among Indonesian governmental officials. Enthusiasm for this journey has been so current in recent years among governmental officials that many of them bear the title of *Haji*. Even the more mundane-oriented celebrities like film stars, artists, and pop-singers have begun to be *Hajis*, and they have been increasingly open in their religious life.

Although Sukarno performed many great services for Islam in Indonesia, these were religious only in their outward appearance. It was really Suharto's New Order that has fundamentally changed Islamic religious life in the country. Although Sukarno coined the slogan "Religion is an Absolute Ingredient for Nation Building", it was Suharto's Government that applied it to political life, if only out of fear of the Communist comeback. In Suharto's Indonesia atheism is considered a crime, and no Indonesian is foolish enough to publicly call himself an atheist.

> In the period since independence until 1965, the right to freely adhere to one's own religion and to worship according to one's belief (article 29 of the Constitution) was also implemented as the right not to believe in God.... In the New Order, however, every citizen must have a religion and people who stubbornly insist on the freedom to be atheists, can be branded as communists and perhaps arrested.... Thus in Indonesia there are officially no non-religious people. (Oey, *op. cit.*)

This situation provides a possible explanation for the growing religious enthusiasm among Indonesian Muslims and the overflow crowds in mosques, despite their increasing number and capacity. It is also a possible explanation for the limited revival of Hinduism and Buddhism in Java, and for the mass conversion of the *Abangan* Muslims to Christianity (estimated number is up to three million) that resulted in the issue of Christianization as mentioned before.

However, as discussed earlier, Suharto's involvement with religion is still fully consistent with his version of the meaning of *Pancasila* philosophy that religion should not interfere with politics and state affairs. (Federspiel, *op. cit.*) The encouragement of the religious life of Islam has been invariably accompanied by vehement suppression of its political expressions. Some observers even note that what is being followed by the present regime is a repetition of Dutch colonial policy towards Islam, especially as advised and formulated by C. Snouck Hurgronje, the notable Dutch Islamicist of the last century. His advice was that the enemy of Dutch colonialism was not Islam as a religion but Islam as a political doctrine. He therefore formulated "twin policies of tolerance and vigilance", that is, tolerance towards the religious aspects of Islam and vigilance against its political activities. Hurgronje went even further as to encourage modern education for Indonesian elites to free them from what he called "the narrow confines of the Islamic system", because "Islam held no keys to healthy social growth." (Benda, *op. cit*)

Assuming that the New Order Government has consciously taken over the Dutch colonial policy concerning Islam based on Hurgronje's ideas, the question may be asked, will this policy be successful? That is, will Indonesian Muslims be really "emancipated" — as sometimes the purpose of this policy is described — from the "narrow confines of the Islamic system"? A straight negative or affirmative answer to this question would be simplistic. Given the immense complexity of Indonesian society, it would certainly be safe to leave it to history to answer such questions. But looking back to colonial times, one might find some clues to a probable answer.

> ... the then Advisor on Native and Arabian affairs to the colonial government, the famous Islamologist C. Snouck Hurgronje, had said that the *Pax Neerlandica* would inevitably further the consolidation of Islam in Indonesia. Snouck Hurgronje thought, however, that one could split religion from politics, and that toleration of the faith could go hand-in-hand with vigilance against Islamic political action; the adherence to this line of thought in later years allowed the development and growth of such overtly non-

political movements as *Muhammadiyah*. . . . Snouck Hurgronje, writing in the 1890's, believed that Islam would not be able to compete with Dutch education, but in fact the Dutch penetration of the Outer Islands was soon followed by the arrival of students from al-Azhar, and modern Islam spread like wildfire. (Benda, *op. cit.*)

As has already been discussed, *Muhammadiyah* is the main organizational expression of Indonesian modernist Islam which had more far-reaching influence than the politically-oriented *Sarekat Islam*. *Muhammadiyah* was then to become the backbone of the *Masyumi* Islamic political party, the most dynamic political party during the Indonesian revolution, a militant Muslim political movement with an ideologically all-embracing creed fighting for an Islamic state. Although politically modernist Islam, as represented by this movement, has not been an important force in recent years,

. . . its schools, publishing houses, and social organizations are busier than ever, and the long-term goal of the Islamization of Indonesia — in some still unspecified sense — remains intact and surely will reappear in some form as an important influence in political life — perhaps not as an *aliran* but as a number of autonomous religious, social, and economic organizations representing specific interests of their constituents and at the same time espousing a unified modernist view of politics and society. (R. William Liddle, no date).

One could say, therefore, that based on the observation of the growing interest of young people in religion, the "wildfire" of Islam has begun to burn Indonesian soil again. And one might point as an indication for that to the growing strength of the Islamic party, the PPP (*Partai Persatuan Pembangunan* — United Development Party). Although the New Order has been admirably successful in depoliticizing and neutralizing the former mass-followers of the Nationalist and the Communist parties as part of an over-all depoliticization program, "Islam as religion and a way of life has lost none of its powerful hold on its tens of millions of adherents". (R. William Liddle, 1978). PPP was successful in getting more votes — a meager score, but psychologically significant — in the election of 1977 compared to that of 1971. It is interesting to note that in large cities, including Jakarta, PPP won more votes than the Government-sponsored *Golkar* (*Golongan Karya* — The Functional Group, the New Order's ruling party).

But one might argue that PPP would never be able to contribute significantly to a long-run fundamental resurgence of Islam in Indonesia compared with the politically inactive but socio-religiously very active modernist organizations like *Muhammadiyah*. The reason is that PPP is being dominated by the traditionalist *Nahdlatul Ulama* which, according to Abdurrahman Wahid, himself a leading figure of the association, "does not fully appreciate the significance of development program, has never standardized its policies, and the organizational pattern of which, in almost every respect, has remained the same since 1926 when it was founded until the present year of 1980!". (*Kompas*, 1980). This is to be contrasted against the modernists who "foster a belief in the power of individual initiative rather than a blind acceptance of *takdir*, which often served to rationalize inaction and a piously stagnant mode of life". (Allan A. Samson, in *Asian Survey*, Vol. VIII).

Nevertheless, whether the modernist Muslims in Indonesia would be able to revive their dynamic modernism of the first decades of this century remains a big question mark. For one thing, the prevalence of a new type of conservatism and traditionalism, and the heavy stress on solidarity in their struggle, must have hindered them from being fully creative and responsive to the ever-changing social and political problems. Or perhaps Wertheim was right when he assessed the current situation of Indonesian Islam as "an example of the operation of Jan Romein's 'Law of the Retarding Lead': precisely because Islam was rightly being viewed by Muslim people as progressive throughout the colonial and imperialist period, it has not yet felt the challenge to become really progressive in a changed world". (Wertheim, *op. cit.*)

Considering the *Santri-Abangan/Priyayi* split, and the fact that the New Order Government is heavily and disproportionately dominated by the *Abangan/Priyayi* groups, the difficulties that political Islam has been experiencing seem to be fully understandable. But given the fact that Islamic religious life has been much more encouraged than ever before, it would seem reasonable to reexamine the nature of the New Order Abanganism, or even Abanganism as a whole in its history. With regard to the New Order Abanganism, William Liddle doubts very much that Abanganism as an ideological force is still operating among the current Indonesian ruling elite. Although *Abangan/Priyayi* nationalists are predominant among them, "these men neither face competition for power and office from outside their cultural group nor enjoy any organizational links with the *Abangan* urban and rural masses ... At the highest governmental levels, then, Abanganism is no longer the ideology of a cultural group which can, in the conceptualization of cultural politics, be counterposed to Islam as the ideology of the *Santri* cultural group." The political attitudes of the New Order are predictable not from their position as *Abangan/Priyayi* leaders, but from "their position in power hierarchy, their ambition to greater power, and their fears of those who might displace them . . . New Order Ideology has become in great part a rhetorical weapon, a defensive wall erected to protect the leaders from the consequences of their policy mistakes and their drives toward self-enrichment." (Liddle, *op. cit.*)

This analysis would give us a better understanding of the nature of the recent New Order policy of rapprochement with Islam — if only limited to initiating regulations dear to the hearts of the Muslims such as the decisions concerning the issue of Christianization. This policy can be interpreted within the context of the balancing act of the Government, as we have seen earlier. It may also be explained from the need of the ruling elite to find a new and broadened basis of power. Since Abanganism, after the downfall of Sukarno and his death, as an ideology appears to be a spent force at the mass level (Liddle, 1978, *op. cit.*), and has become, in Benedict Anderson's term, "the doctrine rather than ideology, an empty shell of slogans which masks the absence of any real vision of what Indonesia might become or how it might get there" (as quoted in Liddle, n.d., *op. cit.*), Islam as the religion and the value-system of the majority of the population could serve the purpose.

> Most Indonesians are believers of the Islamic faith. Consequently, the largest part of the population in the Indonesian archipelago submit themselves to the values and norms of Islam. Not denying the existence of a great diversity of interpretations and conceptions of Islamic teachings, there are basic values which any individual, especially he who aspires for leadership positions, is expected to take seriously and to conform to them. A leader who fails to subject himself to these basic values will soon lose his position as a legitimate leader among his fellow believers. (Harsja W. Bachtiar, 1972)

It is therefore quite plausible that Islam in Indonesia would have still better chance to grow and flourish. In fact, some Muslim optimists are beginning to see that what is happening in the New Order Indonesia is a process of further Islamization or, rather, a "Santrinization" of the Indonesian elite who happen to come from *Abangan/Priyayi* cultural variants and therefore have had better education in modern terms that the *Santri* because of the colonial policy. One of the indices for this is the attitude of *Golkar,* the political organization of the governing Army. While in the general elections of 1971 *Golkar* pursued an anti-Islamic policy and actively cultivated the support of the Abangan people through the devotees of *Aliran Kepercayaan* (Javanese mysticism), by 1977 *Golkar* recruited many local

Muslim leaders into its camp, and later was forced to a "me-too" position on the religious questions vis-a-vis the Islamic PPP. (Liddle, 1978, *op. cit.*)

In spite of all these promising developments for Islam in Indonesia, one should always be reminded, however, that it is very improbable that the New Order will foster political Islam. The Government's policy following a kind of improved version of Snouck Hurgronje's advice to Dutch colonial government — tolerating, even encouraging, religious aspects of Islam, but curbing any indication of its political revival — has always been there and too obvious to be wished away. The best that Islam could have within the New Order Indonesian political system is to be an inferior co-holder of power. Except that, "The Crescent is too big to become anybody's innocuous satellite, a mere Sputnik" (Wertheim, *op. cit.*), culturally, or even politically, in Indonesia.

One can see, therefore, the position of Islam in Indonesia in terms of challenges and opportunities. It is of course very much up to the creativity of the Muslims themselves to be able to meet the challenges and to benefit from the opportunities. Looking back to the revolutionary period of the nation, one could find that the Muslims, under the leadership of the *Masyumi* intellectuals, have demonstrated their aptitude to cope with Indonesian social changes. "*Masyumi* was the Islamic party considered best able to deal with the secular problems usually associated with socio-economic development. Its religious and philosophical ethos was development-oriented." (Samson, *op. cit.*) Perhaps all that Indonesian Islam needs today for a resurgence is for the modernists like *Masyumi* intellectuals and others to undertake a general revision of their modernism and to rework it, getting rid of the neo-conservatism that has begun to tangle their creativity. After all most Indonesians look on themselves as true Muslims, and have chosen Islam as their religion, whatever their differences on other issues may be.

Bibliography

Bachtiar, Harsja W., *The Function of Some Institutional Arrangements in the Formation of the Indonesian Nation.* Jakarta:

Universitas Indonesia, Berita Antropologi, Terbitan Khusus No. 2, 1972.

Benda, Harry J., *Continuity and Change in Southeast Asia*. New Haven: Yale University Southeast Asian Studies, 1972.

Crouch, Harold, *The Army and Politics in Indonesia*. Ithaca: Cornell University Press, 1978.

Federspiel, Howard H., "The Military and Islam in Sukarno's Indonesia", *Pacific Affairs*, Vol. 46, No. 3, (Fall 1973).

Feith, Herbert, and Castles, Lance, *Indonesian Political Thinking, 1945-1965*. Ithaca: Cornell University Press, 1970.

Geertz, Clifford, *The Religion of Java*. Glencoe, Ill.: Free Press, 1960.

Henderson, John W., et. al., *Area Handbook for Indonesia*. Washington D.C.: The American University, Foreign Area Studies, 1970.

Kahane, Reuven, *The Problem of Political Legitimacy in an Antagonistic Society: The Indonesian Case*. London: Sage Publication, 1973.

Kahin, George McT., *Nationalism and Revolution in Indonesia*. Ithaca: Cornell paperbacks, 1970.

Lee, Oey Hong, *Indonesia Facing the 1980's: a Political Analysis*. Hull, England: Europress, 1979.

Lev, Daniel S., "Judicial Authority and the Struggle for an Indonesian Rechsstaat", *Law and Society Review*, Vol. 13, No. 1 (Fall 1978).

Liddle, R. William, *Cultural and Class Politics in New Order Indonesia*. Athens: Ohio University, Institute of Southeast Asian Studies, n. d.

_____ , "The 1977 Indonesian Election and New Order Legitimacy", *Southeast Asian Affairs*, 1978.

Noer, Deliar, *The Modernist Muslim Movement in Indonesia*. Singapore: Oxford University Press, 1973.

Samson, Allan A., "Islam in Indonesian Politics", *Asian Survey*, Vol. VIII, pp. 1001-1017.

Soedjatmoko, "Indonesia: Problems and Opportunities", *Austrialian Outlook*, December 1967.

Vandenbosch, Amry, *The Dutch East Indies*. Berkeley: University of California Press, 1942.

van der Kroef, Justus M., *Indonesia Since Sukarno.* Singapore: Asia Pacific Press, 1971.

Ward, Kenneth, "Some Comments on Islamic Reactions to Recent Development in Indonesia", *Review of Indonesian and Malaysian Affairs,* Vol. 2, No. April-June, 1968.

Wertheim, W. F., "Islam Before and After the Elections", in *Indonesia After the 1971 Elections,* ed. Oey Hong Lee. London: Oxford University Press, 1974.

XXIII

ISLAM IN THE PHILIPPINES

William L. Yam, S.J.

> Tucked away in the southern extremity of the Philippines archipelago the islands of Mindanao, the Sulu group and Palawan offered ideal sancuary for Muslims who resisted assimilation by Spaniards since the sixteenth century and subsequently by Westernized Filipinos of the northern islands. Yet they had to struggle hard to preserve their religion and the integrity of their traditions, including their political system. In recent years this struggle has intensified to the point of becoming open warfare against the Manila government. The apparent links between the "Moros" of Philippines and Middle Eastern Muslims would make us wonder what, if any, is the influence of the so-called Islamic revival on the current Moro militancy. Brother Yam here addresses this question and provides an historical sketch of the Muslim minority problem in the Philippines.
>
> William L. Yam, S.J. who has lengthy experience in the Philippines is currently working on a doctorate in political science at Northern Illinois University.

In late October, 1972, a month after Philippine President Ferdinand Marcos declared martial law in the country, the Moro National Liberation Front declared open war on the national government by attacking Marawi City in Lanao del Sur Province on the island of Mindanao. Shortly thereafter, fighting broke out in other parts of Lanao, North Cotabato, Zamboanga, and Sulu provinces. Suddenly, the world, and most non-Muslim Filipinos for that matter, were made aware that there was a Moro problem. For well nigh fifty years, after the Moro wars and since the new American military government replaced Spanish authority over the archipelago, the non-Muslim

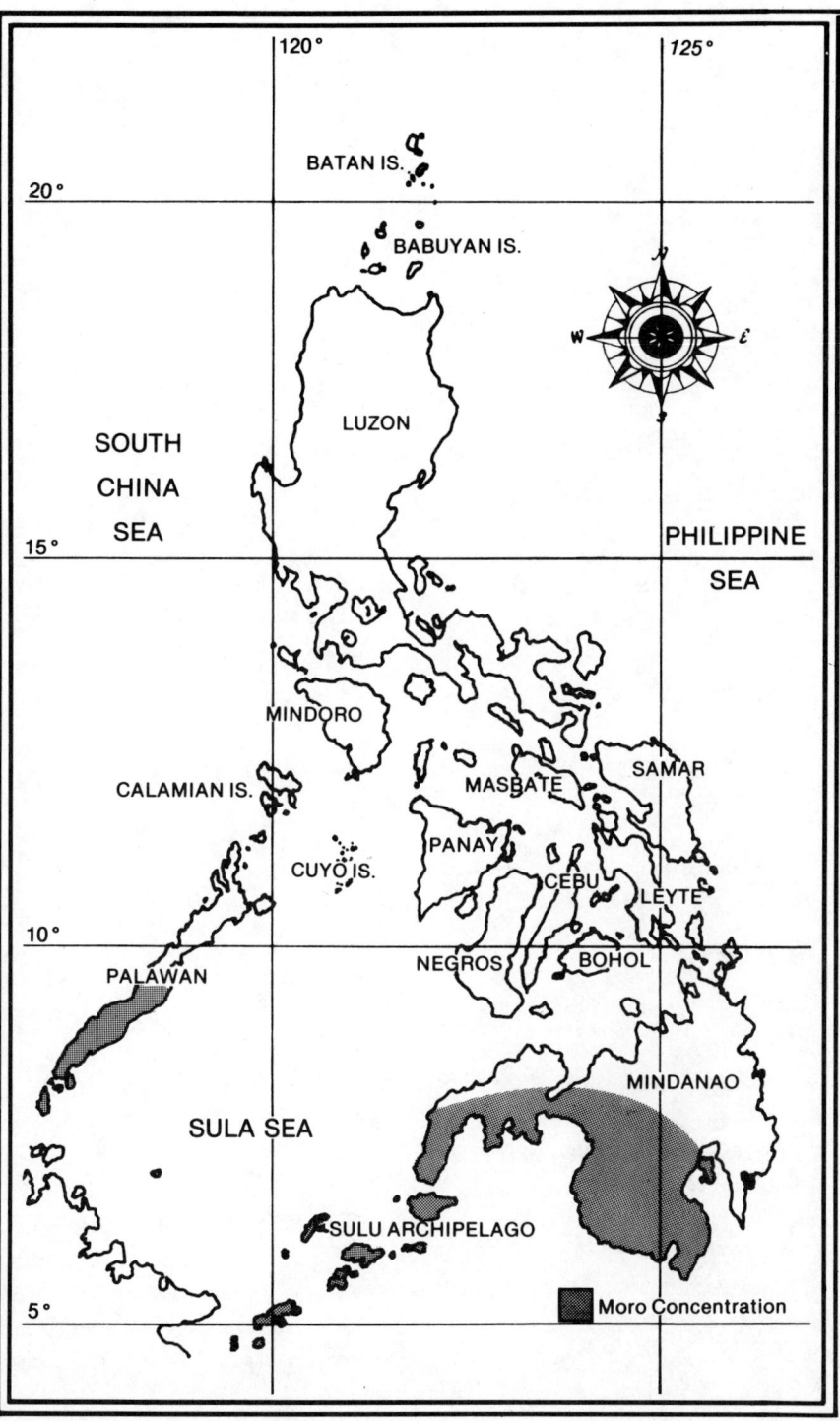

population (the Philippine population does not consist of just Christians and Muslims as popular literature would have us believe) had been blissfully ignorant of the festering problem in the south. To be sure, it was not the lack of locally published material that accounted for this ignorance. There had been numerous studies of a sociological nature and numerous reports of armed conflicts between Muslim and Christian settlers, and constabulary skirmishes with "outlaws" in southern Mindanao. But such is human nature that people do not pay attention to others unless and until a big problem arises between them.

Islam Comes to Southeast Asia

In the island world of Southeast Asia, then as now, the sea was the highway. Arab traders dominated this highway from the late 7th century until the intrusion of the West, when Vasco da Gama rounded the Cape of Good Hope in the 15th century. At every trading center on the Southeast Asian littoral and island world, they established trading settlements because a roundtrip voyage normally took a whole year, relying on the direction of the monsoon winds and having to sit out the typhoon season in between the changes of wind directions. By the end of the 8th century, Arab traders had reached as far east as the southern Chinese port of Canton and established a flourishing settlement there.

Generally, the Islamization of the Southeast Asian peoples followed a similar pattern. When a culturally and economically developed people interact with a less developed people, it is generally the less developed people who take and follow the model of the more developed. In this way, the acceptance of Islam was largely a painless process in Southeast Asia. Being more sophisticated in commerce and armaments, the Arab traders, some of whom stayed permanently in the trading centers, did not find it difficult to command the respect of the animistic aborigines. They then taught their religion to the aborigines, married into their ruling families, and gradually took over the local chiefdoms. From then on, the spread of the faith and the establishment of Islamic institutions became a matter of time.

The establishment of the first sultanate in the southern Philippines in the late 15th century (now the City of Jolo in the Sulu Islands) followed the above general pattern. It was the first organized government in the Philippines. The authority structure placed the sultan at the head of a group of datus (chieftains of clans) and by virtue of his armed might and shrewd alliances (usually reinforced by marriages) he was able to maintain his power. The sultan and datus were both political and religious leaders, and the relationships among the sultan, datus, and their people — the whole web of duties, prerogatives, rights, and obligations — were codified in the *Tariq*. It was a clear and specific set of rules which was highly conducive to the maintenance of stability of the society. However, as in all human organizations, rivalry for power among the leaders prevented the rise of any effective challenge to Western intruders. Except for short periods in the early 17th and 18th centuries, when they were able to mount fierce raids on the northern Spanish-held islands, the Muslims of the south could only hold off subjugation by the Spanish conquistadores from the north. To their credit, the Philippine Muslims were able to accomplish up to the 20th century what none of their Southeast Asian brethren could do, that is, maintain their freedom from the colonizers. In the early 20th century, the weakness created by internal political rivalry finally cost them their freedom when they were confronted by American power.

It should be noted that the expansion of Islam was gradual, beginning from centers in the Malay peninsula and Sumatra and island-hopping to the southern Philippines. It took over seven centuries of expansion before the first sultanate was established in Jolo, but this very slowness assured solid acceptance of transplanted customs, religion, political structures, and the firming of familial ties among distant ruling elites scattered around the island world. And, this process gave a large part of the Southeast Asian island world a strong community of identity, the divisive policies of Western colonial regimes notwithstanding. If, in 1970, 65% of the southern Philippine Muslims could identify themselves as "Muslims" rather than as "Filipinos," there could be no quarrel as to the strength of Islam as an integrating force in that region.

The Spanish Regime

Significantly, Islam met the same antagonist in its easternmost expansion as in its westernmost expansion: Spanish Catholicism. Both being militantly aggressive religions, it was no surprise that the meeting was an explosive one. And, out of this three-hundred-year war came the hatred and prejudices which have plagued the Philippine polity to this day. In Spanish histories, these wars were always referred to as *guerras piraticas*, punitive expeditions to avenge Muslim slave raids on the Christian north. For the Muslims, this three-hundred-year war was a matter of preserving their religion, which involved their very way of life, defending their land and their traditional freedom to rove the seas and trade with relatives and friends to the south. Moreover, the Spaniards used mostly northern Christianized natives to do their fighting for them, and this established the bad blood between southern Muslim Malays and northern Christian Malays. From this three-hundred-year conflict rose the stereotyped epithets on both sides which still perpetuate the division. To the Christian, "Moro" was a pejorative label. It meant cunning, cruel, treacherous, pirate, slaver. To the Muslim, "Christian" meant coward, cheat, bully, landgrabber, one who would destroy Islam if he could. In the 1950's, Filipino Muslims reacted strongly to the use of this Spanish label on themselves because of its derogatory connotations, and they preferred to be called Muslim Filipinos or just plain Muslims. But after the escalation of the fighting in the early 1970's, the term "Moro" returned to acceptable use on both sides of the conflict. In fact, the main group of Muslim rebels called itself the Moro National Liberation Front and its military arm the Bangsa Moro Army. The rationale behind this new usage is more political in intent than evidence of more self-awareness and self-confidence on the part of the Muslims, although this may be one of the reasons for the change in usage.

After three hundred years of warfare on land and sea, to the day they relinquished the archipelago to the Americans, the Spaniards could accomplish nothing more than establishing one stronghold in Moroland and extracting a grudging acknowledgement of Spanish sovereignty from the sultan of Jolo and the datus of southern Mindanao. They were never able to impose actual rule over the Muslims; as a result Philippine Muslim society did not suffer the wrenching of their social fabric as had happened in the north.

The American Regime

The United States acquired the Philippines from Spain after the Spanish-American War. And forthwith, President William McKinley sent soldiers, bureaucrats, public school teachers, and volunteers, to develop, civilize, educate, and train in the science of self-government all those benighted "Little brown brothers" across the Pacific. It seems that then as now, American governments could not appreciate socio-political systems different from their own. They came to Moroland with their *mission civilisatrice* and ran right into the "Moro problem". Little did they realize that to this group of dark-skinned, kris-carrying sea rovers, they were the "American problem." The Americans, in keeping with their experience with the pacification of the Native Americans back home, made treaties with the Sultan of Jolo, who was by then a mere shadow of his powerful forebears, and then they were perplexed and angered at the sultan for the noncompliance and defiance of the datus. Moreover, the Americans themselves undermined what little authority the sultan had by often dealing directly with the datus. The result was a needless spilling of blood, mostly Moro blood. The outcome was never in doubt. Even then, at the turn of the century, Chairman Mao's dictum was borne out, that political power comes out of the barrel of a gun. The Moros were finally "pacified."

To a certain extent, the Americans saw the differences and potential problems between the Muslims and the northern Christian Filipinos. So at the beginning of their regime, they kept the Moro Provinces separate from the civil government they were then establishing in the rest of the country. They made a wise decision in assigning Najeeb Saleeby to deal with the Muslims in his capacity as Assistant Chief of the Bureau of Non-Christian Tribes and as the Agent for Moro Affairs. Saleeby was a Syrian by birth, a Muslim, and came to the Philippines in 1900 as a surgeon in the U.S. Army. The American intent was to integrate as soon as possible the governance of the Muslim areas of Mindanao and Sulu into the civil government of the Philippines as a necessary preparation for independence. The Moros were allowed to regulate their internal affairs, permitted their traditional free trade, and were not taxed. However, integration into the American-sponsored government meant to the Moros the imposition of a Christian government with all its attendant Christian values. In short, it meant the destruction of their whole way of life which was built around Islam. Consequently, while they did not have the power to prevent the imposition of the external forms of the national government, they rejected the substance of those forms.

Furthermore, aside from their leaders' opposition to accepting the modernization services of the government, Muslims found the government's avowed integrationist goals repulsive. Integration both in its political and social aspects was and is abhorrent to the Muslim, for the Muslim does not see any distinction between political and religious power, much less conceive of social interaction devoid of religious implications. To be integrated was tantamount to being assimilated and, hence, cutting one's self off from the *Dar ul-Islam*. For this reason, anything that the government did was regarded with deep suspicion. And, for all the local government structures created in Moroland and the respectable number of Muslims appointed or elected to man these structures, integration did not penetrate much below what one could see on the surface.

And so, the Muslims entered the 20th century and the new political arrangement disadvantaged both by the new colonial rulers and, worse, by their own traditional rulers. They lived under laws which they were not aware of. Further, their leaders did not bother to educate them about these laws. And, when they ran afoul of the unknown laws, they were confused, then angered. After trading with their relatives and fellow Muslims to the south for centuries, suddenly navy cutters intercepted their *vintas* (slim and swift outriggers with colorful square sails) and they were arrested for the crime of smuggling, a concept they neither understood nor had even heard of. When they traded and made a profit, they now not only had to give the datu a cut but the government as well. But, the biggest surprise of all came when the land they lived on, and which they assumed they possessed, could now be expropriated by the government at any time. Traditionally, they knew that their land, though theoretically belonging to the datu, was theirs to live on and work on as long as they wanted. But now, a distant Christian power owned their land, rivers and forests and could take them all away at any time.

The traditional leaders, now garbed as mayors and governors and congressmen, were in part to blame for the disadvantages of the Muslim people. They failed to educate their people about the new system in which they now lived. And, by far the most serious problem which arose from this ignorance of the new system was the land problem. It began in the mid-1930's when Mindanao was billed as the "land of promise."

With the population in the upper two-thirds of the archipelago rapidly increasing and its natural resources declining, Mindanao was seen as the solution. It was sparsely populated, had vast virgin forests, and untapped mineral resources. To relieve the population pressure in the north, the government encouraged migration southward and began establishing settlements for poor northern peasants in the fertile Cotabato valley in the late 1930's, and leasing huge tracts for commercial agricultural enterprises. After the interruption of World War II, the projects were resumed in the early 1950's. In President Ramon Magsaysay's well-known solution to the Huk problem of Central Luzon, one of the key incentives he offered to Huks to surrender was a new beginning in life on a parcel of land in

Mindanao. And so, more than anything else, this competition for land perpetuated and heightened the Muslim-Christian animosity and heaped fuel on the fire until it blew up in the early 1970's.

Post-World War II Developments

After World War II, a new generation of Muslims was growing up, and Islam in the southern Philippines was experiencing a renaissance. Young Arab volunteers from the Middle East were coming in to teach both the religion and the Arabic language. More and better madrasah (Koranic) schools were founded, new and more impressive mosques were built and, generally, Muslims showed the effects of the revival in more regular observance of religious practices, the creation of Islamic clubs and organizations, and many young men departed for studies at Middle Eastern schools, notably at the University of Cairo. What all this meant was that besides having a religious revival in the country, Muslims were also being drawn outward and closer to the larger Islamic community abroad. Thus the conditions for secessionist thinking were laid. It would be out of this postwar generation that the present crop of young Moro National Liberation Front (hereafter the MNLF) members and adherents would be drawn.

In 1962, when talks were underway to make Sabah (in North Borneo) a state of the Malaysian Federation, President Diosdado Macapagal of the Philippines formally laid claim to Sabah as a part of the Philippines on the strength of its formerly having been a territory of the now defunct Sulu sultanate. Nothing came of this claim at the time. When Ferdinand Marcos became president in 1966, he decided to do something about it. In 1968, part of Marcos' plan was the creation of a Filipino Muslim commando force to infiltrate Sabah, and this after he had re-established diplomatic relations (broken off by President Macapagal earlier) with Malaysia and joined her in forming ASEAN in 1967. But something went wrong during the training of the secret force on Corregidor Island and the Muslim recruits mutinied. They were massacred to a man by their officers. Conflicting reports clouded the truth of the incident. But certainly, to the Muslims, it was a clear message that the government was insensitive to Muslim lives and was using them against fellow Muslims to the south. MNLF leaders have cited this as one of the causes of the MNLF's formation. Still, no rebellion broke out immediately following the incident.

But, right after this Corregidor incident, a prominent Muslim of Cotabato announced the formation of the Muslim Independence

Movement (MIM). But since the MIM did not have the strength to pose any threat to the government, no action was taken against it. Meanwhile, other articulate regional Muslim organizations surfaced: the Darul Islam in Cotabato, the Lanalip in Lanao, the Muslim Brotherhood in Jolo, and the Green Guards in Zamboanga. By March, 1970, newspaper reports revealed that young Muslim Filipinos were being trained in Malaysia. This was confirmed in later interviews with MNLF leaders during the war. In any case, Malaysia was only returning Marco's favor.

Many of these young trainees at the Malaysian camp were under the patronage of an older generation Muslim congressman, Lucman Rascid, who was well-connected with Islamic leaders abroad. It was through Lucman that the younger and more ideological generation made contact with such generous supporters of liberation movements as Col. Moammer Qaddafi of Libya. With the patronage of older politicians as a cover, the younger generation organized a movement of their own that was decidedly more radical. And, when they had gathered enough strength, they would eventually break off and denounce their former patrons as part of the oppressors of the people.

This younger generation who were to become the MNLF leadership are highly educated young men with degrees from Manila universities and colleges. Among them are a lawyer, a municipal judge, an elected vice-mayor, and a college instructor. They run a sophisticated political organization with specialized functional bureaus and a military force estimated at about 20,000 men, led by allegedly Malaysian-trained leaders who are experts at guerrilla warfare. And, the MNLF is said to be supported in part by Libyan arms and funds channeled through Sabah.

Ideologically, the MNLF has tried to walk a tight rope. On the one hand it must maintain a strong Islamic character in order to retain the support of the Muslim world. And so, it must reject and deny any semblance of a link with the northern Maoist New People's Army (NPA), a link which government propagandists tried hard to establish. On the other hand, the MNLF recognizes the fact that they must not overemphasize their Islamic character so as not to alienate unduly non-Muslims who now outnumber the Muslims in their own homeland. In interviews, various MNLF leaders make an effort to emphasize the non-religious image of the organization and of the conflict itself, and the inclusion of non-Muslim inhabitants of Mindanao in their definition of the term "Moro." But definitely, the MNLF's Islamic character has been an asset. Their issues have been and still are before the International Islamic Council, and pressure, especially the threat of oil supply cut-off, has been used effectively on Marcos to restrain him from seeking a purely military solution by ordering an all-out offensive by his better equipped forces.

In the long continuing war, the MNLF has had its troubles also. It has been hard hit by defections of high ranking field commanders as well as political leaders, "returnees" as they are called by the government-controlled press in Manila. And, as with the Palestinian cause, the Islamic Council has been long on threats and urgings to the Marcos regime but short on action. In the smaller Islamic world of Southeast Asia, there has been a reconciliation among state leaders who see the need for more solidarity among ASEAN countries in the face of a gradual U.S. pullout from the area. Marcos, for his part, has tried to lessen the dissatisfaction in the south by pushing development projects in the area. He also set up two semi-autonomous regions there in July, 1979, with their own regional legislative assemblies and executive councils of limited powers and conducted elections for these.

However long the MNLF war may last and whatever the outcome, in the end there will still be the problem of political integration to be solved. This is a problem common to all new countries born of former European colonies, simply because their boundaries as a juridical entity were drawn for the convenience and benefit of their former colonial masters without regard for ethnic, linguistic, or religious realities. To overcome the centrifugal tendencies of such an artificial entity, these states must integrate their peoples in a process vaguely called "nation-building."

Political integration requires, among other things, a basic uniformity of political structure and laws within a state. The people should hold some uniformity of values which bestow legitimacy on the political structure and the laws. Then, there must be a sense of identity with the body thus created by the structure and laws. These are the requirements on the part of the people being integrated. But if political integration is to be firm, the state must also reciprocate with rewards. There must be reciprocity, and the reciprocity (sometimes regardless of the reality) must be perceived as satisfactory by both sides.

In the case of the Muslim Filipinos, the government has been attempting to achieve a uniformity of political structure and laws since the American regime. And, while it is true that some degree of uniformity of structure and laws has been achieved, this uniformity has been more a surface dressing than a reality accepted by the

Muslims. For the Muslims, their very identity and way of life as a people are derived from Islam and its legal system. It was Islamic law which bestowed legitimacy on the authority and institutions which held their society together. If the Muslims have acquiesced to the national laws, it is because they are powerless to do anything about it. So they have done what most helpless minorities do — superficially accept the imposed laws and institutions, pay lip service to them, and go about holding on to their traditional way of life quietly, avoiding open confrontation if they can help it.

This issue of political identity poses some rather interesting questions. As mentioned earlier, in an extensive survey carried out by a private foundation in 1970, at a time when Islamic consciousness was high and anti-government feeling was approaching the exploding point, 65% of the Muslim population queried replied that they identified themselves as "Muslims" and only 29% would call themselves "Filipinos." On the other hand, when asked about their attitude towards secession, 55% expressed a definite preference for remaining within Philippine polity while only 21% definitely preferred secession. This is a hopeful sign for the eventual political integration of the Muslims into Philippine polity: in spite of the strong conflict over values and political structures, many are willing to remain within the state called the Philippine Republic.

A contributory factor to this willingness to stay within the Philippine polity may have been brought about also by the looseness of the political integration process thus far. Even when the early American regime imposed a uniformity of laws on the Muslims, the formal organization was merely superimposed on the communities, and their different customs and institutions were recognized, and an effort was made to respect them. Also noted in the survey mentioned earlier, the negative attitude towards the national government was directed not so much against the form of government *per se*, but rather against those in power. If they have now come to accept the system, it may be that their leaders' ability to participate in and use the system to reinforce their traditional position of power showed the common people that acceptance of the system was not so bad after all. And, from the 1930's on, Muslims have been elected as local and national officials such as mayors, congressmen, and senators.

To the young MNLF leadership, then, exclusion from the political system could not be a credible complaint. Neither could they truly say that integration was threatening to destroy their particular way of life, as enforcement of a uniform code of law had not really been complete in the south. Even so, to counter the complaint against "Christian" law, Marcos has taken steps to give a little bit of legislative power, though directly controlled by himself, to the assemblies of the newly created autonomous regions. Little as this may be, still, it gives hope that Philippine law as applied to the Muslim areas may be gradually adjusted in matters touching on Islamic beliefs.

Integration, then, cannot be just a change of titles of the traditional leaders: from sultan to governor or from datu to ward heeler. Effective, beneficial, and genuine, political integration requires that the people accept and be educated in the "rules of the game," rules which up to now remain strange and unfamiliar, but which nonetheless supercede their own traditional rules. This genuine integration is what the MNLF seems to mean in its description of "autonomy." They want a more selfless leadership and a more equitable share of the resources produced by a land traditionally theirs and the right to control these resources. But within the national government, which sees subversion in any demand for rights or questioning of its prerogatives to complete control, the MNLF's attainment of its aspirations must be remote indeed, especially when international Islamic support remains mere words and opposition from other factions within one's own people threatens betrayal of the cause.

The predicament of the Muslims in the southern Philippines is by no means unique. It is a problem shared by many minority peoples in the new states in Asia and Africa. It is unfortunate that in their rush for development most new states have paid scant attention to minority aspirations, be they ethnic, cultural, or religious. In the Philippines, this problem reaches back through four-and-a-half centuries of politico-religious conflict and mutual ignorance. Today (Fall 1980) the conflict is still nowhere near a solution, after thousands have lost their lives and thousands more rendered homeless refugees. And, because the Muslims in the Philippines are a transnational minority, the repercussions of the strife affect not just the Philippines' internal security but also its economic and political relations with Southeast Asian neighbors (Malaysia and Indonesia) as well as the distant oil-rich Middle Eastern states. Meanwhile, amid news reports of ambushes and air strikes and body counts, the people of southern Mindanao, both Muslim and Christian, must steel themselves for more suffering.

Bibliography

Asiaweek (Hong Kong), September 1972 —

Far Eastern Economic Review (Hong Kong), September 1972 —

Filipinas Foundation, *An Anatomy of Philippine Muslim Affairs.* Manila, 1971.

Gowing, Peter G., *Mandate in Moroland.* Quezon City: Philippine College for Advanced Studies, University of the Philippines, 1977.

Human Relations Area Files, *The Philippines.* New Haven, Conn., 1955. 5 vols. ("The Moros", vol. 4, pt. 5, pp. 1729-1775).

Laquian, Aprodicio A., "The Political Integration of Muslim Filipinos," *Philippine Journal of Public Administration,* XIII, 4 (October 1969) 357-380.

Majul, Cesar Adib, *Muslims in the Philippines.* Quezon City: Asian Studies Center, University of the Philippines Press, 1973.

Noble, Lela Garner, "The Moro National Liberation Front in the Philippines," *Pacific Affairs,* XLIX, 3 (Fall 1976) 405-424.

XXIV

WOMEN IN ISLAM: YESTERDAY AND TODAY

Darlene May

One of the most serious grievances Shiite Muslim leaders cited against the Shah of Iran was his liberation of women. Understandably enough, then, one of the most visible signs of the return of true Islam to Iran after the revolution was the veiling of the women. Yet, uncharacteristic of Islamic tradition — so at least thought some Western observers — women were/are playing important roles in the revolution in Iran. Apparent discrepancies such as this, the real differences that are observed in the status of women between various Muslim societies and the continuing debate in many Muslim countries over what women's role should be in the modern society cause us to ask questions such as: What is the role of women from the point of view of orthodox Muslim theology and Islamic law? What role did women play historically in Islamic societies? Should Islamic theology and law be reinterpreted in view of the imperatives of our time? Is there a new role for women emerging in the Islamic world and if so what is it? Professor May addresses these questions.

Darlene May, who has had extensive research experience in the Middle East, is currently professor of Arabic Language and Islamic Studies in the Department of International Studies at Southwestern University at Memphis. As a convert to Islam, she is able to offer views from inside the Islamic community.

Scarcely half a century ago a husband-and-wife team of missionaries assigned to serve the United Church of Christ in Arabia and Egypt penned a damning indictment of the status of women in Islamic society:

> "No one can study the tragic story of women under the Moslem faith without an earnest longing and prayer that something adequate may be done.... We think with pity and sorrow of the veiled women of Islam."[1]

Furthermore, these two authors painted a grim and entirely unwholesome picture of the home life to which the woman was relegated and labeled its low ideals as one of the chief causes of the moral decay prevalent in Islam:

> "Sound family life is impossible. The children grow up in a poisonous atmosphere of intrigue, fleshly lust, bad language, and shameless licentiousness. They are polluted from youth up."[2]

Finally, they attributed this ignominious position of the Muslim woman, not to some accident of her society, but to "the doctrine propounded in the Koran, of an essential inferiority of woman to man."[3]

Indeed, it has been only recently that Western observers have begun to acknowledge that "the Koran by and large improved the position of Arabian women" and that the picture of these women's family life "was not as bad as Westerners often used to paint it."[4] Nonetheless, the status and role of the woman in Muslim society remains one of the most grossly misunderstood and misrepresented aspects of Islam in the West. In fact, it is undoubtedly the source of much of the prejudice against Islam that is current in the non-Muslim world today. It is important, therefore, to know the Muslim woman for what she truly is!

I. The Traditional Status of Woman according to Islamic Theology

The traditional Islamic view of woman is, of course, firmly rooted in the two basic sources of Islamic theology: the Quran, which Muslims hold to be the Word of God exactly as it was revealed to the Prophet Muhammad; and the *Sunnah*, the collection of *Hadiths*, or inspired sayings uttered by the Prophet, as well as the actions performed by him. Within Islamic theology there can be found several sets of beliefs about the nature of woman which establish her status in Islamic tradition and contribute towards determining her role in Islamic society.

First of all, man and woman alike were created by God, Who made them full and equal partners in the process of procreation.

> "O mankind! Be careful of your duty to your Lord Who created you from a single soul and from it created its mate and from them twain hath spread abroad a multitude of men and women." (Quran IV:1)[5]

> "O mankind! Lo! We have created you male and female, and have made you nations and tribes that ye may know one another."
> (Quran XLIX: 13)

Thus, both man and woman are absolutely essential for life, and both stand equally before God.

> "All people are equal, as equal as the teeth of a comb. There is no claim of merit of an Arab over a non-Arab, or of a white over a black person, or of a male over a female. Only God-fearing people merit a preference with God." *(Hadith)*

In the Quran woman is not regarded as the handmaiden of the devil, the seed of evil, the seductive cause of man's downfall. She did not play the primary role in committing the First Sin; indeed, Adam bears the greater responsibility for their eviction from the Garden.

> "And verily We made a covenant of old with Adam, but he forgot, and We found no constancy in him. And when We said unto the angels: Fall prostrate before Adam, they fell prostrate (all) save Iblis; he refused. Therefor We said: O Adam! This is an enemy unto thee and unto thy wife, so let him not drive you both out of the Garden so that thou come to toil. . . . But the Devil whispered to him, saying: O Adam! Shall I show thee the tree of immortality and power that wasteth not away? Then they twain ate thereof, so that their shame became apparent unto them, and they began to hide by heaping on themselves some of the leaves of the Garden." (Quran XX: 115-121)[6]

Both Adam and Eve sinned by disobeying God, and both repented and were forgiven. Succeeding generations of their children have not been made to pay for their sin; womankind has not been singled out to suffer the curse of regular menstrual cycles, the discomforts of pregnancy, and the pain of childbirth as punishments for this First Sin. Rather, these are all natural biological phenomena experienced by the females of many of the species of mammals created by God.

Second, man and woman share certain physiological and psychological characteristics; therefore, they share certain rights and responsibilities. Before the *Shari'a*, the Revealed Law of Islam, they are equally responsible and independent agents who are equally required to observe the ordinances of this Law. Likewise, the Law entitles them to equal enjoyment of human dignity, respectful treatment, free choice, freedom of expression, and freedom of action — whether it be to learn, teach, work, preach, contract, possess, inherit, trade, or otherwise act in daily life. Man and woman receive identical punishments for failing to carry out their obligations and identical rewards for fulfilling them and performing good deeds.

> "Lo! I suffer not the work of any worker, male or female, to be lost." (Quran III: 195)

> "Lo! men who surrender unto God, and women who surrender, and men who believe and women who believe, and men who obey and women who obey, and men who speak the truth and women who speak the truth, and men who persevere (in righteousness) and women who persevere, and men who are humble and women who are humble, and men who give alms and women who give alms, and men who fast and women who fast, and men who guard their modesty and women who guard (their modesty), and men who remember God much and women who remember — God hath prepared for them forgiveness and a vast reward." (Quran XXXIII: 35)

Third, man and woman each has certain physiological and psychological characteristics that the other does not have. Indeed, God deliberately made man and woman different so that they would complement each other.

> "He created for you mates from your selves that ye might find rest in them, and He ordained between you love and mercy." (Quran XXX: 21)

Accordingly, God has warned that no one should tamper with His creation and the natural laws under which it operates.

> "Cursed are the men who behave effeminately; and cursed are the women who behave in a masculine manner." *(Hadith)*

Thus, in those areas of life where sexual characteristics have nothing to do with one's status and function, man and woman can enjoy the same status and perform the same function. For example, both can be teachers, and both can buy and sell property. However, in those areas of life where sexual characteristics do affect one's status and function, man and woman cannot share the same status and function. Therefore, because sexual differences have a bearing upon the structure of the family, husband and wife cannot play identical roles. In fact, whenever sexual differences are relevant to role-playing, "men are a degree above women" (Quran II: 228).

> "Men are in charge of women, because God hath made the one of them to excel the other, and because they spend of their property (for the support of women). So good women are the obedient...." (Quran IV: 34)

This does not in any way imply that the wife is inferior to her husband in status and function, for the degree given to man is, as we have already seen, certainly not one based on character, intelligence, virtue, or spirituality. Neither is it a position of supremacy that authorizes him to dominate and oppress the woman. Rather, it simply indicates that man has been entrusted with some responsibilities and rights that do not pertain to woman, and vice versa. Moreover, the rights and obligations of both are proportionate. Accordingly, since man bears more responsibilities than woman in certain areas of life, as a compensation, he has additional rights in those areas, e.g., additional authority over certain family matters. Woman, on the other hand, has been granted certain rights and exemptions from obligations which man has not in order to compensate for her having to submit to man's authority. Man and woman thus enjoy a complementary and reciprocal relationship.

II. The Traditional Role of Woman According to Islamic Law

Being multi-faceted, the traditional Islamic view of woman enables her to play a variety of roles during her lifetime. Each of these roles engenders its own particular set of rights and obligations that apply to every woman who undertakes that role. All these rights and obligations are spelled out in great detail among the ordinances of the *Shari'a*, the Revealed Law, which is derived from the principles and precepts mentioned in the Quran and preserved in the *Sunnah* of the Prophet. The Law thus regulates not only the actions of woman as she plays a certain role but also the actions of all the persons with whom she interacts while playing that role. The roles which are legally open to the Muslim woman through the course of her lifetime can neatly be placed into three categories: the roles which she plays as a member of mankind, the roles which she plays as a member of her family, and the roles which she plays as a member of her society.

A. *Woman as a Member of Mankind*

Because woman is a human being, a part of God's Creation, the first role to which she must devote herself is that of Servant of God. Indeed, this is the primary role which she must exercise throughout her lifetime, from the precise moment of her birth to the very moment of her death — and beyond until the end of time. As Servant of God, woman owes God certain rights. Chief among these are the Five Pillars of the Faith, the major ritual acts of worship which include reciting the Testimony of Faith, performing the five daily prayers, keeping the fast of *Ramadan*, paying the annual legal alms, and making a pilgrimage to Mecca. While it is incumbent upon every Muslim — male and female — to observe all of these Pillars, woman, because of her particular characteristics, enjoys certain exemptions from them that man does not.

(1) Foremost of the Pillars, of course, is bearing witness to the oneness of God by reciting the Testimony of Faith: "There is no god but God." A disavowal of God's oneness amounts to apostatizing from the Faith. According to the Law, the penalty for such apostasy is death. Female apostates, however, have customarily received less severe punishment, and, indeed, the Hanifite school of law declares that only men shall be put to death for apostasy.

(2) Second in importance is the ritual prayer, which all Muslims must perform at five specified times during the course of each day.

> "And the believers, men and women, are protecting friends one of another . . . and they perform the ritual prayer and they pay the legal alms, and they obey God and His Messenger." (Quran IX: 71)

Woman is, however, totally exempt from these prayers for a maximum of ten days during menstruation and a maximum of forty days after childbirth and is not required to make up these legitimately omitted prayers at a later time. Furthermore, while it is obligatory for men to perform the Friday noon prayer in congregation at a mosque, it is permissible for women to perform this prayer at home since attending the mosque service may be a hardship for any woman whose presence is necessary at home, e.g., to care for a small child or an ailing relative. When females do choose to exercise their option to pray in public, they must pray together in the last lines of the congregation behind the front ranks of adult males and the intermediate ranks of male children. This system of ranks is not designed to demonstrate a hierarchy of superiority and inferiority. Rather, it is designed to allow a maximum degree of spiritual concentration by eliminating visual and tactile distractions of a sexual nature. Because of this system as well as the stipulation that men are to be in charge of women in certain settings, a woman is never permitted to lead a mixed congregation of males and females in prayer.

(3) All Muslims are enjoined to keep a total fast from food and drink during the period from dawn to sunset each day throughout the month of *Ramadan*, the holy month during which God revealed the Quran to His Prophet Muhammad.

> "O ye who believe! Fasting is prescribed for you. . . ." (Quran II: 183).

However, women who are menstruating or in confinement after childbirth are not permitted to fast, just as both males and females who are ill, on a journey, or in combat are not. The reason for this exemption is that

> "God desireth for you ease; He desireth not hardship for you."
> (Quran II: 185)

Likewise, pregnant women may elect not to fast if fasting would present a hardship for them. In all these cases, each day missed is made up later in the year at a more convenient time.

(4) Men and women alike bear the duty of paying legal alms, which is a kind of welfare tax levied annually to help relieve the distress of poor and needy Muslims. Moreover, men and women pay these alms at the same rate — a minimum of 2½% of the net wealth that one has accumulated as savings and investments by the end of each year. Women enjoy the special privilege of being able to exempt from their tax base whatever wealth they have converted into personal ornaments.

(5) It is incumbent upon every Muslim who is physically, mentally, and financially capable to make a pilgrimage to Mecca at least once in a lifetime.

> "Perform the pilgrimage and the visit to Mecca for God." (Quran II: 196)

The rites for male and female pilgrims are identical except that during menstruation the latter are relieved from performing certain of these rites, such as the ritual prayers, and are required to postpone performing others, such as the circumambulation of the Ka'ba and the run between mounts Safa and Marwa. In addition, while males are required to don a special dress that consists only of two large pieces of white seamless cloth, females are permitted to wear any clothing that leaves only the face and the hands exposed.

Such are the primary duties of woman to God which are spelled out in the ordinances of the Revealed Law. However, beyond the Law woman has the same obligation as man to develop spiritual virtues to the highest degree possible and thereby worship God in an interior as well as an exterior way. Indeed, women are recognized to have played an important role in the development of the Islamic community through their strong, untiring faith. Moreover, because sexuality has nothing to do with matters of faith, virtue, and spirituality, "there is full equality between the sexes in the field of saintliness."[7] Women are, in fact, frequently mentioned in the biographical dictionaries of saints, and one of the most famous of the early saints of Islam is Rabia al-Adawiyya (d. 801), a woman who introduced the concept of pure love into Sufism. Farid ad-Din al-Attar (d. 1220), the most famous biographer of Sufis (Muslim saints), explained the inclusion of women in his work by declaring:

"Attainment of the divine lies not in appearance but in [sincerity of] purpose. . . . If it is possible to have learnt two-thirds of the Faith from 'A'isha the Righteous [the wife of Muhammad], then it is possible to learn some of the truth of religion from one of her handmaidens. Since a woman on the path of God becomes a man, she cannot be called a woman."[8]

Thus, male and female saints share equally great renown for their religious learning, enjoy the same power to work miracles, and receive like honors in life and after death.

Many women — like Sayyida Nafisa (d. 824), the great-granddaughter of the Prophet's grandson Hasan, and Sayyida Zaynab, sister of Hasan — are well remembered for their virtue and piety, and their tombs are still thronged by Muslims of both sexes. Some women have established hermitages to function both as a haven for husbandless women in need of security and as places of instruction for women dedicated to the pursuit of spiritual life. Women saints have also served as the *murshids*, or spiritual guides, of Sufi orders and, like men, have even attained the high spiritual function of prophecy. Moreover, the Sufis also view women as being spiritually superior to men. Ibn Arabi (d. 1240), "the greatest master" of Sufism, asserted that God "is seen more perfectly . . . in woman than in man," since the female is "the true revelation of God's mercy and creativity."[9] For this reason, the Sufis show a special love for Mary, mother of Jesus, regarding her as one of the greatest saints and even a prophet, for she is the perfect "symbol of the spirit that receives divine inspiration and thus becomes pregnant with the divine light."[10] The Prophet Muhammad himself affirmed women's unique spiritual value in his mystical pronouncement:

"I was made to love three things of your world: women, perfume, and the refreshment of the eye in prayer."[11]

B. Woman as a Member of her Family

The family is certainly the single most important institution in Islam, for it is the basic unit of society, the unit within which each individual establishes and develops his primary relationships before going on to forge links with other members of the society at large. Within this family unit, a female will, during the unfolding of her life, play a succession of different roles: daughter, sister, wife, and mother. Each of these roles carries with it its own particular set of obligations and rights. Yet all of them are subject to one basic, simple principle — a principle which the Prophet left as a legacy to his Community in a *Hadith:*

> "He is not one of us who does not have mercy on the younger, or does not respect the older."

This principle serves as a permanent and timeless guide for all the interaction between the various generations that constitute the family.

(1) The newborn female, of course, begins her life within the family unit in the role of daughter. The first obligation which she must then assume is to her parents. As soon as she becomes aware of her role, she must begin to treat them with respect, obey them, and give them help and understanding just as God has commanded her to do.

> "Thy Lord hath decreed, that ye worship none save Him, and that ye show kindness to parents. If one of them or both of them attain to old age with thee, say not 'Fie' unto them nor repulse them, but speak unto them a gracious word. And lower unto them the wing of submission through mercy, and say: My Lord! Have mercy on them both as they did care for me when I was little." (Quran XVII: 23-24)

Indeed, the Prophet often reminded the members of his Community that, whereas they owed their first concern to God, they owed their second to their parents.

> "Somebody asked the Prophet which work pleases God most? He replied 'the service of worship at the appointed hour,' and when it was continued: 'And what afterwards?' the Prophet replied: 'To be bounteous to your father and mother.'" *(Hadith)*

The male child bears this obligation to the same degree as the female, and, in addition, as an adult he must pay for his parents' maintenance if they are needy.

As for the rights of the female child, the Quran makes special mention of them, for in pre-Islamic Arabia it was not unusual for a father to bury alive his infant daughters and show exaggerated preference for his sons. The Quran first of all charges parents not to be disappointed with the sex of their child but to accept it joyfully since it has been determined by God Himself.

> "When if one of them receiveth tidings of the birth of a female, his face remaineth darkened, and he is wroth inwardly. He hideth himself from the folk because of the evil of that whereof he hath had tidings, (asking himself): Shall he keep it in contempt, or bury it beneath the dust!" (Quran XVI: 58-59)

> "Unto God belongeth the sovereignty of the heavens and the earth. He createth what He will. He bestoweth female offspring upon whom He will, and bestoweth male offspring upon whom He will." (Quran XLII: 49)

Secondly, the Quran explicitly forbids the practice of female infanticide.

> "Say: Come, I will recite unto you that which your Lord hath made a sacred duty for you: that ye ascribe nothing as partner unto Him and that ye do good to parents, and that ye slay not your children because of penury — We provide for you and for them.... And that ye slay not the life which God hath made sacred, save in the course of justice." (Quran VI: 151)
>
> "And when the girl-child that was buried alive is asked for what sin she was slain . . . then every soul will know what it hath made ready." (Quran LXXXI: 8-9, 14)

In addition to the right to life, the daughter is entitled to love, compassion, protection, and gentle discipline as well as to a good education and the provision of all her material needs until the time of her marriage. The parents are likewise obligated to fulfill all these rights for their son, except that he is entitled to financial support only until he comes of age or completes his education. Moreover, Ali, the cousin and son-in-law of the Prophet, counseled Muslim parents to respect their sons and daughters alike.

> "Do not compel your children to accept your manners. They belong to a generation different from yours."[12]

(2) The female will also play the role of sister if her parents bear other children. (As a sister, she and her siblings are mutually obligated to treat each other with love, respect, and concern on a footing of equality.) However, the sister is due a special right from her brother: if she has no husband or father or grandfather to take care of her, her brother must assume the responsibility for her maintenance. In return for this right she inherits from her parents' estate a share that is only half the size of her brother's.

The Prophet Muhammad had no sisters himself, having been left an orphan and an only child by the death of his father before he was born and the death of his mother when he was only six. However, as the father of four daughters, he was able to acquire a great deal of experience with female children. He urged the men of his Community to discharge their duties to both daughters and sisters with no grudge or rancor.

> "Whoever is blessed with two daughters or is taking charge of two sisters, and treats them well and patiently, he and I shall be in Paradise like these . . . [the index and the middle fingers side by side]." (Hadith)

(3) The adult female usually takes on the role of wife, for marriage is a religious duty as well as a moral safeguard and a social commitment. Indeed, the Prophet proclaimed that "to marry is to perfect half of one's religion." Moreover, not only does marriage provide a legitimate

channel for the individual to obtain personal fulfillment on a physical, an emotional, and a spiritual level and thus maintain stability; it also contributes to the good of society by furnishing an accepted means for reproducing and thus perpetuating the species. Accordingly, marriage is much encouraged, while monasticism and celibacy are greatly discouraged.

Marriage in Islam has two aspects — sacramental and contractual — for, while it is based on a legal contract, God is its first Witness. Indeed, the Prophet emphasized its sacramental aspect when he advised the men of his Community to select women on the basis of their permanent interior qualities rather than their ephemeral external ones.

> "A woman may be chosen in marriage for her wealth, or for her beauty, or for her nobility or for her good religious conduct. Pick the one who is morally motivated and hold fast to her." *(Hadith)*

In order for the marriage contract to be validly concluded, three conditions must be fulfilled. First, both parties to the contract should know each other. Second, the woman must voluntarily give her consent, not be forced into the marriage by her male guardian. Third, the contract must stipulate the payment of a suitable dowry to the woman.

Once the contract of marriage is concluded, both the man and the woman are able to make claims, each upon the other, while at the same time retaining rights. Each makes an exclusive commitment to treat the other with love, concern, and loyalty. Nevertheless, neither one loses his/her individual identity, for each one keeps his/her own name and remains an independent agent who is personally responsible for all his/her own actions — and only his/her own. The two are to be equal partners in running the home and rearing the children. They should cooperate with each other, sacrifice for each other, and consult with each other. The Prophet regularly sought moral support and wise counsel from his wives and shared with them in cleaning, sweeping floors, mending clothes, preparing food, and taking care of the children. Thus, it is clear that the roles which husband and wife play are not attached to specific areas of labor; rather, they relate to certain attitudes and responsibilities. The husband's role is to act as protector and guardian of the household, provide the finances necessary for its operation, and to formulate the policy by which it should function without being arbitrary, authoritarian, tyrannical, or inconsiderate. He should under no circumstances exploit his role, for the degree which he has over his wife is one of responsibility, not

superiority. Indeed, the Prophet informed the men of his Community that "the best among you is the one who is best towards his wife."
In her role as wife, the woman bears several general obligations: to bring joy, warmth, and peace to her marital relationship, to see to the comfort and well-being of her husband, to be chaste and faithful to him, to be honest and careful with his possessions, and to obey him. The Prophet devoted a large part of his Farewell Sermon, which he delivered to his Community during the Last Pilgrimage, to the role of the wife, and in it he elaborated upon these duties.

> "... they should not let your beds be trampled by others than you, should not allow those to enter your houses whom you do not like without your authorization, and should not commit turpitude. If they do commit that, then God has given you permission to reprimand them, to separate yourself from them in beds, and to strike them but not hard. If they abstain and obey you, then it is incumbent upon you to provide their food and dress in accordance with good custom. And I command you to treat women well. ..."[13]

In order that these obligations might be balanced, the wife has been entitled to make a number of demands upon her husband.

First of all, it is her right to be treated with kindness, patience, generosity, understanding, and respect. The husband should never hurt her feelings, cause her emotional grief or physical harm, or keep her in suspense as regards his intentions for their marriage or divorce.

> "... a woman must be retained in honor or released in kindness."
> (Quran II: 229)

> "But consort with them in kindness, for if ye hate them it may happen that ye hate a thing wherein God hath placed much good."
> (Quran IV: 19)

> "I urge you to treat women kindly. They are a trust in your hands. Fear God in His trust." *(Hadith)*

Secondly, the wife is due full maintenance by her husband at the same level of comfort to which she was accustomed before marriage. This includes food, a dwelling with privacy, and a reasonable amount of new clothing each year but not personal luxuries. She is not obliged to do household chores, to prepare food for consumption, or to nurse her infants if she does not wish to do so. Likewise, if she performs any of these tasks, she is entitled to compensation if she desires it.

> "Lodge them where ye dwell, according to your wealth, and harass them not so as to straiten life for them. And if they are with child, then spend for them till they bring forth their burden. Then, if they give suck for you, give them their due payment and consult together in kindness." (Quran LXV: 6)

Thirdly, the wife is entitled to retain full control over her dowry, all other property that she owns, and whatever wages she earns.

Fourthly, the wife has the right to demand monogamy from her husband in the marriage contract. If she does not exercise this right and her husband chooses to take one, two, or three other wives, then she has the right to demand from him an equal share of his kindness, attentions, and financial support.

> "... marry of the women, who seem good to you, two or three or four; and if ye fear that ye cannot do justice to so many then one only...." (Quran IV: 3)

This divine command virtually amounts to a prohibition of polygyny, the taking of multiple wives, because it is extremely difficult, if not impossible, for a man to treat several wives equally. Thus, polygyny is to be practiced only in unusual and extenuating circumstances.

Fifthly, the wife's right to receive a specified portion of her deceased husband's estate is guaranteed.

> "And unto them [the wives] belongeth the fourth of that which ye leave if ye have no child, but if ye have a child then the eighth of that which ye leave, after any legacy ye may have bequeathed, or debt ye may have contracted, hath been paid." (Quran IV: 12)

Sixthly, just as the wife has rights in marriage, she also has them in divorce. It is lawful for her to stipulate in her marriage contract that she be entitled to obtain a divorce from her husband whenever she desires without stating the grounds. If she has not made this stipulation, then it is nonetheless lawful for her to seek a divorce through the court on specific grounds: impotence, insanity, leprosy or other grave disease, non-payment of dowry, non-payment of maintenance, apostasy from Islam, lengthy absence or desertion, physical or emotional abuse, or false accusation of adultery. However, the Prophet cautioned his Community — male and female alike — not to exercise the right to divorce without a compelling reason on account of its gravity.

> "Among all permissible things, divorce is the most hated act to God." (Hadith)
>
> "Divorce causes the Throne of God to shake." (Hadith)

If the wife is divorced by her husband, she has the right to receive full maintenance from him throughout the prescribed waiting period at the end of which the divorce shall be final and the woman is free to remarry. Since the purpose of this waiting period is to determine the existence of a pregnancy and definitively establish paternity, its length is at least three months and, in the event of a pregnancy, as many as twelve, i.e., until the child is born.

> "Provide for them [divorced women], the rich according to his means, and the straitened according to his means, a fair provision." (Quran II: 236)

(4) If God so wills, the marriage of man and woman produces fruit, and the woman will then embark upon the most special and honored role which she can play within her family: the role of mother.

> "Or He couples them, males and females, and He maketh barren whom He will." (Quran XLII: 50)

As for the duties involved in rearing a child, the mother shares these jointly with the child's father. Both mother and father are equally responsible for keeping the child from harm, treating him with compassion, and attending to his proper intellectual, moral, and spiritual development. However, it is the father who must provide for all the child's material needs, whereas it is the mother who takes care of most of the child's bodily needs. Moreover, for fulfilling this function, she is entitled to fair recompense from the child's father.

> "Mothers shall suckle their children for two whole years; that is for those who wish to complete the suckling. The duty of feeding and clothing nursing mothers in a seemly manner is upon the father of the child. No one should be charged beyond one's capacity. A mother should not be made to suffer because of her child, nor should he to whom the child is born be made to suffer because of his child.... If they desire to wean the child by mutual consent and after consultation, it is no sin for them; and if ye wish to give your children out to nurse, it is no sin for you, provided that ye pay what is due from you in kindness." (Quran II: 233)

Although the mother's responsibilities to the child are commensurate with the father's, her claims upon the child are actually much greater than his on account of her greater involvement in the child's conception, birth, and care.

> "And We have commended unto man kindness toward parents. His mother beareth him with pain, and the bearing of him and the weaning of him is thirty months, till, when he attaineth full strength and reacheth forty years, he saith: My Lord! Arouse me that I may give thanks for the favor wherewith Thou hast favored me and my parents...." (Quran XLVI: 15)

Indeed, the Prophet declared that the mother is due a full three-quarters of the child's love and attention.

> "Someone asked the Prophet: 'Who deserves my service most after God?' The Prophet said, 'Your mother.' The person asked again: 'And who is next?' The Prophet said, 'Your mother.' The man asked further, 'And who is next?' The Prophet replied, 'Your mother.' The man asked once more, 'And who is next?' The Prophet. peace be upon him, said: 'Your father.' " *(Hadith)*

Moreover, the mother deserves the child's veneration, for her role has made her exalted in the sight of God, Who has placed her higher than the father.

"Paradise is under the feet of the mother." *(Hadith)*

In the event of divorce, it is the mother who automatically has the right to custody of the children unless she has caused herself to be disqualified on moral grounds. Further, she retains this right until she remarries. If she is still unmarried when her male child reaches the age of seven, then he is free to choose to live with whichever parent he prefers. Her female child, likewise, is free to make this choice when she turns nine. In addition, the divorced mother is entitled to receive from the father not only a reasonable amount of money for the maintenance of the children but also fair wages for herself for taking care of them.

Finally, if the mother outlives her child, she is to be allotted a certain share of the estate of that child: a third if the latter died childless; a sixth if there is a surviving child or sibling.

> "And to the parents [of the deceased] a sixth of the inheritance if he have a son; and if he have no son and his parents are his heirs, then to his mother appertaineth the third; and if he have brethren, then to his mother appertaineth the sixth, after any legacy he may have bequeathed, or debt hath been paid. Your parent or your children: Ye know not which of them is nearer unto you in usefulness."
> (Quran: IV: 11)

C. Woman as a Member of her Society

In addition to playing the roles of daughter, sister, wife, and mother within her family unit, the Muslim woman is entitled — indeed, *enjoined* — by the Revealed Law to play certain other roles outside the family. This is because the society, like the family, is an extremely important unit of relationships in the Islamic world. Just as there is a close bond between the individual and the other members of his family, there is a strong link between the individual and the rest of his society. This Islamic view of the individual and his place in this world is a natural outgrowth of the keystone of Islamic faith and action: *tawhid*, which is a verbal, intellectual, practical, and spiritual affirmation of the Unity of God. The concept of Divine Unity is, of course, the very core of the Testimony of Faith, the most basic credal statement in Islam: "There is no god but God." The essence of the Quran, it is the sole subject of the final chapter:

> "Say: He is God, the One! God, the eternally Besought of all! He begetteth not nor was begotten. And there is none comparable unto Him." (Quran CXII)

Because humanity was created in the image of God, humanity also is fundamentally one despite its great superficial diversity. This belief in the Oneness of God and His Creation sacralizes all the lawful actions of the individual and renders one's service to fellow humans an integral part of one's service to God.

Thus, every man and woman is obligated to contribute however possible to the welfare, prosperity, and advancement of society. This duty is one owed not only to society but also to God, the Creator of mankind. In return, the society as a whole is responsible to God for the material and spiritual welfare of each of its individual members. Man and woman claim the same rights from society: the right to dignity, respect, and honor as well as the right to security of person and property. No woman is to shirk her social obligations because of her sex; nor is society to discriminate between man and woman and deny woman her social rights.

Man and woman share many of the same specific obligations to society, and so they also share many of the same roles in society. Woman, like man, is able to exercise an intellectual role, a vocational role, a political role, a military role, a legal role, and an economic role. However, in playing these roles the woman enjoys some special rights and exemptions from obligations that the man does not enjoy. These rights and exemptions arise out of (1) the particular physiological and psychological characteristics which distinguish her from the man and (2) the particular roles which she plays in the family, for her roles as wife and mother take precedence over her various social roles. Indeed, no person — neither man nor woman — should ever devote so much of one's time and talents to society as to neglect one's own family.

(1) Woman as an Intellectual Agent

(In order for woman to take her rightful place as a helpful and productive member of society, she must first receive an education. Indeed, the acquiring of knowledge is one of the most basic and serious obligations incumbent upon Muslims, for Islam is, more than any other religion, a Way of Knowledge.) That is, Islam presents as the major road to follow toward salvation, neither fear nor love of God, but knowledge of Him and His creation. Numerous verses of the Quran and sayings of the Prophet exhort the believers to learn to their full capacity and promise rich rewards to those who comply.

"Say: My Lord! Increase me in knowledge." (Quran XX: 114)
"Seek knowledge even if it be in China." *(Hadith)*
"God will exalt those who believe among you, and those who have knowledge, to high ranks." (Quran LVIII: 11)

Moreover, the duty to learn is so crucial in Islam that no exemptions are made from it, neither on the basis of age nor on the basis of sex.

> "Seek knowledge from the cradle to the grave." *(Hadith)*
> "The search for knowledge is a duty for every Muslim, male or female." *(Hadith)*

Within the Islamic tradition, then, education is not meant to be linked to a sexual function since God has purposely given both man and woman the capacity to acquire knowledge as well as disseminate it. In fact, throughout the history of Islam many women have become renowned for their scholarship. Aisha, wife of the Prophet, is well remembered for her outstanding memory and is regarded as one of the greatest teachers of *hadiths*, having reported more than one thousand. Nafisa (d. 824), great-granddaughter of the Prophet's grandson Hasan, was considered such a great authority on *hadiths* that the Imam ash-Shafi'i, founder of one of the four Sunni schools of jurisprudence, sat in her circle in Cairo during the height of his fame. Shuhda bint al-Ibari (d. 1178), who was given the title "the pride of womankind," came to be ranked among the foremost scholars of her age through her public lectures to large audiences in Baghdad. Zaynab bint Ahmad of Jerusalem, who instructed the learned traveller Ibn Battuta in *hadiths*, left a camel load of diplomas upon her death in 1339.

(2) Woman's Vocational Role

It follows from the importance which Islam places upon education for all Muslims that men and women alike have the obligation to put their education to some useful purpose. Every individual, male and female, should cultivate his special God-given abilities and exercise them for the benefit of himself, his family, and his society. One might accomplish this in many ways, e.g., by being a helpful neighbor, by volunteering time and talents to a charitable organization, by pursuing a particular vocation for pay. Of course, whereas men bear the obligation to engage in gainful employment in order to earn a livelihood and support their families, women do not. Indeed, the woman's obligations to society are tempered to a large extent by her obligations to herself and her family. Thus, she is to expend of her efforts outside the home only if, in doing so, she does not lose her dignity, disobey her husband, or neglect her family. Notwithstanding, Islamic history records numerous examples of women who have taken up some occupation. It is known that several of the Prophet's wives and daughters worked at various tasks for wages and that the Market Inspector whom the second Caliph, Umar, appointed for his capital city was a woman. Countless other Muslim women after these have been employed, and many have become famous in their own right as religious scholars, writers, poets, teachers, and physicians.

(3) Woman's Political Role

Because the Islamic society attaches great value to learning, it encourages its members to use their education not just to contribute to it vocationally but also to participate actively in its political life. Thus, all adult Muslims — male as well as female — enjoy two rights crucial for the effective operation of any truly Islamic government: the right to formulate and freely express personal opinions on issues of public interest and the right to nominate candidates for public offices and share in their election.

It is a matter of record that in the early days of Islam women as a whole exerted a fair amount of influence on the conduct of political affairs in their community. Instead of being asked to veil, hide, and separate themselves from the rest of their society, they were invited to engage in serious discussions on public affairs and their views were received with all due consideration. The Prophet Muhammad exacted oaths of allegiance from women, just as he did from men,[14] and permitted women to challenge his stand. Indeed, the Quran preserves the account of a woman who had first complained to the Prophet that her husband had divorced her for no good reason by proclaiming — as was the wont of the pagan Arabs — that her back was for him as the back of his mother and later had disputed with the Prophet when he refused to take action against the man. A subsequent revelation clearly rendered punishable such treatment of one's wife.

> "God hath heard the saying of her that disputeth with thee (Muhammed) concerning her husband, and complaineth unto God."
> (Quran LVIII: 1)

Moreover, women are known to have debated the highest government officials publicly. A woman once took issue with a pronouncement made in the mosque by the Caliph Umar and was able to prove her point with sound arguments, whereupon he declared to the assembly, "A woman is right, and Umar is wrong."

Some women were able to wield considerable power as the mothers, wives, or daughters of men incumbent in important posts. Such was the case with Zubayda, the still revered wife of the Abbasid Caliph Harun ar-Rashid (786-809), and the mother of the Abbasid Caliph al-Muqtadir (908-932), who regularly held public audience to receive petitions from her son's subjects and redress injustices. However, the

Revealed Law does not permit that a woman herself hold any office that would put her in charge of men. A woman could never, therefore, serve as Caliph or even as a judge. The bases for this restriction are to be found in the Quran and the sayings of the Prophet:

> "Men are in charge of women." (Quran: IV: 34)
> "A people will not prosper if they let a woman be their leader."
> *(Hadith)*

This restriction, or exemption from an obligation, corresponds, on a social level, to the same pattern of authority that exists in the family setting, i.e., man enjoys additional authority as a compensation for his additional responsibilities, whereas woman enjoys certain exemptions as compensation for her having to submit to man's authority.

(4) Woman's Military Role

Within the Islamic society the duty of protecting and defending family and community falls squarely upon the men. While women are totally exempt from this duty, they nonetheless have often assisted fathers, brothers, husbands, and sons in fulfilling their military obligation and, in so doing, have risked danger and even suffered death. Moreover, women have taken an active part in warfare in a variety of capacities: as transporters of wounded and dead soldiers from the front lines to the rear, as nurses for the wounded, as gravediggers, as procurers and managers of rations, as cooks, as water-carriers, as sources of moral support, and as actual fighters. In fact, women have at times played a major military role. Aisha, wife of the Prophet, was commander of her own troops in the Battle of the Camel, which she waged against the Caliph Ali in 656. In the Battle of Qadisiyyah, fought between the Sassanid Persians and the Muslims in 637, a group of Muslim women cleverly made war banners of their aprons and marched in ranks carrying them, giving the enemy the impression that reinforcements had arrived and thus disheartening them and turning the tide of the battle.

(5) Woman's Legal Role

As regards the Revealed Law of Islam, men and women are equally responsible for observing all the ordinances that apply to them. All those — males and females — who fail to carry out an obligation or who commit a forbidden act are subject to one and the same penalty. For instance, anyone who steals is to lose the right hand; anyone who indulges in intoxicants is to receive eighty lashes.

> "As for the thief, both male and female, cut off their hands." (Quran V: 38)

> "Strong drink . . . [is] only an infamy of Satan's handiwork. Leave it aside in order that ye may succeed." (Quran V: 90)

All those — males and females — who are the victims of certain criminal acts for which there exists a legal retaliation in kind or compensation in cash are entitled to identical redress. For example, anyone who deliberately takes another's life is either to suffer execution or to pay a suitable sum of money to the victim's next-of-kin — whichever the latter demands. Anyone who willfully cuts off the hand of another must either lose his own hand or pay compensation to his victim — whichever the latter demands.

> "O ye who believe! Retaliation is prescribed for you in the matter of the murdered; the freeman for the freeman, and the slave for the slave, and the female for the female." (Quran II: 178)

Men and women alike have a certain legal obligation to their society; namely, they both must witness the signing of contracts and provide testimony about events of which they have knowledge whenever they are asked to do so. However, in performing these acts of bearing witness and testifying a woman in most cases enjoys only half the legal status of a man.

> "And call to witness, from among your men, two witnesses. And if two men be not at hand then a man and two women, of such as ye approve as witnesses, so that if one erreth through forgetfulness the other will remember. And the witnesses must not refuse when they are summoned." (Quran II: 282)

This legal equation of "two equals one" is intended to lighten the woman's burden as a witness in recognition that women as a group are usually less experienced than men in public affairs. Yet, in those matters which are generally considered to be within the special province of female expertise, a single woman can be accepted as a conclusive witness and no man can even be considered.

(6) Woman's Economic Role

Within the Islamic society men and women alike enjoy full freedom of economic action. Both have the right to acquire property through various legitimate means: by inheritance, as a gift, in payment of labor, or by purchase.

> "Unto the men of a family belongeth a share of that which parents and near kindred leave, and unto the women a share of that which parents and near kindred leave, whether it be little or much — a legal share." (Quran IV: 7)
> "Unto men a fortune from that which they have earned, and unto women a fortune from that which they have earned." (Quran IV: 32)

Women, like men, can enter into contracts, conduct business, dispose of wealth, lend and borrow. Each individual — male or female — is directly responsible for whatever personal debts he or she incurs. Women alone, however, possess an absolute right over their property. That is, they bear financial responsibility for nothing except personal luxuries, whereas men are under a legal obligation to use portions of their property to maintain their wives, children, parents, and sisters, to pay a dowry to their brides, and to provide alimony for their ex-wives.

Sexual Morality: A Basic Requirement for All Social Roles

Islam soundly condemns any and all intrusions of immorality into the behavior of its followers — men as well as women — as they execute whatever roles they have assumed as members of their society. Thus, the Quran prescribes that the same severe penalty be applied to all those Muslims who fornicate or commit adultery.

> "The fornicator and the fornicatress, scourge ye each one of them with a hundred stripes." (Quran XXIV: 2)

In addition, as a measure of precaution the Revealed Law forbids Muslims to engage in any of the social practices that might lead to a manifestation of immorality. Accordingly, the Quran enjoins both men and women to be modest and chaste in their behavior.

> "... men who guard their modesty and women who guard (their modesty) ... — God hath prepared for them forgiveness and a vast reward." (Quran XXXIII: 35)
>
> "Tell the believing men to lower their gaze and be modest. That is purer for them. Lo! God is Aware of what they do. And tell the believing women to lower their gaze and be modest. ..." (Quran XXIV: 30-31)

Islam, nevertheless, emphasizes modesty for the female, and so there are more regulations governing her appearance and conduct in the society than there are governing the male's. Indeed, the Quran specifies that the woman is always to dress and behave in such a way as not to stir men's passions or cause suspicion of her own morality. Neither should she expose her beauty to any male who is not forbidden by law to marry her on account of degree of kinship; nor should she be alone with such a man.

> "And tell the believing women ... to display of their adornment only that which is apparent, and to draw their veils over their bosoms, and not to reveal their adornment save to their own husbands or fathers or husbands' fathers, or their sons or their husbands' sons, or their brothers or their brothers' sons or sisters' sons, or their women, or their slaves, or male attendants who lack

> vigour, or children who know naught of women's nakedness. And let them not stamp their feet so as to reveal what they hide of their adornment." (Quran XXIV: 31)

To balance these additional restrictions upon the woman, Islam provides special measures to protect her reputation from false accusations of immorality.

> "And those who accuse honourable women but bring not four witnesses, scourge them with eighty stripes and never afterward accept their testimony." (Quran XXIV: 4)

By way of summary, then, the traditional status and role of the Muslim woman is three-fold in nature. In certain roles, the woman is a degree lower than the man by virtue of her sex. While this degree requires her to submit to the man's authority, it in no way implies that she is inferior. Rather, it entitles her to full maintenance and protection by her male relatives, relieves her from certain responsibilities, and endows her with special rights. In certain other roles, the woman is an equal complement of the man. Thus, the man and the woman share many obligations and rights and receive identical rewards for fulfilling like obligations and identical punishments for committing like violations. The differences between them which arise out of differences in sex indicate a relationship that is complementary rather than competitive. In still a third set of roles, the woman enjoys a rank that is higher than the man's. The woman as mother is given greater honor than the man as father. In addition, the Sufis regard the woman as spiritually superior to the man by virtue of her being a more perfect reflection of God.

II. The Current Status of Women and Their Emerging Role in the Islamic World

Notwithstanding the ideal presentation of the woman in Islamic theology and law, Muslim women have in certain periods and in certain societies suffered from either a misinterpretation or an abuse of particular doctrines and ordinances. Local customs and the ascendant role of the man in society, in particular, have at times led to the practice of some forms of discrimination against women. The most glaring of these, in Western eyes, include requiring the woman to veil and keep herself strictly segregated from the male portion of society and denying her the right to an education, thereby barring her from access to information about her rights under the law. (Indeed, in some regions women are frequently discouraged and, in some instances even forbidden, from exercising any of their rightful roles outside the family. The problem which, as a result, has arisen for the contemporary world is how to reconcile the Islamic ideal of equity with the ways in which women are viewed and treated in actuality.

A. Current Status and Treatment of Muslim Women: Saudi Arabia and Egypt as Contrasts

It would be useful here to examine the specific circumstances of women in two countries — Saudi Arabia and Egypt — that represent opposite ends of a spectrum of the prevailing Muslim attitudes towards women.

1. Saudi Arabia is typical of the countries of the Arabian Peninsula in its highly conservative and restrictive view of the proper participation of women in society. The Saudis have officially pronounced the social mingling of sexes to be morally wrong and therefore unacceptable. As a result, girls are placed in separate schools at the age of six and are forced to don the all-concealing black cloak and face-veil as soon as they reach puberty. Those who advance to the university enjoy the most modern classroom facilities, replete with elaborate electronic systems that permit instantaneous communication with their segregated male professors via closed-circuit television and telephone. These expensive measures are necessary because qualified women who could lecture to them directly are in pitifully short supply. In addition, female students have access to the university library only on the one or two days per week when males are denied entrance. After completing their education, women can seek employment only in all-female institutions like schools and hospitals. As regards the routine of their daily lives, women have very few, if any, opportunities for even visual contact with strange men. Forbidden by law to drive cars, women are limited in their mobility to riding in private chauffeur-driven cars or on public buses that have a special closed section for females. Public buildings that need to serve women as well as men, e.g., the telephone central office, have separate entrances and reception areas for males and females. All but the two or three largest mosques in the capital city bar their doors to women. Women at home are sealed off from the outside world by opaque window-glass, which is required by law for all private dwellings. Needless to say, a good many Saudi women, particularly those who have traveled outside their country, complain about what they label "a lack of freedom".

2. Egypt, in stark contrast to Saudi Arabia, was the scene of the earliest calls for Muslim women's liberation, no doubt because it was

the very first area of the Middle East which the West happened to penetrate. Indeed, since Napoleon's full-scale invasion in 1798, Egypt has had constant contact with the West. By the end of the nineteenth century male social and political reformers, well acquainted with trends in Europe, had made an important place for women in their programs aimed at improving the over-all conditions of life in Egypt. The men who took the lead in this reform movement — among them Rifaʻah at-Tahtawi, Muhammad ʻAbduh, and Qasim Amin — all emphasized the institution of universal education as the most significant measure for elevating the status of women and increasing their contributions to society. They also strongly advocated the removal of the veil, the abolition of polygyny, and the transfer of the right of divorce from the husband to the court as supportive measures for bettering the lot of women. Then in 1923 Huda ash-Shaʻrawi, wife of a respected political figure, founded the Feminist Union to fight the conservative political establishment for recognition of women's educational, vocational, and political rights.[15] Later that year, following this lady activist's example, Egyptian women began discarding the veil, and by 1930 there were unveiled women attending classes with men in universities. However, it was not until 1956 after Nasser's Revolution, that women were able to secure for themselves the right to vote and participate in political life as elected members of the National Assembly of the Arab Socialist Union and as appointed members of the Cabinet of Ministries.

In present-day Egypt women enjoy full equality with men educationally and professionally, for there is no sexual discrimination in admitting applicants to institutions of higher education or in hiring employees and setting their wages. Indeed, women can now be found in sizeable numbers in a variety of professions — as teachers, physicians, lawyers, engineers, architects, managers of companies, deans of university faculties, and even cabinet ministers. Nonetheless, women in Egypt are still seeking to put an end to some forms of discrimination that remain within the family structure. For instance, they would like to rescind or at least regulate men's right to multiple wives, revoke men's right to absolute divorce and confine the right of divorce to the court, and cancel men's right to automatic custody of older children in the event of divorce. Only this year did the women succeed in convincing the Sadat government to abolish the much hated House of Obedience, an exclusively Egyptian institution which gave police the authority to detain forcibly any recalcitrant wife who left her husband and return her to him.

B. Women's Liberation in the Contemporary Islamic World

There is no question that Muslim women's rights for participation in their society are staunchly supported by the Revealed Law and Islamic tradition. Yet it is certainly true that in many parts of the Islamic world today these rights are often poorly understood and hardly exercised. In fact, according to a recent report based on figures obtained in the mid-1970's:

> "In comparison with other major culture areas, the Muslim-majority nations of the world have low rates of reported economic activity by women, low female literarcy, and low female school enrollment at all levels."[16]

It is indeed, disheartening, if not alarming, that the 1974 United Nations statistics show that adult females in the Arab nations suffer from the highest illiteracy rate in the world: approximately 86%. It would appear, then, that in order to exercise their divinely-ordained rights a great many women who themselves have no religious training are forced to rely, first of all, on their male relatives' personal knowledge of Islam and, secondly, on the dictates of the individual consciences of these males for implementing that knowledge.

This state of affairs has led most concerned men and women to conclude, in agreement with the nineteenth-century reformers in Egypt, that education of both males and females is still the major means for rectifying the existing discrepancies between the traditional ideal and reality. Indeed, an Arab social scientist who based his Ph.D. thesis on the premise that education is the remedy for the Arab-Muslim woman's ills has categorically stated:

> "Those [Arab women] who are enlightened see in education, for themselves and their sisters, the solution to their problems and, more importantly, the essence of their liberation."[17]

Through proper education women could become aware of public issues and needs and develop skills helpful to their societies in a variety of areas, not only in religion and child care but also health, agriculture, arts, and industry. Thus, they would keep in step with their husbands and children and be able to cope more easily with the tremendous changes being wrought in their societies by industrialization, modernization, and Westernization. Conversely, without this education women will become increasingly isolated from the male members of their families as rapid changes continue to occur in their environment; as a result, they would eventually become crippled even in the only roles left open to many of them: their roles as wives and mothers.

Accordingly, women's liberation in the contemporary Islamic world focuses on developing the roles in family and society which traditionally have always been accessible to them — their roles as wives, mothers, and nation-builders. The majority of Muslim women do not understand women's liberation as a liberation from the male, for within the traditional Islamic perspective male domination of the female has been mandated by God. Indeed, the Muslim women's movement places a high value on maintaining femininity and modesty and avoids inciting its members to wrest from men their position in family and society, with all the privileges and responsibilities that it entails. This, of course, presents a sharp contrast to the Western women's movement and its prevailing philosophy of feminism, which often focuses on issues like sexual freedom, lesbianism, revealing fashions, abortion on demand, denunciation of the institution of marriage and the status of the housewife, deglorification of motherhood, assertiveness training and the development of aggressive and even rude behavior, the forfeiture of rights to financial maintenance by the husband and payment of alimony, and the portrayal of men as oppressors.

In fact, Muslims see the so-called "liberated" Western women as anything but liberated, for in Muslim eyes what they have achieved is simply the freedom to receive training to work alongside men in full-time paying careers outside the home while at the same time bearing their original obligations inside the home. Moreover, they view these women as having achieved this "freedom" by force, not through divine revelation or even male consent, at the expense of their security and many of their natural rights. A leading American spokeswoman for Muslim women has disparagingly defined feminism as "an unnatural, artificial and abnormal product of contemporary social disintegration which in turn is the inevitable result of the rejection of all transcendental, absolute moral and spiritual values."[18] Indeed, she categorically denounces the society wherein feminism reigns triumphant:

> "A society which makes no cultural or social distinction between the sexes, a society without marriage, home and family, where modesty, chastity and motherhood are scorned, does not represent 'progress' or 'liberation' but degradation at its worst."[19]

Moreover, she fears that the emergence of feminism in America and the concomitant disintegration of the home and family cannot but lead to the decline and eventual collapse of the country. Only a few Western scholars outside the Islamic tradition have been able to comprehend this Muslim point of view and acknowledge that Muslim women's liberation "must be defined in terms consistent with the Qur'an and with what Muslims understand as the divinely-ordained principles of Islam."[20]

C. The Emerging Role of Muslim Women

(It is clear that in the Islamic world the status of women has, for nearly a century, been undergoing discernible change — slight in some countries, radical in others.) In the wake of this alteration of status the roles of women within the family have begun to shift as they develop new, but nonetheless traditional, roles outside the family. Indeed, the political leaders in many Muslim countries have had a direct hand in initiating, guiding, and encouraging these shifts, for they have tried to provide opportunities for the education of adult women without disrupting the existing male-female role patterns in the society and to effect innovations in the environment through legal reforms without directly confronting the society. The usual strategy, then, has been to involve women as much as possible in the socio-economic development of the nation.

(Of all the Muslim countries, Turkey and Tunisia have been at the forefront of increasing educational opportunities for women and introducing reforms in personal status law — with Egypt not far behind. For example, as of 1973, 83% of the young girls in Tunisia were attending primary school as were 61% of those in Turkey and 55% of those in Egypt. In addition, as of the same year the governments in Tunisia and Turkey had instituted a number of legal reforms significantly affecting women's status: a minimum legal age for marriage was established; the registration of all marriages was required; the women's share of inheritance was allowed to be increased; women were permitted to initiate divorce; polygamy was either restricted or altogether abolished; and men's right to absolute divorce was cancelled. All but the last two of these reforms had been carried out in Egypt by 1973. At the other end of the scale are Saudi Arabia and the Yemen Arab Republic. As of 1973 only 18% of the young girls in Saudi Arabia and scarcely 1% of those in Yemen were attending primary school, and not one of the just mentioned reforms had been made to raise women's status.[21])

Of course, even these educational and legal changes have not guaranteed any actual improvements in the lives of individual women. For instance, a secluded woman might simply not be aware of the new opportunities and rights available to her, and an aware woman might be reluctant to pursue them out of fear of personal reprisals from her male relatives. Even an aware and courageous woman might face the insurmountable barrier of a conservative judge who would refuse to make and enforce any judgments that are in accordance with these reforms but, in his view, at variance with the traditional ordinances of the Revealed Law. It is comforting, however, that more and more Muslims are coming to view these reforms as issuing from a new yet valid interpretation of the Law that, while on the surface divergent from the original legal formulations of the traditional authorities, preserves and reflects the spirit of the Quran and the *Sunnah* to a much greater extent.

In any case, it is obvious and beyond question that changes in women's status and roles are under way in even the most conservative of Islamic societies. In Saudi Arabia, for example, females now receive the same official encouragement to obtain an education as do males. Tuition and books are free to all, regardless of sex, and all receive from the government a monthly allotment of expense money equivalent to $65 while attending high school and $195 while attending college. In addition, several Saudi universities are now in the process of developing for women special Master's programs in a variety of fields, and the University of Riyadh has concrete plans to begin graduating women Ph.D.'s from a number of departments within the next ten years.' The Saudi government has allowed the expansion of professional opportunities for women, e.g., with the establishment of women's banks, and has eased somewhat the laws forbidding the employment of women alongside men so that now women may be employed in privately owned non-Saudi companies, with certain restrictions. Furthermore, the society has relaxed the women's standards for public dress; as a consequence, one may now see foreign women freely walking in the streets without a veil, head covering, or long skirt. In fact, it would be difficult to challenge anyone who points to the changing status and role of women as the most critical social issue facing Saudi Arabia today. The burgeoning national wealth, the rapid modernization and industrialization, and the increasing contacts with the West — all are placing traditional Saudi society under a great deal of stress. One might well ask what their effect will be on the status and role of Saudi women in particular. Obviously, whatever changes are made should be made slowly and carefully within the framework of the Islamic tradition in order to avoid an irreparable disruption of society and a severe shock to its individual members, male as well as female.

It is interesting, indeed, to compare the newly emerging role of women in Saudi Arabia to that of women in Egypt. As Saudi women move from their extremely conservative position toward a less restricted way of life, Egyptian women — who took the lead in Muslim women's liberation! — are now returning to a more traditional way of life. One of the most visible signs of the Egyptians' shift in direction is their widespread donning of the dress demanded by the Revealed Law. Within just the past five years a broad cross-section of women — well-to-do and poor, urban and rural, educated and illiterate, Westernized and traditional, young and old, attractive and plain — have willingly left their particular fashion to adopt traditional garb that identifies them instantly as Muslims. Many observers from the outside are regarding this phenomenon with bewilderment and wondering why it has occurred. Some insiders are responding that it is the result of the Saudi conservative view of Islam — a view which oftentimes has impact precisely because it is backed up with Saudi money. Others believe that it arises out of Egyptians' fear that their own society, heavily influenced by the West, will disintegrate if it continues in the path laid out by the West. One Egyptian woman has explained her reaction against things Western and her embrace of the traditional in this way:

> "Once we thought that Western society had all the answers for successful, fruitful living. If we followed the lead of the West, we would have progress. Now we see that this isn't true; they [the West] are sick societies; even their material prosperity is breaking down. America is full of crime and promiscuity. Russia is worse. Who wants to be like that? We have to remember God. Look how God has blessed Saudi Arabia. That's because they have tried to follow the Law. And America, with its loose society, is all problems."[22]

The question now remains: How can we interpret these seemingly opposing trends in Saudi Arabia and Egypt? Each of these two Muslim countries has provided for women in its society a position that appears to be the very antithesis of that accorded women in the other. In the one, women have found themselves restricted and prevented from assuming their traditional Islamic status and roles; in the other, women have found themselves bombarded with Western attitudes and customs and lured from undertaking their traditional Islamic status and roles. In both Saudi Arabia and Egypt women are at present moving from their un-Islamic positions at opposite ends of a spectrum towards a common center that represents the ideal Islamic position. Perhaps these opposing trends indicate an imminent return of Muslim societies to the true spirit of Islam. Perhaps they will meet in this center from which Muslim women will emerge as possessors of an authentically traditional status and set of roles. One Western scholar has wisely counseled her fellows not to assess the circumstances of Muslim women from a Western perspective:

> "What we as Westerners might hope for them in the way of greater steps toward equality and improvement in general status may very well not be what many Muslims want for themselves."[23]

In this vein, Westerners and Muslims alike would do well to wish that once again Muslim women will take their rightful place in Islamic society and enjoy their traditional rights and carry out their traditional obligations and contribute fully to the development of their communities.

Footnotes

[1] Dr. and Mrs. Samuel M. Zwemer, *Moslem Women.* West Medford, Massachusetts: The Central Committee on the United Study of Foreign Missions, 1926. p. 5.

[2] *Ibid.,* p. 31.

[3] *Ibid.,* p. 35.

[4] Beck and Keddie, *Women in the Muslim World.* p. 26.

[5] In citing this verse and all the others that follow, I have used as my source for the verse numbers as well as for the English translation the 1977 Muslim World League edition-translation of Muhammad Marmaduke Pickthall's *The Meaning of the Glorious Qur'an.*

[6] See also Quran II: 35-37 and VII: 19-27.

[7] Ignaz Goldziher, *Muslim Studies,* Vol. II, ed. by S. M. Stern and tr. by C. R. Barber and S. M. Stern. Albany: State University of New York Press, 1971. p. 274.

[8] Reuben Levy, *The Social Structure of Islam.* London: Cambridge University Press, 1971. p. 132.

[9] Annemarie Schimmel, *Mystical Dimensions of Islam.* Chapel Hill: The University of North Carolina Press, 1978. p. 431.

[10] *Ibid.,* p. 429.

[11] *Ibid.,* p. 431.

[12] See Abdul-Rauf, *The Islamic View,* p. 93.

[13] See Muhamed Hamidullah, *Introduction to Islam.* Beirut: The Holy Koran Publishing House, 1977. p. 156.

[14]See Quran LX: 12.

[15]For a detailed and entertaining picture of Egyptian women's activities during this period, see Afaf Lutfi al-Sayyid Marsot, "The Revolutionary Gentlewomen in Egypt," in Beck and Keddie, eds., *Women in the Muslim World*. pp. 261-276.

[16]Elizabeth H. White, "Legal Reform as an Indicator of Women's Status in Muslim Nations," in Beck and Keddie, eds., *Women in the Muslim World*. p. 52.

[17]Zuhayr Khalidi, "The Present Situation of the Arab-Muslim Women: Problem Assessment and Remedy for Consideration" in *Proceedings of the 6th Annual Conference of the Association of Muslim Social Scientists*. Indianapolis, Indiana, 1977. p. 24.

[18]Maryam Jameelah, *Islam and Muslim Women Today*. Lahore: Mohammad Yusuf Khan, 1978. p. 37.

[19]*Ibid.*, p. 47

[20]Jane I. Smith, "Women in Islam: Equity, Equality, and the Search for the Natural Order," *Journal of the American Academy of Religion*, Vol. XLVII, No. 4, p. 518.

[21]For this and additional statistical information, see White, "Legal Reform." Also see Noel Coulson and Doreen Hinchcliffe, "Women and Law Reform in Contemporary Islam," in Beck and Keddie, eds., *Women in the Muslim World*. pp. 37-51.

[22]John Alden Williams, "A Return to the Veil in Egypt," *Middle East Review* (Spring 1979), p. 54.

[23]Smith, "Women in Islam," p. 528.

Suggested Reading List

Abbott, Rabia, *Aishah: The Beloved of Mohammed*. Chicago: 1942.

Abdal-Ati, Hammudah, *The Family Structure in Islam*. Plainfield, Indiana: American Trust Publications, 1977.

Abdul-Rauf, Muhammad, *The Islamic View of Women and the Family*. New York: Robert Speller & Sons, 1977.

Alireza, Marianne, *At the Drop of A Veil*. Boston: Houghton-Mifflin, 1971.

Badawi, Gamal A., "Woman in Islam." In *Islam: Its Meaning and Message*, edited by Khurshid Ahmad. London: Islamic Council of Europe, 1976.

Beck, Lois and Nikki Keddie, eds. *Women in the Muslim World.* Cambridge, Mass.: Harvard University Press, 1978.

Dickson, Violet, *Forty Years in Kuwait.* London: 1970.

Fernea, Elizabeth Warnock, *Guests of the Sheik.* Garden City, N.Y.: 1965.

Fernea, Elizabeth Warnock, *A Street in Marrakech.* Garden City, New York: 1975.

Fernea, Elizabeth W., and Basima Bezirgan, eds. *Middle Eastern Muslim Women Speak.* Austin: The University of Texas Press, 1977.

Gordon, David C., *Women of Algeria: An Essay on Change.* Cambridge, Mass.: 1968.

Kramer, Jane, *Honor to the Bride.* New York: Ballantine Books, 1972.

Lemu, B. Aisha and Fatima Heeren, *Women in Islam.* Leicester, U.K.: The Islamic Foundation, 1976.

Makhlouf-Obermeyer, Carla, *Changing Veils: A Study of Women in South Arabia.* Austin: The University of Texas Press, 1979.

Maududi, Abul Ala, *Purdah and the Status of Women in Islam.* Lahore: Islamic Publications Ltd., 1972.

al-Qazzaz, Ayad, *Women in the Middle East and North Africa: An Annotated Bibliography.* Middle East Monographs, No. 2. Austin: The University of Texas Press, 1977.

Siddiqui, Muhammad Mazheruddin, *Women in Islam.* Lahore: The Institute of Islamic Culture, 1959.

Smith, Jane I., ed. *Women in Contemporary Muslim Societies.* Lewisburg: Bucknell University Press, 1979.

Smith, Margaret, *Rabia the Mystic and her Fellow Saints in Islam.* Cambridge: 1928.

Vaka, Demetra, *Haremlik: Some Pages from the Life of Turkish Women.* Boston and New York: 1909.

Vreede-de Stuers, Cora, *Parda: A Study of Muslim Women's Life in Northern India.* New York: Humanities Press, 1968.

Woodsmall, Ruth Frances, *Moslem Women Enter a New World.* New York: Round Table Press, Inc., 1936.

XXV

Concluding Statement

ISLAM: LEGACY AND CONTEMPORARY CHALLENGE

Fazlur Rahman

At the beginning of this book the question, "What is the situation of Islam in the Islamic world today?", was raised. Professor Seyyed Hossein Nasr addressed it. Now that we have examined contemporary Islam from a variety of angles, it is appropriate to conclude this book with an enquiry into the predictable future of Islam in the Islamic world. Professor Rahman addresses this question. He does so by analyzing the various trends in historical Islam and the forces behind them and by assessing the relative strengths of the same forces or their modern successors in their current configuration.

Fazlur Rahman, born in undivided India, educated there and in Europe, has traveled, taught and lectured in many parts of the world. The author of some of the classic works on Islam, he is respected as an eminent elder statesman of Islamic scholarship. Currently he is Professor of Islamic Studies in the Department of Near Eastern Languages and Civilizations at the University of Chicago.

Islam arose in the early seventh century Mecca as a response to certain spiritual-moral and social problems, primarily to polytheism and a grave socio-economic disparity, that prevailed in the prosperous merchantile community of Mecca. There is strong evidence in the Qur'an itself that, in its eyes, the two, monotheism and humanism — i.e., human egalitarianism — were organically linked from the very beginning. The Qur'an asked Meccans to "recognize the right of the poor" in their wealth and to be grateful to the one God who had "satiated them from hunger and given them immunity from war," thus underlining peace and prosperity as the greatest blessings of God. When the Meccan merchants rejected the Prophet's call saying that he had no right to interfere in either their faith or their wealth because "nobody can tell us what to do with our wealth," a thirteen-year long and protracted struggle followed after which Muhammad moved from Mecca to Madina.

In Madina, the Prophet was able to put through the reforms for which he had lacked the necessary political authority in Mecca. The *Zakat* (tax) was imposed on the relatively well-to-do to create a welfare state; usury was prohibited and, instead, investment in the uplift of the poor sectors of society was constantly stressed and characterized as "establishing credit with God" as opposed to investments in usurious institutions. The rights of slaves, women, orphans, captives, wayfarers, etc. were emphasized and, in general, a sustained and massive effort was made to improve the lot of and strengthen the weaker segments of society. Justice in economic matters, fair-play in political affairs and kindliness in social relations were constantly upheld as the true ideal of piety; forgiveness "to those who have been transgressing against you" was declared to be the mark of true faith. Familial relations were to be based on "mutual love and mercy"; the husband and the wife called "garments unto one another" and husbands were prohibited to take back any gifts from their wives in case of divorce "even if you may have gifted them a heap of gold." The age-old Arab institution of vengeance *(th'ar)* was abolished; divisions of tribes and nations, tongues and colors were considered to serve certain useful functions, as they contributed to the variety and richness of the human race, provided they did not tend to produce any essential distinctions between man and man in terms of superiority or inferiority.

Whenever the Qur'an and Muhammad could bring reform through legislation, this was done; otherwise, issues were clarified at the ethical level and "clear guidance" was provided in the direction in which human society ought to move. Thus, in the almost parallel cases of slavery and polygamy, these were legally but restrictively permitted; yet clear direction was given to the abolition of both. However, historical forces did not allow their abolition. In particular, the rapid and vast Muslim conquests soon after the Prophet's death, which immediately resulted in a massive increase in the number of slaves and slave women, represented developments that ran counter to the sociomoral purposes of the Qur'an on these issues.

What is extremely important to note is that the Qur'an and Muhammad's practice had provided two basic factors whose constant interaction is ideally the source of all Islamic dynamism. One is the moral-spiritual factor — the values of the Qur'an under whose impact the individual Muslim is to be reformed and trained as one who "surrenders himself to God." This factor, which is so essential for being a Muslim, is denoted in the Qur'an by the term *taqwa*. *Taqwa means that state of mind whereby a person becomes capable of discerning right from wrong* (one might call it "conscience") *and acts choosing the right with the full awareness that the criterion of judgement upon his perception and action lies outside him.* The second part of this statement is absolutely important since the Qur'an recurrently emphasizes and warns against the subjectivity of human perceptions, whether this subjectivity has its source in conditions that are individual, national, racial, cultural or, indeed, communal. "(Truth) is not your (i.e. Muslims') wishful thinking, nor is it the wishful thinking of the People of the Book (i.e. Jews and Christians)." The human self-deception is of such an order that "When it is said to them 'Do not sow corruption on the earth,' they reply 'We are only reforming (the earth)'; beware! These are the corruptors, but they do not realize this." Hence *taqwa* and self-deception are mutually incompatible.

The Qur'anic accounts of the Last Day or the End are an amplification of the theme of *taqwa*. If one develops true *taqwa* or conscience within himself, he must keep his gaze at the long-range purposes or "ends" of life and cannot allow himself to get lost in immediate, short-term expediencies, for these latter make man myopic and blind to the real ends. This is the meaning of the end or the *akhira* as opposed to the short-sighted and vagrant view of life called the *dunya*. Again, in the End — Judgment, man's inmost thoughts and intentions will become public and the Qur'an says that a person's own "hands, feet, eyes and ears" will bear witness against him." It is the hour of truth when man will be faced with a candid stock-taking of his deeds. But *taqwa* requires that man has this experience constantly *in this life;* he must face the truth, do his stock-taking and conduct himself accordingly.

Islam wants to build individuals with this kind of sense of responsibility. Myopic individuals, totally immersed in the immediate pressures and insatiable appetite for consumer goods, are hardly the stuff with which a higher and a healthy life could be built for future generations. Here we may be told that it is too utopian to hope to create a whole society like this and that what can be attained at best is the formation of a small minority of such individuals. Such criticism notwithstanding, we must have goals that may seem immediately not attainable. If a society should set its goals at no better than the creation of a plastic world of consumer goods and then boast that there is no gap between its ideal and the actuality, one can only say that its estimation of itself is extremely low. Just as there has to be a positive and intelligible link between the ideal and the real to make the forward movement of the real possible, it is equally imperative to keep the ideal constantly higher in order for that movement to become possible.

This, then, is the account of true conscience without the cultivation of which, at least to some degree, no individual can be prepared to serve a higher or "more distant" end. The second aspect which is equally a *sine qua non* for the Quar'an to achieve its goals concerns the "Community that surrenders itself to God *(Umma Muslima)*", a concept whose origin the Quar'an attributes to Abraham. This is a community constituted of individuals such as we have described above. When, after a protracted criticism of earlier communities for the way they divided mankind through their proprietory claims over truth, the Qur'an announces the formation of an actual, historic Muslim community and calls it "the mediam community," "the best community that has been produced for mankind, for you command the good and prohibit evil and you believe in God." But it also clearly tells Muslims that they cannot take God for granted, that God is not the prisoner of their wishful thinking, and, indeed, that if Muslims would not come up to His purposes, He is capable of raising another people "who will not be like you," for God gives the "inheritance of the earth to those who will deserve it."

Just as God passes judgment upon individuals, indeed, so does He judge peoples, nations and communities. This judgment is according to well established laws or "practice of God which is unchangeable." The mandate of man, being God's vice regent on earth is that he removes corruption from the earth and reforms its affairs in such a way that God's law shall work. When a nation or a community has been given power on earth but it misuses this power and does not stop the rot but eventually itself becomes rotten, it becomes ripe for harvest: it is removed from the scene and "neither heavens nor the earth weep for it." And the Qur'an almost invariably adds, "We did them no injustice, they did injustice to themselves." It is for this purpose, that is, in order to discover why nations rise and fall that the Qur'an asks people "to travel on the earth and see how the criminal (nations) fell" and to develop "eyes that can see, ears that can hear and hearts that can understand."

In sum, then, individual conscience and the collective will to act, that is, *taqwa* and the community, are the twin pillars upon which the entire edifice of Islam rests. As long as the two remain strong and alive and mutually supportive, the whole edifice will stand, but should one weaken or should the bond between the two be severed or distorted, the end will be tragic. This is not the place to detail the developments in Islam subsequent to the Prophet, but certain crucial points must be noted. Although it is correct that, generally speaking, the Muslim concepts did not result in the kind of exploitative imperialism seen in several pre- and post-Islamic instances and Islamic society showed, on the whole, a much greater racial and religious tolerance, nevertheless, the bond envisaged by the Qur'an between individual morality and community action came, in course of time, to be weakened and then distorted as well.

We have already noted how, on the issues of slavery and polygamy, the orientation of the Qur'an was distorted and, in fact, reversed through the early Islamic conquests. The Muslim Community, indeed, came to arrogate to itself that very status of infallibility, for which the Qur'an had denounced earlier communities, and came to see itself not as an aspirant to righteousness but as the possessor of it. Besides the politics of the inter-community rivalry, there were undoubtedly certain internal causes for the development of this self-image, some of which were primarily legal. The concept of the normativeness of the *Ijma* or consensus of the Community materially contributed to that of the idea of the infallibility of the Community. The idea of the intercession of Muhammad on behalf of the sinners of his Community, which appears to have developed — in the teeth of the Qur'an — as an answer to the Christian doctrine of "justification of faith," was further bound to weaken the moral sensitivity. But, above all, it was the development of Islamic Law as a comprehensive formulation of Islamic behavior that shifted the delicate balance between conscience and action, and tipped the scale to the side of the latter. It is correct that Islamic Law is permeated by moral considerations and is not law in the secular sense of the word, but all law, as such, is mechanistic and is construed in terms of do's and don'ts. Worst of all, after a period of brilliant growth, this Law reached a point of virtual halt in about four centuries, probably because of its very comprehensiveness and success, and gave way to almost unmitigated traditionalism, with the general decline in Islamic intellectual creativity.

We have also pointed out elsewhere that an Islamic ethics proper, systematically based upon a genuine understanding of the purposes of the Qur'an, did not develop in Islam. The leaders of the *Shari'a* made practically no distinction between ethics and law, as hinted above. If, first, an ethics of the Qur'an had been systematically constructed and then law derived from it with due regard to the changing social situations, Islamic conscience could have been kept more or less fully alive and the emerging phenomenon of Sufism could have been directed into more healthy and constructive channels. But in the absence of a truly Qur'anic ethics, the spirit of Islam was stormed by an unbridled growth of wilder forms of spirituality ranging from extravagant esoteric doctrines to orgiastic antinomian cults. Despite the fact that Sufism did take several middle of the road, orthodox and quite sober forms, the massive injurious effects of its uncontrolled expressions on the body of the Community can never be overestimated. How does one square, for example, the insistent Qur'anic call for establishing an ethically just and viable social order on earth with the vagrant intoxicants of the various popular Sufi practices? Is the ill-balanced dancing of the glass-eating dervish the proper stuff for satisfying Qur'anic requirements? To crown all, since Islamic law was reduced practically to a lifeless shell in the late medieval centuries, the Sufi adepts often took the greatest pleasure in ridiculing it and advocating rebellion against it, for the lawyers only "worshipped a pile of dry books" whereas Sufi initiates worshipped the true God!

With the decline in intellectual creativity and the onset of ever-hardening conservatism, the curricula of education in the *madrasas* (institutions of higher Muslim learning) shrank and intellectual and scientific disciplines expurgated, yielding the entire space to the so-called *Shari'a* sciences, that is, religious disciplines in the narrow sense. Mechanical learning largely took the place of original thought. With the thirteenth century, the age of commentories and super-commentaries begins and it is not rare to find an author who wrote a highly concise text in a certain field, in order to be memorized by students, and then, in order to explain the enigmatic text, himself authored both a commentary and a super-commentary! The human spirit cannot, of course, be completely killed — witness men like Nasir al-Din al-Tusi and Ibn Khaldun — but whatever of this spirit survived was inspite of rather than due to the *madrasa* system. It has been correctly said by Muhammad Iqbal that in the later Middle Ages the more original and creative minds moved from orthodox Islam into Sufism.

From the eighteenth century, with the advent of the Wahhabi and the Indian reformist phenomena, up to the last years of the nineteenth, a strong and agitated throb of life appeared in the greater part of the Muslim world. These reformers, for the most part, were convinced that Muslim societies had degenerated because they had strayed from the original teaching of the Qur'an and the example *(sunna)* of the

Prophet and their proposed remedy was to return to these pristine sources of Islam. In the Qur'an and the example of the Prophet, however, these reformers, for the most part, found little beyond the doctrine of the Unity of God, which they contrasted to the cults of saints and their shrines prevalent among Muslims. There can be little doubt that the doctrine of the Unity of God is of the essence of the teaching of the Qur'an and the prophet's *sunna* but, as we have said at the outset, this monotheistic idea is organically linked with the idea of socio-economic justice and a general ethical "reform of the earth." That these aspects were hardly seen by these reformers, except, to an extent, by Shah Waliy Allah of Delhi (d. 1767) — who was distinguished among them by intellectual sophistication and much wider learning — is at least understandable since they were sharply reacting to the deluge of popular Sufi religion with all its superstitions and degrading beliefs and practices.

But while, in a limited way, these movements did represent a sign of new life in Islam, their effect in the all-important field of education proved disasterous. If the traditionalist conservative had expelled philosophy and science from his *madrasa* centuries earlier, the new fundamentalist reformist sought to exorcise all elements of intellectualism even from within the religious sciences themselves — including theology and whatever rationalist base the legal science had built for itself over the centuries. When one considers this fact along with the insistence of all of these movements on *Ijtihad* — responsible original thought on the part of competent thinking individuals — the situation seems truly paradoxical; while insisting on *Ijtihad*, these movements effectively destroyed the very intellectual instrument whereby *Ijtihad* could be achieved. The explanation of this paradox is that just as these movements arose against Sufism, so they arose in revolt against almost all the medieval intellectual heritage which they accused of having encouraged *Taqlid* (blind acceptance of authority as against *Ijtihad*) and of having obscured the original teaching of the Qur'an. They, therefore, drastically curtailed their educational program in the conviction that Islam, in its original form, was quite a simple religion which had been unnecessarily made complex and cumbersome by medieval Muslim intellectuals. Now, of course, in a sense, original Islam, like any other religion was indeed, simple. Yet, in a more important sense, it was quite complex, in fact, more complex than any other religion. The basic failure of the Wahhabis and other similar fundamentalist movements was not to see this. From such a simplistic perception of Islam, what *Ijtihad* could possibly mean is difficult to see except that Muslims should be able to perceive how much actual Islam deviated from the Qur'anic monotheism — even though, as we have pointed out, the concept of monotheism rediscovered from the Qur'an by these reformists was highly truncated, as it was sheared of its basic moral, social and economic implications. There is hardly a trace in the writings of Ibn 'Abd al-Wahhab, the founder of Wahhabism, or any other Middle Eastern fundamentalist reformer of this basic original elan of the Qur'an.

Let us now dwell for a moment on an explanation of what we mean by the complexity of Islam. The Qur'an and Muhammad's activity had what might be called a "macro-background" in the conditions prevailing in pre-Islamic Arabia in general and in the Meccan milieu in particular, as we have pointed out at the very opening of this paper. The Qur'an itself bears the most eloquent testimony to this when it speaks of Muhammad's "burden which was breaking your back." Besides this general socio-historical background, the individual pronouncements of the Qur'an in matters social, moral, political or economic, all had their backgrounds rooted in the flesh and blood of history; the Qur'an is hardly a speculative document except in some of its theologico-metaphysical statements. This background material is largely preserved, although it has its own internal problems, in the Qur'an commentaries, and is called "occasions of Qur'anic revelation." This material is absolutely crucial for an adequate understanding of the Qur'an both as a whole and in terms of its individual statements. Indeed, what gives cohesiveness to the Qur'an is just this social-historical background which, of course, prominently includes the activity of the Prophet himself, and without which Qur'an must appear, as, indeed, it has appeared to many Westerners, a jumble of disconnected and even discordant ideas. Fundamentally important though the fact of this background is, for that is precisely where the dynamics of Islam are displayed as a living force, it has been hardly made use of in classical Islamic legislation. The fundamentalists, who have an innate propulsion towards literalism, are almost entirely innocent of it and the Muslims of today totally ignore it because they are totally ignorant of it.

It is only by understanding the background of the Qur'anic pronouncements, particularly those concerning the society, that their true import can be appreciated. And it is only by appreciating the full import of these pronouncements that their *raisons d'etre* or their purposes can be best grasped and distinguished from wording of the law. This all-important distinction was, indeed, made by Muslim jurists who called the letter of law "rule *(hukm)*" and its purpose *ratio legis (illat al-hukm)*. This was theoretically the basis from which they developed the principle of analogical reasoning *(qyas)* for deduction of further laws from the Qur'an. But this distinction was, first, used mostly in theory and was seldom applied in practice, and where it was applied it was sometimes applied much too widely but often much too narrowly so that much more often than not the letter of the law, not its purpose or *ratio legis,* prevailed. The second most important failure which, in fact, ensured that the body of the *Shari'a* would remain more or less a chaotic jumble and will not develop into law proper was that ethics was not distinguished from law. Since a proper and systematic Qur'anic ethics was never formulated, the Qur'an was not seen or appreciated as a unity but only as a series of pronouncements essentially unconnected with each other. This, to my mind, is the greatest problem still today which should be dealt with before any attempt is made at a reconstruction of Islamic society. In other words, before we start any reorganization, an ethical system which will do justice to the over-all purposes of the Qur'an as an organic unity should be formulated. And then we should derive law from it, systematically keeping in view both the spirit and the letter of the Qur'anic pronouncements.

This was not achieved by our classical jurists. But the fundamentalists of the eighteenth and nineteenth centuries deprived themselves even of this medieval legacy — which, despite its grave failings was, nevertheless, both rich and profound — and, in their marauding anti-intellectualism, reduced Islam to the barest bones. From about the middle of the nineteenth century arose the phenomenon of what is called "Islamic Modernism." In a definite sense, Islamic modernism departed from the earlier fundamentalism described above. The fundamentalists had emphasized *Ijtihad* or new thinking, but their real or substantive accomplishment was not any new *Ijtihad* but the elimination or at least minimization of the popular superstitions in religion and recovery of some of the essential aspects, if not the whole, of original Islamic monotheism and insistence on a puritanical way of life. Its formal *Ijtihad* was just this insistence on *Ijtihad.* The modernists took over this legacy of the incumbency of *Itjihad* and gave it a new content. This new content they took from the modern West, just as their early forefathers had taken much of the content of their law from Iran and Byzantium. We need not go here into the details of the modernist doctrines — they range from the role of reason in faith through political democracy to rights of women. We have detailed these reforms in several places, especially in our book *Islam*. But it is not in any particular doctrine or reform that the basic contribution of the modernist achievement lies, even though these are, of course, important in their own right and with regard to several of them modernist thought exhibits a considerable range of differences. The real revolution wrought by the modernists lies rather in the fact that, in contradistinction to the traditionalist conservatives and the fundamentalists, they declared Islam to be not only a religion in the usual sense of the word — guiding private life and ordaining rituals — but covering the totality of individual and collective life. The modernists, who were in intimate touch with the West and, as we have said, were tangibly influenced by some of its modern doctrines, did not regard Islam and Christianity to be coextensive and comparable but rather regarded Christianity *plus* Western secular institutions — political, educational, economic, etc. — to be commensurate with Islam. They, therefore, talked about an Islamic state, Islamic law, Islamic education, Islamic society etc. and not of secular law, polity, education, etc. within the context of Islam. They showed, with remarkable consistency, that the Qur'an had Islamically given Muslims the principles of a democratic system which they failed to work out and, instead, yielded to autocratic rule; that the Qur'an had Islamically given women rights which Muslims themselves not only failed to develop further but, with regard to which, they even gravely retrogressed; that the Qur'an had Islamically and insistently called upon Muslims to use reason, to study nature and to exploit it for man's good and that Muslims failed to follow the teaching. It was the Muslim modernists, not the fundamentalists or the traditionalists, then, who recovered the integral Islam of the earliest days, and, having adapted certain key modern Western institutions and integrated them with Islam as being Islamic *par excellence*, offered Islam as a successful substitute for and the only viable alternative to the secular West, as the secularism of the West began to show serious cracks in its inner moral human structure.

The idea that Islam centrally aimed at the creation of a social order and that even its rituals like prayer, fasting, *zakat* and pilgrimage had obvious and fundamental social and political meaning and dimension was a truly revolutionary rediscovery. Some modern Western educated Muslims also went secular and sought to bifurcate life into a public sector which they made over to secular activity — exactly as though religion, effectively killed through secularization, had to be effectively nailed into the coffin of conscience lest it turn into a dracula, while conscience was perceived more as an effective grave for religion than as an oven where moral values are baked and molded. But, for the vast majority of modern educated Muslims, Islamic modernism came as a fresh breath of life. Yet, modernism has not as yet succeeded in the Muslim world and, for the time-being at least, appears to be submerged under a flood of what I call neo-fundamentalism, so much so that even its strengths appear to be its weaknesses. Unless we can perceive the real nature of this enigma, we will not be able to point to any solution for the problem, let alone predict its future.

The modernists, on the whole, had argued for their reformist theses brilliantly and correctly. But the basic fault with the modernist reform was that its leaders proceeded selectively, the guiding principle for their choice of themes being the actual needs of the Muslim community as they perceived them or the points where they thought Islam needed a defense against Western attacks, for example, the principle of *Jihad* (i.e. struggle for the cause of Islam, often called Holy War in the West). They, like the classical Muslim jurists, made little attempt to treat the Qur'an as a whole and formulate its world-view, then formulate its ethics and finally derive its particular doctrines and laws from it, giving due weight either to the *ratio legis* of the Revelation or to the existential situation of today. The theses they chose for their reform needs were actually inspired from the modern Western milieu, which was bound to be the case. This gave the conservatives, the guardians of traditional Islam, the occasion to suspect that the modernists were actually advocating Westernism because they had been brain-washed. Two highly sensitive points lent themselves particularly to re-invigorate this suspicion and extend it to the entire field of modernist reform. The conservatives, although they might concede that many of the Muslim woman's rights, which in fact the Qur'an gave her, are denied to her either by her parents or her husband, were, nevertheless, dead against the emancipation of women after the Western model. They thought this would eventually destroy the family institution which the Qur'an regards as basic for society, and they also pointed to what was happening in the West with increasing poignancy: a wild growth of whole generations which, without any reliable sense of right and wrong, would not only menace their own societies but, before long, the world at large. Secondly, the conservatives objected vehemently both to the Western attacks on the Islamic concept of *Jihad* and equally to the defense of *Jihad* offered by a number of prominent modernists. Islam was not spread by the sword as the West alleged, the conservatives would say, but supposing it did, then while the sword at least spread Islam, what has the Western bomb spread? The reply, that modern Western wars were not religious but for the sake, say, of economic markets, would, of course, carry no weight for the Muslim since for Islam the economic market, the school or the political activity are as much a proper field of religion as is the mosque.

This rejecting attitude of the conservatives towards the modernists was fundamentally determined by their anti-Westernism. So far as borrowing of institutions from other cultures is concerned, the early generations of Muslims had done it patently and on a large scale in various fields, and far from having any qualms about it they definitely viewed it as strengthening Islam. But these borrowings Islam had done on its own terms and as much as it was able to assimilate. What facilitated this psychologically was the fact that Muslims, being politically ascendant, were and considered themselves to be masters of their own destiny. But very different was the situation of Islam vis a vis the modern West. While Islam was defeated militarily, politically and economically, the West remained culturally and socially arrogant. Never before in the history of mankind has any cultural system so unashamedly claimed to be so unreservedly righteous as to pose as the ideal culture for the entire human race and felt entitled to impose itself on all the others. While the conservative Muslims might recognize the technological and scientific achievements of the West as amazing and even admirable, the Western *society* progressively seemed to them as a vast exploitative and highly dangerous tribe of economic animals. One can well imagine the yawning gap between the two. The Muslim modernists were caught in the middle. The conservatives, as they recoiled into their medieval shell, suffered from such a terrible psychological hiatus that the advocacy of even genuine and urgent reforms upset him. There appeared an equally yawning gap between the courageous and appropriative mentality of their early Muslim forefathers and their own unthinking negativism.

There were, however, two very important pieces of legacy which fairly large segments of conservatives inherited from modernism, thus giving rise to the contemporary phenomenon of neo-fundamentalism which must be distinguished from the pre-modernist fundamentalism spoken of earlier. These two very important pieces of modernist legacy are the desire for the cultivation of science and technology and the conviction that Islam does not exist only in the mosque and does not consist of certain rituals only, but encompasses the entire field of life. At the beginning of its career in the twenties and thirties of this century, this neo-fundamentalism had the promise of a liberating and positive force. Although it was intemperate in its critique of modernism, it was highly critical of conservative traditionalism as well which it accused of having turned Islam into some kind of Brahmanism or papal Christianity. But not long after its birth, it began to show certain alarming symptoms. Its main motivation settled down as establishing Islam as something quite unique and, indeed, utterly different from the West. Although its representatives declared that safeguarding the integrity of the Muslim family through raising moral standards was only a first step in their program, they have done precious little about this; nor have they been able to do anything to genuinely reform the system of education. Their Islamic needs seem to be satisfied by declaiming ad nauseam that whereas Western democracy believes in the sovereignty of the people, Islam believes in the sovereignty of God, thanks to their sheer confusion between the modern notion of political sovereignty and that of the Qur'anic idea of God's being the "kingdom of the heaven and the earth." This terrible confusion, of course, must lead to further, more disastrous ones. For example, in modern democracy people's representatives are lawmakers whereas in Islam who can be a law-maker except God? Again, Western economy works through banking institutions which charge interest, and interest, as our medieval lawyers told us, is utterly unIslamic. In modern days Keynes expressed his disapproval of interest and Karl Marx declared it absolutely forbidden. Their arguments provide new justification for the Islamic position on interest, although on different grounds. But, since the former was a socializing thinker and the latter an uncompromising socialist, our neo-fundamentalists can never, never accept their position for that would be truly Satanic.

Two things must be kept in mind about neo-fundamentalism. By and large, its banner-bearers are not trained scholars of Islam: in fact, a vast majority of them are not at all scholars of Islam. They are essentially laymen with a strong emotional attachment to Islam and a strong desire to see it vindicated against the West. Khomeini is the only significant example of a trained traditionalist scholar whom historical forces have turned into a fundamentalist. For that reason, even his fundamentalism appears to be of quite a different sort. In his draft constitution, he does not dabble in the grandiose but confused ideas like God's sovereignty but plainly states that sovereign power lies with the people. Nor does his draft constitution talk about the desirability of closing down banks — although it has a heavy emphasis on social and economic justice and the safeguarding of Islamic values through a properly organized family life. The second point, allied to the first, is that because the neo-fundamentalists, unlike the pre-modernist fundamentalists, are not scholars; they do not think and argue about issues — they are not equipped to do that — but they mechanically declaim. To be sure, they can and do change their views but rather unpredictably. They are not embarassed by blatant and frequent self-contradictions. And by denying themselves the benefit of recourse to their long heritage which, as we have said earlier, is highly rich and flexible, they have made their cliches and slogans almost devoid of any meaning. Since this situation cannot continue indefinitely, particularly when the fundamentalists are in positions of power and decision-making, there seem to be only two possibilities. Either they will change which is quite likely, and, in some cases is happening now, in which event there may be a two-pronged development of deriving inspiration from Islam's medieval heritage and evolving a form of neo-modernism. If such developments do not occur, then fundamentalism will be a very transitory phenomenon and will be replaced either by modernism or some form of secularism. Since secularism does not seem to me to be a real possibility in Muslim societies, except as an extreme reaction to a stolid fundamentalism, some kind of neo-modernism seems to be the most likely possibility.

So that these developments may take place under the light of authentic Islamic principles, let us suggest a methodology for interpreting the sources of Islam. As alluded to earlier, the first imperative in this methodology is to understand the Qur'an and the Prophet's activity in their socio-historical setting. This will lead to an appreciation of the world-view and ethics of the Qur'an. The next step would be the formulation of laws, based on the Qur'anic ethics and the specific needs of our time. In other words, the first movement should be from the specifics of the Qur'an to general principles governing an ethical and legal system; and the second, from these general principles to specific laws suitable to life today. These interrelating processes, when successful, will also serve as checks against each other, as we have elaborated more fully in the *introduction* to our monograph *Islamic Education and Modernity* which is currently in press.

INDEX

A

Abbassids 130, 131, 317
Abd al-Qādir 7
Abdül Hamid II
 (Ottoman Sultan) 319
Abdülmecit
 (Turkish Sultan) 335
Abu Bakr 32, 180, 286
Achnacarry Agreement 108
al-Adawiyya, Rabia 376
Adonis
 (Ali Ahmad Said) 60, 67
al-Afghānī 10
AGIP 113
Ahl al-Kitab,
 (People of the Book) 47
Ahmad, Mirza Ghulam 264
Ahmadis 264
Ahmadiyah 7
Alexander the Great 73
Ali, Sonni 286
Aligarh School 262
Aliran Kepercayaan
 (Javanese Mysticism) 340, 346
Aman
 (safe conduct) 48, 49
Amanullah 252
Amnesty International 208, 209
Anglo-Persian
 Oil Company 107
Anti-Christ 42
al-Arabi, Ibn 27
Arabian Marker 118
Arafat, Yasser
 (Yasir) 81, 168
Architecture, Islamic 41
d'Arcy, William Knox 107
Askia, Muhammad Toure
 (the Great), ... 286
Atatürk
 (Mustafa Kemal) 12, 34-35,
                97-99, 117,
                321-22, 324-25
Atheism 222
al-Attar, Farid ad-Din 376
Ayati, Muhammad Ibrahim 185
Aytmatof, Cengiz 248
al-Azhar 11, 159-60,
                162, 165

B

Baader-Meinhof Gang 201
Bābi-Bahā'ī 8
Bakr, Ahmad Hasan al- 310
Balfour Declaration 135

Bakhtiar, Shahpour 214
Ball, George 204, 205
al-Banna, Hasan 151, 160, 161
Barkan, Ömer Lüfti 318
Ba'thism 14, 311-312
al-Bayati, Abd al-Wahhab 68
Bayezid II
 (Ottoman Sultan) 319
Bazargan, Mihdi 178, 215
Bektasis 318
Bergson 7
Bhutto, Zulfikar Ali 264, 265
Bihbihani, Sayyid
 Muhammad al-Musavi al- 174
Bill, James A. 202-203
                209, 211
al-Biruni 248
Brinkley, David 205
Burujirdi, Ayatullah
 Sayyid Muhammad Husayn 172
Byzantine Empire 47, 73,
                76-77, 132

C

Caesaro-papism 73
Caliphs (Caliphate) 10, 12,
                46-48, 76-79,
                148, 159, 167
Camp David Agreement 165, 166
Cemal, Kemal 247
Churchill, Winston 107
Colonialism 39
Communism 38, 82
Compagnie Francaise
 de Petroles 113
Constantine 45, 73
Council on Islamic Ideology ... 268, 269
Crusades 5, 6, 78-79
Cyprus 100

D

Dahbour, Ahmad 59
Dār al-Harb 3, 39-41,
                48, 76
Dār al-Islam 2, 3, 5,
                39-41, 48, 76, 80
Dār al-Sulh 2, 3
Darwinism 33
Darwish, Mahmoud 66
Daoud, Muhammad 252
Data Ganj Baksh 270
Descartes 7
Dhimma 47, 48
ad-Din, Mustafa Jamal 58
Divorce 382

416

Draft Memorandum
   of Principles 108

E

Edict of Gülhane 319
Eliot, T. S. 8
Equality 76
ERAP 113
Erdman, Paul 216
Eskandari, Iraj 186
Evans, Ahmad 292
Evolution 33
Evren, General 317, 337

F

Falsafi, Hujjat al-Islam
   Muhammad Taqi 173, 174
Family in Islam 377-84
Fanon, Frantz 178
Fida'iyan-i Khalq 186
Fida'iyan-i Islam 12, 173
Fiqh 297, 298, 301
Five Pillars of Faith 225, 374
Free Officers Movement 172
Frost, David 206
Fulanis 280
Fundamentalism 10-13, 17

G

Gailani family 256
Galief, Sultan 244
Garvey, Marcus 289
Ghaffari, Abu Zarr 182
al-Ghazali 17, 26, 42
Golden Horde 239
Gölkap, Ziya 320
Golkar
   (The Functional Group —
   Indonesia's ruling party) 352, 354
Grand Mosque 154
Green Book 301, 302-304
Guénon, R. 8
Guided Democracy 344
Gurevich, Georges 178

H

Habash, George 168
Haddad, Qasim 61
Hagia, Sophia 335
al-Hājj 'Umar 7
al Hallaj 62, 63, 64
Hanafi 146
Hanbali 146
Hausas 279, 281
Hawatmeh, Nayef 168
Heads of Agreement
   of Distribution 108

Hekmatyar, Gulbudin 254
Hellenization 73
Herzl, Theodor 135
al-Hijazi,
   Abd al-Mu'ti 67
House of Obedience 393
Hume 7
Hurgronje, C. Snouck 351
Husain, Saddam 310
Husayn 56, 57, 58,
                  59, 60, 61, 62, 63
Husayn, Taha 162
Husayniyah Irshad 178, 182
Hussein, King
   (Jordan) 207, 217
Hussein, Sharif 320

I

Ibn Arabi 377
Ibn Battuta 286, 289
Ibn Khaldun 286
Ibn Yasin 286
Indian National Congress 262
Iqbal, Mohammad 262
Islamic revival 122
Ismail,
   Shah of Iran 319
Ismailis 149, 150
International Energy
   Agency 114
Ivan the Terrible 239

J

al-Ja'fari, Salih 58
Ja'afaris 149, 150
Jadid 241
Jakarta Charter 343, 345
Jamaat-e-Islami 262, 264,
                    265, 268, 270
al-Jayyusi,
   Salma al-Khadra' 68
Jihad 279-81
al-Jīlānī 17
Jizya 47
Jordan 83

K

Kajamberdiev, Turar 248
Karbala 56, 59, 62, 63
Kashani, Sayyid Abu
   al-Qasim al- 173, 174
Keita, Allakoi 286
Kemalism 99, 100
Kennedy, Edward 205
Kharajite-Ibadi sects 276-77
Kharijis 308

417

Khomeini (Khumayni),
 Ayatollah Ruhollah
 al-Musavi, ... 40, 176, 182-86
Kissinger, Henry 204, 207
Knowledge, pursuit of 385-86
Komsomol. 231
Kurds 307-308

L

Last Judgment 24, 25, 33
Lausanne, Treaty of 321
Lenczowski, George 202-203, 207
Lenin (Leninism) 222, 242
Leo Africanus 286
Liberalism 79
Locke 7

M

Macapagal, Diosdado 364
Magsaysay, Ramon 363
Magic 36
Mahdi 7, 10, 12,
                          15-16, 154
Mahmud II
 (Ottoman Sultan) 319
Mahmūd,
 Abd al-Rahim 66
Mahmut II
 (Turkish Sultan) 335
Malari 348
Maliki 146
Manzikert, Battle of 317
Marcos, Ferdinand 358, 364,
                          366, 368
Marxism 12, 14-15, 222, 231
Mashaikh 269, 270
Masyumi 342, 344-46, 348, 355
Maūdudī,
 Maulānā Abul 'Alā 11, 262, 268
McCaulay, Lord 270
Mecca 154
Mehmed VI
 (Ottoman Sultan) 322
Mehmed Fatih
 (Ottoman Sultan) 319
Memorandum
 for European Markets 108
Mevlevis 318
Milani, Ayatullah
 Sayyid Hadi 179
Modernism, Islamic 410-413
Mongols 5-6
Monogamy 382
Monthly Religious Society 176, 182
Moorish Science Temples 290, 291
Moro National
 Liberation Front 358, 364-68
Mu'awiya 77

Muftis 253
Mughals 131
Muhammad, Elijah 289
Muhammadiyah 342, 352
Mujahidin 252, 257, 258
Mujahidin-i Khalq 179, 186
Mujtahid 173, 176,
                          177, 178
Mullah *(Mollah)* 38, 40, 231,
                          253, 255
al-Muntazar, Muhammad 149
Murshid. 232
Musa, Mansa Kankan 286
Musahibans 252
Muslim Brotherhood 151, 152,
                          158, 159
Muslim Independence
 Movement 364-65
Muslim League 261, 262
Mussadiq (Mussadeq),
 Muhammad 99-101, 173-74,
                          213, 215
Mutahhari,
 Shaykh Murtaza 175, 185
Mysticism 21, 22, 34,
                          42, 64, 65, 79

N

Nabhani, Sheikh Takieddin 167
Nafisa, Sayyida 377
Nahdlatul Ulama 342, 344, 352
Napoleon 6
Naqshbandiya 232
al-Nāsir, Jamāl 'Abd 12
Nasser, Gamal Abdel 80, 172-73
Nastir, Muhammad 346
National Front 212, 213
Nationalism.................... 79
"New Order" 346, 349, 350,
                   351, 352, 353-54, 355
Niazi, Muhammad 254
Nietzsche 291, 292
Nizam-e-Mustafa. 264, 265
Nizami 248
Noble Drew Ali
 (Timothy Drew) 289, 290-91
Noorani, Maulana
 Shah Ahmad 266
Nūrsi, Sayyid Sa'id 12

O

"Objective Resolution" 262
"Old Order" 346
OPEC 106, 113,
                   114-15, 116, 118,
                   119, 121, 122, 123
Orf 240
Ottomans 50-51, 77,
                          81, 88-91, 92,
                   146, 159, 309, 317

Ozenbashly, Ahmet 244

P

Pahlavi, Mohammed Reza
(Shah of Iran) 99, 100, 204
Pahlavi, Reza Shah 97, 99
Pakistan 83
Pakistan National Alliance ... 264, 265
Palestinians 66
Pan-Arabism 311
Pancasila
(Five Principles) 341, 343,
344, 345, 348, 351
Pan-Islamism 10, 83, 122-23
Parmusi
(Muslim Party of Indonesia) 345
Pasha, Cevdet 240
Persia 77, 88, 89, 91, 96
PKI
(Indonesian Communist Party) .. 344
PLO 81, 168, 201
Polygyny 382
PPP
(United Development Party) . 352, 355
Prester, John 132

Q

Qadhdhafi (Qadhafi),
Mu'ammar 14, 297-304, 365
Qadiriya 232
Qajars 81
Qazaf 267
Qazis 253
Quran (Koran) 2, 12,
22-25, 33, 42,
45-46, 55, 74-75,
130-32, 300-301,
325-26; and women, 371-73

R

Rabani, Burhanuddin 254
Rahman, Abdur 262
Rascid, Lucman 365
Red Army 243
Red Army Faction 201, 202
Red Brigades 202
Red Cross, International 209-210
Republic of Turkey
(founding) 322
Reynolds, Frank 206
Rumi, Jalal ed-din 318, 336
Russia 96

S

al-Sabur, Salah Abd 62
Safavids 131, 308-309
Safiq, Mussa 254

Salafiyyah 11
Saleeby, Najeeb 362
Sanjaby, Karim 213
Sarekat Islam 341, 352
Sartre, Jean-Paul 178
al-Sa'ud, Abd al-Aziz
(Ibn Sa'ud) 147
al-Sa'ud, Muhammad 147
Sayyid Ahmad (of Breli) 262
Sayyid Outb 12
Schimmel, Annemarie 328, 329
Selim I (Ottoman Sultan) 319
Seljuks 131, 240, 317
Seven Sisters 107, 108, 109, 110
Sexual Morality 390-91
Seyyed Amir Ali 262
Shafi'i 146
Shah Wali Allah
(of Delhi) 262, 408
Shahid (Martyr) 55
Shamanism 240
Sha'rawi, Huda ash- 2, 393
Sharia (Shari'ah) 2, 4, 17,
23, 37-38,
46, 75-77, 83,
87-88, 90, 92,
159, 171-72,
240, 253, 256, 263,
266-68, 297-303, 343, 374
Shari'ati, Dr. Ali 178-82, 215
al-Sharqawi, Abd al-Rahman 62
Sheikh 232
Sheykh ül-Islam 318
Shiites,
(Shia, Shiism) 2-3, 12,
22, 40, 57, 75, 79, 83,
87-88, 228, 268
el-Siba'i, Mustapha 167
Sirhindi, Shaykh Ahmad 17
"Sixty Minutes" 203, 205, 217-19
Smith, W. C. 6
Socialism, Islamic 13, 14
Spengler 8
Spencer 7
Spiritual Boards 229-31
Stalin 242
Sufi Brotherhoods 231-33, 280
Sufism (Sufis) 2, 7, 10,
13, 17, 21, 23,
27, 34-37, 43, 79,
161, 178, 231, 407-408
Suharto 345, 346, 348,
350, 351
Sukarno 344, 345,
346, 349-50
Sultan 77
Sunjata Epic 278-79
Sunnah (Sunna) 23, 24-26,
31, 33, 46, 374

Sunnis (Sunnism) 2, 3, 75, 83, 87-88, 145-47, 308-309

T

al-Tabari 48
Tabari, Ihsan 188
Tariqa (Tariqah) 4, 23, 36, 280
Tatar 241
Togan, Zeki Velidi 243
Touqān, Ibrāhīm 65
Tudah
  (Tudeh — Communist Party) 186
Turkish Petroleum Company 107
Twelvers 308

U

Ullama (Ulama, Ullema, 'Ulemā).. 8, 46, 77-79, 87-99, 159, 172, 175, 178-80, 184, 240, 253-56, 262-63, 265
Umayyads 131
Umma 75, 76, 159, 235
Usman dan Fadio 7
Usher 266, 267, 268, 270

V

Voltaire 7
Vurgun, Somet 247

W

al-Wahhāb, Muhammad ibn Abd ... 146
Wahhābī 7, 10, 11, 13, 31, 83
Wallace, Mike 203, 205, 217
Westernization 91
White Army 243
White Revolution 100
Women: scholars 386
  vocation role 386;
  politics 387-88;
  property rights 389-90;
  in military 388;
  current status 391-93;
  liberation movements 394-96;
  emerging role 396-99

Y

Yazdi, Ibrahim 215
Young, Andrew 204, 218
Young Turks 34, 51
Yusuf, Sa'di 67

Z

Zakat 266, 267, 268, 269, 270

Zanjani, Sayyid Abu
  al-Fazl al-Musavi al- 173, 174
Zaydis 148, 149
Zaynab, Sayyida 377
Zia, General
  (Mohammad Zia ul Haq) 265-67, 268, 269, 270
Zionism 126, 134, 135, 165, 166, 168
Zoroastrianism 48